South-East England

South-East England

Oliver Mason

John Bartholomew & Son Limited
Edinburgh and London

Other titles in this series:

Cumbria   JOHN PARKER
Devon & Cornwall   DENYS KAY-ROBINSON
The Scottish Highlands   JOHN A. LISTER
South Wales   RUTH THOMAS

In preparation:

Somerset & Avon   ROBERT DUNNING
Dorset & Wiltshire   DENYS KAY-ROBINSON
Eastern & Central Scotland   EDWARD PECK

British Library Cataloguing in Publication Data
Mason, Oliver
    South-East England. – (Bartholomew guide books).
    1. South East, Eng. – Description and travel
    I. Title
    914.22′04′857   DA632

    ISBN 0–7028–1019–3

First published in Great Britain 1979 by
JOHN BARTHOLOMEW & SON LIMITED
12 Duncan Street, Edinburgh EH9 1TA
And 216 High Street, Bromley BR1 1PW

ISBN 0 7028 1019 3

All maps © John Bartholomew & Son Limited

Printed in Great Britain by
Hazell Watson & Viney Limited,
Aylesbury, Buckinghamshire

Contents

Preface

If obliged to pick out one outstanding quality of this bottom right-hand corner of England one could do worse than choose *gentleness*. Lacking the drama of the North, the mystery of East Anglia, or the awesomeness of the mountain regions, its wooded hills and valleys, its rolling chalk uplands, its warm buildings, are friendly and re-assuring. Within these limits there is great variety, owing to the tightly-packed succession of geological strata, so that the region comes nearer than any other to being England in microcosm.

If it is dangerous to generalize about landscape, it is much more dangerous to do so about people. Yet there is surely some justification for seeing the gentleness of the landscape reflected in the character of the people here. Their gentleness – politeness, even – is seen as hypocrisy or slyness by the forthright Northerner, as slowness or softness by the quick, take-it-or-leave-it Londoner. Better communications, and the all-pervading media, have not yet smoothed away local variations in speech and de-meanour; it will be a sad day if they ever do.

The quality of gentleness in the landscape has been bestowed upon it largely by the efforts of Man. It was not always gentle. The wooded hills and valley were impenetrable swamps and dangerous forests; the rolling chalk uplands provided the only safety, the only communications, the only place to live. Even when the Romans came, the Weald presented them with a problem, a barrier between the coast and the Thames that they never really succeeded in breaking down. Communications have always been difficult, through the chalk and in the stiff clay. But gradually Man has cut, cleared, built, drained, tilled, and moulded the land, not from any other motive than self-interest perhaps, but with, on the whole, happy results; only on the coast has he grievously offended, almost beyond hope of restitution. Now at last he has become aware of the importance of preserving the best of what he has helped to create, but it is a vulnerable landscape, and Man's greed is still a powerful force.

Writing this book has proved a labour of love. There are so many who have helped me in my task that it would be foolish to try to mention them all. As time has gone by they have grown from a handful to a host. But four must be named: I owe special thanks to Irwin Prowse and John Hardcastle for their expert advice; to Valerie Cottington for her patient typing, enthusiasm, and helpful suggestions; and to Mercia Mason for her constant encouragement, as well as many penetrating criticisms.

Oliver Mason
Sussex
May 1978

Landscape

Most of this south-east region falls within the geographical feature known as the Weald or within the chalk hills of the North and South Downs. The Downs run in the shape of an elongated horse-shoe from Folkestone round to Beachy Head. The North Downs pass above the towns of Ashford, Maidstone, and Sevenoaks, in Kent; then Reigate, Dorking, Guildford, and Farnham, in Surrey. They then curve round above Alton and Petersfield in Hampshire, where they become the South Downs and pass above Storrington and Lewes in Sussex. The coast from Beachy Head back to Folkestone lies across the open end of the horse-shoe.

Between the North and South Downs is a third line of hills, very different in character from the Downs, known as the High Weald, running from Horsham to Hastings, bordered on either side by a wide valley known as the Low Weald. Interposed between the North Downs and the Low Weald is a fourth range of hills, those of the Lower Greensand. All these hills and intervening valleys run roughly from west to east, and form one clearly defined and basically simple geological unit known as the Wealden Anticline.

The parts of our region which lie beyond the Wealden Anticline are the northern strip of Kent from Dartford to Deal, the part of Surrey between the North Downs and the Thames valley, and the coastal strip of Sussex from Chichester Harbour to Shoreham.

Let us first consider the geology of the Weald and the Downs, leaving aside, for the time being, the parts which lie beyond their confines. Nearly all the rocks within this formation were laid down during the geological period known as the Cretaceous period, which lasted for some 70 million years, from about 135 million years ago to about 65 million years ago. Vast though this time scale is (man appeared upon the earth less than two million years ago), it is fairly recent in geological terms. All these cretaceous rocks were deposited in water; the rocks of the High Weald, known as the Hastings Beds, and consisting of Ashdown Sands, Tunbridge Wells Sands, and Wadhurst Clay, were deposited in a large inland lake that covered the area. After this, during the so-called Upper Cretaceous period, the whole region was flooded by the sea, and the succeeding depositions were therefore made in salt water; these rocks are the Lower Greensand, the Gault (a kind of clay), the Upper Greensand, and the Chalk.

By the end of the Cretaceous period, then, all these rocks had been laid down, and were lying in more or less horizontal layers, with the Hastings Beds at the bottom and a thick layer of Chalk on the top.

The world then entered upon the period of geological development known to us as the Tertiary period, during which – about 20 million years ago – there took place the last of the great cataclysmic earth movements, resulting in the formation of most of the world's great mountain ranges, including the Alps, Andes, and Himalayas. Although at a very considerable distance from the centre of this upheaval, the rocks of what is now England were folded or creased into a series of corrugations, the ridges being anticlines and the troughs synclines. The Weald is one of the major anticlines, situated between the two synclines of the Thames basin to the north and the English Channel to the south.

The arch formed by this Alpine movement was now attacked by wind, rain, and frost, a process that has been continuing ever since. During this time the arch has been gradually worn away, so that the Chalk, together with the Upper Greensand, Gault, and Lower Greensand, has disappeared from the centre of the area altogether, exposing the older rocks of the Hastings Beds. The formation of the valleys of the Low Weald is due to the softness of the clay compared with the rocks on either side, causing it to be eroded more quickly. The differences in thickness of the beds determine the heights of the ridges and the breadths of the valleys.

As the traveller crosses the Weald from north to south he may fairly easily pick out the characteristic features of the geological strata. Although it has its minor complications, there is probably no part of England where the landscape more clearly reflects the geology. Entering the area from, say, London, one comes first to the chalky North Downs. Owing to the undercutting action of the rivers, the Downs, both North and South, present their steeper slope, or scarp, towards the centre and their gentler slope, or dip slope, outwards. Coming from London, you are on the North Downs without realizing that you have done any climbing, so gradual is the incline. (But you will notice it on a bicycle.) Not until you come to the top of the scarp and look south do you appreciate that the Downs are, by the standards of southern England, a considerable range of hills.

People familiar with the chalk downs of Wiltshire, or with the South Downs for that matter, tend to find the North Downs rather tame in comparison, since they are less bare of vegetation, and much more built upon. Nevertheless they display at least some of the typical characteristics of chalk hills: they are generally rounded and smooth, bare in comparison with the surrounding countryside, and contain many dry valleys. Beech is pre-eminent among the larger trees, not because it thrives on chalky soil, but because it is the tree that tolerates it best.

The band of Upper Greensand and Gault, which originally lay immediately underneath the Chalk, now succeeds it horizontally. The Upper Greensand is a very narrow belt at the foot of the Chalk scarp. It is so narrow that it has no noticeable effect upon the landscape, but it may be distinguished here and there as a strip of sandy soil mixed with, or lying alongside, the chalk.

At the foot of the South Downs the Gault Clay is equally insignificant, but below the North Downs it forms the vale known as the Holmesdale. In places the clay, a stiff blue marine mud, gives rise to extensive green pastures, being too heavy for cultivation; elsewhere, where the gault is mixed with sands washed down from the scarp of the Downs, the soil is much lighter and more fertile.

The Holmesdale, then, is a valley situated between the North Downs and the next range of hills, those of the Lower Greensand. These are considerable, and are often mistaken for the North Downs. They are, however, quite different in character: they have a generally sandy, rather than a chalky, soil; and they are more thickly wooded. Their north slopes dip gently, while the south slopes form a real scarp, with concave, land-slipped sides. The line of these hills runs from Selborne in Hampshire, through Hindhead in Surrey, then south of Godalming, Dorking, Sevenoaks, and Maidstone, to Ashford. They culminate in Leith Hill, south of Dorking, at 294m. or 965ft the highest point in the South-East. (The tower at the top is 40ft high, and has a spiral staircase, which bestows upon the visitor the right to say that he has climbed to a thousand feet.)

The well-drained sandy soils of these hills are sometimes rather poor, and are given over to heathland and pine woods; but there are steep-sided fertile valleys. There is considerable variation in the scenery. South of Sevenoaks and Maidstone, for instance, fruit is extensively cultivated on the lower slopes of the hills. Here too the hard stone called Kentish Rag is quarried; in former times it was much used in building throughout its own county and beyond. In complete contrast is the famous feature called the Devil's Punchbowl, near Hindhead, a steep, precipitous, and thickly wooded valley, the head of which has been carved into the shape of a bowl by the undermining action of springs at the junction of the sandy rocks and the underlying clay. Everywhere in this Lower Greensand country there are trees; indeed thick woods are characteristic of it, particularly south of Haslemere, Guildford, Dorking, and Sevenoaks, and from Maidstone to Hindhead the outcrop of the Greensand is marked by tall church towers and stone houses.

The Greensand belt lines the inner edge of the Chalk for its entire circuit, although it is much wider and more noticeable in the north and west than in the south. Then, moving again towards the centre of the horse-shoe, we come to the clay land of the Low Weald, which almost completely surrounds the High Weald. The clay begets heavy, sodden soils and a somewhat featureless landscape. So glutinous is the ground that before the invention of the tarmac road it was sometimes necessary to employ oxen rather than horses to draw heavy loads. Defoe, in his *Tour through the Whole Island of Britain* (1724–7), tells us that at a village near Lewes he saw 'an ancient lady, and a lady of very good quality I assure you, drawn to church in her coach by six oxen . . . the way being so stiff and deep that no horses could go in it'. There are numerous sunken tracks and lanes, often running as much as three or four yards below the level of the adjoining fields owing to the action of man and the elements.

This country, too, is quite thickly wooded in places, although the swamps and dense oak forests of old have been cleared. Much timber has been used as building material, while the clay has gone into the making of bricks and tiles. Where this area of clay reaches the coast, in the open end of the horse-shoe between Eastbourne and Hythe, there are large marshy tracts, Pevensey Levels in the west, and Walland and Romney Marshes in the east. These have been efficiently drained, and afford good grazing for cattle and sheep respectively.

Finally, we move up on to the High Weald – sometimes known as the Forest Ridges – the core of the region, and its oldest part in geological terms. This is an area of steep hills and deep valleys whose broken-up, irregular character is due to the jumbled alternation of the sands and clays of the Hastings Beds. In one sense the seams of Wadhurst Clay constitute the heart of England, for here grow the finest oaks in the country, the trees that once provided timber for her ships, and on which, therefore, her very safety depended. At the centre of the High Weald, rising in places to well over 600ft above sea-level, the sandstones predominate, forming poor, sandy, acid soils and giving rise to the wild heathland of Ashdown Forest, once thick with trees. The High Weald as a whole, stretching, as we have seen, from Horsham to Hastings, is densely wooded. Many of the trees were cut down in days gone by for shipbuilding, and to supply fuel for the hungry furnaces of the Wealden iron industry. But there are plenty left; indeed it has been said that Sussex, in which the whole of this area lies, has more trees for its size than any other county in England.

We have said that the High Weald runs down to the coast at Hastings. The sailor plying eastwards up the English Channel can see this most clearly, for he gets an end-on view: the chalk of the South Downs descends to the coast at Beachy Head; then there is a gap, where the clay belt terminates in the Pevensey Levels, before the brown cliffs of the sandstone rise up, as high as Beachy Head itself. Here Hastings Castle, and the tower of Fairlight church, are prominent landmarks, before the coastline sinks once more to Rye Bay, running out to Dungeness.

After descending to the clay plain, south of the High Weald, the land climbs over the narrow bands of Greensand and Gault to the scarp of the South Downs, the most obvious and prominent feature of the region. It is the South Downs by which Sussex is chiefly remembered in popular imagination. Viewed from the north, they can be seen as a narrow wall of chalk bordering the coast, but the walker on these hills soon discovers that they are surprisingly wide, and the lack of pronounced landmarks can easily lead him to lose his sense of direction. The dip, or reverse, slope runs gently down to the coast, broken up by numerous dry valleys and coombes marking areas of weakness in the rock structure.

No account of the Wealden landscape would be complete without mention of its rivers, for it is they, created by rain and assisted by frost, that have given it its present form, by wearing away, over millions of years, the central roof of chalk, and cutting through the outer ring of the Downs. The High Weald is the great watershed, the Channel or the Thames the destination, of most of these rivers; among the major streams only the Wey and the western Rother rise well to the west of the High Weald.

Originally all the rivers were 'consequent' streams, that is, streams that run down the natural slope of the rocks. In the case of the Weald this meant that they ran to north and to south. Later, when the central part of the chalk arch had been worn away and the broad vales of the Low Weald began to form, 'subsequent' streams, running at right angles to the slope of the rocks, started to flow along the clay valleys. When they met a 'consequent' stream, one of two things could happen: either the consequent would sweep up the subsequent and carry it on down the valley it had carved for itself through the Chalk, or the subsequent would lop off the head of the consequent and carry it down the clay plain. An example of the former is the subsequent western Rother flowing into the Arun near Pulborough, while the latter is exemplified by the Medway's capture, through the agency of its tributary the Eden, of the head waters of the Darenth. On the dip slopes of the Chalk are many dry valleys, originally filled with less successful streams at a period when possibly the water-table was higher.

As we have seen, the undercutting action of the rivers running along the clay valleys has caused the Downs to present their steeper slopes towards the centre; to the north and south they decline more gently, to the Thames Basin in the north, the Thames estuary in the north-east, and the English Channel in the south. Ancient settlements known as 'gap towns' developed where rivers cut through the Chalk, for example, Guildford on the Wey, Leatherhead and Dorking on the Mole, Lewes on the Ouse, Maidstone and Rochester on the Medway. Often castles were built at such points to guard the river approaches.

Where the whole anticline sinks into the sea, as at Beachy Head, the pattern begins to repeat itself in the syncline: the lighthouse at the foot of the cliff actually stands on a ledge of Upper Greensand, while beyond it, a little further east, a band of Gault Clay is exposed to view. South of Dover, Gault Clay is found at the bottom of the cliffs, overlaid by dull-white chalk. Water seeping from the base of the chalk produces ideal conditions for the development of landslips, contrasting with the firm vertical cliffs at Dover itself, where the Gault lies below sea level.

Something must now be said about those parts of our region that lie outside the Weald and its ring of chalk.

In the north, a small corner of Surrey extends into the middle of the so-called London Basin. In this, the process of sedimentary deposition continued after the chalk was laid down. These deposits belong to the Tertiary period, and consist of sands known as Reading Beds, then London Clay, then another layer of sands known as Bagshot Beds, in that order of deposition – that is, from bottom to top. Then, as in the Weald, folding took place, but this time in the opposite direction, so that the whole area became a syncline – a saucer, or basin, of chalk holding within it these later deposits. Finally the River Thames wore down the chalk at Goring, and has ever since been slowly but inexorably widening its valley.

Essentially the London Basin today consists of a triangular-shaped area of low ground, widening from west to east, and extending roughly from Reading eastwards to Clacton in Essex, and to Ramsgate and Deal in Kent. On either side of it are chalk uplands: the Berkshire Downs and the Chiltern Hills to the north, and the North Downs to the south. Within the enclosing chalk is a narrow band of sandy soil above the Reading Beds and then a much broader band of London Clay. Finally, surrounded by the London Clay are 'islands' of the sandy Bagshot Beds, the largest being in the area of Bagshot itself, which is in Surrey.

The portion of Surrey that extends across the London Basin is, of course, that part of it which lies north of the Downs. Guildford is at the southern edge of this stretch of country. To the west of the gap formed by the River Wey, the Hog's Back, bearing the A31 road, is the last sliver of the North Downs before the chalk peters out momentarily, to reappear as the Hampshire Downs beyond Farnham. Here on the Hog's Back one can gaze far across the London Basin to the north and north-east; with binoculars, individual buildings in central London, 30 miles away, can be picked out and identified, while at night the whole north-eastern sky is one huge neon lamp.

Below the chalk on the northern side is a narrow band of sandy soil, the Reading Beds. In the old days, when drainage was more of a problem than it is today, settlements were sited on this base, above the soggy clay but with a good water supply from numerous springs. Guildford is one such settlement; Canterbury, near the far eastern end of the London Basin, is another.

If we follow the A320 road from Guildford to Staines, we are in Surrey all the way. (It is often not realized that Surrey has extended itself northwards to include Staines, north of the Thames, and even to lap the runway at Heathrow.) The route of the road is indisputably suburban in character, but if we look beyond the rash of housing we can see the change from soil to soil. First we cross the clay country whereon stand the northern suburbs of Guildford – at this point the band of clay is unusually narrow. Soon we notice heaths and pine trees: this is Whitmoor Common. This sort of terrain continues right through Woking – pine, bracken, gravel, sand.

To the east of us the Wey and the Mole meander through the clay to their final resting places in the Thames, while to the west the heath extends to Camberley. This heathland is too sterile, because too acid, to support farming; it does, however, provide the Army with training grounds, and has some excellent golf courses: West Byfleet, Sunningdale, and, rather on the edge of it, Wentworth. Then at Chertsey we return to the clay. Here we reach the Thames itself. We follow the river valley for the short distance up to Staines, passing on our left the old gravel pits at Thorpe, now worked out and promoted to the status of a marina.

Part of Kent, too, lies beyond the confines of the Weald and the Downs: the strip along the north coast from Dartford to Thanet, and the east coast from Ramsgate to Deal. Much of this coast is flat, marshy, and even dreary, given over to oil refineries and other industrial development. Elsewhere, as on the north coast of the Isle of Sheppey and at Whitstable, there are cliffs of London Clay subject to erosion. Behind the coast, subsidence has caused the channels of estuaries and streams to join up, thus forming the islands of Sheppey and Grain, and numerous muddy islets in the Medway estuary.

The isle of Thanet, a knob or outlier of chalk, was a true island in Saxon times, separated from the rest of England by the Stour to the south and the Wantsum to the west; the latter, however, has silted up and is no more than a drainage channel wandering across the marshes west of St Nicholas at Wade. The Stour has altered course more than once, and now makes a great loop southwards to Sandwich before turning north and finally achieving an outlet to the sea at Pegwell Bay, whence hovercraft roar across to Calais in 40 minutes.

The last corner of our region lying beyond the Downs is the strip of Sussex coast between Chichester Harbour and Shoreham. At Chichester, as at Guildford in the north, alternating strips of sands and clay run from west to east, ending with the sands of Selsey Bill, while a finger of similar soil runs east from Chichester through Arundel to Worthing, between the chalk of the Downs to the north and of the coast to the south.

Early in the Ice Age (although the ice never reached so far south as this) the channels of Chichester Harbour were rivers running into the main river at Spithead, whose mouth was probably somewhere south of the present Selsey Bill. In other words, the land was higher in relation to the sea than it is now. But towards the end of the Ice Age, say about 12,000 years ago, when the melting ice caused the water level to rise, the whole of this area is thought to have been covered by a shallow sea. Finally it fell back, Selsey and Thorney being uncovered as islands and later becoming peninsulas. The process continues today as part of the ceaseless war between land and sea.

Man in the Landscape

The story of Man in the south-eastern landscape starts tentatively about 400,000 years ago. If Man was there before this Palaeolithic time, or Old Stone Age, we know nothing of it. This was the era of alternate advance and retreat of the ice, with long intervals of many thousands of years marking the climatic rhythm, before the long-drawn-out withdrawal of the ice, round about 9000 B.C. There are no remains of human habitations before the latter date – only a collection of tools such as hand-axes found in the river gravels of the Thames and Wey valleys in Surrey, of the Thames, Medway, and Nail Bourne valleys in Kent, and below the South Downs in Sussex, west of Arundel.

The next, or Mesolithic, period dates from about 9000 to about 3000 B.C., when a general westward movement of Man brought settlers to Britain. The ice had retreated and the climate was warmer. Now for the first time sites of crude dwellings appear, such as the pit dwelling at Abinger; there are signs of temporary occupation, too, on Holt Hill, south-west of Aylesford, consisting of a scattering of flint implements. Typically, Mesolithic dwellings were pits roofed with furze; as these people had inadequate digging tools they tended to scoop out their pits in soft sandy rocks and clays such as are found about Tunbridge Wells, East Grinstead, and Horsham. There is evidence, too, as at Iping Common, near Midhurst, that they began clearing the dense forests of the Weald by burning – partly by accident no doubt, but also partly on purpose to provide grazing for the animals they hunted, for this was before the days of farming; or perhaps they were making open spaces into which the animals could be driven and thus more easily killed.

The next period, the Neolithic or New Stone Age, lasted from about 3000 to about 2000 B.C. Now for the first time farming was carried on, and pottery was introduced. There are a number of Neolithic sites, such as the causewayed camps at Bignor Hill, at Whitehawk (in the eastern part of Brighton), and at The Trundle (see Goodwood); the flint mines of Cissbury Ring (see Findon); the long barrows at Badshot Lea, near Farnham, and Jullieberries Graves near Chilham; and the once chambered tomb of Kits Coty near Aylesford, now a jumbled group of four huge stones without a roof.

As the Neolithic Age merged almost imperceptibly into the Bronze Age, the Beaker Folk began to settle in south-east Britain. They came from the Iberian peninsula via the Rhineland and the Netherlands, and acquired their name from their custom of placing cups or beakers beside their dead on burial. From the evidence of the tools and ornaments they left behind they appear to have been more warlike and yet more highly civilized than previous settlers. Some of the round barrows or burial mounds of Sussex and Kent may be theirs. In Surrey, however, there are almost no traces of the Beaker Folk, apart from the single beaker found at Titsey, and indeed the Mesolithic culture here seems to have lasted until the Bronze Age, when metal implements were made for the first time. Most of the round barrows of Sussex and Kent are thought to date from the early Bronze Age, and there are many round barrows in Surrey dating from the same period, although most of them are hidden by trees, or spoilt by unskilled excavation. Sometimes they are arranged in groups, as on Reigate Heath.

The period that succeeded the Bronze Age is known as the Iron Age. It started about 600 B.C. with the arrival in south-east Britain of iron-using immigrants from northern France and the Netherlands, who seem to have settled peaceably with their Bronze Age predecessors; in many places bronze implements continued to be used well into the Iron Age. Then about 250 B.C. a second, more warlike, people appeared from northern France; they were the builders of the great Iron Age forts that are dotted about the Downs, especially the South Downs of Sussex. Finally, about 100 B.C. the first of the Belgae arrived in Kent, bringing gold coinage, wheel-turned pottery, and other refinements. They gradually spread over the rest of the region, and revolutionized its agriculture by the use of the heavy wheeled plough with which they were able for the first time to drain and cultivate the heavier soils. These were the people who were dominant in the region when the Romans came.

★

The history of this south-east corner of England is that of England itself writ small, for being closest to the Continent it has been in the forefront of events, bearing the brunt of foreign invasions. On the other hand it presented, at any rate until the nineteenth century, an awkward and intractable terrain, an annoying obstacle, rather than a convenient stepping-stone, between the coast and the Thames valley, and remained, apart from the iron of the Weald, comparatively undeveloped.

An invader had made no worthwhile progress until he had crossed the Thames. Julius Caesar's 'invasion' of 55 B.C. was little more than a reconnaissance. In the following year he made a more serious attempt; he did in fact cross the Thames, and many of the chiefs of the Belgic tribes did homage to him. Having received hostages, however, and a promise of tribute, he returned to Gaul. It was not until A.D. 43 that the Emperor Claudius sent an army to attempt the permanent subjugation and occupation of the island. The Romans then claimed, in the wonted style of invaders, to be liberating the local population from the oppressive yoke of the powerful Belgic tribe known as the Catuvellauni. Having landed, probably at Richborough (Rutupiae) in Pegwell Bay, they pushed on to Canterbury and thence along the direct route to the crossing of the Thames, the only major obstacle being the River Medway, where a two-day battle was fought. Later they spread out along both coasts, establishing defences at Dover (Dubris), Lympne (Lemanis), and Pevensey (Anderida), and important towns at Canterbury (Durovernum) and Chichester (Noviomagus). Perhaps owing to its proximity to London, Rochester (Durobrivae) was of less importance.

Apart from exploiting the Wealden iron, the Romans left Surrey and the Weald almost untouched, although they did have to build roads connecting London and the coast, notably the road to Chichester, which the Saxons later named Stane Street. As for Kent, once the Roman invaders had crossed the Thames it became something of a peaceful backwater, with dense civilian settlement. Military installations were designed to repel invasion from the sea rather than counter-attack from the land. In Sussex, too, resistance to Rome was slight; indeed Cogidubnus, king of the Regni, the tribe that dominated the area at the time, eagerly came to terms, and was rewarded with the high-sounding title of *Rex et legatus Augusti in Britannia*. Chichester became the Roman capital of the region round about, and here the puppet king's court was established. There are no other Roman towns in Sussex, although there are remains of several villas, as well as the grandest building of all, the palace at Fishbourne (q.v.).

The South-East enjoyed peace and prosperity under the Romans during the first two centuries A.D., but the next two were a time of ever-increasing threat and danger from pirate raids. At the port of Lympne, the chief base of the *Classis Britannica*, the defences had to be massively reinforced in the late third century. Little of them now remains, but, as can be seen today, Dover and Richborough were also strengthened, and a new fort was built at Reculver. These precautions were, however, unavailing; Lympne was abandoned first, perhaps owing more to land-slipping than to military assault. Little is known of the last days of Dover and Reculver, but it seems that only Richborough held out well into the fifth, when Rome herself fell prey to the Goths.

Ironically, it was in the vicinity of Richborough that the Jutes from northern Denmark, under Hengist, are supposed to have landed in 446, perhaps not as invaders but rather at the urgent invitation of Vortigern, king of the hard-pressed Cantii, who were threatened from the north by the Picts. Hengist seems to have beaten the Picts, and then to have taken over the territory he had rescued. Kent became a Jutish kingdom.

There were other landings on the east and south coasts of Britain at about this time. The Saxons, from the northern coast of Germany, landed, probably at Selsey, in about 477, under their leader Ella, and the kingdom of the South Saxons, or Sussex, came into being. As for Surrey, this is the Saxon *Suthrige*, or South Region, implying that it lay south of some other important area; it probably means the region south of London, its wild and hilly terrain being a useful barrier against raiding bands.

Although there were frequent feuds and squabbles between the Saxon kingdoms, and between the Saxons and the Angles to the north, it is almost certainly wrong to imagine a state of continuous strife. The newcomers gradually mixed and merged with each other, and when St Augustine brought back Christianity it acted as a further healer of divisions. St Augustine landed in Kent in 597, having been sent by Pope Gregory to 'preach the word of God to the English nation'. He was well received by King Ethelbert, whose wife Bertha was already a Christian, and was allowed to preach freely, and even to lodge with his followers in the city of Canterbury, where eventually he established his see. From this corner of England Christianity spread once more over the southern half of Britain.

In 681 St Wilfrid, from Lindisfarne, came to Sussex and founded a church at Selsey. The South Saxons resisted Christianity longer than any of the other kingdoms, but once they accepted it they were active in church building. Indeed, the number of Saxon churches in present-day Sussex is above average; this is probably due to dwindling prosperity in the later Middle Ages, which meant that there was less reason here than elsewhere to replace small humble churches with large grand ones. Most of the Saxon churches, like Arlington, Bishopstone, Chithurst, Jevington, Selham, are in the southern part of the county close to the Downs, where the agrarian recession of the fourteenth and fifteenth centuries was most marked, although Worth is a notable exception.

The coming of the pagan Danes late in the eighth century presaged more bloodshed and fiercer battles, just when it looked as if England would become truly united under one royal house. Surrey was not immune, for the Danes came into it across the Thames and along the east–west trackway previously mentioned. Ethelwulf, king of Mercia, defeated them at 'Aclea', identified by some as Ockley, below Leith Hill. The Benedictine abbey at Chertsey, founded in the mid seventh century, suffered frequent raids, as did most of the Saxon churches in the area. Peace ruled for about a hundred years after Alfred's victory at Ethandune in 878 and the Treaty of Wedmore concluded in the following year, under whose terms Saxon and Dane each recognized the other's boundaries. During this time, under the influence first of Alfred and later of Edgar and his great archbishop and adviser Dunstan (*see* Mayfield), the English at last became welded into a nation; and although Danish invasions were renewed from about 980, they culminated in another period of peaceful progress under the wise Danish king Canute (1017–35, *see* Bosham). After Canute's death, however, the struggle was once more resumed, until finally, in 1066, William of Normandy stepped ashore at Pevensey.

This is not the place to analyse the rival claims of William the Norman and Harold the Saxon to the throne of England. Whatever the legal niceties, might if not right proved to be on William's side – together with considerable luck. William was making for Hastings as a strongpoint and base for future supplies, but was blown off course and landed at Pevensey. He was not to know that his men and horses would be able to wade ashore and strike across country towards Hastings unopposed. Having secured Hastings, William sallied forth to meet Harold and his army, weary after their battle at Stamford Bridge in Yorkshire against Harold's brother Tostig, and their astonishingly rapid march southwards to meet the new threat. William's victory at Senlac (*see* Battle) had a profound and lasting effect upon the course of English history.

Like the Romans, William had a sharp eye for the strategic points of the terrain, and was an efficient administrator. The land was parcelled out among those who had been his most faithful supporters, and in each area a castle was built, from which the tenant-in-chief could rule the surrounding countryside. In Sussex these districts were known as 'rapes'. The hastily erected wooden structures were soon replaced by stone. In addition, some Roman strongpoints such as Dover and Pevensey were refortified. The Norman castles were built at strategic sites, mainly guarding river valleys: Arundel, Bramber, Lewes, Camber in Sussex; Rochester and Allington in Kent; Guildford in Surrey. The building of castles was carefully controlled from the first: a 'licence to crenellate', granted by the King, had to be obtained. However, during the turbulent reign of Stephen a number of unlicensed castles sprouted, many of them subsequently destroyed by Henry II; Farnham Castle in Surrey is an example.

The Conqueror's firm rule brought peace, but only for a time. Invasions ceased, but the years that followed saw growing rivalry between monarch, barons, and Church, of which Becket's murder in 1170, and the signing of Magna Carta at Runnymede in 1215, were symptoms. The South-East, which had hitherto occupied the centre of the stage because it bore the brunt of invasions, began to yield pride of place to London, the Midlands, and the North. Nevertheless, although there were no invasions, there were threats of them, and numerous raids. During the Hundred Years' War against France castles were built and houses fortified in response to these dangers (*see* Amberley, Bodiam, Cooling).

There were also sporadic outbursts of unrest. The Peasants' Revolt in 1381, widespread throughout eastern England, found its chief leader in Wat Tyler, a Kentish man, inspired by another, John Ball, called by the irate landowners 'the mad priest of Kent', who for 20 years had been preaching inflammatory doctrines. Wat Tyler was killed by the royal forces at Smithfield. Discontent again flared in Kent in Cade's rebellion (1450). This was a more local affair, the men of Kent having supplied ships to seize the Duke of Suffolk, who was pursued on his way to France and beheaded in an open boat off Calais. Cade and his 20,000 followers marched on London, where they were repulsed with great slaughter; Cade himself was eventually killed by the Sheriff of Kent.

One of the demands that had been made by the rebels was the return to favour of Richard, Duke of York, and chief leader of the Yorkists in the Wars of the Roses. These wars were fought out in the Midlands and the North, and hardly touched the parts south of the Thames. It was different, however, when the reign of the Tudors was ushered in at Bosworth Field in 1485. No part of England remained unaffected by those ruthless, colourful characters. Great houses were built or enlarged: Knole, Otford, Parham – and, of course, Nonsuch Palace, built for Henry VIII himself, of which there is now no trace. Great religious houses were destroyed at the Dissolution or fell into ruin: Bayham Abbey, St Augustine's Abbey at Canterbury, and most of Boxgrove Priory. Forts were built along the coast as invasion threats from France were again renewed: Sandown, Deal, Walmer, Sandgate, Camber.

In 1554 Kent spawned yet another rising: Wyatt's Rebellion, caused by Mary Tudor's proposed marriage to Philip of Spain, which was, understandably in the climate of the times, extremely unpopular. Sir Thomas Wyatt led the men of Kent in a march on London that ended in ignominious failure. He himself was executed, as was the young Lady Jane Grey, who it had been planned should occupy the throne in Mary's place; Lady Jane's husband, father, and uncle shared the same fate, and even the Princess Elizabeth, the future queen, was imprisoned in the Tower.

Henry VIII's coastal forts already mentioned – Sandown, Deal, and the rest – which were never needed in the end, were the forerunners of the Martello towers, built in the early 1800s along the coasts of Kent and Sussex against the threatened invasion by Napoleon. These were modelled on the tower at Cap Mortella in Corsica, which had so successfully resisted the British fleet a few years before. ('Mortella' was corrupted to 'Martello' through a signalling error.) From this time too dates the Royal Military Canal, built at Pitt's urgent demand, to stop Napoleon crossing the flat plain of Romney Marsh, and the subject of scornful remarks by Cobbett.

No account of the region's history, however brief, would be complete without mention of the trade for which Sussex, especially, was renowned: that of smuggling. Its heyday was from the end of the seventeenth century to about 1830. During this period taxes on imports were steadily increased and bitterly resented as an infringement of personal liberty, particularly as they were imposed largely to pay for foreign wars. The fact that the enemy was more often than not France was no discouragement: 'honour among thieves', perhaps. Agricultural labourers preferred to join in the lucrative trade rather than toil for a pittance on the farms; the smugglers struck a bargain with the farmers, 'releasing' their men to get the harvest in on condition that the farmers 'forgot to lock the barns' at night. After the final defeat of Napoleon at Waterloo, the British government was able to spare men and ships to tackle the smuggling problem in earnest, and the tide began to turn in favour of the excisemen. The trade was finally killed by the drastic reductions in import duties made by Peel in the 1840s.

As in other parts of England, Victorian development of the South-East, and particularly the coming of the railways, fundamentally affected the demography and landscape (*see below*, p. 21). In the eighteenth century, Surrey, for instance, was a wild, heathy county, sparsely cultivated and sparsely populated. In 1801 the population of the county – excluding the part transferred to London under the Local Government Act of 1888 – was 106,000; in 1921 it was 930,000. It would be misleading to claim that the railways were the cause of this increase but they were certainly a factor determining where people lived and the structure of employment; and by the turn of the century they were carrying a significant number of workers to and from London, the presence of which came to dominate much of Surrey and Kent.

The railways also encouraged the development of the coastal resorts with which the region is so liberally supplied. It was in the eighteenth century that the health-giving properties of sea air were first promoted, especially at Brighton by Dr Russell of Lewes, and gave rise to the popular pastime of sea-bathing. The bathing-machine is said to have been invented by Benjamin Beale of Margate, also in the eighteenth century. The Prince of Wales's period of residence at Brighton from 1784 gave a fillip to the fashion of going to the seaside, and by the end of the nineteenth century the gradually increasing leisure of the working classes – and the railways – had translated it from a dream to a reality for the masses.

In the Second World War the region bore the brunt of enemy air attacks, Kent earning the nickname of 'Bomb Alley'. It also provided many of the bases from which the Battle of Britain was fought and won. Meanwhile the whole coast became a 'prohibited area', protected by wire, mines, and gun emplacements, and difficult for the visitor of today to remember or to imagine.

★

The buildings of the region reflect both geology and history. Unfortunately, as everywhere in England, in the urban and suburban parts – and even in the rural parts, albeit to a lesser extent – a deadening and ugly uniformity of building materials, colours, and shapes has tended to swamp the individuality, the inherent rightness, of the local products, largely as a result of the countrywide improvement in communications ushered in by McAdam, and by the canal and railway engineers of the eighteenth and nineteenth centuries. It must in fairness be said, however, that of recent years local authorities have made efforts to build in local styles, and with traditional local materials, or, where that has been impracticable owing to the cost, at least in colours that have toned with them.

Dull uniformity has in any case done no more than make inroads; it has not obliterated. Stone, brick, tiles, and wood combine to make the buildings of Surrey, Sussex, and Kent among the most varied and interesting – if not outstanding – in the country, and it is still possible, so far as stone is concerned, to trace in the buildings the path of geological strata. In these counties the strata run roughly in east–west bands across the region, and we can look at each in turn, starting with the youngest in geological terms, the Thames basin in the north. This, as we have seen, belongs to the Tertiary period, and consists of sands and clays. Stone for building has been in short supply and of inferior quality. Indeed there are only two kinds of usable stone at all: sarsens, which are lumps of grey sandstone, and puddingstone, a conglomeration of flint pebbles and crumbly sandstone held together by a cement of iron oxide. Of the two, puddingstone is much the more plentiful. Alec Clifton-Taylor has described it as 'one of the least attractive of English stones and one of the least durable'. Nevertheless, for lack of anything else, it was much used in the churches of this part of the region, mainly in the northern parts of Surrey. Its inferiority to sarsens, which are themselves by no means first class, being too hard to give anything but a pretty rough surface, is well demonstrated at Chobham, where the tower of the church is of sarsens and the rest of puddingstone. Other churches where puddingstone has been used extensively are at Albury, Byfleet, Cobham, and Woking.

Passing to the next geological band, we come to the chalk of the North and South Downs. The chalk itself has been little used as a building stone externally; certainly less in the South-East than in Hampshire, Dorset, or parts of Wiltshire. Its chief use has been internal, as in the churches at Great Bookham, Compton, Farnham, and Fetcham, as well as in others further from the source of this material, such as Godalming, Pyrford, and Stoke D'Abernon. It is also found, in the form of calcareous tufa, at East Malling church in Kent, in association with Kentish Ragstone, and in the twelfth-century tower at Leeds. The main drawback of chalk as a building stone for outside walls is its lack of durability, whereas for interior work its softness lends itself to the elaborate carving beloved of medieval craftsmen, while its lightness makes it suitable for vaults.

The chief importance of the chalk of the Downs, however, so far as building materials are concerned, is as a source of flint. The main characteristic of flint is the very opposite of that of the chalk in which it lies buried: it is exceptionally durable. For this reason it is specially common in older buildings in the coastal towns, for it is impervious to the ravages of the salty air. But it is also common in Surrey, from the ridge of the North Downs northwards; indeed at least half the walls of the old churches of Surrey are faced with it. Since in most cases it is unknapped, the result is usually far from elegant, in contrast with the much more sophisticated churches of East Anglia. The inelegance of unknapped flint is exemplified in a secular building of importance too: Goodwood House in Sussex, whose architect, James Wyatt, was instructed by the Duke of Richmond to build it in this material because it was obtainable locally. This normally sound idea was certainly a mistake in this instance, for the large areas of mortar are considerably darker than the lumps of flint they are holding together, and the result lacks dignity.

Knapped flint – that is, flint that has been split, and then set into the wall with the split, or shiny black, face showing outwards – is also seen in several buildings along the coast, at Sandwich in Kent, and particularly in the Brighton area of Sussex, where in Georgian and Victorian times, by a further refinement, the flints were not only knapped but also squared off. Examples of this may be seen at St Michael's church, Lewes (exterior of the south aisle), at Court Farm, Falmer, at the Hall at Southwick, and at No. 69 Ship Street in the centre of Brighton itself.

As we move off the chalk ridges we descend first to the Upper Greensand. The narrow belt of it running along the southern slope of the North Downs has produced Reigate stone, or Firestone, much used for building in the Middle Ages. This stone was quarried, or more usually mined by running gently sloping shafts into the hillsides, at such places as Brockham and Betchworth to the west of Reigate, Merstham and Gatton to the north-east, and Bletchingley and Godstone to the east. These places provided stone for such notable buildings as Southwark Cathedral, Windsor Castle, and Henry VII's chapel at Westminster Abbey. The stone is also found further west, near Farnham, where it is known as Malmstone. It lends itself to moulding and carving, but it weathers badly, as may be seen to this day at Westminster.

From the Lower Greensand belt of Surrey comes a tougher and coarser stone, whose high iron content gives it a brownish hue. This is called Bargate stone, although curiously enough there is no such place as Bargate in Surrey. It is sometimes known as Burgate stone, and is thought by some, therefore, to be connected with Burgate House, Hambledon, near Godalming, although this was not built of it and is some distance from the nearest known deposit of the stone. Here is a minor mystery.

Bargate stone used to be quarried in the Guildford–Godalming area. It was used in the twelfth century as a facing stone for Guildford Castle. Charterhouse School, built by P. C. Hardwick in the nineteenth century, is largely composed of it, and Lutyens used it in the courtyard at Munstead Wood, near Godalming, at Tigbourne Court, near Witley, and in several other houses in Surrey. It is a hard, intractable stone, and cannot be used where a smooth surface is required. Nevertheless its colour and texture are attractive in a crude, no-nonsense way.

Another stone of the Lower Greensand belt of Surrey is Carstone, seen at various places in the vicinity of Albury and Tilford, where it was used for both church and bridges. Carstone, too, contains a high proportion of iron, and comes in various shades of brown. (In Norfolk it is called Gingerbread Stone.) It was once used for 'galleting'. This is the practice of inserting small pieces of the stone – sometimes flint was used – in the mortar of an outside wall. It may originally have been done to help to keep the mortar together, but later it became a purely decorative device. It is hardly ever seen on large or ambitious buildings, but is quite common on humbler dwellings in south-west Surrey and north-west Sussex, as well as over the border in Hampshire, around Selbourne. It is also used to give a rustic effect to more pretentious buildings, as at Tigbourne Court. On really large expanses of wall it merely looks absurd, as at Albury Park and at Deal Castle.

However, the most important building stone from the Lower Greensand belt of the region is Kentish Rag or Ragstone, a limestone quarried mainly between Maidstone and Sevenoaks. In the county itself it is found at Old Soar near Plaxtol, at Rochester Castle, at Knole, and at many of the county's churches, such as Chart Sutton, Hoo, Lympne, St Peter's, Maidstone, and Newchurch on Romney Marsh. It is a coarse, brittle stone, lacking elegance. Nevertheless, owing to the dearth of durable building stone in the South-East, and the ease with which Kentish Rag could be transported down the Medway and up the Thames, it has been much used in London and in south Essex. The Romans made use of it for building London's wall, the Normans for the White Tower of London (which they faced with Caen stone), and the medieval builders for a number of London churches. It is in London particularly that another of its drawbacks is apparent: owing to its rough, uneven texture, it harbours the dirt, and this intensifies its crudity. But in the Kentish countryside its down-to-earth simplicity, as at Ightham Mote or Old Soar, looks entirely right. Its ruggedness also accords well with the somewhat martial air imparted to many a Kentish church tower by the stair turret rising from one corner, which is so characteristic of this county.

As we move in from the Lower Greensand towards the centre of the Weald, we come to the source of the freshwater limestones, composed largely of the shells of snails and molluscs, and known locally as 'marble' because they take a polish – Bethersden marble in Kent and Sussex marble in Sussex, the chief quarries for which are at Bethersden, near Ashford, and Kirdford, near Petworth. Bethersden marble paves the village church itself, and the pavement at Biddenden; Biddenden church tower is built of it, and it provides the stone for many fonts and monuments throughout the county.

Sussex marble provides the stone for the font at Kirdford and for many other fonts in Sussex, and it was widely used for floor slabs. It was formerly known by the charming name of 'winklestone'. There were other quarries near East Grinstead, at Petworth, at Laughton, east of Lewes, and at Charlwood, Outwood, and Ewhurst, in Surrey.

Finally, so far as indigenous stone is concerned, we come to the Wealden sandstones of the so-called Hastings Beds. These sandstones have no rival among the building stones of the South-East. They are fine-grained, and capable of being 'ashlared', that is to say, cut, squared, and smoothed. They are varied in colour, even from the same quarry, and this gives a pleasingly warm effect, the overall hue being sandy, although often shot or streaked with greys, browns, and rusts. Their durability and impermeability varies, it is true; but on the whole the Wealden sandstone is an efficient and attractive building stone, with a 'warmth', both to eye and hand, quite lacking in, say, flint. Good examples are seen at Bodiam Castle and Wakehurst Place in Sussex, and Cranbrook church and Penshurst Place in Kent.

Another use for the Wealden sandstones of Surrey and Sussex is as roofing slates, known as Horsham slates, although these have been obtained from many other sites in the Weald than Horsham. Dark brown in colour, and often covered with moss, which they appear to attract to an almost excessive degree, these roofs are pleasant to look at. They are very heavy, and a roof made of these slates often sags in consequence; the burden of them has proved intolerable to many a rafter.

A notable building stone which must be mentioned, although not an English stone at all, is Caen stone, which the Normans were used to and which they found quite easy to bring across the Channel and up the river estuaries of the South-East, a practice carried on right through the Middle Ages and even into Victorian times. Fortunately this stone, although not a native, so to speak, blends well with its English surroundings, being a limestone similar in appearance to Clipsham. The outstanding example of it in our region is the central tower of Canterbury Cathedral ('Bell Harry'), which, though built of brick, is faced with Caen stone, and is a thing of beauty. In an entirely different setting it is combined with flint to give a chequerwork effect on the south face of The Marlipins at New Shoreham, Sussex, a mainly fourteenth-century house which is now a museum.

For all our talk about stone, it is not the stone buildings of the region that make the predominant impression upon the mind of the traveller, but the bricks and tiles; nor is the impact of wood by any means negligible.

All three counties have areas well endowed with clay suitable for making bricks of high quality, and there are examples in all three of old buildings made from them. There are examples of Roman brickwork in the chancel of St Martin's church in Canterbury and in the church walls at Ashtead, Mickleham, Fetcham, and Stoke D'Abernon. Curiously, there appears to have been no brick-making in England for about a thousand years after the departure of the Romans. Examples of fifteenth-century brickwork are Farnham Castle tower and Bishop Waynflete's gatehouse at Esher in Surrey, and Herstmonceux Castle in Sussex; from the sixteenth century the gatehouse of Sissinghurst Castle in Kent is a fine specimen, as is Great Fosters near Egham in Surrey. Also in Surrey is the seventeenth-century Abbot's Hospital at Guildford, and many excellent brick houses of the eighteenth century, while an example from the present century is Guildford Cathedral.

Good brick buildings can be found everywhere, if one keeps one's eyes open. Unfortunately it is not necessary to be observant to realize that the vast majority of brick buildings in all three counties are characterless efforts of the nineteenth and twentieth centuries, made as like as not of mass-produced bricks used with callous disregard for the local landscape.

Closely related to bricks are tiles. The process of manufacture is essentially the same: clay is pressed into a mould, then fired or baked until hard. They are often made at the same kiln, although the clay is baked harder in the case of tiles.

The Romans made roofing tiles in England, but after their departure, as with bricks, there was a gap, and tiles were not re-introduced until about the twelfth century, probably as a substitute for wooden shingles in the first place. Certainly their use in the Middle Ages became widespread long before that of bricks, which to begin with were known as 'waltyles' (wall-tiles).

These three counties form the area of England where tiles are commonest and at their best, and where tile-hanging is so characteristic. This method of wall-covering was begun in the seventeenth century, with the object of protecting the walls, particularly wooden walls, from the damp. The commonest shape for tiles used in this way is the plain rectangle, with the surface of the tile slightly curved, but other more fanciful shapes are often employed, such as the fish-scale, in which the tile is rounded at the lower end. Sometimes a mixture of shapes appears on the same wall, but this tends to look fussy.

In the eighteenth century the fashion started of covering walls with tiles made to resemble bricks. These became known as 'mathematical' tiles, for reasons that are obscure. The practice was given added impetus after 1784, when a brick tax (which did not apply to tiles) was introduced; it was not withdrawn until 1850. Examples of such tiling may be seen in many places, notably at Lewes, Brighton, and Rye, in Sussex, and at Canterbury, Hythe, and Tenterden, in Kent.

Perhaps because the use of tiles for roofing is so common in the region, the use of thatch for the same purpose is comparatively rare.

In a region where wood was plentiful we should expect it to have been used extensively for building, and so it was. Timber-framed houses are common – more so than is at first apparent, for there are many houses, such as Rampyndene at Burwash, Sussex, which look from the outside as if they were constructed from some other material, usually brick. Sometimes the timber-framing is masked from the outside by tile-hanging or weatherboarding.

The timber-framed houses of this region are among the finest in England. The majority, as elsewhere, date from the sixteenth and seventeenth centuries, although the region contains more of them dating from before 1500 than any other part of the country except Essex. Examples are the late-fourteenth-century yeoman's house at Larkfield, north of East Malling, Kent; the fifteenth-century Old Shop at Bignor, Sussex; and the exquisite fifteenth-century farmhouse at Brewer Street, north of Bletchingley, Surrey. The last of these is an example of the so-called Wealden type, which is found in Kent more than anywhere else, specially in the Greensand area east of Maidstone; Corner Farm, Langley, is an excellent example here. This type of house consisted of a central portion, which was the main hall of the house and which extended from floor to roof, and two side portions, one of which contained the solar and other private rooms, while the other side contained the service rooms, notably the kitchen; both wings had two floors. All three sections were covered by one roof, hipped, or sloping, at both ends. The upper floor of each wing was jettied – that is to say, it overhung the rooms below. This meant that the roof had to protrude a considerable way from the wall of the centre portion, and it was necessary to support this overhang by means of curved braces rising from the jettied wings and running parallel to the face of the wall. Sometimes the support afforded by these braces was augmented by others rising from the studs, or uprights, of the central wall itself, and set at right angles to it.

The reason for jettying or overhanging in timber-framed houses – in the Wealden type it was invariably carried out on the front, but sometimes also at the back and the sides – is a subject of discussion and conjecture among experts, which cannot be gone into here; whatever the original purpose, it may well be that it later became simply a matter of following the fashion.

The days of the Wealden timber-framed house were of short duration; the discomforts of the central hall were not to be tolerated by the affluent gentry of Tudor times; besides, it lacked refinement. Brick fireplaces began to appear, and an extra floor was put in half way up the hall. Today, if a Wealden timber-framed house has a central hall reaching from floor to roof, it will most probably be a restoration or imitation.

The material used to fill up the space between the studs of timber-framed houses varied. On the humbler dwellings it was plain wattle and daub. On others a coating of plaster was added, which helped to keep the draught out. At a later stage it was sometimes brick; this is known as 'nogging'. In some cases the bricks are laid horizontally, in others in a herringbone pattern, and in yet others higgledy-piggledy, betraying poor workmanship. Brick-nogging can look very attractive, although as a draught-excluder it is less effective than plaster.

So far as colours are concerned, there are no black-and-white half-timbered houses in the South-East, other than a few modern imitations of the genuine ones to be found in such counties as Hereford and Worcester, Shropshire, and Cheshire; in the South-East they saw no good reason to paint their lovely oak timbers black (oak was almost invariably used), and if plaster was employed as a filling it was more often given a softer tone such as ochre rather than a staring white.

Wood was, of course, used in a variety of ways. Weatherboarding has been mentioned. This method of wall-covering is outstandingly characteristic of these three counties, commoner here than anywhere else in England. Its name proclaims its purpose. It consists of wooden boards fixed, usually horizontally but not always so, on to the sides of a building to give extra warmth and protection from the weather. The boards normally overlap, which helps to keep out the damp. Farm buildings are often tarred, whereas houses are usually painted white or cream. The use of weatherboarding was originally due to its being cheaper than bricks or tiles; it is never seen on a building with any pretensions of grandeur. On a modest building it always looks good, if properly preserved. It is quite often seen on church towers, especially in Surrey; Burstow church is a good example. Nowadays it is also used on houses without any intention other than to harmonize with the local style.

Another use for wood, also very characteristic of this region, is as a roofing material in the form of shingles. These wooden 'tiles' of silver-grey are common on the spires of churches in all three counties. They were formerly made of oak, but now for economy's sake they are almost always replaced with Canadian cedar, when restoration is necessary. (At Sissinghurst Castle, however, oak was used on the gatehouse turrets by Sir Edward Maufe in his sympathetic restoration of 1958.) Canadian cedar is quite satisfactory, and can be cut in larger sizes of shingle than oak; it also weathers to a pleasant grey colour, which, however, lacks the silvery tone that only oak can display.

Wood and brick combine in a type of building still seen in East Sussex and west Kent: the oast house, formerly used for the drying of hops employed in the production of beer. Many are now derelict, and others have been converted into attractive – although not, in view of their round shape, entirely convenient – dwellings. Where they are still preserved in their original form, with their distinctive conical roofs, their white wooden cowls fresh-painted, they are a considerable enhancement of the landscape.

Wood and brick are also used for windmills, of which there are still a number of good examples in the region: brick for the tower mills, such as at Nutley in Sussex, and wood for the smock and post mills. There is a fine smock mill at Cranbrook, Kent, still in commercial use, while Jack and Jill, the two windmills at Clayton, Sussex, are respectively a brick tower mill and a wooden post mill.

★

Land communications have never been easy in this region, and even today they leave much to be desired. We have seen that the geological strata run east and west, rather than north and south, and this means that the lines of hills and valleys tend to run in the same direction, which would therefore be the easiest way for roads and tracks to take. But the looming presence of London at the apex has been a dominant influence in the development of south-eastern communications ever since the arrival of the Romans, and it continues to dominate them today, when so far as communications are concerned the whole region is describable, in cynically basic terms, as a tract of land separating London from the coast; and the main lines of communication go across the 'grain', that is, north–south.

In ancient times, settlements and the tracks leading in and out of them were sited on the higher ground, away from the swamps and dense forests of the valleys. Gradually, however, the swamps and forests were cleared, and human settlements were established in the valleys, where water was more easily available and life was generally easier. Nevertheless, travelling still remained less laborious on the hills. The so-called Pilgrims' Way, following as it does the line of the North Downs, existed long before the murder and subsequent veneration of Becket, and is thought to date from the Iron Age at least; but it was still the easiest way for the pilgrims of the Middle Ages.

When the Romans came, they lost no time in establishing a network of roads linking their military stations. Their coastal forts of Regulbium (Reculver), Rutupiae (Richborough), Dubris (Dover), and Lemanis (Lympne) had roads converging on Durovernum (Canterbury), whence a single route was driven straight to the crossing of the River Thames at Londinium. The road they built from Dover to London remained 'The Dover Road' right up to our own times, when it finally proved quite inadequate to carry modern traffic. Once they had traversed the chalk at the south-east end of the North Downs, and apart from the crossing of the Medway at Durobrivae (Rochester), the Romans may well have found this road one of the easiest they ever had to build in the South-East. When they came to constructing a road from Noviomagus (Chichester) to Londinium, for instance, they had a much more difficult task. This road, later named Stane Street by the Saxons and bearing that name still, first had to climb over the South Downs between Chichester and Pulborough, then traverse the sticky clay vale around Billingshurst before tackling the Lower Greensand hills south of Dorking. Next came the North Downs. To avoid the steep Box Hill, the road was driven along the Mole valley towards Leatherhead, but this was so difficult to penetrate that at the first opportunity, which occurred at Mickleham, the road veered off to the right, over Mickleham Downs towards Epsom and Ewell.

Anderida (Pevensey) posed even greater problems, since Pevensey Levels were in those days something like Chichester Harbour today, an arm of the sea completely covered by water at high tide. It would seem that the way north from here was therefore along the north side of the South Downs to Lewes (not a Roman town); thence the Romans built a road that follows the Ouse valley a little way, then climbs up to the middle of Ashdown Forest, then turns slightly to the left and descends to the clay lands around Edenbridge, climbs again over the Lower Greensand to the west of Westerham, and crosses the North Downs along the line of the present boundary of Surrey and Greater London between Warlingham and Biggin Hill.

The Saxons, when they came, were no road builders. They settled in the valleys, and used the Roman roads that already existed without bothering to maintain them. Where there were no roads already made, they simply picked a way across the plain or over the hill, which after a time became, through usage, the recognized route; thus the roads grew up from local necessity, haphazardly and without any co-ordinated plan.

As ways were gradually developed through the valleys, the settlements in, or on high ground at the sides of, those valleys developed with them. These are the 'gap' towns one can see on the maps of today, principally where river valleys cut through the chalk of the Downs. The most obvious of these towns are Maidstone and Guildford under the North Downs, and Lewes under the South; it is significant that they all have castles. Yet not one of them owes its *existence* to the fact that a way was struck through the valley; only its later development. They were settlements that grew up in the first place because they were at river crossings on east–west, not north–south, routes.

By the end of the Middle Ages, then, the outline of the present-day communications map was already laid down, with three notable exceptions: railways, motorways, and airports. The canals were also missing, but they are not so easily discernible today.

All through the ages, from the departure of the Romans onwards, the roads have been notoriously inadequate. Until Tudor times, travelling and carriage of goods were done almost entirely on horseback. Then, as London's importance as a centre of population and trade became more firmly established, and wheeled vehicles were more and more used, the inadequacy of the roads was fully revealed. 'Sussex full of dirt and mire' (Leland, writing in the sixteenth century); 'very ill for travellers' (Sussex again, by John Speed, 1611); 'one of the dirtiest counties in England' (Surrey, thus castigated by Salmon in 1736); these are but a tiny sample of the sort of comments called forth by the roads in this corner of the country. It is worth making a fuller quotation from the section on roads in *A General View of the Agriculture of the County of Kent* (1796), by John Boys of Betshanger [Betteshanger]: 'The turnpike roads in other parts are also, in general, very good, except some cross turnpike roads in the Weald, which are as bad as can be imagined; being even impassible [sic] for coaches and chaises very frequently in winter. . . . The cause of the badness of these roads is a want of materials; the soil being a deep soft clay, without any mixture of gravel, flints, stone, or chalk, or any other good materials within a moderate distance'. Boys then goes on to suggest an ingenious remedy: 'The cause of the evil being thus seen, a remedy should be sought; and what Nature has denied, Art and Industry should endeavour to supply. Bricks, burnt very hard, would make an excellent road, if laid on green furze, and covered over thinly with gravel. Fields, along the roads where there are no woods, might be sown with furze, for the purpose of burning bricks; and kilns might be erected at proper intervals. Thus the bricks would be made on the spot, and brought into use at an easy expense'. It is interesting to speculate whether McAdam, who was even then beginning to formulate his theories of road-building and to carry out experiments, would have considered bricks laid on green furze, rather than stone, had he lived in Kent.

To redress the balance somewhat, this time in Surrey, it is only fair to quote from the seventh edition of the *Little Guide* to that county, published in 1952: 'The Surrey main roads of today are for the most part excellent; indeed those who drive, cycle, or walk cannot fail to wish from time to time that they were not so good, for they are often sorely hustled by the rush and tear of motorists, who make intelligent observation an impossibility'. This must surely be the only instance in history of the Surrey roads being described as too good.

Any detailed account of road-building practice would be out of place here; suffice it to say that it was McAdam who in the early nineteenth century laid down the principles on which about half the present roads of Britain were constructed. On a firm subsoil, shaped to the finished camber, McAdam laid one foot of small broken-up stones, no large stones or other material being allowed. The wheels of vehicles ground the stones, and the resultant dust filled the interstices. Later it became the practice to bind the stone surface together by the addition of tar and chippings. Before McAdam, the roads of Britain were the worst in Europe, and those of the Weald, owing to the terrain, probably the worst in Britain. Even today, the two great ridges of chalk, the sticky clay plains, the dense population and the consequent scarcity of land available for recreation present the road builder with considerable problems. And there is much that needs doing. No road is more urgently needed, for instance, than the M25 and the 'South Orbital Road' round the south side of London to provide access to the Channel ports from the industrial heart of England.

As for canals, their commercial life in this part of England was even shorter than in most. None ever made a profit. The first was the River Wey Navigation, opened in 1653, connecting Guildford with the Thames and London. The Basingstoke Canal was built in 1796, and linked the town of Basingstoke with the River Wey near Byfleet. Next, in 1816, came the Wey and Arun, from the River Wey at Shalford to the Arun near Wisborough Green. This was followed in 1817 by the Chichester Canal, connecting Chichester with Chichester Harbour, and in 1823 by the Arundel and Portsmouth Canal. All except the first were part of a grandiose scheme to connect London with Portsmouth, thus giving London access to the English Channel without the need to face the hazards of the journey round the North Foreland. One of these hazards, molestation by the French, faded away after the defeat of Napoleon at Waterloo.

Wellington, by winning that battle, had a hand in bringing about the demise of the Wey and Arun Canal, or rather in causing it to be born a weakling, just as Nelson, by his victory at Trafalgar ten years earlier, which put paid to Napoleon's plans to invade

England, had rendered the Royal Military Canal, hastily constructed at Pitt's command along the northern edge of Romney Marsh, redundant before it was even completed – redundant, that is, from a military point of view, although it carried barge traffic for many years, taking some £50,000 in revenue over a period of fifty years. Like many other canals, it was finally killed off by the railway – in this case the Hastings to Ashford line, now itself threatened with closure. Similarly the Wey and Arun was extinguished by the opening of the Guildford to Horsham line in 1865. Today, a devoted band of enthusiasts is working, mostly at weekends, to re-open the canal to pleasure craft.

It is the railways that have brought about the biggest social revolution in the region. The first railway to penetrate the chalk wall of the North Downs was the London to Brighton line in 1841, which gave birth to whole new towns, such as Purley and Redhill. The Portsmouth line reached Guildford in 1845, Godalming in 1849, Portsmouth in 1858. In the east, Dover was reached in 1844, and Margate in 1863.

Now the wheel has come full circle, and several of the old lines have been closed. The Canterbury to Whitstable line, opened in 1830 and the first in the country to carry fare-paying passengers, is one of them. The Guildford to Horsham line, which killed the Wey and Arun Canal, is itself dead. The well-known Bluebell Line, running from Sheffield Park to Horsted Keynes, is all that is left of the line connecting Lewes and East Grinstead. It is now run by a private company, whose summer trains are often filled to capacity. The same may be said of the Kent & East Sussex Railway, which uses a small section of the old Headcorn to Robertsbridge line at Tenterden. The line is gradually being reclaimed from Tenterden towards Robertsbridge by indefatigable volunteers (see Tenterden).

Despite this process of retrenchment, the railways are a potent influence in shaping the demographic pattern of the South-East. The presence of thousands of commuters in the area is due to the railways, and this has brought prosperity. To work in London and live in the country or by the sea is to be a member of a club; and although the club has no longer any pretensions to exclusiveness, membership of it is still held to be worth considerable sacrifice. Three hours' travelling a day, from door to door, is common-place; four is not unknown. Nearer in, the county of Surrey has been partly swallowed up by the metropolis – transformed from wildness to cosiness in less than a century. Yet even this county has retained an individuality and a local pride, for in England such things are unquenchable.

So far we have been thinking in terms of communications inwards, so to speak; that is, communications within the region and between it and the rest of England, notably London. But the region also looks outwards, across the sea to the Continent. Through London's international airport at Gatwick it looks even further afield; but the presence of Gatwick, although its effect on the surrounding area is considerable, is coincidental. Not so the ports of the coast, the gateways to the rest of Europe. No road is more historic than 'The Dover Road', no port more historic than Dover. Come to that, the whole of this coast has historic associations. At Pegwell Bay the Romans landed in A.D. 43, Hengist and Horsa in 446, St Augustine in 597. At Pevensey, William landed in 1066. Napoleon, on the other hand, and Hitler, could only gaze across the strait at those maddening white cliffs, while the English hastily assembled their makeshift defences.

Departures vie with arrivals in history. The Dover Road, a Roman road, has been trodden, ridden, driven over, by a large and varied company, spanning the centuries, setting out for Rome, Paris, Florence, the Netherlands, and battlefields without number – soldiers and sailors, prelates and politicians, painters and poets, saints and sinners, eloping lovers and fleeing felons. Now the aeroplane and the hovercraft make light work of what can be a troublesome crossing in a ship. And still the traffic grows. Will there ever be a Channel tunnel? Those who live in and love this corner of England devoutly hope not – almost to a man. Is it surprising?

★

Compared with the rest of the country, the proportion of agricultural land of first-class quality in the region is high. The outstanding areas in this respect are north Kent, Romney Marsh, Pevensey Levels, and the coastal plain running westwards from Worthing to the Hampshire border. There is comparatively little really low-class land. The region is blessed with more sunshine than any other part of Britain, and a moderate rainfall. All these factors – soil, sun, and the right amount of moisture – combine to place it among the best agricultural regions of England.

There is great diversity of agricultural activity: fruit and hops in north and mid Kent; fruit again around Kirdford and Wisborough Green in Sussex; grazing of sheep on Romney Marsh, and of cattle on Pevensey Levels; market-gardening in glasshouses on the coastal plain of West Sussex; vegetables and barley in Thanet; and dairying and poultry-rearing in areas dotted about over most of the region.

So far as there is a pattern to it all, it reflects the basic geology of the region more closely than in most of the rest of England – certainly than that part of the country lying, say, north of the Thames; this is because in those other areas the soils that are the natural concomitant of the underlying rocks have themselves been overlaid, to a much greater extent than in the South-East, by post-glacial deposits resulting from the melting of the ice cap.

However, it has to be admitted that social factors have as much bearing on the matter as geological ones. We may perhaps best illustrate this by two examples.

Why is north Kent the great fruit-growing area it is, earning the county the honourable title of 'The Garden of England'? The soil is right: the fertile, well-drained Tertiary Beds, largely covered with rich brick-earth, below the dip slope of the North Downs. There is plenty of sun; rainfall is moderate. And yet – there are other regions where fruit is grown perfectly satisfactorily. Excellent soil, maximum sunshine, moderate precipitation – these are advantages, but none of them is critical. The reasons for the fruit-growing pre-eminence of Kent are at least partly social and historical: in the days when land communications were poor, the Kent growers had the great market of London near at hand, and the sea and the Thames estuary were the road by which their produce reached it. Then again, it has been suggested that the Romans introduced cherry-growing into Kent. If this is true, then the probable reason for their choice of north Kent is that it was quite simply the first suitable place they came to. It has remained a great cherry-growing area ever since.

For our second example let us take Romney Marsh. For long it was almost synonymous with sheep-grazing. They used to say you could fatten twelve sheep to the acre without any fodder other than the grass there. To suggest growing crops on the Marsh was heresy. Then, shortly before the Second World War, some East Anglian farmers arrived upon the scene. 'What's all this nonsense?', they said; 'the sheep is a sacred cow!' – and they started to plough up the land. When the war came, much more of the land was ploughed. It yielded wonderful crops, and most of the very best of the superbly fertile soil of Romney Marsh has remained arable ever since. Why was the sheep formerly sacred? Because it was traditional – and exceedingly profitable; and because it was much less trouble to graze sheep than to plough that heavy land, and to cut a lot of extra drainage channels. If you can make as much money as you want without too much effort, why work harder?

Another area of marshland that used to be purely pastoral but is now largely arable is the area between Herne Bay and Margate. Here, too, the break with tradition came in wartime, and the area has been under cultivation ever since, particularly for the production of barley, broccoli, and early potatoes. The change from pastoral to arable has been given added impetus here as elsewhere by modern machinery, which not only saves labour, but also enables the farmer to take quick advantage of sudden improvements in the weather. Its only and considerable drawbacks are that it does not make manure, and that you can't talk to it – except perhaps to curse it.

The chief fruit-growing areas of Kent are the belt of first-class land stretching from the boundary with London right down to Canterbury, below the north-east slopes of the North Downs, and the country extending from the Lower Greensand around Maidstone through the Weald clay to the sandstone area in the vicinity of Cranbrook. Here for an all too brief period in May is a glorious sight: first the white blossom of the pear tree and the cherry, then the pink-and-white apple blossom. The pattern of fruit-growing has changed fundamentally in the last few years, for now the miniature trees, or 'spindles', are in vogue: they are more easily sprayed, and the fruit more easily picked; and the trees bear fruit only three to four years after planting, instead of the 10 or 12 years the larger trees used to take. The quality, it is held, does not suffer. Unfortunately research has not yet succeeded in producing a satisfactory miniature cherry tree. It is a race against time, for many people seem to think that this tree in its present form will simply have to die out. It is uneconomic: it is almost impossible to find anyone to pick the fruit; methods of keeping the birds away are very expensive and not very effective; and the trees take 15 years to come into bearing.

The apple is the chief of these fruits, in point of quantity produced; the pear and the cherry come next, but far behind. Soft fruits – strawberries, raspberries, gooseberries – are grown in considerable quantities, mainly on the lighter soils of north Kent. But the fruit, or rather flower, most characteristic of Kent and East Sussex must be the hop, used in the production of beer. It is distributed all over a wide band of country between Sittingbourne in Kent and, say, Wadhurst in Sussex, except on the North Downs themselves. It is also grown on a fertile strip south of the Hog's Back in Surrey. It is not difficult to grow, although it needs a deep soil for its long roots, with a good water supply and adequate drainage, and a reasonable amount of sunshine. As he passes through this countryside in springtime the traveller can hardly fail to notice the serried ranks of tall hop-poles, with the strings on which the hops are to be trained arranging and re-arranging themselves in intricate geometrical patterns. Throughout the summer the hops creep steadily up the strings, until they are ready to be harvested in September.

Hop-farming, however, has undergone great changes. To begin with, the area under cultivation has been drastically reduced (and the price thereby 'stabilized'); the area is less than one quarter of what it was at the end of the last century. Production is on a quota system, organized by the Hops Marketing Board at Paddock Wood in Kent.

Picking is done by machinery, so that the traditional annual invasion by the pickers from London is a thing of the past, its only tangible legacy the groups of derelict brick or tin huts in which the pickers were 'housed'. Even these are, mercifully, disappearing by slow degrees. The older folk of these areas can still recall stories of the 'goings-on' that occurred at these times – most of them rather lurid – and the 'missions' the churches ran in an effort to make the strangers feel welcome, and perhaps to convert some of these visitors from 'heathen lands afar'. These praiseworthy attempts were not notably successful; there was little integration, mainly because the natives, rightly or wrongly, regarded the Londoners as a rough lot, to be tolerated as a necessary evil. A few, however, married and settled down in the area.

Late frosts are one of the hazards of fruit-farming. In order to minimize this danger, the valley floors, where frost pockets are apt to collect, tend to be used for the hops, which are less sensitive to frost, while the higher ground is reserved for the orchards and the cultivation of small fruits, although this pattern is by no means invariable.

Moving westwards, we come to the clay plains of the Weald. Here the emphasis is on dairying. There is a general tendency for sheep to be replaced by cattle. This applies not only to Pevensey Levels, where the soil is very similar to Romney Marsh, but even to the South Downs, once pre-eminently the domain of the sheep, a notable breed of which, the Southdown, takes its name from the area, yielding mutton and wool of the highest quality. In recent years the disappearance of the sheep and the rabbit has resulted in the encroachment of shrubs such as hawthorn, blackthorn, and gorse upon these once bare hills.

The south-west corner of Sussex, between Worthing and the Hampshire border, is the other area of first-class agricultural land already mentioned. A variety of crops are produced, but the speciality is the growing of tomatoes and other fruit in glasshouses, for here there is plenty of light, and a mild winter climate, which reduces heating costs. There is a Glasshouse Crops Research Station at Littlehampton, an indication of the importance of this activity in the area, but it would be a mistake to think of it, or of any part of the region, as being exclusively given over to any one form of agriculture, or, for that matter, of any form of agriculture being confined to one part of the region. The agriculture of these counties is, indeed, outstanding for its variety. A crop that is becoming steadily more important throughout the region is maize, now being used on an increasingly large scale, for economic reasons, as fodder for cattle. Here the South-East's climate holds a great advantage, for this grain needs plenty of light, and will not grow at all further north than, say, the Chilterns.

In Surrey, the chief agricultural activity is once again dairying, with herds averaging about 80 head of cattle, compared with the national average of about 35. This is largely a matter of money: not infrequently, the owners of dairy herds in these parts derive the greater part of their income from sources more urban in character. Nursery gardens are a feature of the Surrey landscape on the poorer soils, such as the Bagshot Beds, in the north of the county.

As we have seen, the whole region is heavily wooded. On some of the relatively low-quality land, where trees will grow better than other vegetation, there are large areas of commercial forest. The Forestry Commission owns something like 50,000 acres wholly or partly in the region, and over 90 per cent of this area is under plantations. Yet the area under Forestry Commission management is less than one-eighth of the total area of woodland. Indeed the area of Forestry Commission land under plantations in their New Forest and South-East England Conservancy is the smallest in any of their conservancies. From an employment point of view commercial forestry is not an important factor in the South-East.

In the Weald, the character of the natural woodlands varies with the geology. The chalk outcrop of the North Downs forms a plateau on which there is an appreciable deposit of clay-with-flints. Beech predominates on the chalk, whereas oak, hazel, and hornbeam coppice characterizes the clay-with-flints. On the heath soils of the Lower Greensand, birch and pine grow naturally, while on the Weald clay plain, between the Downs and the High Weald, the slow-growing oak, often with an undercover of coppice, is ubiquitous. On the sands of the Hastings Beds, birch and pine flourish, while the Wadhurst Clay produces the finest oak trees in England.

This region was noted, from the Middle Ages right up to the Second World War, for a system of forestry known as 'coppice-with-standards', that is to say, short, spreading oak trees with a continuous layer of coppice underneath. Originally the oak yielded short planks and curved timber for shipbuilding, while the coppice, which was usually hazel or hornbeam, was used to produce the charcoal employed in the iron industry. Both these requirements no longer exist, but there is a keen demand today for good-quality chestnut coppice, usually cut on a 15-year cycle, and used to produce cleft chestnut pale fencing. To obtain the quality required, the trees are grown on the most suitable soils, notably the clay-with-flints of the North Downs plateau, and free of the baleful effect of the 'standards', the oak trees whose shade would inhibit the growth of the coppice. The industry is peculiar to this part of England.

The Forestry Commission is often criticized for planting conifers where deciduous hardwoods would look better, especially on the chalk Downs, where it is usually considered that beech trees are the most suitable. The critics should take a closer look. It is the intention of the Commission that beech should be the final 'crop' here, but this is best achieved if the plantations are formed in the first place with an admixture of conifers; the conifers 'nurse up' the beech, after which they can be cut out as 'thinnings' and sold for a good price, leaving, ultimately, a pure beech wood. This was the method used in the eighteenth and nineteenth centuries to produce the famous beech woods on the Goodwood estate on the South Downs.

There is in any case little demand for hardwoods nowadays. About 90 per cent of the total commercial timber requirement is for softwoods. Where hardwoods are being planted, either by the Forestry Commission or by private individuals, it is usually being done for aesthetic reasons and for the benefit of future generations.

★

Despite some urbanization, agriculture remains the chief industry of the region. No industry other than agriculture and forestry has made much impact upon the landscape; those that come nearest to doing so are coal-mining, oil-refining, cement manufacture, and gravel extraction.

In the past it was iron, the only major industry to affect all these counties, though it was chiefly centred in Sussex. It flourished particularly during the sixteenth and seventeenth centuries. The main source of iron ore was on the High Weald at the base of the Wadhurst Clay, close to its junction with the Hastings Sands, where there was also a plentiful supply of the other essentials, wood and water. The most important centres in Sussex were at East Grinstead, Hartfield, Maresfield, Buxted, Mayfield, Wadhurst, Ashburnham, and Penhurst; in Kent they were Brenchley, Horsmonden, and Lamberhurst, now wholly in the county but then partly in Sussex; in Surrey there were ironworks around Haslemere, Cranleigh, Dunsfold, Abinger, and Shere, and on the heaths of Thursley and Witley. Iron was worked in these parts from earliest times, and certainly during the Roman occupation. Yet after the departure of the Romans there is no record of its continuance. Only one 'ferraria', or ironworks – at East Grinstead – is mentioned in Domesday. It was not until the bloomery was replaced by the blast furnace at the end of the fifteenth century that the industry assumed any importance.

In the bloomery process, iron ore, previously washed, was laid in layers alternately with charcoal, on a platform made of sandstone or beaten clay. The heap of iron ore and charcoal was roofed with clay. The charcoal was then set alight and heated by means of bellows placed at the sides and worked by hand. This would separate out the iron from the ore, and the iron would drop to the bottom and be extracted, spongy and malleable, ready to be beaten into whatever shape was required.

The blast furnace evolved quite simply from the bloomery. In order to obtain greater output, larger and larger heaps of iron ore and charcoal were made, and the working of the bellows became more and more onerous. So did the beating out of the iron with hammers. Then someone thought of harnessing water power to do these things. A dam could be constructed across a stream to create a pond, the contents of which could be released at a controlled rate over a waterwheel, which in turn could operate the opening and closing of bellows and the raising and releasing of hammers. This meant that even larger quantities of fuel and ore could be heated and higher temperatures obtained; instead of the separated iron coming out as a soft but still solid mass, it now came out in liquid form, and could then be reheated and made into wrought iron, or poured into moulds for the making of cannon and other cast-iron products.

Cannon was probably the most profitable, if not the chief, product of the industry. Firebacks were another, much admired and prized today – and, unfortunately, easily and widely imitated. Bellfounding was carried on at Chiddingly and Hailsham, although it was mainly an itinerant trade. Graveslabs were produced in fair quantity; there is a splendid collection in the church at Wadhurst. The forge at Lamberhurst, beside the River Teise a mile west of the village, is generally claimed to be the one where the railings for St Paul's Cathedral were made. Wren's accounts giving all the details are still in existence, and show a total cost of about £11,400. The total weight was just over 200 tons.

The Wealden iron industry reached its peak in Elizabethan times, but it prospered until the eighteenth century, when it went into fairly rapid decline owing to the discovery that coal, in the form of coke, could be used more efficiently than charcoal in iron-smelting, resulting in the removal of the industry to the source of coal in the Midlands. The last forge to close was at Ashburnham, in about 1830.

Until coal ousted timber as the source of fuel, the Weald was specially suitable for the operation of the blast furnaces, having a good supply of the ore, plenty of trees to provide charcoal, and many streams with narrow, steep-sided valleys, easily dammed. The ore of the Weald has in fact a considerably higher iron content than that found elsewhere in England. One can imagine how different the South-East would look today if coal had been available as well. As it is, the visual remains of the industry consist of the hammer-ponds that still abound in the area, and of the numerous bumps and hollows that betoken the sites of ancient bloomeries and of 'mines' from which the iron ore was dug. All these remains present something of a challenge to the industrial archae-ologist, since they tend to be buried in woods and thick undergrowth, nature having recaptured the territory formerly denuded by Man. To the layman the most pleasing reminders of the industry in the landscape are the handsome houses, mainly built in the seventeenth century, of the ironmasters, of which Bateman's at Burwash is a good example.

Other industries of the past, which, however, never attained the importance of the iron industry, are glass manufacture and the production of gunpowder. Glass was made in Surrey around Chiddingfold, and also at Thursley, Alfold, Dunsfold, and Ewhurst; and in Sussex at Petworth, Loxwood, and Wisborough Green. It was being made at Chiddingfold in the early thirteenth century, and possibly before that. Some of it found its way to Westminster Abbey and St George's Chapel, Windsor, in the thirteenth and fourteenth centuries, and there is a window filled with fragments of it in the church of Chiddingfold itself. The industry died out at the beginning of the seventeenth century, perhaps owing to the proclamation of 1615 forbidding the use of timber for fuel, in order to conserve it for the Navy.

As for gunpowder manufacture, this was carried on by the Evelyns at Wotton from the late sixteenth century, but was soon transferred to Godstone, where there was a larger supply of charcoal. Godstone closed down in the mid seventeenth century when the powder mills at Chilworth were opened; here the industry continued until as late as 1918: the First World War was the occasion of its final fling before the Armistice struck its death knell. Faversham in Kent was another major centre of the industry for 300 years, and the mills there were working until 1934, when they were compelled to close because the site was considered too vulnerable in the event of war. One of the mills has been imaginatively restored by the Faversham Society.

So far as modern industries are concerned, none is exclusive to the region except gypsum quarrying near Mountfield in Sussex. Gypsum, a sulphate of calcium, was discovered there in 1872 during a survey carried out in a vain search for coal; it is mostly used in the manufacture of cement, which is made in the chalk of the North and South Downs – in the Medway valley between Maidstone and Rochester, and near Lewes, Newhaven, and Shoreham in Sussex. Indeed the northern strip of Kent from Dartford to Maidstone is a largely industrial landscape, with cement and paper works, sand and gravel quarrying, and oil refineries on the Isle of Grain. Brewing is an important industry of Maidstone, Faversham, and elsewhere.

A coal of high calorific value is mined in the small Kent coalfield, which has been operating since the end of the nineteenth century. There are collieries at Betteshanger, Tilmanstone, Snowdown, all more or less due west of Deal, and at Chislet, south-east of Herne Bay. Like the discovery of gypsum at Mountfield, the discovery of the Kent coalfield was fortuitous: in 1886 they were boring a shaft at the foot of the Shakespeare Cliff at Dover in connexion with the Channel Tunnel project when the coal was struck.

In Surrey the British Aircraft Corporation's factory at Weybridge employs between 5,000 and 6,000 people, but in general the wide diversity of light industry in the county has preserved it from the worst effects of economic blizzards. It has, however, suffered, and still suffers, from the violation of the environment caused by gravel extraction, part of the concrete-making process, in the Thames valley. Some 300,000 people live in the part of the county liable to be affected. The quality of life is lowered by dust, noise, and ugliness. The nuisance of vehicles going in and out of the works seems to cause the most annoyance. Apart from this, some of the land is also suitable for agriculture, so that there is a further conflict of interests. But it would be a pity to end on a sour note, for it can truthfully be said that on the whole this thickly populated region remains relatively unspoilt by industrial development.

Short-stay Guide

The following list is intended for the person whose time in the South-East is limited to a few days. What, out of all that is described in this book, is most worth visiting? The list is subjective and tentative.

Towns and Villages
Bosham
Brighton
Canterbury
Chichester
Elham
Faversham
Guildford
Rye
Sandwich
Smarden
Tenterden
Winchelsea

Cathedrals (*) and Churches
Barfreston
Berwick
Boxgrove
*Canterbury
Chaldon
*Chichester
Cobham
Compton (also Watts Memorial Chapel)
*Guildford
Lancing College Chapel
Lingfield
Lydd
*Rochester
Romney
Shoreham, West Sussex
Sompting
Winchelsea

Monasteries
Battle Abbey
Bayham Abbey
Canterbury, St Augustine's Abbey
Mayfield, Convent
Michelham Priory

Castles
Arundel
Bodiam
Deal
Dover
Herstmonceux
Hever
Leeds
Rochester
Saltwood
Scotney
Walmer

Houses
Clandon Park
Firle Place
Glynde Place
Goodwood House
Ightham Mote
Knole
Lullingstone Castle
Newtimber Place
Parham
Penshurst Place
Petworth House
Polesden Lacey
Quebec House
Royal Pavilion, Brighton
Smallhythe Place
Squerryes Court
Uppark

Gardens
Borde Hill
Great Dixter
Leonardslee
Nymans
Sheffield Park
Sissinghurst Castle

Wakehurst Place
Wisley

Antiquities
Chanctonbury Ring
Cissbury Ring
Kits Coty
Mesolithic Pit Dwelling, Abinger
Wilmington, Long Man

Roman Remains
Bignor, villa
Fishbourne, palace
Lullingstone, villa
Pevensey Castle

Miscellaneous
Weald and Downland Open Air
   Museum, Singleton

Key to Map

Abinger	Surrey	C3 1
Albury	Surrey	B3 2
Alfold	Surrey	B4 3
Alfriston	E. Sussex	D6 4
Amberley	W. Sussex	B5 5
Appledore	Kent	F4 6
Ardingly	W. Sussex	D4 7
Arundel	W. Sussex	B5 8
Ashburnham	E. Sussex	E5 9
Aylesford	Kent	E3 10
Barfreston	Kent	H4 11
Battle	E. Sussex	E5 12
Bayham Abbey	E. Sussex	E4 13
Berwick	E. Sussex	D6 14
Bewl Bridge Reservoir	Kent/	
	E. Sussex	E4 15
Biddenden	Kent	F4 16
Bignor	W. Sussex	B5 17
Bishopsbourne	Kent	G3 18
Bishopstone	E. Sussex	D6 19
Bletchingley	Surrey	D3 20
Bodiam	E. Sussex	F5 21
Bosham	W. Sussex	A6 22
Boxgrove Priory	W. Sussex	B5 23
Bramber	W. Sussex	C5 24
Brede	E. Sussex	F5 25
Brenchley	Kent	E4 26
Brightling	E. Sussex	E5 27
Brighton	E. Sussex	c6 28
Burton	W. Sussex	B5 29
Burwash	E. Sussex	E5 30
Canterbury	Kent	G3 31
Chaldon	Surrey	C3 32
Charing	Kent	F3 33
Chevening	Kent	D3 34
Chichester	W. Sussex	A5 35
Chiddingfold	Surrey	B4 36
Chiddingstone	Kent	D4 37
Chilham	Kent	G3 38
Clandon Park	Surrey	B3 39
Clayton	W. Sussex	C5 40
Cobham	Kent	E2 41

Compton	Surrey	B3 42
Cooling	Kent	F2 43
Cranbrook	Kent	F4 44
Cuckfield	W. Sussex	C5 45
Deal and Walmer	Kent	H3 46
Ditchling	E. Sussex	C5 47
Dover	Kent	H4 48
Dunsfold	Surrey	B4 49
Eastbourne	E. Sussex	E6 50
East Clandon	Surrey	B3 51
East Grinstead	W. Sussex	D4 52
Edenbridge	Kent	D3 53
Elham	Kent	G4 54
Etchingham	E. Sussex	E5 55
Ewell	Surrey	C3 56
Ewhurst	E. Sussex	F5 57
Fairlight	E. Sussex	F5 58
Farnham	Surrey	A3 59
Faversham	Kent	G3 60
Findon	W. Sussex	C5 61
Firle	E. Sussex	D5 62
Fishbourne	W. Sussex	A6 63
Folkestone	Kent	H4 64
Glynde	E. Sussex	D5 65
Godalming	Surrey	B4 66
Goodwood	W. Sussex	B5 67
Goudhurst	Kent	E4 68
Guildford	Surrey	B3 69
Hadlow	Kent	E3 70
Halnaker	W. Sussex	B5 71
Hastings	E. Sussex	F5 72
Herstmonceux	E. Sussex	E5 73
Hever	Kent	D4 74
Hindhead	Surrey	A4 75
Hove	E. Sussex	c6 76
Hythe	Kent	G4 77

key continues on page 34

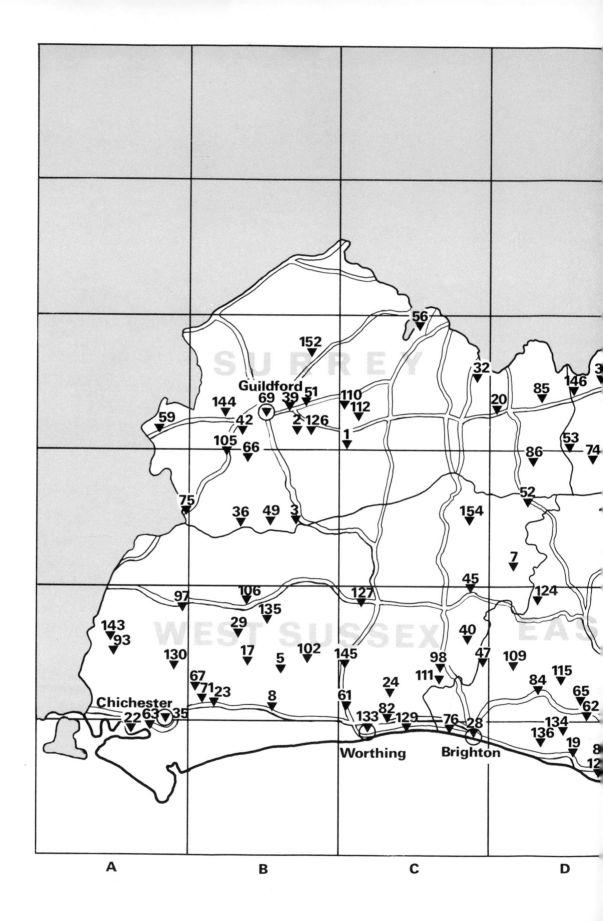

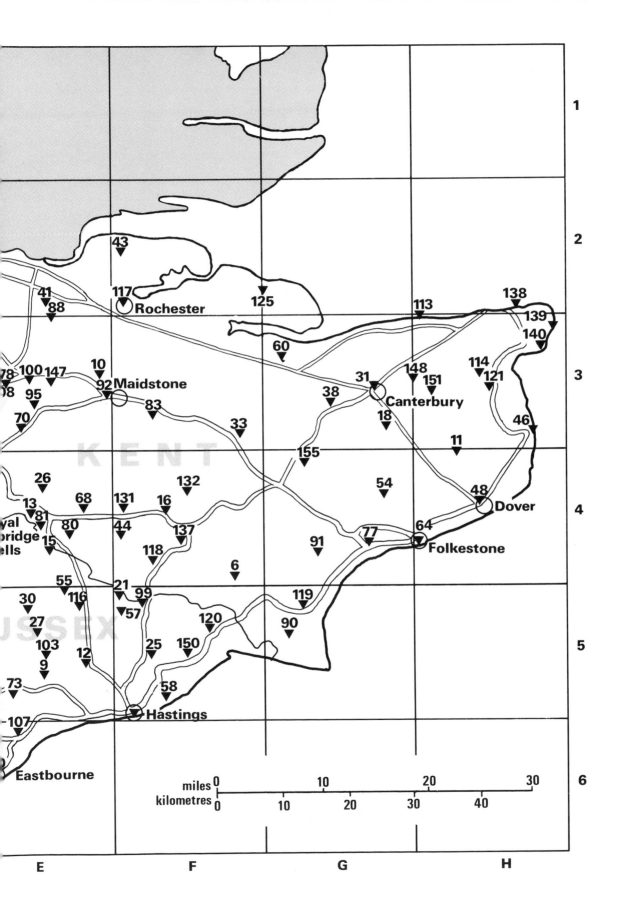

1

43

2

41
88

117 ⊙ Rochester

125

138

113

139

60

140

78 100 147   10

114

148
151

31

121

92 Maidstone

38

⊙ Canterbury

3

95

83

18

46

70

33

11

155

K E N T

26

132

54

13
81

68

131

16

48

yal
bridge
ells

80

44

137

⊙ Dover

4

15

118

91

77

64

⊙ Folkestone

55

21

6

119

30
116

99

90

27
103

57

120

9

12

25

150

5

73

58

107

⊙ Hastings

Eastbourne

miles 0   10   20   30

kilometres 0   10   20   30   40

6

E   F   G   H

KEY TO MAP

key continued from page 31

Ightham	Kent	E3 78	
Jevington	E. Sussex	D6 79	
Kilndown	Kent	E4 80	
Lamberhurst	Kent	E4 81	
Lancing	W. Sussex	C5 82	
Leeds	Kent	F3 83	
Lewes	E. Sussex	D5 84	
Limpsfield	Surrey	D3 85	
Lingfield	Surrey	D4 86	
Litlington	E. Sussex	D6 87	
Luddesdown	Kent	E3 88	
Lullingstone	Kent	D3 89	
Lydd	Kent	G5 90	
Lympne	Kent	G4 91	
Maidstone	Kent	E3 92	
The Mardens	W. Sussex	A5 93	
Mayfield	E. Sussex	E4 94	
Mereworth	Kent	E3 95	
Michelham Priory	E. Sussex	E5 96	
Midhurst	W. Sussex	A5 97	
Newtimber	W. Sussex	C5 98	
Northiam	E. Sussex	F5 99	
Offham	Kent	E3 100	
Otford	Kent	D3 101	
Parham	W. Sussex	B5 102	
Penhurst	E. Sussex	E5 103	
Penshurst	Kent	D4 104	
Peper Harow	Surrey	B4 105	
Petworth	W. Sussex	B5 106	
Pevensey	E. Sussex	E6 107	
Plaxtol	Kent	E3 108	
Plumpton	E. Sussex	D5 109	
Polesden Lacey	Surrey	C3 110	
Poynings	W. Sussex	C5 111	
Ranmore	Surrey	C3 112	
Reculver	Kent	H3 113	
Richborough Castle	Kent	H3 114	

Ringmer	E. Sussex	D5 115	
Robertsbridge	E. Sussex	E5 116	
Rochester	Kent	F2 117	
Rolvenden	Kent	F4 118	
Romney	Kent	G5 119	
Rye	E. Sussex	F5 120	
Sandwich	Kent	H3 121	
Seaford	E. Sussex	D6 122	
Sevenoaks	Kent	D3 123	
Sheffield Park	E. Sussex	D5 124	
Sheppey	Kent	F2/G2 125	
Shere	Surrey	B3 126	
Shipley	W. Sussex	C5 127	
Shoreham	Kent	D3 128	
Shoreham by the Sea	W. Sussex	C6 129	
Singleton	W. Sussex	A5 130	
Sissinghurst Castle	Kent	F4 131	
Smarden	Kent	F4 132	
Sompting	W. Sussex	C6 133	
Southease	E. Sussex	D6 134	
Stopham	W. Sussex	B5 135	
Telscombe	E. Sussex	D6 136	
Tenterden	Kent	F4 137	
Thanet	Kent		
Margate		H2 138	
Broadstairs		H3 139	
Ramsgate		H3 140	
Tonbridge	Kent	E4 141	
Tunbridge Wells	Kent	E4 142	
Uppark	W. Sussex	A5 143	
Wanborough	Surrey	B3 144	
Washington	W. Sussex	C5 145	
Westerham	Kent	D3 146	
West Malling	Kent	E3 147	
Wickhambreaux	Kent	H3 148	
Wilmington	E. Sussex	D6 149	
Winchelsea	E. Sussex	F5 150	
Wingham	Kent	H3 151	
Wisley	Surrey	B3 152	
Withyham	E. Sussex	D4 153	
Worth	W. Sussex	C4 154	
Wye	Kent	G4 155	

Gazetteer

Abbreviations
c. for century
B.T.A. for British Tourist Authority
D.O.E. for Department of the Environment
N.M.R. for National Monuments Record
N.T. for National Trust

Entries in the Gazetteer
The letter and figure supplied to each entry are a grid
reference for the map on pp. 32–3

Abinger Surrey C3

There are two villages in one long narrow parish, nine miles from N. to S. and nowhere more than a mile from E. to W. This shape is common in the parts of Surrey below the Downs, and also in Kent (cf. Chevening); it originates in Saxon times, when the parish boundaries, based on tithings, were drawn so as to include a fair share of the various kinds of soil – Chalk, Gault, Greensand.

High up on the N. slope of the Greensand hills, ABINGER COMMON is a rather spread out place without any proper centre, and despite its glorious rural situation it has a somewhat surburban look. The approach from Ockley, over the w. side of Leith Hill, is amazing: a steep climb between high sandy banks and a varied assortment of trees – beech, birch, pine, oak, holly. Then a shorter drop down the other side brings one to the beginning of the village, at a fork of two roads, the right-hand fork leading off to Wotton. Here on the left is Goddards, the only house of any architectural interest, for with its characteristic asymmetry and original use of materials it is unmistakably by Lutyens. It was built in 1898–9 as a home of rest for lady social workers, becoming a private house about ten years later. The C. 17 cottage on its s. side was converted by Lutyens for use as a post office, but is now a cottage again.

Further on, also on the left, is the church of St James, opposite the Abinger Hatch pub. The old village stocks stand here beside the road, roofed over, and surrounded by high railings. The medieval church was all but totally destroyed by a flying bomb in 1944 and was rebuilt by F. Etchells in 1951. There are some old treasures, such as the three alabaster reliefs – one in the porch, one by the font, and one on the s. wall of the chancel near the altar – and the C. 16 carved chest in the N. chapel. The C. 19 bronze relief of the Crucifixion on the w. wall of this chapel is dramatic; but the most exciting feature of this otherwise rather arid interior is the splendid modern (1967) E. window by Lawrence Lee on the theme of Life through Death.

A path leading from the w. side of the churchyard takes one past Abinger Manor, built by John Evelyn in the C. 17, but much altered and added to. The path passes round the back of a Norman motte of c. 1100, situated in the manor garden – a fine example, more or less complete, and still retaining part of its moat.

Towards the SW. corner of the large field beyond, which is private land, is an unprepossessing hut surrounded by a wire fence. The hut, whose key may be borrowed on application at Abinger Manor, covers the excavated site of a Mesolithic pit dwelling thought to be the oldest man-made dwelling still preserved in Britain. Charts and diagrams explain the mode of life

Abinger Roughs
(A. F. Kersting)

of these ancient people, and there is a display of implements found during the excavations, which were carried out in 1950.

The road running down the hill to the N. from church and pub joins the A25 at Crossways Farm, the sturdy C. 17 house featured in Meredith's romantic novel *Diana of the Crossways* (1885). A left turn at the main road brings one to the other village, ABINGER HAMMER. This attractive place derives its name from its connexion with the Wealden iron industry. The old hammer ponds, made by diverting the Tilling Bourne, which flows through the village, have been turned into watercress beds, and stretch along the valley floor on either side of the cricket field. The most famous building is the Clock House of 1891; the clock overhangs the road on a corner, and a Jack strikes the hours with a hammer.

Albury Surrey B3

Albury is situated in the Tilling Bourne valley E. of Guildford. The story starts at Albury Park, further E. along the valley, a mansion standing on the site of a Tudor manor house, which after many changes of owner and numerous alterations was bought, in 1819, by Henry Drummond, the banker. In the 1840s Drummond called in Pugin, who completely altered the appearance and character of the house.

Externally it is now much as when Pugin had done with it. Specially remarkable are the immense 'Tudor' chimneys, each one different from the next, and the battlements, which accord ill with the wholly domestic nature and history of the place. The mixture of brick and flint is also far from happy, while the galleting, which covers the house like a rash of the measles, is quite unsuitable here. To be fair to Pugin, it should be mentioned that the work was done during his last years, when his health was failing and much of his practice was being taken over by his teenaged son, E. W. Pugin.

The house is now owned by the Mutual Households Association, and a few of the rooms are shown to the public, including the entrance hall, with a late-C. 17 overmantel attributed to the Dutch craftsman J. van Santvoort, and the main staircase, built by Sir John Soane in 1800.

Originally the village of Albury and its church crowded right up to the house, and the road to Shere, the line of which can still be seen on the s. side, passed close by. Successive owners must have found the lack of privacy irksome, and indeed one of them, the Hon. William Clement Finch R.N., in the late C. 18 obtained an order to close the road, which was diverted round the perimeter of the park; in due course he enclosed the village green and annexed the NE. corner of the churchyard. A later owner, Charles Wall, continued the good work, demolishing cottages after moving their occupants to new dwellings he had had built for them at the nearby hamlet of Weston Street. By the time Henry Drummond acquired the estate almost the entire village, except the

Looking towards Alfriston from Lullington Heath, to the E of Litlington; Firle Beacon is in the background

(A. F. Kersting)

church, had disappeared and had been rebuilt at Weston Street.

Drummond was an adherent of a sect known as the Catholic Apostolic Church (sometimes referred to as 'Irvingites'), who believed that the Second Coming was imminent. This led to his estrangement from the vicar of Albury, and, in 1840, to his commissioning a new church from W. M. Brooks, who was possibly assisted by Pugin; the result was the extraordinary building at the corner of the park. This church is no longer in use. Since the village had moved from his gates and he himself no longer worshipped in the parish church, Drummond offered to build the villagers another one. This offer was accepted, not without loud protests from some quarters, and the result is the equally bizarre building at Albury itself, a red-brick imitation-Norman church, also by W. M. Brooks.

The original parish church still stands in the grounds of Albury Park, close to the house and open to visitors, although seldom used. It is by far the most interesting of the three, having a Saxon nave, a Norman tower, an c. 18 cupola, a c. 13 chancel, now open to the sky, and a late-c. 13 transept converted by Pugin into a wholly Victorian mortuary for Mr Drummond, with vivid walls, ceiling, and windows. T. R. Malthus, author of the controversial *Essay on the Principle of Population*, became curate here in 1798.

The gardens at Albury Park were laid out by John Evelyn, the famous c. 17 diarist and landscape gardener. His most interesting work here was on the far, or N., side of the Tilling Bourne, which ran through the grounds, but this part of the estate is not owned by the Mutual Households Association and is not open to the public. Nevertheless something of what Evelyn did can

be glimpsed from the s. side of the stream, including the semi-circular wall that partly enclosed a pool and fountain. One can also make out the line of the canal he built at a lower level, but the tunnel through the hillside, a sort of grotto, is out of sight.

Up on FARLEY HEATH, two miles s. of the village of Albury, is the site of a Roman temple. Our forebears did not scruple to take the stone for their own building and road-mending, and there is now nothing left of this c. 1 temple except two square fragments of wall level with the ground.

To the N. of Albury is the famous and popular NEWLANDS CORNER, where there is a view to the South Downs framed between ridges of wooded hills.

Alfold Surrey B4

Hard by the Sussex border s. of Cranleigh, the village straggles along the B2133 road up to Alfold Crossways. But the old part, at the s. end, is the very perfection of a Wealden village – pub, pleasant houses well grouped, and an old church among the trees.

The church is approached along a paved path in front of two small Wealden houses, brick and timber, with scallop tile-hanging. Opposite the second house, Church Cottage, are the old stocks and whipping-post. Then the church, entered by the N. porch and c. 14 door. This church has much to offer: Norman font, near the s. door, one of the oldest fonts in Surrey; Jacobean pulpit and sounding-board; massive oak timbers at the w. end, supporting the bell-turret and shingled spire.

Alfold was once a centre of the Wealden glass industry. In the c. 16 it was given a new lease of life by a Frenchman, Jean Carré, who brought glassmakers from Lorraine to these parts. His final resting-place in the churchyard here is thought to be at the foot of the war memorial, and is marked by an iron plate suitably inscribed.

Alfriston E. Sussex D6

A much visited place in the Cuckmere valley under the Downs, with a long street lined by lovely old houses; there are tea-rooms, antique shops, boutiques, cars and coaches. Go mid-week if you can. At any time it is worth making the effort to walk the length of the main street. There is a free car park at the N. end of the village. From there, the first thing of interest is the stone market 'cross', now with only a shaft; even that is but a modern replacement of the original, which was smashed by a lorry. Opposite, on the E. side of the street, the South Downs Way heads off again across the Cuckmere towards its completion at Beachy Head.

Soon, on the same side of the street, comes the George Inn, a c. 15 timber-framed building with closely set 'studs' or uprights. The Star Inn, opposite, is another old timber-framed building of the same period, with heraldic figures of men and beasts holding up the projecting roof. Next comes a small timber-framed house, also c. 15, followed by various weatherboarded and tile-hung houses and cottages. At the s. end of the village, on the left, is the hotel and restaurant called 'Chateau Anglais'; turning left here we come to the Clergy House (N.T.), close to the river. This was the first building bought by the Trust; they paid £10 for it in 1896.

The timber-framed Clergy House dates from the c. 14, and has a thatched roof. It is a typical small Wealden house, with central hall, projecting solar wing to left and service wing to right, and braces supporting the overhang of the central portion. The solar wing contains an exhibition of photographs of other Wealden houses, while in the service wing is the N.T. shop. As this was the priest's house, and medieval priests were – at any rate officially – celibate, being looked after by a housekeeper, there is no connexion between the solar wing and the rest of the building; thus were the proprieties observed.

The house stands at the s. end of the large green, one of the best features of Alfriston, on the E. side of which stands the c. 14 flint church, with a shingled broach spire.

Allington Castle Kent *see* Maidstone

Amberley W. Sussex B5

The village, church, and castle stand on a low E.–W. ridge between the South Downs and the River Arun. They make a pretty picture, and the old part of Amberley is fortunate in being well away from the main Storrington to Arundel road. A train roars along the valley below from time to time, but most people can tolerate that.

Church and castle stand side by side at the E. end of the ridge. The church has a Norman nave of the early

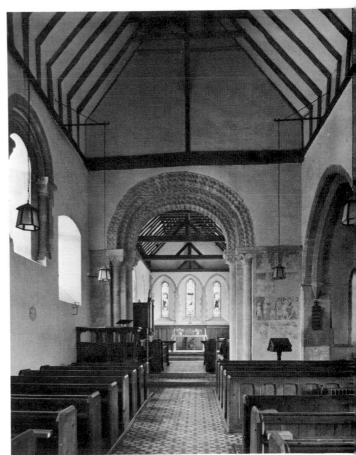

(A. F. Kersting)

Amberley church: the chancel with its elaborately carved arch

c. 12, and chancel, s. aisle, and tower of 1230. The roof covering the s. aisle is a straight extension of the roof of the nave, giving the exterior of the building on this side a grand barn-like appearance. There is a blocked-up Norman doorway on the N. side; the s. doorway, by which one enters, is Early English, with ornate carving. Inside, one's attention is immediately arrested by the Norman chancel arch, elaborately, if not very imaginatively, carved; to the right of it are traces of medieval wall-paintings.

Amberley, like Bodiam in E. Sussex, stands near the head of what was in medieval times the navigable part of a river. They both have castles built in the second half of the c. 14, during the Hundred Years' War. Neither was put to the test of military attack. Amberley's castle was built by Bishop Rede of Chichester, who enlarged and fortified the manor house and built a great curtain wall that still rises sheer from the valley floor. The castle is a ruin, but the manor house is still lived in; neither is open to the public.

The village is one of the most charming in Sussex.

Houses of all shapes, sizes, materials, and ages make up an unfussily harmonious whole, ranged round and within a quadrilateral of roads.

From the N. side of Amberley a signed footpath leads down to the valley, here known as the Wild Brooks, and follows the river northwards, whence one can look back at the outline of castle, church, and village, while to the W., across the river, rises the spire of Bury church.

Appledore Kent F4

The village has something of the seaside about it. It stands on the edge of Romney Marsh, and indeed sea-going ships used to sail up to it in the early days of its medieval prosperity, until the River Rother altered course after a violent storm in 1287. Even then, Appledore continued to prosper as a centre of the cloth-making trade.

There are many pleasant houses in the main street, mostly of brick with tiled roofs, although weather-boarding, tile-hanging, and half-timbering are also to be seen.

The church is tucked away in a corner on the E. side, behind the Red Lion. Near the gate leading to it is a board giving an excellent potted history of Appledore, always a prey to invaders or the fear of invasion: the Danes, until Alfred chased them away; the French, who virtually burnt the place down in 1380, and who, under Napoleon, threatened to pay it another visit but never did. The Military Canal, below the bank at the marsh's edge, was built to frustrate Napoleon, and refortified in the Second World War to stop Hitler.

Rebel armies, too, have marched through Appledore: Wat Tyler's in 1381, Jack Cade's in 1450, both with Appledore men in their ranks. Here, where the board stands, was the old market place; an annual fair, authorized by Edward III, was held on this site until 1899.

The church itself was rebuilt and enlarged after the French raid of 1380. It is mainly C. 15, but there is a good deal of C. 19 restoration. The N. and S. transept roofs, for instance, are original, while the roof of the nave is partly, and that of the chancel wholly, restored. There is also an old wooden screen, again partly restored. The chancel arch is also timber and the nave roof has crown-posts on tiebeams with pierced spandrels. It is the timbers, here, that catch the eye.

At HORNE'S PLACE, nearly a mile N. off the Kenard-ington road, is a C. 14 domestic chapel (D.O.E.), attached to a farmhouse that encloses an earlier timber-framed house attacked by Wat Tyler's mob in 1381. Until its restoration in the 1950s the chapel had been used as a cellar and a hay loft.

Ardingly W. Sussex D4

The church, which stands some distance to the NW. of the village, is mainly C. 14, and has a stumpy square C. 15 tower and a dark interior. There is a fine C. 15 screen, and

an ancient and curiously rustic set of steps to the belfry. Within the chancel is the effigy of a priest, early C. 14, an altar tomb and brass of Richard Wakehurst, d. 1454, and his wife Elizabeth, and on the floor in the centre of the chancel the splendid brasses of Richard and Margaret Culpeper, and of Nicholas and Elizabeth Culpeper with their ten sons and eight daughters. Margaret and Elizabeth were Richard Wakehurst's grand-daughters: by marrying two Culpeper brothers they brought nearby Wakehurst Place into the possession of the Culpeper family.

WAKEHURST PLACE is an Elizabethan house about a mile to the N., built by Sir Edward Culpeper in 1590. But it is now the gardens that most people come to see. The estate, which dates from the C. 11 and was owned by the Culpepers for over 200 years, was eventually bought in 1902 by Gerald W. E. Loder, who later became the first Lord Wakehurst of Ardingly. He was a keen gardener who specialized in conifers, rhododendrons, and hardy flowering shrubs. When he died in 1938 the estate was bought by Sir Henry Price, the clothier, who added to the collection of trees and shrubs. He be-queathed the estate to the N.T., who in 1965 leased it to the then Ministry of Agriculture as a second garden for the Royal Botanic Gardens, Kew.

Building on such good foundations, 'Kew' has done a magnificent job, and the public can now enjoy walking round a huge (but well-signposted) area containing pinetum, lakes, heath garden, Himalayan garden, water garden, rhododendron garden, and a beautifully tended walled garden planted as a memorial to Sir Henry Price. The grounds are so spacious that they never seem unduly crowded.

The original house has been greatly altered. The present S. front was once the N. range of a courtyard house of which all but the N. range and the stumps of the E. and W. ranges was demolished in the C. 17 and C. 19. On the other hand considerable additions were made in the 1870s. The house contains a first-class exhibition as well as a bookstall and tea-rooms, but the rest of it is not open to the public.

Most of the area on the W. side of the road between Wakehurst Place estate and the village of Ardingly is occupied by the South of England Agricultural Show-ground. The show itself is held annually in early June, and lasts three days.

S. of the village, on the right of the minor road leading to Haywards Heath, is Ardingly College, one of the Woodard schools (see Lancing). The buildings, among which naturally the chapel is dominant, are in rather stark red brick, and were designed in the 1860s by Slater and R. H. Carpenter.

Arundel W. Sussex B5

The sight of the town from the S., dominated by its castle and Roman Catholic cathedral, is impressive indeed. It stands nobly, climbing up from the River

ABOVE: *Arundel: castle, town, and cathedral*
(A. F. Kersting)

BELOW: *the C12 gatehouse and C19 curtain
wall of Arundel Castle*
(A. F. Kersting)

Arun and looking s. out over the flat lands towards the
sea, and towards the Downs on the other sides.

The castle is the irresistible attraction. The oldest part
was built by William I's friend Roger de Monte
Gomerico (Montgomery). His son, Robert, rebelled
against Henry I, who deprived him of the castle and left

it as a dower to his own second wife, Adeliza of Louvain,
who after Henry's death married William de Albini, a
powerful Norman from Norfolk. From them, through
many vicissitudes and complicated processes of inheritance, the property has passed to the Fitzalan-
Howards, Dukes of Norfolk, Earls Marshal of England

41

since the time of Richard III, and the foremost Roman Catholic family in the land.

The castle was bombarded and largely destroyed by the Parliamentarians under Waller in 1644, so that the edifice we see today, apart from the gatehouse, the keep, and other fragments, is a late-c. 19 reconstruction, put in hand by the 15th Duke. Visitors can ascend to the keep – 'a long and arduous climb', a notice warns. Thereafter they can tour some of the rooms of the castle: the private chapel, a late-c. 19 exercise in Early English inspired by Salisbury Cathedral, with pillars of Purbeck marble; the Barons' Hall, a reconstruction of a medieval hall; the picture gallery, lined with portraits of the Howards down the ages; the dining room; the drawing room, with a huge, carved fireplace adorned with heraldic devices; the Victoria Room, so named because it recalls the visit to the castle of Queen Victoria and Prince Albert – the bed and matching furniture being specially made for the occasion; the library, the only room shown to visitors that dates from Regency times – the books are behind grilles, but a c. 16 Bavarian chest and c. 17 Portuguese ebony cabinet are outstanding exhibits; and the breakfast room, where above the fireplace is the sword taken from James IV of Scotland by Thomas, Duke of Norfolk, Earl of Surrey, at Flodden Field in 1513. Also within the castle precincts and open to visitors is the Fitzalan Chapel, which is the chancel of the parish church. This was used as a stable in the Civil War by the Parliamentarians, who sited cannons in the tower to bombard the castle. As the chancel is a Roman Catholic place of worship it is separated from the rest of the church, which is Church of England, by an iron grill and glass screen. This screen represents an ecumenical advance, since it replaces the former brick wall put up in the c. 19.

A little further along the London Road, on the opposite side, is the Roman Catholic cathedral of Our Lady and St Philip Howard. (Philip Howard, who died in 1595 while a prisoner in the Tower of London, was declared a saint by the Pope in 1970.) The church, built in 1870–3, is uninteresting, but from a distance it dominates the town even more than does the castle. It also gives it a distinctly Continental air, built as it is in the French Gothic style of c. 1300.

Back along the London Road the High Street tumbles down the hill and opens out into The Square, a mixture of styles and periods. Beyond the Norfolk Arms it narrows once more into the High Street; close to the bridge at the bottom are the remains of the Maison Dieu, a c. 14 hospital, or almshouses.

Past these remains, Mill Road leads on to Swanbourne Lake, a famous beauty spot, then on again to the Wildlife Park, a sort of miniature Slimbridge run by the same Wildlife Trust.

Ashburnham   E. Sussex   E5
A scattering of houses strung along the road running s.

(Janet & Colin Bord)

A crowded semicircle of medieval symbolism: the S doorway of Barfreston church

from Pont's Green passes for the village of Ashburnham, and it is a voyage of discovery to find the parish church. It is signed from a gateway by a lodge at one of the entrances to Ashburnham Park, on the B2204 road between Battle and Boreham Street. Through the gateway is a drive curving through woods. Finally we come to a bridge over a Capability Brown lake, and are confronted by the sadly truncated remnant of Ashburnham Place, made out of the dark Ashburnham bricks. The modern box of a building on the right is a Christian conference centre, for the present owner of Ashburnham Place is also the incumbent (in the ecclesiastical sense) as well as being a descendant of the Ashburnhams, who have lived in this place for centuries.

On the left is the c. 18 stable block, built of stone, and ranged round three sides of a courtyard. To the E. of this is the parish church, built in 1665 (except the tower, which is older) by John Ashburnham. Inside, the church is a good, and well-kept, example of late-C. 17 church architecture and furnishings, notably the w. gallery with an ordinary domestic staircase leading up to it, the plain pulpit, the plain box pews – truncated, like the house – and the Decalogue, or table of the Ten Commandments, formerly the reredos but now hung on the s. wall of the nave.

The site of Ashburnham Forge, the last of the old Sussex forges to close down (about 1830), is at the bottom of a steep hill on the road between Pont's Green and Penhurst, about half a mile from the latter place. Here the road crosses the Ash Bourne, the stream that supplied the power. Vestiges of the forge can still be seen, and lumps of iron lie about or are found embedded in nearby tracks and footpaths. Upstream is the site of the old furnace, where the ore was smelted. Ashburnham brickworks, where the bricks were fired by wood, thus acquiring their characteristically dark hue, were only a short distance w. of the forge, and were in operation until about 1970, when they finally capitulated to the mass-production methods of Fletton and similar places.

Aylesford Kent E3

An ancient place, known to the Romans for its ford across the Medway just below the point where it becomes tidal. Here, in the mid c. 5, Hengist and Horsa defeated the Britons in a battle recorded in the Anglo-Saxon Chronicle. Now it is an old huddled village tumbling down the steep hill to the river, crossed since medieval times by a splendid stone bridge. This idyllic place is hedged in by industry and new housing, and choked with traffic. From time to time a train clatters past, and a continuous if subdued roar comes from the M20 motorway. The industry is diverse: to the w. is the vast complex of the Reed Paper Mills, while to the E. along the road to Forstal is a sizeable industrial estate.

The old parish church, the lower half of whose tower is Norman with pieces of Roman tiles embedded in its Kentish ragstone walls, calmly surveys the scene from the hill above Aylesford. It is a large church standing in a well-kept churchyard; on the s. side is a curious turret, an entrance to the former rood loft, while inside is a double nave supported by graceful c. 15 pillars. The most dramatic part of the church, however, is the N. chancel, with its Culpeper and Banks memorials. The former is a tomb of alabaster and marble on which lie the figures of Sir Thomas Culpeper, d. 1604, and his wife. On either side are the smaller figures of their three sons and three daughters. But even this elaborate monument is completely overshadowed by the huge c. 18 memorial in the NE. corner, where stand Sir John Banks, in wig and semi-Roman garb, and his wife Elizabeth, dressed as a Roman matron, while below them, semi-recumbent, is their son, Caleb, in wig and Roman armour.

Beside the river to the w. stands The Friars, a Carmelite foundation of 1242, which after seven centuries, and many vicissitudes and changes of owner-ship, returned to the Carmelites in 1949. The Friars is charming, with its open-air church and side chapels, its garden and 'Rosary Walk', despite the rather insistent Carmelite symbolism.

About a mile and a half NE. of Aylesford are KITS COTY HOUSE and LITTLE KITS COTY HOUSE (both D.O.E.), remains of Neolithic communal burial chambers, signed from the A229 road from Maidstone to Chatham. A left turn off this road, a mile and a half after it passes under the M20 motorway, leads to a fork in the minor road; both Kits Coty Houses are now two minutes' walk away but in opposite directions.

It is better to visit Little Kits Coty House first, down the left fork, as it is the less impressive of the two. It stands in a field on the left, surrounded by smartly painted railings. What remains of this 4,000-year-old tomb is a jumble of stones, some huge, lying about under two large elm trees. Originally there was a chamber of large stones surrounded by a roughly square kerb of smaller stones; the tomb was demolished in about A.D. 1690.

Returning to the fork in the road, we see a track crossing the Pilgrim's Way and leading straight up the hill between hedges, over-arched with trees. Half-way up on the left, again in a field, is *the* Kits Coty House, three huge upright stones with a capstone lying across the top. This burial chamber is thought to be about the same age as the other, and to have been a long mound with stone kerb.

The view from up here, with the North Downs sweeping round in a great arc on the skyline, is more exciting than the stones, which are tightly enclosed by iron railings, not to mention the litter receptacle thoughtfully provided.

Although these ancient tombs are both now out in the open, the name Kits Coty is thought to be derived from the Celtic *Kid Coit*, meaning 'tomb in the wood', and the *Coit* to be connected with the *Quoit* found in Cornwall (*see* the volume on Devon and Cornwall in this series). The modern Kits Coty is an 'estate' of houses dotted about the wooded hillside to the N. in a maze of unmade roads.

Barfreston Kent H4

This village on the edge of the Kent coalfield (of which one is hardly aware) is little more than a hamlet. Although pleasant enough, it has nothing outstanding except its church, the most appealing Norman church in the county. Small in size, and having neither tower nor spire, it possesses, especially in its famous s. doorway, the richest of late-Norman carving. A puzzle is why so much skill and energy was expended in the adornment of what can surely never have been an important church. One theory is that in the late c. 12 the lord of the manor, Adam de Port, added the elaborate decoration to an earlier building as a thank-offering for his marriage.

Outside, the lower half of the building is of flint and

the upper of Caen stone, in which all the superb carving is done. The s. doorway is undoubtedly the *pièce de résistance*. At the centre of the tympanum is Christ in Majesty, with symbolic figures all round. Over it are arches, elaborately carved: first a narrow band of leaves, then a wider band, with animals playing musical instruments, presided over by an archbishop, and finally the widest band, depicting country labours and biblical scenes. The whole crowded semicircle of stone is heavy with medieval symbolism.

The N. doorway, which is blocked up, also has good carving, although far less elaborate. The wheel-like E. window is remarkable, while all the way round the outside of the church is blind arcading, a frieze, and numerous grotesque heads.

Within, a drastic restoration was necessary in 1840, especially in the chancel, which was in danger of toppling over; but fortunately the architect, R. C. Hussey, was meticulous in replacing everything in its original position wherever possible, the only serious casualty being the wall-paintings that formerly adorned the chancel. Now in the last quarter of the c. 20 another kind of restoration has been necessary, for rain and salty winds – the sea is not far away – had begun seriously to affect the carvings of the s. doorway and the surrounding stone. Silicone has been used in an attempt to stop the rot.

Bateman's E. Sussex *see* **Burwash**

Battle E. Sussex E5

This small, attractive town about six miles NW. of Hastings owes its name to the most famous battle fought on English soil, and has an abbey to commemorate it whose gatehouse is the climax to the main street.

The best plan is to start at the N. end of the High Street and approach the abbey on foot, for there are some interesting buildings on the way. On the right, for instance, the Nonsuch Hotel bears an inscription to the effect that this was 'formerly the Bull Inn, rebuilt 1688 AD with stone from Battle Abbey. Kitchen demolished 1685'. (It is surprising that there was any stone from the abbey left by 1688.) Then on the left the c. 13 half-timbered Clock Shop is surely worth a glance, while on the right is The Old Pharmacy (established 1740), in a half-timbered house bearing the date 1500, followed by the handsome, Georgian, George Hotel. This jumble of periods and styles, characteristic of many English towns, is what makes the street so pleasing. At the end of it the triangular Market Place, a car park most of the time, leads gently up to the gatehouse of the abbey.

The gatehouse was built after 1338, the year when the abbot was granted a licence to crenellate, or fortify, the abbey. It is thus more recent by two and a half centuries than the original abbey buildings, which were completed by the end of the c. 11, the Conqueror's

thank-offering for his famous victory in 1066. (The church was consecrated in 1094, in the presence of William II and several bishops, its high altar sited at the very spot where Harold fell.) Neither church nor monastic buildings were very big; both were enlarged later, the monastery in the c. 13, the church early in the c. 14.

After the Dissolution of the Monasteries the abbey was handed over to Sir Anthony Browne, Master of the King's Horse (*see* Midhurst), who pulled down the church and adapted many of the monastic buildings to his own domestic use. Most of these were made into a Gothic mansion in 1857, now occupied by a girls' school and not open to the public.

As one passes through the c. 14 gatehouse, the school is ahead, and the site of the church, of which only fragments of the s. aisle remain, is to the left. A memorial erected in the early c. 20 marks the site of the high altar. The excavations to the E. of this are of the E. end of the church as enlarged in the c. 14.

To the s. one can see the only monastic building still standing, the dormitory, whose s. end rises to its full height, with a gable and lancets. This dates from the c. 13. Running E. from the s. end of this building was the reredorter, or monks' lavatories, slight remains of which may be seen. To the w. are the c. 13 remains of the cellars that were under the gatehouse, eight barrel-vaulted chambers, all but one interconnecting. The ruins to the w. of them, with two turrets, are Tudor, the remains of 'Princess Elizabeth's Lodging'. Sir Anthony Browne was an executor of Henry VIII's will, and after the King's death in 1547 the young princess was put in his care. He started to build a house for her here, along the s. side of his property, but he himself died the following year, before it was finished, and the princess never came to live at Battle. Sir Anthony and his lady, recumbent alabaster figures, now rest in the parish church, on the N. side of the sanctuary.

As one returns to the gatehouse it is sobering to think that this is the very path by which the Normans came storming up the hill to turn the English right flank and so gain the day, over 900 years ago.

Through the gatehouse on the left is the Pilgrims' Rest, a c. 15 hall house, a cosy thing compared with its formidable neighbour. It is now a restaurant. But if we turn right out of the gatehouse we come to the parish church of St Mary, a little way along the road and on the left.

Battle Abbey grew up as a result of the battle; the town grew up as a result of the abbey. At first the townspeople were allowed to worship in the abbey church, but this became inconvenient for the abbot and his monks, and in the early c. 12 a church was built outside the abbey walls. The incumbent was appointed by the abbot, and was called a dean. To this day Battle shares with Stamford and Bocking the distinction of being a 'peculiar', that is, or rather was, a parish exempt

The Dormitory of Battle Abbey   (A. F. Kersting)

from the jurisdiction of the bishop of the diocese. Nowadays there is little difference between a peculiar and any other parish, except that the vicar is called 'the Dean', and his house 'the Deanery'.

The present church bears scant resemblance to the original c. 12 edifice. The only Norman parts are the arch of St Catherine's Chapel at the end of the s. aisle, a wall panel in the s. wall of the chancel, and the bowl of the font. The nave and chancel are Early English; the s. aisle and N. chapel are Decorated; the N. aisle and tower are Perpendicular. And over all is evident the hand of William Butterfield, who carried out a major restoration in the middle of the c. 19, during which the wall-paintings on the N. wall of the nave were white-washed over. Now once more they stand revealed.

Back in the High Street, across the road from the bottom end of the car park in front of the abbey gate-house, is the town museum. This is in Langton House, a c. 16 house to which a third floor was added in about 1700. The building is named after Elizabeth Langton, who endowed the local school. In the Museum, which is on the first floor, there is a diorama, or lighted three-dimensional representation, of the Battle of Hastings, depicting the crucial phase when the Saxon right impetuously pursued the retreating Norman left, allowing itself to be cut off from its own main body and annihilated. There is also a replica of the Bayeux tapestry, exhibits of the Sussex iron industry, and other objects of local interest.

Bayham Abbey   E. Sussex   E4
Beside the infant River Teise, on the border with Kent, the D.O.E. maintains the ruins of an abbey to challenge those of the North and West. Reached now by a long narrow drive leading N. off the B2169 road midway between Bells Yew Green and Lamberhurst, the abbey was sited, like most medieval abbeys, in delectable surroundings. Even today there is little to disturb the peace of this rural valley.

The abbey was founded in the early c. 13 through the amalgamation of the monasteries at Brockley in Kent and Otham in Sussex, and lasted until 1525, at which comparatively early date it was dissolved by Wolsey. It was a Premonstratensian foundation, which means that

45

it was a 'daughter', or offshoot, of the head abbey at Prémontré, in Aisne, NE. of Paris. It was, of course, ranged round a cloister. The church was on the N. side, the abbot's quarters on the w., the refectory or dining hall on the s., and the dorter, or sleeping quarters, on the E. At Bayham there is little left of the w. range. The undercroft below the dorter can be seen to the s., and to the E. there are substantial remains of the chapter house, and the warming room below the dorter. Part of the wall of the dorter itself still stands, and the doorway in it that led to the reredorter, or latrine.

By far the most complete remains, however, are of the church to the N., standing to a considerable height. The visitor enters the ruins at the w. end, so that he gets an immediate impression of great height and length, and in place of an E. window he sees a beech tree, its roots clinging to the apsidal end of the presbytery, behind the high altar.

It is important to realize, when examining the ruins here, that the church has had two pairs of transepts in its time. The first crossed the nave opposite the E. side of the cloister, continuing the line of the buildings ranged along this side of it. But in about 1270 the E. end of the church was considerably extended, and the transepts now seen are those of the extended church. This is the most splendid part, with fluted shafting to the pillars, and elaborately carved corbels. There are considerable remains of both transepts, and of the chapels leading out of them eastwards.

Beside the stream to the NW. are the ruins of the gatehouse. This was converted into a lakeside summer-house in the c. 18 by the Pratt family, who owned the ruins by then, and who continued to do so until their descendant, the Marquess of Camden, handed them over in the present century to the then Ministry of Works. The lake, sadly, is more or less dried up.

The large mansion on the hill to the NW. is the other Bayham Abbey, built in about 1870 in the Tudor style, until recently the home of the Camdens. The thin-spired little Victorian church half hidden in the trees across the stream from the abbey ruins was also built by them. Now it, too, is in a ruinous state. Both mansion and Victorian church, being N. of the river, are in Kent.

Bedgebury Park Kent *see* **Goudhurst**

Berwick E. Sussex D6
A hamlet under the Downs, much visited, but quiet because well away from through traffic. The church is at the far end, and is approached on foot past a private house. There is a beautiful view of the Downs from the footpath on the far side: superb emptiness, with only a few buildings to be seen, and none of them ugly.

Inside the church are what most people come to Berwick to see: the wall-paintings done during the Second World War by Duncan Grant, Vanessa Bell, and her son Quentin Bell – biblical scenes, with Sussex characters set against a Sussex landscape. Perhaps nowadays they seem rather conventional, and the Nativity by Vanessa Bell a trifle sentimental, but there is no denying that they transform the rather unexciting and drably furnished church. It must be difficult for a preacher here to hold the attention of the congregation, distracted not only by these pictures but also by the real Sussex landscape beckoning from beyond the clear-glass windows.

Bewl Bridge Reservoir Kent/E. Sussex E4
This is the largest sheet of inland water in the South-East, having a surface area of some 770 acres, and a total area of about half as much again if the surrounding Water Authority land is included. The reservoir is on the borders of Kent and East Sussex, between Lamberhurst and Wadhurst; the needle-like spire of Wadhurst church on its ridge to the w. soars skywards, an unmistakable landmark, answered by Kilndown's more modest spire to the E. Like all stretches of water, the reservoir is subject to sudden changes of mood: now grim and grey, now sparkling in the sun, now reflecting the tranquil blue of the sky, now, as the sun sets, streaked with red. The gentle valleys of the Bewl and its tributary the Hook are flattened by the huge level surface, which is quite out of scale and can never look natural. Never-theless, its highly irregular shape saves it from mere dullness, and great pains have been taken with the landscaping.

Most of the water in the reservoir is pumped up from the Medway and released to the Medway towns as required. Vast numbers of water birds have made their homes here, to the delight of ornithologists. For the delectation of fishermen the water is stocked with many thousands of trout. Sailing, rowing, aqualung – there is room for all these sports on, or in, the water, while walkers and riders are catered for on the perimeter, which is 17 miles round.

Biddenden Kent F4
The fame of Biddenden rests on the legend of the 'Biddenden Maids', the twin sisters Eliza and Mary Chalkhurst, or Chulkhurst, born joined at the shoulders and hips in 1100, who lived to the age of 34. They bequeathed a parcel of land to the churchwardens and their successors for ever, and stipulated that bread and cheese should be given annually to the poor of the parish. This distribution is still made every Easter, and paid for from the income of the land, which is known as the 'Bread and Cheese Lands'. The legend is generally accepted, except the date of the Maids' birth, which is thought to have been something like 1560 rather than 1100 (the sign in the village depicts the Maids in Elizabethan costume).

However, Biddenden deserves fame for better reasons than a freak of nature bravely borne, for it has a beauti-ful street, several interesting old houses, and a noble church. The church is built mainly of sandstone, except the tower, which, like the pavements of the main street, is made of Bethersden marble – but do not expect a smooth white stone: Bethersden marble is a brownish-grey colour, and quite rough.

The tower is battlemented, with a turret in one corner. As you enter the church by the s. porch the first thing you see is the c. 13 font. There is a good Jacobean pulpit, and a nasty c. 20 altar and reredos. There are several fairly late brasses, including a wall brass to John Mayne, who died in 1566, and after whom is named the Church of England school just across the road from the church.

Out in the village again, we go down the lovely main street of timber-framed houses to the T-junction at the other end, walking carefully on the 'marble' pavement, for there are rather large spaces between some of the slabs. Turning right, we soon come to an early-c. 18 red-brick house, Hendon Hall, with a gazebo, or summer house, on the wall further along the road. Across the road facing Hendon Hall is Biddenden Place, another red-brick house of about the same date, but enclosing an earlier building, of which the date stone of 1624 is evidence.

Back the other way, past the end of the main street, is the large Old Cloth Hall, mostly c. 16, recalling the former importance of the cloth trade in these parts. The building may be glimpsed through the hedge from the roadside, just past the Rose public house.

Bignor W. Sussex B5

They were ploughing a field to the E. of the little village here; the plough struck a large stone; the stone was removed – and there underneath was a mosaic picture of a dancing girl. This was in 1811. Further excavations revealed the site of a large Roman villa, and one of the finest collections of Roman mosaics in England.

The villa dates from the c. 4, and is on the line of Stane Street, the Roman road from Chichester to London. It must have been a most desirable residence, the property of a wealthy owner, for it was ranged round four sides of a large garden measuring 205ft by 114ft. A corridor ran round the sides of the garden, opening out into rooms on the N., S., and W. sides; on the E. side were farm buildings and servants' quarters. The villa was at the centre of a farm estimated to have comprised about 1,900 acres. It was a large and luxurious dwelling, sited on slightly rising ground with a grand view of a wooded stretch of the South Downs.

To get his bearings quickly, the modern visitor must appreciate that the main car park occupies the site of the central courtyard of the villa. One enters, then, into the N. corridor, and most of the mosaics revealed are on the N. side. A well-laid-out museum contains a clear model of the villa and other interesting exhibits; sometimes the villa must have been visited by un-authorized characters who trod on the floor tiles before they were properly set, for here we see the footprint of a

cat, a dog, or even a wolf – and in one case the imprint of a man's sandal.

A tour of the rooms reveals some splendid mosaics. The freshness of the colours and the liveliness of expression are perhaps their most exciting feature. One of the most striking is the representation of the head of the goddess Venus, and – on the same floor – gladiators at practice, got up as cupids to make it all seem a jovial sport rather than grim and mortal combat. A section of corridor has its mosaic floor exposed to a length of 82ft, or little more than a third of the total, which emphasizes how very large this villa was. The dancing girls, one of whom has already been mentioned, are on the floor of a room containing a decorative water basin, which may have had a fountain springing up from its floor. The original lead pipe to the basin is still in position. At the N. end of the floor is a vivid mosaic picture of Ganymede being carried off by an eagle.

On its own in the SE. corner of the courtyard (car park) is a superb portrayal of the head of Medusa, on the floor of an *apodyterium*, or dressing room, conveniently situated next to the *frigidarium*, or cold plunge. Of course one would expect a villa like this to have under-floor heating, and there are extensive remains of the hypocaust that provided it.

The village of Bignor itself is dotted about round a quadrilateral of roads. At the NE. corner is a splendid c. 15 house with timber-framing, brick-nogging, a large overhang, and a thatched roof – 11 centuries later than the villa and no doubt less comfortable. The church is at the NW. corner of the quadrilateral. It has an early-Norman font of the most basic design, without decoration of any sort, and a fine c. 14 screen, much restored. The ancient chest, until recently used as an altar, now stands in the nave to the right of the screen, having been replaced by a modern table of good design. The building is, however, mainly c. 13, Early English, descended upon by G. E. Street in 1876–8. He is responsible for the fussy little lychgate, the ridiculous bellcote, the incongruous s. porch, the scraping of the interior, and the tiling of the chancel, to mention no more. Amazing to think that this is the architect of London's Law Courts, whose main hall is so grandly ecclesiastical that it is sometimes taken by foreign visitors for a cathedral.

Birchington Kent *see* Thanet

Bishopsbourne Kent G3

A hamlet beautifully situated in the valley of the Nail Bourne below Barham Downs. Here all is peace, save for the muted roar of the A2 road up the hill to the NE. In this place Richard Hooker (1553–1600) was the incumbent during the closing years of his life. The old rectory where he wrote most of his great book, *The Laws of Ecclesiastical Polity*, was pulled down in 1954; it stood across the road from the church.

Hooker more or less asked for a country living where

he could live in peace and quiet and devote more time to his writing; after the hurly-burly of London, where he was Master of the Temple church and continually embroiled in controversy, Bishopsbourne must have been a veritable haven. It was presented to him by Elizabeth I, who is said to have 'loved him dearly', and this gentle scholar seems to have been much loved by his parishioners too.

The present rectory, Oswalds, a white house next to the church, was occupied for a time by Joseph Conrad, who wrote some of his books there. The flint church itself is rather severe-looking, with a Perpendicular tower buttressed almost to the top – indeed the stair turret is lost somewhere within the buttress at the sw. corner. The lack of a chancel arch gives added spaciousness to the interior. Against the pillar by the pulpit is a delightful statuette of Hooker, which was formerly in a niche in the old rectory. There is also a wall monument to him on the s. side of the chancel, and the glass of the E. window is another Hooker memorial, put in in 1890.

There is good stained glass in the chancel dating from the C. 13 and C. 14, and in the s. chapel is glass of the C. 16 showing several coats of arms of the Beckingham family, and C. 17 Dutch glass depicting biblical scenes, the most vivid being the Building of the Tower of Babel, and the Massacre of the Innocents. The w. window by Burne-Jones, in memory of Dr Sandford, Rector of Bishopsbourne and later Bishop of Gibraltar, seems tame by comparison, although it has a certain quiet beauty.

The font is C. 14, standing on a modern plinth. The pulpit is C. 17, Hooker himself being a contributor: 'I give, and bequeth', ran his will, 'three pounds of lawful English money, towards the building and makeing of a newer and sufficient pulpitt in the p'ish Church of Bishopsbourne'.

Bishopstone E. Sussex D6

There are two Bishopstones between Newhaven and Seaford: the old village up the hill, and the large group of C. 20 villas lower down near the main road, on the s. slope of Rookery Hill.

Nearly 500yd of flat land, traversed by the railway, lies between these villas and the sea. Here at one time was the mouth of the River Ouse, until nature and man combined in the C. 16 to divert its course to form the New Haven to the w. Even so, there was a tide mill opposite Bishopstone until well into the C. 19; now only the remains of its foundations can be traced.

The church of St Andrew, up the hill in the old village, is the pride of Bishopstone. Most of it is either Saxon or Norman. The Saxon parts are the nave and the porch – although originally this was not a porch but a side-chamber, the entrance to the church itself being through the w. end. However, when the Normans built the w. tower, they blocked off the Saxon doorway in the process and had to build an entrance into the side-chamber,

ABOVE: *the Clayton monument in Bletchingley church:
Sir Robert Clayton (left); a mourning cherub (right)*

(N.M.R.)

OPPOSITE: *the C12 coffin lid in Bishopstone church*

(A. F. Kersting)

North Downs between Reigate and Westerham; its wide High Street climbs quite steeply from E. to W., and curves gracefully as it climbs.

Near the bottom, standing back, is the large church, mainly Perpendicular; the tower, however, is Norman, with a C. 17 top, the whole restored in 1910. Inside, there is much unfortunate Victorian meddling, such as the pseudo-Early English lancets at the E. end inserted by Butterfield in 1870. He even threw out the fine Jacobean pulpit; it was removed to Orsett in Essex, but returned to Bletchingley in 1937. Street's reredos also dates from 1870; among its apostles and saints appears the figure of Samuel Wilberforce, Bishop of Winchester, unjustly famous as the person who, when Bishop of Oxford, attempted to deride Darwin's Theory of Evolution in public debate and was made to look exceedingly foolish by T. H. Huxley. His dignity is fully restored here at any rate, for he stands next to St Mark.

Dominating the S. aisle, if not the entire church, is the stupendous monument erected in 1705 by Sir Robert Clayton in honour of his wife. Husband and wife stand, larger-than-life figures flanked by mourning cherubs, while below is the infant figure of their only son, who had died in 1669.

Leading up the hill from the church is an alley called Church Walk, with some picturesque old cottages, the first dated 1522. Opposite, across the High Street, is the White Hart, which might be Tudor, although it bears the date 1388. Then up the hill is a pleasing variety of styles and colours all the way to the top, where on the left is the site of the C. 12 castle. Hardly anything is left of it now beyond the names Castle Hill, Castle Square, Castle Close, Castle Lodge, Castlefield, and, inevitably, Castle Antiques.

A lane to the S. drops steeply; here is a tremendous Wealden view, with the M23 motorway snaking along the valley floor in the foreground. Down in the plain to the N. is the hamlet of Brewer Street, where stands Brewer Street Farmhouse, a famous and much photographed timber-framed house of the C. 15. It is close-studded, has two overhanging gables, and a roof of Horsham slate. It has been considerably and sympathetically restored, and is altogether delightful.

Bodiam E. Sussex F5

The village is approached down a winding, sunken, wooded road, opening out a little at the village itself, which tumbles down the last bit of hill to the bridge over the Rother. On the left, just before the bridge, is the car park for Bodiam Castle (N.T.).

This castle, with its romantic moat and superb setting in the Sussex countryside, must appear on more calendars than any other castle in Britain. It deserves its fame. No matter what the weather, it always impresses; this is probably due as much as anything to the contrast between the grimness of the castle itself and the tranquillity of its surroundings.

which thus became the porch. Evidence that this was originally a side-chamber is the doorway connecting it with the nave; this was placed to W. of it, to allow space for an altar to the E. The present doorway is a Norman rebuilding of the earlier Saxon one.

Over the gable of what we must now call the porch is a Saxon sundial, inscribed with the name Eadric; who he was is not known.

Inside, there is more Norman work, shading into Early English. There is also Victorian restoration, notably of the nave roof, originally C. 15. Weak Victorian stained glass fills the windows.

Of the furnishings, the font is Norman. Perhaps the most interesting object, however, is the C. 12 coffin lid, now on the S. wall of the tower. This has a charming design of three circles formed by interlacing ropes and containing a cross, the Lamb of God, and two doves drinking from a pitcher.

Bletchingley Surrey D3

A village on the sandstone ridge that runs parallel to the

As a defensive stronghold it was never put to the test. Yet if it proved in the end to be something of a white elephant, one can hardly wonder that in 1385 it was thought necessary to build it. The Hundred Years' War with France was dragging out its dreary length; in 1377 a French fleet had sacked and burnt the port of Rye at the river's mouth; control of the Channel was in French hands; further raids – even, conceivably, an invasion – were likely. Small surprise that a royal licence was issued to Sir Edward Dalyngrigge granting him permission 'to strengthen and crenellate his manor house of Bodyham near the sea in the county of Sussex'.

Actually this is not what Sir Edward did. His manor house of Bodiam was in all probability situated near the parish church, above the village, too far from the river to be of much use for defence. The castle, then, was purpose-built from the start, and a very thorough job was made of it. The chances of taking the defenders by surprise were fairly slim. By the time one had disembarked down by the river (the only practical approach route in those days), the drawbridges would be raised, the portcullises lowered, and the oil brought to the boil.

So if the castle was never attacked, why is it now only a shell? It was surrendered to the Yorkists in 1483, but as it was continuously occupied during the following century, it seems unlikely to have suffered as a result of this incident. It is more probable that it was slighted by the Parliamentary forces who seized it in the Civil War.

The castle is a rectangle, almost a square, in the middle of a wide moat. (The water-lilies, although undoubtedly picturesque, have rightly been cleared away.) In each corner is a round tower, on the E. and W. sides are square towers, on the N. side is the main gate and on the S. the postern gate.

The modern visitor enters by the main gate. His approach to it is first by a causeway on to an octagonal island in the moat, then on to another island on which part of one wall of a barbican building remains, then on to the main island of the castle itself. He passes under the portcullis into the gatehouse. Originally the causeway on to the first, octagonal island came not from the north bank of the moat as now, but from the W., which meant that any attackers in traversing it would have presented their right, unshielded flanks to the defenders in the castle.

Once inside, one can appreciate the more peaceable aspects of the building. Along the W. side, starting from the main gate, is first a large apparently waste area in the NW. corner, then the retainers' kitchen, with huge chimneys in its N. and S. walls, then the retainers' hall. It is possible to climb up a spiral staircase to the roof of the NW. tower; but this also applies to the postern

Bodiam Castle
(Eric Chalker)

BOSHAM

tower, and those who do not feel up to both might be best advised to reserve their energies for the latter.

In the sw. corner is the lord's kitchen, with access to the sw. tower and the castle well, still full of water, beneath it. In this kitchen also are two huge chimneys, with an oven at the side of one of them. A passage, flanked to N. and s. by buttery and pantry respectively, led from the kitchen to the lord's hall, which had access to the postern gate and tower. By the time this castle was built, towards the end of the c. 14, it was common for the lord of the manor and his family to take their meals in a separate room, not with their retainers.

Beyond the hall, purely a dining room, is the great chamber, or business room, with access to the SE. tower, which probably contained the lord's personal sleeping quarters.

Along the E. side from here is the main living room of the lord's family; this leads in turn into the chapel, from which some steps lead up into the sacristy, or priest's room. Spiritual and secular life were not separated and compartmentalized then as they are today. More household apartments running in from the NE. tower bring us back to the main gate.

Borde Hill W. Sussex *see* **Cuckfield**

Bosham (*pron.* Bozm)   W. Sussex   A6
The village lies on a creek of Chichester Harbour. Lines of flotsam and chunks of seaweed on the roads are reminders that although at low tide the water is a distant ribbon curling through shingly mud, at high tide the village sits with its feet in the sea, rather like King Canute, whose famous confrontation with the waves is supposed to have occurred here (though Southampton also claims the honour).

Tradition has it that Canute lived here for a time, and that the tomb in the nave of the church is that of his eight-year-old daughter; the body is that of a child of the right age, and the coffin is of the right period. It was from here, some 30 years after Canute, that Harold set sail on his fateful visit to Normandy in 1064, praying first in the church, which is depicted imaginatively if inaccurately in the Bayeux tapestry.

The history of the church, however, goes back far beyond Harold or Canute. It is built on Roman foundations; there are Roman bricks in the walls, and the supporting columns of the chancel arch rise from bases that were probably once those of a Roman basilica. Tradition also links the site with a c. 7 Irish monk, Dicul, whom Bede records as having 'a very small monastery in a place which is called Boshanhamm, a spot surrounded by woods and sea', and with St Wilfrid of Lindisfarne.

The church, part Saxon, part Norman-Transitional with some Early English additions, conveys an impression of massive strength, the irregularities of its proportions somehow adding to the bold effect. There is a

(Gerd Franklin)
Bosham church: figure on base of column in N arcade

curious crypt, or semi-underground chapel, in the s. aisle, its roof raised some 5ft above the level of the church floor; the lower part is used as a Lady Chapel, the upper is dedicated to All Hallows; a book records the names of all parishioners who have died. Also unusual are the reptilian creatures (eels?) surrounding the bases of the columns in the N. arcade. The grave of Canute's daughter is marked by a simple slab, bearing the badge of the Danish royal house – a raven; it was given by the children of the village in 1906. No one with any sense of history can fail to be moved by this most ancient church.

The village clustered round it is a pleasing medley of styles and periods. The scent of seaweed fills the air, notice boards proclaim times of tides, prospects of winds, regulations for sailors. Houses facing the harbour have mooring rings clamped in their walls, and steps leading down to captive boats from high-set doors; and everywhere ducks wander, supremely indifferent to traffic, and accorded a measure of amused indulgence by motorists that would never be extended to human beings.

With all its obvious attractions, Bosham remains remarkably unselfconscious and free of synthetic charm.

Boxgrove Priory church

(A. F. Kersting)

You get the best view of it by turning left along the sea road to the far side of the harbour. But watch the tide.

Boxgrove Priory W. Sussex B5

The continuous roar of traffic on the main road just s. of the village of Boxgrove, to say nothing of Tangmere airfield beyond, finds its perfect antidote in the peace of the medieval priory.

The priory was founded in the early c. 12, from Lessay in Normandy, and the church took rather more than a hundred years to build. It then consisted of nave, central tower, transepts, choir, and chancel. The nave was for the parishioners, but at the Dissolution this, together with the monastic buildings, was ruined, and the parishioners moved up, so to speak, into the choir, previously reserved for the monks. That is the situation today.

Entering by a c. 14 room used as a porch, the visitor finds himself in an Early English church of the first part of the c. 13, the only c. 12 bits left being the transepts, the two s. bays of the short piece of the nave w. of the tower, and the upper part of the tower itself. In the early c. 13 the round tower arches were pointed and the pillars on which they rested were encased. The Early English style in which these and all the rest of the church is built had not yet entirely broken away from the Norman, which gives it sturdiness combined with gracefulness. There may be something a little self-conscious in the complicated use of Purbeck marble in the columns and double bays of the choir; nevertheless the total effect is exceptionally satisfying, softened as it is by the unusual c. 16 roof paintings. (Were these the inspiration for Oliver Messel's in the Long Gallery at Parham?) The Victorian E. window is also a success. As for the chantry on the s. side, this is an exquisite piece of Renaissance art. It was built, in 1536 and during his lifetime, for the 9th Earl de la Warr, of nearby Halnaker. This was the time of the Dissolution, and only a year later we find him pleading with Thomas Cromwell to spare Boxgrove Priory, for his 'aunsystorys' and his 'wyffy's mother' were buried there, and he had made himself 'a pow'r chapell to be buryed yn'. In vain: all the monastic buildings and half the church were destroyed; and although his 'wyffy' was buried there, he himself was forced to give Halnaker to Henry VIII and retire to Offington near Worthing. He died in 1554 and his tomb is in Broadwater church.

There is a striking contrast between the magnificent de la Warr chantry and the c. 18 wall monument in the N. transept to Mary Countess of Derby, shown dispensing alms to the poor.

Outside, enough of the former parochial church is left to show that it too must have been of impressive style and proportions. As for the monastic buildings, part of the w. side of the chapter house runs out from the wall of the N. transept – a row of stumpy Norman arches. The roofless c. 13 guest house – or it may have been the Prior's Lodging – stands forlornly in a field to the N.

Bramber W. Sussex C5

On a lofty eminence above this downland village stand the impressive remains (N.T.) of the keep of a Norman castle built by William de Braoze, to whom William I had given the Rape of Bramber in about 1086. (The 'rapes' were the Norman administrative divisions of Sussex, and each had its castle guarding the sea approaches: Hastings, Pevensey, Lewes, Bramber, Arundel, Chichester.) Bramber was then at the head of an arm of the sea into which the River Adur flowed. William de Braoze had completed the castle by about 1090. It had an uneventful history until the Civil War, when the Parliamentarians successfully defended it and then dismantled it, leaving it as it is now. One flint wall of the square keep rises to a height of about 40ft. There are stumps of the other walls, and fragments of the outer wall of the castle appear at intervals round the perimeter; outside that is a steep drop all round to the partly tidal moat, which has now disappeared. After the keep, the largest fragment left is that of the guardroom to the N. In the middle of the area is a mound covered with trees and undergrowth, on which there may well have been a Saxon fort, and even a Norman wooden one, before William de Braoze built his castle of stone.

Immediately below the castle keep is the Norman parish church of St Nicholas, once cruciform; but the chancel and transepts of the old church have long since disappeared. The top of the tower is an c. 18 reconstruction without a roof – you can see the sky through the 'window' on the N. side. There is a good deal of c. 19 restoration too.

Descend the hill into the village and on the right is St Mary's, a timber-framed house of the c. 15. Here in medieval times there was a long bridge and causeway carrying the road across the River Adur. On the bridge was a chapel belonging to Sele Priory at Beeding. In the late 1470s the bridge and chapel, which had fallen into disrepair, were rebuilt by William Waynflete, Bishop of Winchester; and it is thought that he also built St Mary's, as a dwelling for the monks who were wardens of the bridge, and probably as a lodging for pilgrims and other travellers. What is left of it is thought to be one wing of a courtyard house, and is a fine example of a timber-framed house of the period.

In Elizabethan times it was converted into a private house, when chimney stacks were added – before that there had been no heating of any sort. The very unusual painted panels in one of the upstairs rooms probably date from the c. 17. Another room is known as the King's Room, owing to a strong tradition that Charles II stayed here while he waited for a chance to cross the bridge on his way to Shoreham and the safety of France after the Battle of Worcester.

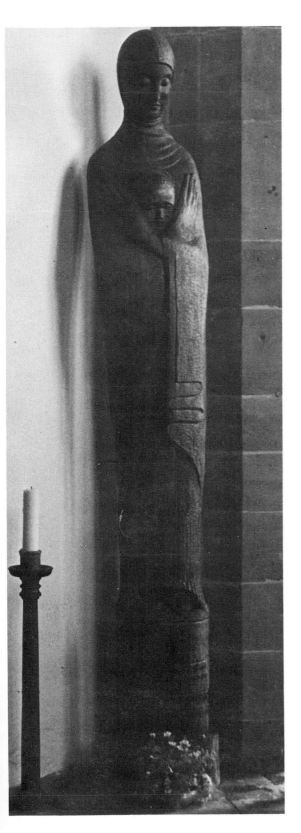

Brambletye E. Sussex *see* **East Grinstead**

Brede E. Sussex F5

In the year 1310 King Edward II reviewed the English fleet from the bottom of the hill s. of Brede. Now at the same spot the River Brede, little more than a large ditch, trickles unnoticed under the brick bridge that carries the A28 road on its way to Hastings. Perched on the hill to the N., the village seems to turn its back on Brede Level, the marshy tract that was once the broad arm of the sea where the proud fleet gathered. The old part of the village, with the church of St George, comes first, but Brede now straggles N. through Cackle Street and on to Broad Oak. Nevertheless, it is a village of much charm, very characteristic of this part of East Sussex, with a number of small, bright, weatherboarded houses.

The church itself is interesting more for the things it contains than for its architecture, in which there are bits of all periods from Norman to Perpendicular. Most interesting, perhaps, because most curious and un-expected, is the flamboyant, swirling tracery of the E. window in the s. aisle, reminiscent of the E. window at Etchingham. For quaintness, the prize must be awarded to the long-drawn-out inscription on the line of the c. 17 gutter fixed to the exterior wall, at the junction of the chancel and the s. aisle, and beginning: 'THIS GVTER . . . .'

Inside the church there are beautifully inscribed notices to tell you about the many interesting things to be seen. Perhaps a personal favourite may be mentioned: in the s. chapel, entered through a Tudor screen of oak, stands the 'Sheridan Madonna', a statue of the Virgin and Child carved from a single oak trunk from Brede Place by Clare Sheridan, in memory of her son who was shipwrecked off the coast of N. Africa in 1937.

Brede Place, about a mile E., was formerly open to the public. It is a c. 15 stone manor house with c. 16 alterations in brick, the home of the Oxenbridge family, one of whom, Sir Goddard Oxenbridge (whose effigy is seen in the s. chapel of Brede church), was said to be a cannibal who ate a baby for supper every night; the children of Sussex disapproved of this practice, and having taken the precaution of getting him drunk, sawed him in half.

Brenchley Kent E4

A typically Kentish village among the fruit and hops SE. of Tonbridge, with the usual mixture of weather-boarding, timber-framing, and tile-hanging. The main street runs W. from a tiny triangle of a green on which a fine oak tree stands. Behind it is the butcher's shop, with its ancient timbers exposed and an overhang all along the front of it. Behind this and to the s. is Church

The Sheridan Madonna in Brede church
(Gerd Franklin)

Mad Jack Fuller's conical folly on Brightling Down (A. F. Kersting)

Close, a small estate of pleasant modern houses. Across the road from the triangle is the sandstone church, approached by a path between enormous yew shrubs, five each side, blocking the view of the building. Standing further back, one can see that the w. tower has a curious concave-sided cap on its corner turret, perhaps a replacement for the steeple blown down in the storm of 1703.

The mainly c. 13 interior was much restored in the c. 19 and is rather disappointing. There is, however, a fine wall monument to Walter Roberts, d. 1652 aged 37, on the w. wall of the N. transept. He and his wife are shown as at a window, hands touching in discreet affection.

The church path comes out into the main street again close to the Old Vicarage, dated 'Circa 1320', its white-painted tiles shaded by a large cedar tree. Further along the street on the right is The Old Palace, once a palace of the Archbishops of Canterbury; its half-timbering, however, is nearly all modern restoration. Opposite, the Bull Inn is aggressively c. 19, but further

on again are several tile-hung houses, culminating in The Old Workhouse, a close-studded building with a timber porch and an oriel window, probably c. 16.

A right turn here, past the handsome c. 18 house on the corner, leads to the top of Pixot Hill, with a vast view across the clay plain to the hills of the Lower Greensand, and the North Downs in the far distance.

Brickwall E. Sussex *see* **Northiam**

Brightling E. Sussex E5
This small village stands splendidly high in the Weald, somewhat off the beaten track. Pre-eminently it is the village of Mad Jack Fuller, its squire, who lived at Brightling Park (then called Rose Hill) until his death in 1834, at the age of 77. Fuller was the eccentric *par excellence*, and something of a megalomaniac, an c. 18 character spilt over into the following century. Four buildings testify to his memory: Brightling Needle; the nearby observatory; the conical folly at Wood's Corner; and his own tomb in Brightling churchyard.

The Needle, sometimes known as Brightling Beacon because it was built on the site of one, is an obelisk erected by Fuller, over 60ft high, standing on ground which is itself nearly 650ft above sea-level and is the highest point in the district, near the crossroads w. of the village.

The observatory, which stands about 400yd s. of the obelisk, witnesses to Fuller's interest in science; it is still used by amateur astronomers.

The folly stands in a field on the NE. side of the hamlet of Wood's Corner, between Brightling and Dallington. The story goes that Fuller made a bet with a friend that the spire of Dallington church was visible from the Grecian temple in the grounds of Brightling Park. When he realized he was wrong he hastily had a conical structure built on the skyline in between, presumably in the hope that it would deceive his opponent and win him the bet – or perhaps he was merely intending to recoup this particular loss by wagers with gullible victims of the future.

Finally, the mausoleum in the churchyard: this is a huge stone pyramid, inside which, according to legend, certainly untrue, Fuller sits upright, wearing a top hat and holding a bottle of claret. The legend, although apocryphal, is at least in character.

Across the road is a house that was once the village inn. Fuller, however, did not relish the idea of rowdies disturbing his peace. At his own expense he had another inn built, at a respectful distance from the village, and named it 'The Fuller's Arms'.

The church contains an c. 18 gallery and pulpit, a bust of Mad Jack Fuller on the s. wall, and the arms of William of Wykeham above the small door on the s. exterior wall of the chancel – he was rector here in 1362, before his great days as Bishop of Winchester and Chancellor of England.

Brighton E. Sussex C6

Brighton is far and away the largest town in the region. It has two unique things, the Royal Pavilion, and The Lanes; another it shares with Hove (q.v.): Regency terraces and squares open to the sea. It is 'London by the Sea' (whereas Southend is only 'The East End by the Sea').

It was once Brightelmstone, a fishing village of little importance and less history, until its health-giving properties were 'discovered' and publicized by Dr Russell of Lewes in the middle of the c. 18; but what finally put Brighton on the map was the arrival of George, Prince of Wales, who, in 1784 at the age of 22, decided to take up residence there. In 1811 he became the Prince Regent, and in 1820 King George IV. By the time he died in 1830, it is estimated that over £500,000 had been spent on his Brighton home.

The story of the Royal Pavilion, from its origins as a severely classical building by Holland in 1787 to its final transformation by Nash into an Indian 'pavilion'

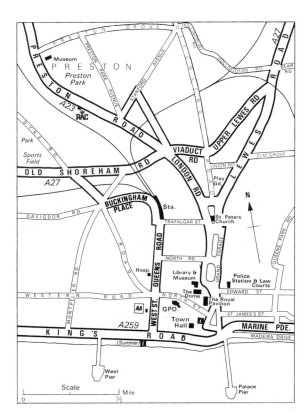

(containing much Chinese decoration introduced nearly 20 years earlier) is too long and involved to be told here. When William IV succeeded to the throne, he continued to live in the Pavilion from time to time, but for Victoria and her earnest consort it was altogether too flamboyant in style, and in 1850, after much argument, it was finally purchased by the town of Brighton for £50,000.

The visitor to Brighton must not miss the Pavilion. The Banqueting Room, with its immense chandelier suspended from dragons' claws and weighing nearly a ton, is an exciting experience, the music room no less so, while the great kitchen, whose iron columns are made to resemble palm trees, seems almost cosy by comparison.

The whole extraordinary edifice has always called forth both admiration and abuse; 'undeniably beautiful in its harmonious proportions', says the official guide-book, while others would agree with Hazlitt: 'a collection of stone pumpkins and pepper boxes'.

The building is situated on the w. side of an open space known as Old Steine. In the Prince Regent's day this was open to the sea, and the view was one of the features of the royal residence. This is no longer so, as the Royal York Buildings partly close off the seaward end of Old Steine, which is now in effect a large round-about and bus turn-round enclosing municipal flower

The Banqueting Room in Brighton Pavilion   (A. F. Kersting)

beds. At the end of Old Steine is the Palace Pier, the younger of Brighton's two existing piers – it was built in 1899. In its heyday it had a landing stage at which quite large cruise-ships could dock, but this is now derelict; the rest of the pier is still open but is a depressing sight, although less so than the West Pier, which was built in 1866, and was finally closed in 1975.

The Lanes, a confusion of narrow streets around Brighton Square, mostly, but not entirely, free of traffic, is the nucleus of the old village of Brightelmstone. There is nothing quite like it in any other English town, although it is faintly reminiscent of certain streets in York.

Just to the E. of the Palace Pier is the underground Aquarium, the highlight of which is the 'dolphinarium', a large pool where four dolphins disport themselves, and at set times perform with diving-boards and hoops. Round the outside of their pool, below water level, is a restaurant where you can sit and eat while watching

the dolphins swimming about on the other side of the glass.

Above the ground again, we can take the narrow-gauge Volks Railway, which runs for one mile westwards along the sea front from here to Black Rock. This was the first electric railway to be built in Britain (1883). From Black Rock one can go up to the top road, on the other side of which is Kemp Town, the smartest part of Brighton. Here is Lewes Crescent, flanked by Chichester Terrace to the w. and Arundel Terrace to the E., and leading at its N. end up to Sussex Square, the whole being a superb example of Regency panache, if not in the first rank architecturally – 'the Crescent and Square are so large that one cannot read the façades together', frowns Pevsner.

Brighton comes to its eastern end in the Marina, about which there was much controversy when the idea of it was first mooted; it was thought by some that it would lower the tone of Kemp Town. These are early

Royal Crescent, Brighton (B.T.A.)

days; but it seems likely to prove in the event an en-hancement of the local scene, as well as a good invest-ment. There is a certain flippant gaiety about the Marina that contrasts with the severity of the barracks-like buildings of Roedean school beyond, announcing the beginning of Rottingdean.

There is Victorian Brighton as well as Regency and modern Brighton, including one of the most exciting Victorian churches in England: St Bartholomew's, in Ann Street, a soaring brick giant, severe, immensely impressive.

Out at Stanmer Park, towards Lewes, stands the University of Sussex, with modern buildings designed by Sir Basil Spence. The lay-out combines compactness with spaciousness, and is visually satisfying. It is ap-propriate to see it at the end rather than at the beginning of one's visit to Brighton, for Brighton is a town that is thoroughly modern in spirit, despite its Regency treasures.

Broadstairs Kent *see* **Thanet**

Burton W. Sussex B5
This place consists of a large house built in 1831 and a tiny church built in about 1075. Both are reached on foot, up the drive that leads off the main Petworth–Chichester road at Duncton, opposite Willett Close. There is no public right of way for vehicles, but the drive is a public footpath: five minutes' walk through woods and another five through open parkland.

The house, now a girls' school and not open to the public, was built as a private house by Henry Bassett, who in 1831 was only 28. It is a severely classical box of a building whose entrance front, with its four great Ionic columns on the first- and second-floor levels, and its blind bays on either side of them, is enough, one would imagine, to strike terror into the heart of any new girl; but the accretion of more modern buildings has had a softening effect.

Beyond the house is the little Norman church, restored in 1636. It is a gem, unspoilt even by the Victorians – except for the tiled floor of the sanctuary, and the E. window, which at any rate might have been worse.

The walls have been adorned with various C. 17 texts, and with a Royal Arms of Charles I, a great rarity. This is on the S. wall, and is delightfully amateurish. Over it is the abrupt text: 'Obey them that have the rule over you. Heb. 13. 17'. It seems to epitomize the attitude of Charles himself, which eventually led to his execution. Underneath are the Latin words 'CHRISTO AUSPICE REGNO' ('I rule with Christ as my guide'), of which the same might be said.

The rood screen is C. 15, and still shows much of its original paintwork. The Decalogue (Ten Commandments) on the wall above is C. 17, and so are the communion rails. The font, crude and basic, possibly Saxon, is thought to be one of the oldest in Sussex.

On the S. side of the chancel is a delightful monument, probably C. 15, to an unknown lady, and on either side of the nave are C. 16 canopy monuments to members of the Goringe family, owners of Burton Park (there have been at least two previous houses on the site). On the N. wall, behind the more elaborate canopy, is a horrific wall painting of a female being crucified upside down on a St Andrew cross. This is St Uncumber, otherwise known as St Wilgefort, said to be the friend of wives who wish to be rid of their husbands.

On leaving the church, one can see, a short distance to the W., two other churches. These are the Victorian churches of Duncton: Church of England on the left and Roman Catholic on the right. A public footpath sign points towards the latter, but unless one is clad in high boots and armed with a bill-hook it is better to return by the drive.

Burwash   E. Sussex   E5

An attractive village with an attractive name, derived from the Old English *burh*, a stronghold, and *erse*, a stubble field. A former centre of the old Sussex iron trade, it stands on a ridge running E. and W. between the river valleys of the Rother and the Dudwell, and has good views of the Weald to N. and S.

The best plan here is to walk along the main street from, say, the free car park near its W. end to the church at its E. The street carries much traffic at times, but is delightful notwithstanding. Brick, tiles, weatherboarding – all kinds of houses are to be seen here, blending harmoniously. The house that stands out supreme is Rampyndene, built in 1699 and situated on the S. side of the street quite near the church (*see also* Lamberhurst). This house, of brick on the outside, is timber-framed, having been built by a timber merchant. Notice the small windows flanking the door, a fashion of the time. The ornately carved hood above the door is the height of elegance.

Beyond the war memorial stands the church, which was largely, and sympathetically, rebuilt in the 1850s by Slater. The old parts that survive are the wide Early English chancel arch and the nave arcades (the S. arcade being partly Norman), and the Norman tower, although there has been some restoration here too. The church contains what is thought to be the oldest cast-iron tomb slab in existence, possibly C. 14. This is now preserved on the N. wall of the S. aisle, on the left of the altar there, and commemorates Jhone (John? Joan?) Colines; beside it is a small C. 15 brass.

A simple, dignified tablet on the wall of the S. aisle commemorates John Kipling, killed at Loos in 1915 at the age of 18. He was the only son of the famous writer, and his memorial serves to remind us also that the parish of Burwash contains BATEMAN's, the C. 17 ironmaster's house which was Rudyard Kipling's home from 1902 until his death in 1936. It was bequeathed to the N.T. by his widow, who died in 1939.

The way to Bateman's from Burwash church is down the hill from the war memorial, turning right at the bottom; or one can go straight to it down another lane (Bateman's Lane) at the other end of the village. The mellow old house of local stone was built in 1634. It makes an immediate impression of friendly dignity. Originally the front of the house was symmetrical, but the right-hand gable, some time, somehow, has been lost. This hardly detracts from the charm of the building.

Inside, the house and its contents are fascinating in their own right, as well as being an interesting memorial to the famous author. One can get the feeling of the house, and examine the more important furnishings, in half an hour. But a thorough visit, including a perusal of the many interesting things in the exhibition room, formerly the guest room, needs an hour and a half or so.

A walk through the garden, which was largely designed by Kipling, and which blends so admirably with the house and the countryside around, takes us to Park Mill, the ancient watermill on a stream running into the Dudwell. Soon after his arrival at Bateman's, Kipling removed the waterwheel and installed a turbine, which drove a generator and supplied electricity to the house, at 110 volts D.C., until 1927. After some years of neglect the mill has been restored to its original use by a band of local volunteers working under the general direction of the N.T. The flour it produces is sold in the shop in the outbuildings of the house.

Canterbury   Kent   G3

And specially from every shires ende
   Of Engelond, to Caunterbury they wende . . .
Chaucer. *Prologue to The Canterbury Tales.*

And not only from 'Engelond', but from 'sondry londes'. After Becket's murder 'pilgrimages' became the chief money-spinner for Canterbury; they still are.

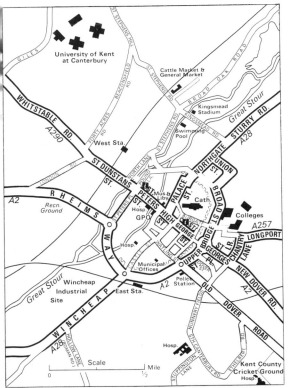

The city suffered grievously from Hitler's bombers in the Second World War; about one third of the buildings in the centre were destroyed. Tragic as this was, it brought benefits: it enabled archaeologists to trace the city's early history, especially its Roman lay-out; it allowed the provision of much more adequate car parking space than most towns enjoy; and it gave an opportunity for imaginative planning of the central area, which it must be confessed appears to have been but clutched at rather than grasped.

So far as early history is concerned, there was certainly an Iron Age settlement here in about 300 B.C., evidence of which has been uncovered in Castle Street, and the area was overrun by the Belgae in about 75 B.C., but the first major development was by the Romans after their successful invasion in A.D. 43. They gave it the name of Durovernum, and it grew into a place of importance, lying as it did at the crossing of the Stour on the route from the coast to London. Much later, it became the supply base for the forts at Reculver and Richborough, and possibly also for Lympne. The Romans built a protective wall round Durovernum, but hardly any of it remains; the considerable portions of wall now standing are medieval, built on the Roman foundations. As for the Roman street plan, it has been established since the Second World War that it bears no relation to today's, which is based on the quite different medieval one. Several Roman buildings have

been uncovered, including a small portion of a town house of the c. 2 or c. 3, with a hypocaust and mosaic pavement, below the E. side of Butchery Lane.

The demise of the Roman empire was a gradual process. Saxon raids began to be a serious menace before the end of the c. 3; not until the middle of the c. 5 was all resistance at an end. The Roman name Durovernum gave place to the Saxon Cantwarabyrig. The two most important local events in the history of Canterbury are the arrival of St Augustine in 597 and the murder of Becket in 1170.

Christianity had been established here in Roman times. In 1962 men engaged on constructing Rheims Way, part of the ring road, unearthed Roman utensils bearing the Christian monogram. Bede stated that St Augustine found churches already in existence; one of them, which he was told had been built 'long ago' by Roman Christians, stood on the site of the present cathedral.

Ever since then, the Cathedral Church of Christ, Canterbury, has stood as the supreme symbol of English Christianity, the seat of the Primate of All England, and in more recent times the mother church of the worldwide Anglican Communion. The present building is a worthy symbol. So far, at least, it has not been dwarfed by huge modern blocks; it still dominates the city. Its lofty central tower of Caen stone, known as 'Bell Harry' after the original bell given by Prior Henry of Eastry, varies in colour with the changing light – grey, silver, golden, pink, never the same but ever beautiful.

Over 300 years before this magnificent Perpendicular tower was built, the scandal of Becket's murder reverberated throughout Europe and turned Canterbury almost overnight into one of the most important places of pilgrimage. This brought fantastic wealth, as the pilgrims streamed in from all parts of Europe, until Henry VIII in 1538 ordered the destruction of Becket's shrine and seized for himself its gold and jewels. Now only a plain and unassuming tablet marks the spot where Becket fell.

Visitors to Canterbury usually start at the cathedral, approaching it through the early-c. 16 Christ Church Gate, restored in 1935. Before entering the cathedral itself it is well to study a simple outline of its history. It is not possible to assign a date for its building; it grew up piecemeal, its development punctuated by disasters, its story interwoven with the city's own.

When St Augustine arrived he repaired the church that occupied the site, founded a monastery alongside, and another outside the city walls. In 851 the Danes came, plundering and pillaging; in 1011 they carried out another, more destructive visitation, sacking the city, burning the cathedral, and carrying off the archbishop, Alphege, whom they later killed. King Canute restored the cathedral and ordered the return of Alphege's body for re-burial there.

In 1067, the year after the Conquest, the cathedral

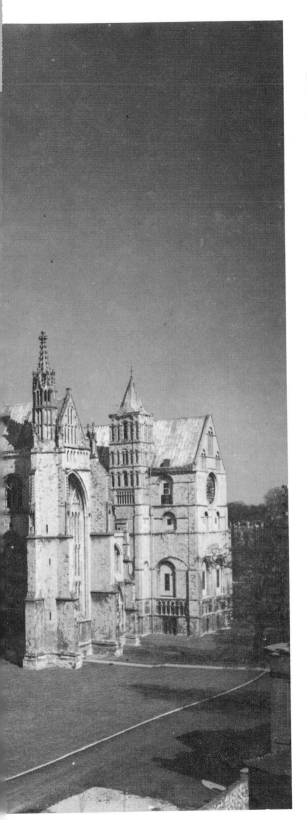

suffered a calamitous fire, and the Normans set about rebuilding it under the direction of the first Norman archbishop, Lanfranc. His successor, Anselm, started to rebuild the choir and eastern transepts, and this was completed by 1130. But in 1170 Becket was murdered, and in 1174 another fire largely destroyed Anselm's work. These disasters, however, must soon have been seen by the worldly as blessings in disguise, and now, to accommodate Becket's shrine and the hordes of pilgrims, the whole eastern part of the cathedral was again reconstructed, this time in Transitional style, first by William of Sens – until he was badly injured in falling from the scaffolding and had to return to Normandy – and next by William the Englishman, who built the eastern crypt, and the Trinity Chapel and Corona at the E. end of the choir.

Meanwhile Lanfranc's nave and western transepts, together with the central tower and two western towers, still stood. By the end of the C. 14, however, most of these had deteriorated so badly that they had to be replaced. The architect of the new nave was Henry Yevele, who completed it by about 1400. About 40 years later the SW. tower was replaced, and by 1500 John Wastell had built a new central tower – Bell Harry. Finally in 1832 the Norman NW. tower was also replaced, by a replica of its C. 15 fellow.

From all this it will be understood that like the majority of English churches and cathedrals Canterbury in its architecture is a strange mixture of dates and styles: crypt, Norman; east of the screen, Transitional; nave, central tower, and western towers, Perpendicular (the NW. tower actually built in 1832). Even this is an oversimplification, but at least it will also be understood that when we start looking at the nave, then move past the screen into the choir, and finally visit the crypt, as many – perhaps most – visitors do, we are going steadily backwards in time. If these points are appreciated, one's enjoyment of the numerous details, only a small selection of which are mentioned in the following description, will be much enhanced.

To complete the catalogue of disasters, however, we cannot omit the destruction wrought by the Puritans at the time of the Civil War in the mid C. 17. One of the glories of the cathedral is its medieval glass, but the Puritans destroyed much of it, as well as a large number of statues. A good deal of the glass that escaped has been moved from its original position, where it formed part of a logical series, and is scattered about the building.

We have already mentioned the Second World War, during which, unlike the city, the cathedral itself was miraculously spared. Today a more patient enemy, atmospheric pollution, gnaws at the fabric. The out-

Canterbury Cathedral from the SW
(A. F. Kersting)

64

come of the battle is uncertain and largely depends upon the generosity of the individual 'pilgrims' of today.

Entering the cathedral, then, by the sw. porch and tower, the visitor will first stand at the w. end and admire Yevele's Perpendicular nave, culminating in the stone screen, or *Pulpitum*, erected by Prior Thomas Chillenden, *c*. 1400, and separating the nave from the choir built 200 years earlier.

The font, on the N. side of the nave near the w. end, dates from the C. 17. Moving up the nave to a point about opposite to it and looking back at the w. window one sees, on the lowest two rows of panes, glass dating from the late C. 12, the oldest in the cathedral.

The *Pulpitum*, from the steps leading up to it, can be seen to bear statues of various kings, spared by the Puritans, who, as was their wont, concentrated instead on destroying representations of saints, of Christ, and of the Virgin. From here, too, one can admire the beautiful C. 15 and late-C. 12 glass in the sw. transept, while in the NW. transept the only medieval glass to survive depicts the family of Edward IV (late-C. 15).

Above the steps is the delicate fan-vaulting in the ceiling of Bell Harry tower; Wastell later brought this particular form of decorative art to perfection in King's College Chapel, Cambridge.

Across the NW. transept from the bottom of the steps leading down into it is the spot called the Martyrdom, where Becket was slain, while through the opening in the *Pulpitum* is the huge choir, whose culmination is the Trinity Chapel behind the High Altar. This was designed to be the focal point and grand climax of the whole cathedral interior, a fitting site for the shrine of the 'holy blissful martyr'. Even the High Altar was relegated to a lower level, where the altar rails are now.

The gate on the s. side of the choir leads into the SE. transept, whose s. windows contain modern glass by the Hungarian artist Erwin Bossanyi (1956). On the E. side of the transept is a chapel restored in memory of the much loved Archbishop William Temple (d. 1944). Moving E. again one comes to the Chapel of St Anselm on the right, with modern glass by H. J. Stammers (1959). Straight ahead are the steps leading up to the Trinity Chapel, worn by pilgrims to Becket's shrine for over 300 years, and by countless visitors ever since. At the top of the steps is the tomb of the Black Prince (d. 1376), son of Edward III and a popular hero, who

(A. F. Kersting)

The C12 crypt

had expressed a wish to be buried in the crypt, but who, it was felt, must be laid to rest in a more sacred place, close to Becket's shrine. On the far side of the Trinity Chapel is the tomb of Henry IV (d. 1413), the only English king buried in the cathedral, while to the w., behind the High Altar, is the c. 13 throne of Purbeck marble known as St Augustine's Chair, which may be a copy of an earlier throne destroyed in the fire of 1174. Archbishops of Canterbury sit on it during part of their enthronement ceremony. Beyond Henry IV's tomb, in the N. ambulatory, there is more stained glass of high quality; these windows are the Miracle Windows, depicting the miracles worked by the intervention of St Thomas Becket. Further w., past the NE. transept, are two windows filled with early-c. 13 glass showing biblical scenes.

Across on the s. side of the *Pulpitum*, off the sw. transept, is the entrance to the crypt, the largest Norman crypt in Europe. In the middle is the Chapel of Our Lady, built by the Black Prince and intended to accommodate his own tomb.

The door on the N. side of the crypt leads out of the cathedral to the buildings of one of the monasteries founded by St Augustine. One comes out opposite a water tower erected in the c. 12. From here a passage leads w. to the Great Cloister, originally Norman but rebuilt *c.* 1400. In the vaulting are colourful bosses, most of them being coats-of-arms of those who subscribed to the cost of the building. On the E. side, next to the passage from the water tower, is the early-c. 14 chapter house; the part above the top of the ornamental arcading round the walls, however, dates from a hundred years later.

The doorway on the other side of the passage leads to the modern library, which replaced the one destroyed in the Second World War. (Although the cathedral escaped damage, buildings in the precincts were less fortunate.) The library occupies the southern part of the monks' dormitory, dismantled at the Dissolution – but some of the old Norman walling can be seen from the other side of the cloister.

On the cloister's N. side were the monks' refectory and buttery, rebuilt in the c. 13 and ornamented with graceful arcading, spoilt in places by the later pillars of the cloister vaulting, which cut into it. On the w. side of the cloister was the cellarer's, or steward's, lodging; next to the doorway in the NW. corner is a small octagonal opening, a medieval serving-hatch through which thirsty monks could obtain refreshment from the cellarer. The doorway itself is the one used by Becket when approaching the cathedral for the last time; he had to make a detour because his usual route by the main w. door was blocked by armed men.

At the other end of the passage leading back to the water tower is the Infirmary Cloister. Passing along its far or E. side one emerges on to the spacious Green Court. In the NW. corner, beside an ancient gateway, much restored, are the roofed steps called the Norman Staircase, which formerly led into a hall for poor pilgrims. At the N. side of Green Court are the buildings of the King's School, a boys' public school of ancient foundation.

From the Infirmary Cloister it is possible to walk round to the E. end of the cathedral, past the ruins of the infirmary and chapel. Beyond the chapel ruins, across a roadway, stands the five-gabled building called Meister Omers, named after a c. 13 lawyer, and now a boarding house for the King's School. Past this is the Kent War Memorial Garden, from the NE. corner of which one can pass through the city walls. On the left is the tower of the Quenin Gate, now blocked; in the wall on the near (s.) side of it are some thin red bricks arranged in the shape of an arch, part of one of the Roman gates into the city.

Only just across Broad Street from here, up Lady Wootton's Green and across Monastery Street, is the entrance to St Augustine's Abbey (D.O.E.) and the imposing Fyndon Gate, built in the first years of the c. 14 under Abbot Fyndon – and restored after bomb damage in the Second World War. This gate is now the entrance to St Augustine's College. The visitor to the abbey ruins passes through the gateway in the wall on the left and turns right; on his left are the modern buildings of Christ Church College of Education, a teacher training college.

The abbey of St Peter and St Paul was founded by St Augustine to accommodate monks and to be a burial-place for himself and his successors, and for the Kentish kings. It was built outside the walls in accordance with the Roman custom for burial-places, and was consecrated in 613. There was always jealousy and wrangling between cathedral and abbey, sharpened in 1011, when the city was sacked by the Danes: although the cathedral was burnt and Archbishop Alphege captured and later put to death, the abbey was spared as a reward to the abbot, who had collaborated with the invaders.

The original abbey was rebuilt and enlarged by St Dunstan (906–88) and re-dedicated to SS. Peter, Paul, and Augustine. Next, Abbot Wulfric started another rebuilding, including a rotunda, in *c.* 1050, but his Norman successor, Abbot Scotland, swept all this aside and started again. Throughout the Middle Ages the monastery was one of the richest and most powerful in England. After the Dissolution it fell into ruin, its stones being used for secular buildings in the city, although part, including the Fyndon Gate, was reserved as a royal staging-post between London and the Channel. Elizabeth I stayed there, and Charles I spent his wedding night in the chamber over the gateway in 1625. Later, these buildings passed into private hands, and by the c. 19 had become a beer-garden and cockpit. Then in 1844 the whole property was bought by the wealthy philanthropist Alexander Beresford Hope (*see* Kilndown), who employed William Butterfield to build the present St Augustine's College as a training college for missionaries. The buildings are now used by the King's School.

The abbey ruins are complicated, as there were several periods of building. Of St Augustine's own building there remains part of the principal abbey church, where St Augustine himself and his five successors as archbishop, and King Ethelbert, his queen, Bertha, and her chaplain, were all buried. In addition there are remains of the earlier church of St Pancras, to the E., parts of which are of St Augustine's time. Also to be seen are the foundations of Wulfric's rotunda, never completed, and parts of Scotland's nave and of the presbytery crypt; to the N. of the abbey church are remains of the old cloister and refectory, and the octagonal foundation of the kitchen.

The adjoining college built by Butterfield is in the same Decorated style as the Fyndon Gate, but more austere. The knapped flint walls accentuate the austerity, but the whole effect is pleasing. Immediately to the right (s.) of the gate are the refectory and chapel, partly medieval. The N. side of the quadrangle, on a raised walk, is all Butterfield, while on the E. side is the library, with a very steeply pitched roof. In the middle stands a well-head.

At the far end of Monastery Street, and facing down Church Street (St Paul's), is Cemetery Gate, another gate of the monastery, dating from the late C. 14; it was heavily restored in 1839. Turn to the left past this gate into Longport, and go past John Smith's Hospital, founded 1657, on the right; then turn left again into North Holmes Road, five minutes' walk from Cemetery Gate, and St Martin's church is on the right. This church almost certainly incorporates part of the church of St Martin where Queen Bertha, who was already a Christian before the arrival of St Augustine, used to worship, and where the saint and his followers worshipped before the conversion of Ethelbert himself. There has been Christian worship here continuously ever since. The present building is not particularly

A section of Canterbury city wall

(N.M.R.)

exciting architecturally, but surely here, if anywhere, is the cradle of English Christianity.

In Canterbury it is hard to escape for long from the influence of Augustine and Becket. There are many churches, and most of them claim some sort of connexion, however tenuous, with the city's ecclesiastical origins. As for Becket, many of the medieval buildings owe their beginnings to the visits of pilgrims to his shrine. Of the churches, two have only their towers left standing. St George's, in St George's Street, now a pedestrian precinct, is one; this tower, and the clock protruding over the street from its flank, were all that was left after the bombings of 1942. The other is St Mary Magdalene in Burgate, the rest of the building having been demolished in 1871; under this tower there stands, among other monuments rescued from the church itself, a large ornate memorial to John Whitfeild, d. 1691: at the corners of a central obelisk are four mourning putti, immensely plump and weeping copiously.

Butchery Lane, where the Roman house already mentioned is to be found, is a short distance along Burgate to the w., on the corner of Longmarket and below the present street level. At the other end of Butchery Lane is the Parade, which a little further w. becomes the High Street. Here on the right is the end of Mercery Lane, where Boots the Chemist almost touches the gift shop on the other side of the street, which is all that remains, after a serious fire in the c. 19, of a large medieval hostel built to accommodate pilgrims, and traditionally known as the Chequer of the Hope.

A little way along the High Street on the left is a building known as Queen Elizabeth's Guest Chamber. It is dated 1573, and has pargetting depicting putti tangled up in vines. The name is apparently of recent invention.

The mock-Tudor Victorian building further on on the right houses a public library and museum, which contains the horde of Roman spoons and other objects found during the construction of Rheims Way in 1962. Soon the High Street crosses a branch of the River Stour on the King's Bridge, where it becomes St Peter's Street. Here on the right, beside the river, is the famous and picturesque Weavers' House, one of the houses used by Flemish and Huguenot weavers who came over in the c. 16, fleeing from religious persecution.

Also on the right, on the corner of St Peter's Lane, is St Peter's church, whose tower is possibly Saxon. The interior, however, is mostly Early English, and very much larger than seems possible to the viewer from the street. Near by to the NE. are the remains of the Black-friars, a Dominican friary founded in the c. 13. Only two of the c. 13 buildings are still standing, the guest hall on the w. bank of the Stour, and the refectory on the E. The former, approached from St Peter's Lane, affords the best view of the latter across the narrow river.

At the far end of St Peter's Street is the Westgate, rebuilt in Kentish ragstone in 1380 by Archbishop Sudbury to strengthen the city's defences on the London side, and now the only one of the medieval city gates still standing. It had a drawbridge over the Stour (another branch of which flows past here), and the usual portcullis and machicolations. Nevertheless it failed to keep out Wat Tyler's rebels in 1381; having plundered Canterbury they moved to London, seized Sudbury himself – as Chancellor he was blamed for the hated poll tax – and slew him on Tower Hill.

The gate served until 1829 as the city gaol. Now it contains a museum, with exhibits recalling its lurid past. The church beside the gate, Holy Cross, was also built by Sudbury, but in knapped flint; it was heavily restored in the c. 19. Beyond Westgate St Dunstan Street launches off towards Whitstable, and is one of the handsomest streets of Canterbury.

Return along St Peter's Street to the King's Bridge. On the right is St Thomas's, or Eastbridge, Hospital, founded in 1175 to accommodate 12 poor pilgrims. (The East Bridge, from which the hospital derives its popular name – 'East' because it spans the eastern arm of the Stour – was also called the King's Bridge because the Crown owned a mill near by.) The building consists of entrance hall and undercroft of the c. 12, a refectory above, and a c. 13 chapel with quaint old timbers. Beside the entrance hall is a c. 14 chantry chapel. A wing built in the c. 17 extends over the river.

Off Stour Street, which leads off the High Street just before the County Hotel, is the Grey Friars, which stands astride a branch of the river behind the houses and on the far side of a garden. This intimate c. 13 building, which may have been the dormitory of the Franciscan friars here, and which was carefully restored in 1920, is supported on pillars rising from the river bed. The walls are a mixture of flint, stone, and brick. On the far bank are slight remains of the original church.

Further along Stour Street, on the right, is the Poor Priests' Hospital. The hospital, or almshouses, was founded in 1200, but the flint buildings that remain are late-c. 14, the chapel on the right, now a family-planning clinic, and the hall on the left, now a regimental museum.

In Hospital Lane, further on on the left, is yet another 'hospital', the Maynard and Cotton, a medieval foundation. The present buildings, however, were run up in 1708, a very humble and rudimentary row of brick bungalows, interesting if only in comparison with the others. This by no means exhausts the number of medieval hospitals, for there are two more in Northgate: St John's, the oldest in Canterbury, founded by Lanfranc in the c. 11, and Jesus Hospital, built in 1595 and enlarged in 1933. Northgate, incidentally, can be reached by way of Palace Street, where the King's School Shop, a half-timbered house of the c. 17, leans quaintly.

Soon Stour Street becomes Church Lane, and on the right is St Mildred's church, largely Perpendicular but with parts going back to Saxon times, where Isaak

Walton was married in 1626. A short distance to the SE. stand the massive and forlorn flint remains of Canterbury Castle, built soon after the Conquest. This is simply the shell of the keep, there being no trace of the other buildings. Nevertheless, the keep is one of the largest in the country, and must have looked formidable indeed when it stood to its full height, about half as high again as it is now. Its defenders, however, seem to have put up the feeblest of resistance: the Dauphin of France took it in 1216 when he came over in support of the barons rebelling against King John (*see* Dover Castle); Wat Tyler took it in 1381, locking up the governor and freeing all the prisoners; and in the Civil War the Royalists surrendered at the first sight of the approaching Parliamentarians – admittedly medieval castles were not much use against cannon.

From near by to the E., it is possible to walk up on to the city walls, which here encircle a large open space known as Dane John. The name is probably a corruption of the Norman word *donjon*; the prehistoric mound, thought to have been an Iron Age burial mound, may have been used as the *donjon* of a temporary castle. It is now climbed by a spiral path and surmounted by a monument, and affords fine views of the city and its surrounding low hills. The monument on top, erected in 1803, commemorates Alderman James Simmonds, the man who in 1790 turned the mound into an amenity and laid out the gardens below, planting the avenue of lime trees there. On the far side of the avenue is a memorial to Christopher Marlowe, Canterbury's most illustrious literary son, born in 1564 and baptized in St

George's church. His memory is kept alive in the modern Marlowe Theatre in the heart of the city.

It is perhaps salutary, after spending so much time in the past, to return to the present by taking a look at the modern University of Kent at Canterbury, which stands on St Thomas's Hill (Becket again), a little over a mile NW. of the city centre. The site is rather bleak and the buildings austere, in striking contrast with the cosy mellowness of the old city below.

Chaldon Surrey C3

Chaldon stands in splendid isolation on the North Downs about two miles w. of Caterham. It is only just in Surrey, for Greater London reaches out to within 160yd of the tiny flint church, which dates mainly from the C. 12 or C. 13, though the shingled spire, hardly more than a spirelet, is a C. 19 addition. Within, there is a 'Jacobean' pulpit, but dated 1657, an unusual date, since this was during Cromwell's Protectorate, when little church building or furnishing was carried out. There is also a memorial tablet of 1562 on the N. wall of the chancel.

But we have eyes for none of this, for here is one of the most important medieval wall-paintings in England. It is on the w. wall, and depicts against a sombre ochre background a kind of Last Judgement scene, on two levels: the lower level is indisputably Hell, the upper level is said to be Purgatory – it does look a good deal less unpleasant; Heaven is represented by the cloudy little circle at the top. Naked figures climb up and fall down the ladder that extends from top to bottom of the

The University of Kent at Canterbury   (A. F. Kersting)

The medieval wall-painting in Chaldon church   (N.M.R.)

painting. The spaces within the main pictures – the usual Weighing of Souls, Harrowing of Hell, and Tortures of the Damned – are taken up with the Seven Deadly Sins. At bottom right is the Tree of the Knowledge of Good and Evil, with the serpent entwined in its upper branches.

The painting was first made about the year 1200, and was rediscovered when the plaster was stripped off in 1870.

Charing   Kent F3
Most of the village is sandwiched between the A20 and the A252. The High Street rises gently up the lower slope of the North Downs, a street of old half-timbered and weatherboarded houses, some with Georgian frontages, and of genuine c. 17 and c. 18 brick houses.

We start at the bottom. There is one house of interest s. of the A20, but it can be seen from the safety of the N. side if one is already in the main part of the village. This is The Filmer House, now called The Old House, and stands in Station Road just s. of the A20. It is a black-and-white timber-framed house, and has a c. 17 front built on to the main, c. 14, part.

In the High Street, which is all N. of the A20, we pass several picturesque houses before coming to the late-c. 15 half-timbered house on the left of which part is, and

always was, a butcher's shop, perhaps the oldest still surviving as such in England. Further up on the same side is Pierce House, standing back a little, a most attractive c. 16 timber-framed house with herringbone brick-nogging.

Further up, again on the left, is Ludwell House, just past School Road. This c. 18 house was the home of Elizabeth Ludwell, who died in 1761 and left many bequests to the parish, including an endowment for a school; until recently the old school house was still standing, a little further up the street on the right.

Opposite Ludwell House is what appears at first sight to be a brick house, but is really a c. 14 timber-framed house bricked over in the c. 17; on closer inspection traces of the timbers can be seen even from the outside. This building was the Swan Inn, built to accommodate pilgrims on their way to Canterbury, but has recently been turned into flats. The King's Head, a little further up on the left, also dates from the c. 14, although the front is a modern jumble and the old bits have got lost somewhere inside. Just past the King's Head is Wakeley House, another handsome c. 18 house. Then newer but pleasant houses line the road on either side until it emerges on to the A252 road.

Immediately above this junction the Pilgrim's Way crosses the main road. Although this route was certainly taken by the pilgrims to Becket's shrine, it was there centuries before that.

Our own route now lies back down the High Street and along the short lane to the E. which leads to the church. The lane widens out just before reaching the church, and the right-hand side is used as a car park. This is the ancient market place, where markets were regularly held from medieval times until the late C. 19. On the left, the sizeable stone ruins are of the old Manor House, owned by the Archbishops of Canterbury until Cranmer was obliged to surrender it, along with much else, to Henry VIII. The gatehouse probably dates from the time of John Stratford, who was archbishop from 1333 to 1348. The large old barn on the N. side of the churchyard was the banqueting hall. The present farmhouse, seen through the archway of the gatehouse, formed part of the complex and was probably built by John Morton, archbishop from 1486 to 1500. Henry VIII stayed at the Manor House in 1520, on his way to 'The Field of the Cloth of Gold'.

Finally, the church. The C. 15 Perpendicular tower is of ashlared Kentish ragstone, battlemented, and with a stair turret in the SE. corner – a typically Kentish tower, in fact, with a fine W. door, probably intended to be a worthy portal for the entry of the Archbishop from the Manor House. To this day Archbishops of Canterbury enter by this door when visiting Charing, and robe in the old Manor House by courtesy of the owner.

We humbler folk, however, enter by the porch on the S. side. This is contemporary with the tower; it has a ribbed vault, and over it another chamber. The nave and chancel are C. 13, witness the lancets in their N. walls, but much of both was destroyed in the disastrous fire of 4 August 1590 in which 'nothing of the church was left but the bare walls, except the floor over the porch, and the floor over the turret where the weather cock doth stand. The fire chanced by means of a birding-piece discharged by one Mr Dios, which fired in the shingels, the day being extreme hot and the same shingels very dry'. The beams of the nave roof are painted, not carved. This, it is thought, may be the Spanish influence of Mr Dios, who was perhaps required to repair the damage he had caused. The easternmost beam bears the date 1592; little time was wasted after the fire. Progress over the chancel was more leisurely, however: the easternmost beam here is dated 1620.

The pews in the N. and S. transepts are the only pews that survived the fire. They have interesting carving, including two 'Jacks-in-the-Green', both in the N. transept, survivals from pagan days when Nature was represented by a man having branches and leaves sprouting from his ears and/or mouth. There is also a third on the organ case in the S. transept; this and the other carvings on the organ case are from pews that replaced those destroyed in the fire and were themselves replaced in the C. 19.

In the N. transept is the mechanism, in working order, from the old clock of about 1600, which was replaced by the present chiming mechanism in 1910.

Charing church boasts a more unusual curiosity: an C. 18 vamping horn, a form of megaphone used to amplify the voice of the choir leader. There are very few known to exist in England, and this is the only one that still has its mouthpiece.

On the N. wall of the nave is a Royal Coat of Arms of 1716, painted over an earlier work whose date, 1685, can be made out underneath.

The vicarage stands open to the churchyard in the NE. corner. It dates, rather surprisingly, from the C. 14; the coating of tiles it was given in 1885 gives a quite different impression. Alongside is the Church Barn, built in the C. 17 at High Halden: it was dismantled, transported to Charing, re-designed, and re-assembled almost entirely by voluntary labour in 1958.

Charterhouse Surrey *see* **Godalming**

Chartwell Kent *see* **Westerham**

Chevening Kent D3
A hamlet of the Holmesdale N. of Sevenoaks, in a long narrow parish (cf. Abinger); it consists of the church, a few cottages, and the big house. The church is C. 13, with a fine Perpendicular tower added 200 years later; it has a stair turret, so characteristic of Kent, in the NE. corner. Inside, there is a longish nave, a much shorter S. aisle, and no N. aisle; we do not know whether there ever was one, or whether one was ever intended, for the purpose of the three arches in the N. wall of the nave is obscure.

The most interesting features of the church are the monuments in the chancel, and in the chantry in the S. aisle. In the chancel are two elaborate wall monuments: that on the S. side of the sanctuary is to Robert Cranmer, who died in 1619 and who was a distant relative of the famous archbishop of the previous century, while the monument on the opposite side is to Robert's daughter, Ann Lady Herries, who died six years before he did. In the chantry, which is kept locked, are alabaster tombs of the Lennards, late-C. 16 and early-C. 17, and a monument in white marble to Lady Frederica Stanhope, who died in childbirth in 1823. The sculptor, Sir Francis Chantrey, has portrayed her lying on her side with her child in her arms.

The modern stained-glass windows at the E. end and in the chantry, replacing three of the five destroyed in the Second World War, are by Moira Forsyth, who also designed the roundel at the E. end of Guildford Cathedral.

As for Chevening Place, formerly the house of the Stanhopes, it stands in red-brick dignity to the W. of the church behind a high brick wall. Built in the first half of the C. 17, perhaps from designs by Inigo Jones, it was bought from the Lennards by James Stanhope, later

1st Earl Stanhope, in 1715. The side wings were then added. Towards the end of the century the 3rd Earl added a top storey and refaced the house with grey tiles, but all this has now been removed. Both he and his daughter, Lady Hester Stanhope, who was born here in 1776, were well-known eccentrics.

In 1969, after the death of the 7th Earl, the estate was put in trust, one of the conditions being that the house should be made available as a residence for the Prime Minister, a cabinet minister, or a member of the Royal Family descended from George VI.

The situation of Chevening is secluded. It is near the A21 and M25, but just about far enough away to avoid serious disturbance. In days gone by the main road to London, and the Pilgrims' Way to Canterbury, passed through here, but both were diverted with typical c. 18 hauteur by the 3rd Earl, making Chevening what it remains today, a pleasant backwater on the edge of the busy stream of life.

Chichester W. Sussex A5

'A Georgian town with a Roman plan' is a description of Chichester that is certainly an over-simplification but perhaps gives something of its flavour, for despite the many medieval buildings the general impression is Georgian, and the Roman plan is clear to see: surrounding walls, of which considerable parts are left, and the crossroads at the centre, where the helpfully named North, South, East, and West Streets meet at the market cross.

The Roman city was the capital of Cogidubnus, the compliant king of the Regni who became a Roman legate. It is the only Roman town in Sussex, and became in due course an important port and trading centre. In 477 it was taken by Ella, king of the South Saxons, and given to his son Cissa, from whom it gets its name, Cissa's *ceaster* (camp), or Chichester. In 681 St Wilfrid landed at Selsey and established a see there. It was transferred to Chichester in 1075, and the cathedral of Selsey lies under the waves.

For the visitor of today the market cross is the obvious starting-point. It was given to Chichester by its bishop, Edward Story, in 1501, to serve as the focus of the market, an ornate 50ft-high Perpendicular building in creamy Caen stone, an arcaded octagon, with a massive central column, a ribbed vault with bosses, and a soaring cupola, the whole edifice bristling with buttresses and pinnacles, and adorned with bishops' mitres, shields, rosettes, and canopies. Sad to say, many of them are badly worn, and the cross is constantly undergoing extensive repair; one hopes the current operation is designed to last. The structure was being continually shaken and not infrequently knocked by passing traffic until in desperation the city fathers decided in 1976 to turn North and East Streets into pedestrian precincts, and South and West Streets into bus streets only; opinion among the citizens about the results seems divided.

A short distance along West Street from the cross, and standing back, is the cathedral, while its detached bell-tower, late-c. 14 or early-c. 15, the only detached cathedral bell-tower in England, stands beside the street. Like Canterbury, this cathedral has suffered a number of disasters since it was built in the early c. 12, soon after the transfer of the see from Selsey: serious fires in 1114 and 1187; Puritan desecration in 1642; collapse of spire and tower in 1861. Yet Chichester and Canterbury are totally different: while Canterbury is colourful and dramatic, Chichester is sober and calm; while Canterbury's interior style is one of violent contrasts, Chichester's parts merge gently into one another; while Canterbury is very much the cathedral, its precincts entered through a lordly gateway, Chichester is the church people drop into casually.

Despite the disasters and the rebuildings, Chichester is recognizably a Norman building still. After the fires, the rebuildings were not revolutionary: after 1187 the retrochoir gallery behind the High Altar was given pointed arches within rounded, and the clerestory was rebuilt in the Early English style, but that is the extent of the revolution. When the spire, built *c.* 1300, collapsed in 1861, bringing the tower down with it, both were promptly rebuilt by Sir Gilbert Scott, and today you can hardly tell the difference. Curiously enough it is the depredations of the Puritans that possibly had the greatest effect; certainly there are few monuments and medieval embellishments in the cathedral, and the glass is mostly Victorian and dull – the c. 20 glass by Christopher Webb on the N. side (1949) is hardly calculated to excite. The medieval highlights are the c. 15 vaulted screen; the tombs of Richard Fitzalan, Earl of Arundel, and his wife, late-c. 14, and (probably) of Maude, Countess of Arundel, *c.* 1300, both on the N. side; the tracery of the great c. 14 window in the s. transept (best appreciated from outside); and above all the c. 12 sculptures in the s. choir aisle, showing Christ arriving at the house of Mary and Martha, and the Raising of Lazarus – at first glance one feels they might have been done by Epstein. Modern excitements are the pulpit and the Chapel of St Mary Magdalene, the former made and the latter furnished by Robert Potter and Geoffrey Clarke – the chapel's central feature being the painting by Graham Sutherland, *Noli Me Tangere*; and the symbolic tapestry designed by John Piper, behind the High Altar. If you like puzzles you will enjoy a boss in the vaulting in the s. choir aisle; stand with your back to the elaborate c. 16 tomb of Bishop Sherburne and look up: the boss has six faces sharing six eyes.

The cloisters are on the s. side, built *c.* 1400 and en-

Chichester: the Perpendicular market cross
(A. F. Kersting)

ABOVE: *Chichester Cathedral: the C12 panel depicting the Raising of Lazarus*

(A. F. Kersting)

OPPOSITE: *Chichester Cathedral from the SE*

(A. F. Kersting)

closing an old graveyard known as Paradise. The s. side of the cloisters is the best place from which to admire the tracery of the s. transept window. Above the window are the carved heads of 15 notables at the time of the 1932 restoration, including King George V, Stanley Baldwin, Ramsay MacDonald. A passage leads from the s. side of the cloisters to Canon Lane. Directly opposite is the Deanery (1725), while to the right is a former residentiary, a c. 19 rebuilding with a c. 12 doorway set into its wall, a curious mixture. The street ends with the c. 14 gateway to the Bishop's Palace, which is a pleasant architectural hotch-potch; the Palace Gardens, on the left through the gateway, are now open to the public and have flower-beds beautifully maintained by the Chichester District Council.

Towards the other end of Canon Lane, on the right-hand side, is The Chantry, mainly c. 13 and the oldest piece of domestic architecture in Chichester. Then at the very end, on the left, is Vicars' Close, a charming row of c. 15 houses originally the homes of the vicars choral. At the far end of the row is the Vicars' Hall, with a c. 12 vaulted undercroft, now a restaurant with its

75

(Gerd Franklin)

Pallant House, Chichester: the entrance

entrance in South Street. Canon Lane itself runs out into South Street through a c. 16 flint gateway.

If we turn right here we can cross the street and turn down Theatre Lane, beside the old Chichester Theatre built in 1791. This comes out into South Pallant, where a right and a left turn brings us into Market Avenue. Here on the left, at the back of a car park, is a stretch of the Roman city wall, with a bastion. (The modern Roman Catholic church, with exciting stained glass, is on the right.) Now back to South Pallant and up to the crossroads where North, South, East, and West Pallants meet. 'Pallant' comes from the Latin *palantia*, an exclusive jurisdiction, for the Archbishop of Canterbury had palatine rights over this part of Chichester until 1552. These streets are Georgian Chichester at its very best. The outstanding red-brick house on the corner of North and East Pallants, called Pallant House, was the home of Henry Peckham, 1683–1764; on each gatepost is an ostrich, which became the Peckham crest. The ostriches were carved from a description sent by

Peckham from abroad, and bear little resemblance to the real thing.

North Pallant goes up to East Street. To the left is our old friend the market cross; to the right the street leads to the site of the East Gate and another stretch of the Roman walls just past the Shippams Paste Factory – the firm was established here in 1750; straight ahead, St Martin's Street runs N., and on the corner where it curves right into St Martin's Square is St Mary's Hospital, which can surely boast the city's most unusual building.

The Hospital of St Mary existed at least as early as 1229, when it is referred to in letters patent of Henry III. From *c.* 1240 until 1269 the present site belonged to the Greyfriars, but in that year they moved to what is now Friary Park; the hospital took the site over, and a new building, completed by *c.* 1290, was put up. It accommodated an infirmary and a chapel under one roof. In the Middle Ages there were many such buildings, but they gave way to those of the collegiate type, with almshouses ranged round a quadrangle (*see* Abbot's Hospital, Guildford), and St Mary's Hospital at Chichester is the only one of the old type left in England.

The internal length of the present building is 128ft; originally it was about 190ft, and reached to the gateway at the street. One enters at the w. end, and an amazing view unfolds. On either side of a central passage, or nave, and under a forest of timbers, are small enclosures for kitchens, rather like the stalls in a stable; behind them are small but comfortable two-roomed flats. Until 1660 all this space was occupied by the beds of the infirmary, and there was no heating of any kind. At the far end is the chapel, separated from the nave by the original carved oak screen; the chapel itself has a beautiful set of misericords, sedilia, and piscina. The glass in the large Decorated E. window was damaged by bomb blast in the Second World War and the design of the new central panel is by Christopher Webb, who designed the modern glass on the N. side of the cathedral.

The roof timbers of the whole building are remarkable, as are the huge c. 17 chimneys that pierce the roof, and about whose aesthetic merits opinions differ. On either side are gardens, a large one to the s. and a small one to the N. Backing on to the latter is a row of old grey-painted cottages whose fronts line St Martin's Square. They form part of the hospital premises and sometimes house married couples, while the eight flats in the main building are for women only. The hospital is administered by the Dean and Chapter of the cathedral; they are responsible for the selection of applicants, who have to be baptized members of the Church of England, to have lived in the city or within five

OPPOSITE: *St Mary's Hospital, Chichester: the nave*
(A. F. Kersting)

miles of its centre for the previous five years, and to be 'of good character'.

St Martin's Square, a charming street of Georgian and earlier houses, continues N. to Priory Park. The old stone building just inside the gates is the chancel of the Greyfriars' church, the rest of which may never have been built. After the suppression of the order at the Reformation this fine c. 13 building was converted into a guildhall. William Blake, the poet, was tried here for sedition in 1804. It is now a museum. The mound to the NW. of it is all that remains of Chichester Castle, demolished in 1217 and without a history. The city walls enclose the park on the N. and E. sides, and here the shaded rampart constructed in the c. 18, which did much damage to the fabric of the walls and necessitated considerable expenditure to preserve them, can best be seen.

To the N. of Priory Park lies Oakland Park, containing the modern Festival Theatre, a well-proportioned 'theatre in the round', with 1,374 seats, none of which is more than 66ft from the stage. The building is in fact a hexagon, and was built in just over a year from the laying of the foundation stone in May 1961.

From near the entrance to Priory Park, Guildhall Street runs w. into North Street. On the corner is the Ship Hotel, a handsome brick house built c. 1790. Inside is a splendid iron staircase and plaster ceiling.

A short distance s. along North Street, towards the city centre, is the Council House, built by Roger Morris in 1731 and extended late in the same century by James Wyatt. The open arcade of Morris's building extends over the pavement, and set into the wall behind is an inscribed stone of Roman origin; on it the letters '. . . IDVBNI . . .' can be made out, part of the genitive case of 'Cogidubnus'. Inside the Council House, the staircase and the fine council chamber are also by Morris; Wyatt's extension at the back provided a small assembly room and various offices. A little further along the street is the c. 13 St Olave's church, now the S.P.C.K. bookshop, squeezed in between the adjoining buildings. Then comes the market house built in 1807 to the designs of John Nash for £1,522 – cheap even in those days – before the market cross greets us once more.

A stroll along West Street is worthwhile. First comes the Dolphin and Anchor Hotel, an c. 18 coaching inn – or rather a union of two inns. On the same side is the church of St Peter the Great, a Victorian church on the site of the one used as a cathedral when the see was transferred from Selsey and before the new cathedral was built.

The best of many good houses in the street is Westgate House, now the County and Diocesan Record Offices. It was begun by John Edes and finished by his widow Hannah Edes in 1696 – their combined initials and crest appear in the tympanum, while hers alone are on the rainwater heads. Behind the house are the neo-Georgian County Council Offices of 1936. Soon the

street peters out at a roundabout, where the West Gate once stood, but collects itself again for a final burst of colour-washed charm as it curves away to the left in true Chichester fashion, modest, uneventful, dignified.

Chiddingfold Surrey B4
Once an important centre of the glass and iron industries Chiddingfold has a large triangular green with a church at the sw. corner and the Crown Inn, c. 15 at least – perhaps even older – on its s. side. Everywhere there are picturesque tile-hung cottages.

The church, a mainly c. 13 structure, was drastically restored by Woodyer in 1869. The lofty nave arcades however, c. 13 but heightened in the c. 15, have grace and beauty. The Victorian E. window, too, with its simple theme of Christ's birth, death, and resurrection, is impressive, especially the dramatic central light depicting the Crucifixion. In the windows of the N. chapel are four panes of c. 15 Dutch glass, telling the story of Tobias and the Angel. But the most interesting window is the w. window of the s. aisle, which is made up of 427 fragments of glass found on the sites of local furnaces, and dating from the c. 14 to the c. 16. Their depth of colour and variety of tone cause one to regret that glass is not still made in the Surrey woods.

Chiddingstone Kent D4
A gem of the Weald of Kent, since 1939 owned and cared for by the N.T.; a really small place, with only two c. 20 buildings, the village hall and the rectory, both well tucked away. What visitors come to see is the church, a short line of old houses across the road, the 'Chiding Stone', and the castle.

The church is mainly c. 14, although the tower is c. 15; it has a stair turret, four octagonal pinnacles, and some amusing gargoyles. There was a disastrous fire, caused by lightning, in 1624; the damage was so severe that a good deal of rebuilding was necessary, and it is not easy to put a date to every part. The porch, certainly built after the fire, is interesting, specially the large flat leaves in the spandrels of the entrance arch.

The interior of the church is very spacious, for the N. and s. aisles are as long as the nave. There is a font of 1628 with a good contemporary cover, elaborately carved and with hinged doors. The pulpit is of the same period. The fine brass chandelier was hung in 1726.

There is a piece of c. 14 stained glass at the top of the side window of the N. chapel nearest the E. end. But the most curious piece of glass is in the E. window of this chapel: the whole window was to have contained a portrayal of the Last Supper; it was begun in 1871, but the money ran out and only one pane was inserted.

In the s. aisle are numerous monuments to the Streatfeild family, the owners of High Street House, which later became Chiddingstone Castle, and in the churchyard is their grand-looking family vault, built by Henry Streatfeild in 1736.

The Jacobean castle at Chilham (A. F. Kersting)

In the row of houses across the road, the half-timbered house at the left-hand (E.) end dates from at least the C. 15, for we know that Roger Attwood, who had taken part in Jack Cade's rebellion but was later pardoned, was living there in 1453. The building now occupied by the post office is of about the same date. In 1517 it was bought by Sir Thomas Boleyn, father of Anne and owner of nearby Hever Castle (q.v.). Later, in 1700, the house passed to the Streatfeilds.

The next house, with a timbered porch, was built about 1550. The date on the next, 1697, is misleading; it belonged to a Henry Streatfeild (Henry was the family name) as early as 1572, and after some changes of ownership reverted to the Streatfeilds in 1739. Finally, what is now the Castle Inn was called Rock House in the C. 17, presumably because the Chiding Stone is just behind it. It became an inn, called the Five Bells, in 1730.

The so-called Chiding Stone is reached by a sign-posted footpath which runs along the E. side of the school, then turns right and runs behind the houses, parallel to the road. Suddenly on the right is a huge bulky outcrop of sandstone, at least 12ft high, but easily climbed and covered with initials. The name Chiding Stone has no significance, and no true connexion with the name of the village.

As for Chiddingstone Castle (*not* N.T.), this has a curious history. It started as a Tudor manor house in the High Street, which ran on past the present Castle

Inn, where the C. 17 wrought iron gates now are. In 1679 the then Henry Streatfeild demolished most of the Tudor house and built himself a fine red-brick mansion. About 100 years later, his great-grandson, another Henry, inspired by the current craze for the romantic, encased the house in stone, built out towers and turrets, and put on battlements and machicolations (now much used by housemartins, who like to build their nests in the angles).

The High Street passed too close for comfort, and was diverted in a great loop to the N., which explains the right-angled bend in the road at the Castle Inn, and a large lake was created just inside it. This lake is full of coarse fish and is very popular with anglers. On the side of it nearest the road is another outcrop of rock, at the base of which are long interconnecting caves or chambers reputedly used as stores by smugglers in the old days.

This Henry Streatfeild's son, yet another Henry, was not satisfied that the house had been sufficiently transformed and added more towers and a Gothic orangery. By 1838 the house stood, a grandiose sham, externally much as it is today, except that in 1895 a covered way was constructed across the courtyard to connect the old kitchen block with the rest of the house – sensible, but visually damaging to the courtyard.

The last of the Streatfeilds died in 1936. After that the castle became a school, used by the Army in the Second World War. In 1955 it was bought by Mr Denys

Eyre Bower, who died in 1977. Here he laid out his unique collection of Japanese lacquer, arms and armour, netsuke, inro, metalwork, theatre masks, etc.; relics of Ancient Egypt; and a large collection of Stuart portraits and relics, from Lely's nude portrait of Nell Gwynn to a letter written by Charles Edward Stuart ('Bonnie Prince Charlie') to his father just before embarking from France for Scotland in 1745. Mr Bower claimed membership of the Stuart family, and considered the Stuarts to be the true Royal House.

Chilham Kent G3

Chilham is fortunate to stand well away from the main road on its little hill, for it is an almost perfect village – so much so that on fine summer weekends there is no room in the village square for all the cars; another car park has been built down one of the streets leading out of it. On the N. and s. sides of the square are brick and timber-framed houses; behind the E. side stands the church, and behind the w. the castle. From each corner of the square streets curve down the hill.

The mainly Perpendicular flint church has a Perpendicular w. tower with a stair turret in one corner and a handsome c. 18 clock. Inside, the church's great size becomes apparent. It is on the whole a trifle dull, its chief interest lying in the several monuments. The heavily 'Decorated' chancel, rebuilt in 1863, has a deadening effect that the monstrous monument to Lady Mary Digges in the s. chancel aisle does nothing to relieve; but the monument on the N. side to James Wildman, by Sir Francis Chantrey, 1822, is appealing.

Chilham Castle, built for Lady Mary's husband, Sir Dudley Digges, is a Jacobean mansion standing well back from the other end of the square. The grounds are open to the public in the summer. Seen from the other side, the house's extraordinary shape is revealed: five sides of a hexagon, ranged round a rather gloomy courtyard, the open end at the back. Beyond is the flint keep of the original medieval castle, equally unusual in shape, for it is octagonal, the only octagonal keep in England except Odiham in Hampshire. The keep at Chilham is wrapped tightly round with a curtain wall.

In a building between keep and Jacobean house is the Kent Battle of Britain Museum, full of nostalgic memories for one generation and amazement for another – amazement that freedom could possibly have hung on such a slender thread. In the grounds are terraced lawns, a lake, some good topiary work, and a heronry first recorded in the c. 13. Demonstrations of birds of prey in flight are given on most days, and jousting takes place from time to time.

Prehistory is represented at Chilham by JULLIEBERRIES GRAVES, a Neolithic burial mound above the far bank of the River Stour about half a mile E. of the village, and past the tall white weatherboarded mill now occupied by the Mid Kent Water Co. The grass-covered mound is beside a clump of beech trees, and is nearly 50yd long,

about 10ft high, and something like 4,000 years old. Before leaving, spare a thought for poor Julius Laberius the Roman, killed in action near here in 54 B.C., from whom 'Jullieberries' is thought to derive its name.

Cissbury Ring W. Sussex see Findon

Clandon Park Surrey B3

A Jacobean house stood on this site near the village of W. Clandon until about 1730, when the owner, Lord Onslow, employed a Venetian architect, Giacomo Leoni, to transform it into a grand mansion. Externally, Leoni's building is no beauty, being a formal red-brick box with stone dressings. All four façades, however, are different, which avoids monotony. The w. façade is spoilt by the heavy *porte-cochère* of yellowish Bargate stone stuck on by the 4th Earl of Onslow in 1876.

The visitor, after himself entering by the *porte-cochère*, passes into the huge two-storeyed Marble Hall, one of the grandest c. 18 entrance halls in England, a truly Palladian creation whose cool whiteness contrasts with the warmth of the brick exterior. One's gaze is first arrested by Rysbrack's superbly ornate marble chimney-pieces, then carried by the marble Corinthian columns to the plasterwork ceiling attributed to the Italian masters Artari and Bagutti, in which some of the figures seem to be tumbling out, as it were, on to the surrounding entablature, while in the centre is a flowing portrayal of the legend of Hercules and Omphale.

Straight ahead, and leading out of the Marble Hall, is the large Saloon, designed as a reception room rather than for sitting. It was the next room the c. 18 visitor would see after the Marble Hall, and by this time he could hardly fail to be impressed if not overwhelmed. The visitor of today, however, first passes through other rooms, containing some splendid furniture and porcelain; much of it comes from the collection bequeathed to the N.T. in 1968 by Mrs David Gubbay, who stipulated only that it should be kept together in one house and not broken up. The Trust's choice of venue was Clandon Park, which sets off the collection perfectly.

After the Marble Hall there is, inevitably, a sense of anti-climax; the many other rooms on view, although formal, are more intimate. Everywhere are portraits of the Onslows and other interesting pictures. One of the most fascinating rooms is the Green Drawing Room, lined with its original green wallpaper; another is the Speaker's Parlour, so called because it contains portraits of all three Onslows who in their time were Speakers of the House of Commons. This room became the dining room early in the c. 19.

The park was landscaped by Capability Brown. Across the lawn s. of the house is an c. 18 grotto containing grouped statues of the Three Graces, while on the E. side is a complete Maori house, probably also c. 18, brought back by the Lord Onslow who was Governor of New Zealand from 1882 to 1892.

The Marble Hall at Clandon   (A. F. Kersting)

Clayton Church: Christ in Glory (N.M.R.)

Clandon Park had been the home of the Onslows for over 200 years when in 1950 it finally passed into the care of the N.T.

Clayton W. Sussex C5

A hamlet on the A273 road between Haywards Heath and Brighton. The London to Brighton railway runs in a cutting, passes under the road, and enters the long Clayton tunnel by grandiose Victorian castellated portals complete with arrow-slits and battlemented turrets. A cottage of later date is perched between the turrets over the tunnel entrance.

The church stands to the E. along Underhill Lane, and is approached by a war-memorial lychgate roofed with Horsham slates. Then comes the C. 15 porch and the simple Norman doorway. Inside is a double surprise, the crude but dignified Saxon chancel arch, and the wall-paintings extending all round the N., E., and S. walls of the nave. The theme is the Last Judgement. On the E. wall, above the chancel arch, is Christ in Glory, with the apostles on either side of the arch. On the N. wall are the Blessed approaching Heaven. St Peter stands at the gate. At the back of the procession, that is at its W. end, is the Fall of Satan. On the sunless S. wall are the Damned, but also more of the Blessed at the E. end of the picture. There was once another, lower, layer of paintings all round, of which little can now be made out; all the remarkable paintings that are left were discovered by E. H. Kempe in 1895. Their date is uncertain, perhaps late-C. 11.

Up on the Downs above Clayton is the famous pair of windmills Jack and Jill. Jack is a brick tower-mill built here in 1896. Jill is a white-painted post-mill, erected at Patcham, Brighton, in 1821, and hauled bodily over the Downs by teams of oxen to its present position, where it continued to work until 1909. A private house stands between the two, and the ground is private property, but there is a car park alongside from which people sally forth on walks.

Cobham Kent E2

This is an unspoilt village, despite its proximity to Rochester and Gravesend. It has a large church dating from about 1220, with an enormous chancel, wider than the nave, and containing no fewer than 14 brasses, mostly commemorating the Cobhams and laid out in two rows on the floor. Arrogantly placed between them and the High Altar (the term seems appropriate here) is an enormous tomb of Flemish workmanship, erected in 1561. On it lie the figures of Sir George Brooke, 9th Lord Cobham, and his wife. Round the sides of the tomb are ranged their ten sons and four daughters.

Outside, immediately S. of the church, is Cobham College, founded in 1362 by Sir John de Cobham as a chantry for the souls of his ancestors. In 1598 it became almshouses, and still is.

Looking westwards along the Downs towards Clayton,
showing Jack Mill

The grand house of the Cobhams, Cobham Hall, stands in parkland to the NE. It dates from 1584, when the 10th Lord Cobham decided to turn his modest manor house into a great mansion worthy of the times – and of himself. He built out two wings, projecting west-wards; these were not completed until 1602. Meanwhile, in 1596 he had died and been succeeded by his son, who in 1603 was implicated in a plot to prevent James VI of Scotland from becoming James I of England. Cobham was imprisoned and his property forfeited to the Crown. In 1613 James I gave Cobham Hall and its land to his own second cousin the 2nd Duke of Lennox (later, Lennox and Richmond).

It was the 6th Duke who in the 1660s carried out the next stage of building, which was to erect the present connecting block between the two Elizabethan wings, in place of the old manor house. The architect was John Webb, who had been a pupil of Inigo Jones. This central block contains the banqueting hall (or Gilt Hall), two storeys high.

Towards the end of the c. 18 the two Elizabethan wings were projected eastwards to form an enclosed Kitchen Court, and between then and 1830 many alterations were made, some of them by James Wyatt. Meanwhile, by complicated processes of inheritance the estate had passed to the Earls of Darnley, who owned it successively until after the Second World War, when on the death of his father the present earl was

obliged to sell the house and part of the estate to help pay the death duties. The house was acquired in 1961 by the then Ministry of Public Building and Works, and later by the present owners, the Westwood Educational Trust, as a public school for girls.

Among the rooms shown to visitors are the Long Gallery of the Elizabethan mansion, on the upper floor of the N. wing, transformed by Wyatt in 1806–9 into a picture gallery and now used as a study hall; the library and the dining hall, both used as such by the school; the Gilt Hall, now the assembly hall; the 'Chapel' (never in fact consecrated), now a second dining hall; the Vestibule, designed by Wyatt as an entrance hall, now the headmistress's drawing room; and the Inner Hall with a granite staircase completed in 1602. Also displayed is the state coach of the Darnleys, built about 1715; the present earl had hoped to use it at the coronation of Elizabeth II in 1953, but the police pronounced it unroadworthy.

The other, very different, house open to the public at Cobham is at the other end of the village: OWLETTS (N.T.), a house of modest size in red brick, built in 1683–4 for Bonham Hayes and his wife Elizabeth, who were local farmers. An outstanding feature is the plaster ceiling above the staircase.

Various alterations and additions were made over the years, until in 1917 Owletts passed to Sir Herbert Baker, the architect, who built on a porch, restored the dining

Watts Mortuary Chapel, Compton   (Gordon Barnes)

room, enlarged the library, removed the side wall on the top flight of the stairs, replaced the duck pond with an octagonal formal garden, and installed the ingenious clock in the living room, which tells the time throughout what used to be the British Empire. The house was acquired by the N.T. in 1965.

Cobham has associations with Dickens: one of his favourite walks from Gad's Hill was through Cobham Park, whose owner, Lord Darnley, gave him a key. The Leather Bottle Inn, in the village, is the hostelry to which the disappointed Mr Tupman retires temporarily in *Pickwick Papers*; it was damaged by fire in 1880 and most of the present building's half-timbering is modern.

Compton Surrey B3
A comfortable if shapeless village s. of the Hog's Back with a church, an art gallery, and a mortuary chapel, all of unusual interest.

The church of St Nicholas, on the right if you approach the village from the N., has a Saxon tower and c. 14 shingled spire, and much Norman work: N. and s. aisles and doorways, nave roof, chancel, and – unique in

Europe – an upper storey to the sanctuary above a vaulted chamber. This upper sanctuary, which was restored in 1953, is late-c. 12, and has a wooden rail of the same date, one of the oldest pieces of church woodwork in England. The purpose of the whole thing is a mystery.

The pulpit with sounding-board, the altar rails, and the oak screen across the tower, formerly at the chancel arch, are all Jacobean. The incongruous dormer windows in the s. roof are a c. 19 addition.

The art gallery in Compton is the Watts Gallery along Down Lane, and houses about 140 pictures by the prolific and highly successful c. 19 painter G. F. Watts (1817–1904). He knew all the pre-Raphaelites, but was never one of them, and he is out of fashion today. His marriage at the age of 47 to Ellen Terry, then a girl of just under 17 (*see* Smallhythe, under Tenterden), was a predictable disaster and was short-lived; his second marriage at the age of 69 to Mary Fraser-Tytler, aged 36, was happy, and for life. He was twice offered a baronetcy but refused; he was awarded the Order of Merit in 1902.

After her husband's death and until her own in 1938, Mrs Watts lived on in Compton at the house called Limnerslease, up the hill opposite the gallery and built by Watts in 1891. It is now divided into flats.

Returning along Down Lane one comes, on the left, to an extraordinary red-brick edifice. This is the mortuary chapel erected by Mrs Watts, who started building it in 1896 with bricks made from local clay, and with the assistance of a local builder and a team of villagers trained at the pottery she had founded.

Both inside and out the building must be seen to be believed. Outside, Celtic ornamentation is superimposed upon an Italianate-looking design. The doorway is 'Norman', the moulding decorated with angels' heads, each the work of a different villager. Inside, the decoration is *art nouveau* while the total effect is almost Byzantine. Mrs Watts herself had hoped that the bright red brick of the exterior would 'tone down', but it never did.

The grave of George Frederic and Mary Watts is above the chapel in front of the cloister.

Cooling   Kent   F2

To the s. of Cooling, across the flat lands where potatoes and cabbages grow and sheep graze, the North Downs rise up behind a double line of pylons; to the N. are the marshes, recalling the forlorn atmosphere of *Great Expectations*; beyond them, ships may be discerned against the background of chimneys on the Essex coast.

Cooling churchyard, also mentioned in *Great Expectations*, is overgrown, and the church is kept locked. At the w. end of the village are the ruins of the castle, privately owned and enclosing a modern house and a number of farm buildings. Quite a lot is left of the castle's outer shell, including the main gate flanked by

two turrets of flint and rubble, with machicolations and battlements. Much can be seen from the road.

The castle was fortified in the 1380s – about the same time as Bodiam and for the same purpose, that is, to repel the French. Also like Bodiam, it was never tested. Its builder, John de Cobham, fixed a self-congratulatory inscription to the right-hand turret of the main gate; it is still there.

In the reign of Henry IV the castle was the home of Sir John Oldcastle, a kinsman of the Cobhams and a friend of Prince Hal. He was burnt as a heretic in 1417 for supporting Wyclif, his friendship with Prince Hal, now Henry V, availing him nothing. He was the model for Shakespeare's Falstaff, although as different from that brilliant creation as chalk from cheese.

Cooling Castle was bombarded and put out of action as a military installation by Sir Thomas Wyatt during his abortive rebellion against Mary Tudor in 1554.

Cranbrook   Kent   F4

A small town that was the centre of a thriving cloth industry. There is a story that Queen Elizabeth I walked from the town to the manor house of Coursehorn, which still stands well out to the E., on a path of locally-made broadcloth. This trade lasted from the Middle Ages to the early part of the c. 19, when it succumbed to the competition from other parts of England more accessible to coal and to the large ports.

The sandstone Perpendicular church of St Dunstan stands hidden at the right-angled bend where the High Street turns into Stone Street. Its size bears witness to the former importance of the town, for it is justly called 'The Cathedral of the Weald'. The tower, with its figure of Father Time, is disproportionately short. Inside, the church is all light and space. Of the many things to see and admire, the following is a purely personal choice: the oak door of the s. porch; the early c. 16 glass in one of the windows of the N. aisle; the c. 18 altar rails, and the brass chandelier in the nave of about the same date; the four large oak bosses on the wall at the w. end; and the marble relief in memory of Thomas Webster R.A. carved in 1889, at the w. end of the s. aisle.

Outside in the town, the High Street has buildings of various periods blending into a harmonious whole. Down a lane on the right past the George Hotel in Stone Street is the Providence Chapel. This curious building of 1828 has a seven-sided front of wood made to look like stone. Another place of worship that should on no account be missed is the tiny Strict Baptist Chapel, further along Stone Street on the right at the bottom of the hill, past the car park: a trim, white weatherboarded building with a single gravestone in its minute graveyard.

On up the hill, on the left, we come to Cranbrook's most conspicuous building, the windmill known as Union Mill. This is a smock mill with a white-painted octagonal tower on a tarred brick base. It has a Kentish

Union Mill, Cranbrook

(A. F. Kersting)

cruck cap, like an upturned boat, peculiar to the county. Its total height is 75ft, all but 10 of which you may climb when the building is open.

The mill was built in 1814 for Henry Dobell. In 1840 a six-blade Sussex fantail and gearing were fitted, and the original wooden staging replaced by the metal staging seen today. In the 1920s new sweeps from the mill at Sarre, near Canterbury, were installed; one of them was rebuilt in 1937 and another restored in 1947. The fantail fitted in 1840 has also been rebuilt.

The mill is called 'Union Mill' because when its first owner, Henry Dobell, went bankrupt in 1819 it was taken over by a *union* formed by his creditors: they ran the mill until 1832, when it was bought by George and John Russell. The mill remained in the Russell family until 1958, since when the Kent County Council have been the trustees. At present it is leased to a company who grind corn commercially. It is many years, however, since the power was provided by the wind; nowadays the mill is driven by electric motors, less romantic but possibly more reliable.

Cuckfield (*pron.* Cookfield) W. Sussex C5
Like Lindfield to the E., this is a village nearly but not quite swamped by Haywards Heath; like Lindfield it manages to retain something of its village character. A glance at the map will show how the main London to Brighton railway sweeps to the E. hereabouts and goes through Haywards Heath, which owes its existence to Cuckfield's refusal to allow the railway any nearer.

The church is c. 13–c. 14, with some rather disastrous restoration by Bodley, 1855–65. The large baroque memorial on the N. side of the sanctuary is c. 18, and commemorates Charles Sergison of Cuckfield Park, who died in 1732. At the foot of the monument his virtues are extolled in fulsome c. 18 prose.

Just outside Cuckfield, a turning off the A272 road towards Cowfold leads into the drive, lined with lime trees, of Cuckfield Park, an Elizabethan house with a small but attractive brick gatehouse, although much of the original brickwork of the house itself is now unfortunately covered with stucco. The house was built at the end of the c. 16 by Henry Bowyer, a wealthy Sussex ironmaster. Later it came into the possession of Charles Sergison, who followed Samuel Pepys as Commissioner of the Navy and Clerk of the Accounts, and served under three monarchs: William III, Anne, and George I. The s. front of the house was added in the c. 19.

Within, six rooms are shown to the public: the hall, which has a good plaster ceiling, half Elizabethan and half an excellent 1931 reproduction; the staircase hall, with the original open well staircase; the Oak Room, with Elizabethan panelling; the morning room, which has an elaborate Elizabethan screen and some good early-c. 17 panelling; and the drawing room and dining room, both in the Victorian s. wing – the latter has

c. 17 panelling, however, and an Elizabethan stone fireplace containing a later fireback dated 1618.

The grounds to the s. of the house drop steeply down to a lake and offer a good view of the Wealden countryside. The lake is formed from one branch of the River Adur, which finally flows out to sea at Shoreham.

About two miles NE. of Cuckfield, on the w. side of a minor road from Haywards Heath to Balcombe, is BORDE HILL, with a large garden containing many rare trees and shrubs of great botanical interest. There are also good walks and a pleasant picnic area. How a staff of four gardeners looks after it all is a mystery. One wing of the house is Elizabethan, but all the rest, which blends in well, is early-c. 20.

There are other attractive gardens in the vicinity. NYMANS (N.T.), about five miles NW. near Handcross, is beautiful from spring to autumn, but perhaps at its best in high summer, when the herbaceous border glows with bright colours and hydrangeas make blue pools under the trees. The garden was created in the early c. 20 by Lt-Col. L. C. R. Messel; he also built the medieval-style house, ruined by fire in 1928; the ruins are a romantic feature of the garden and make an attractive backing for climbing plants. The ground being pretty level, Nymans is a good place for those who find walking hard work.

At LEONARDSLEE, about six miles w. of Cuckfield near Lower Beeding, the garden clothes in colour the sides of a steep narrow valley; magnolias, azaleas, rhododendrons, camelias, acers, and many other shrubs and trees are grouped to produce effects both spectacular and subtle. At the bottom is a stream and a chain of small lakes. In wooded parkland beyond the gardens themselves wallabies live, apparently quite at home among the Sussex beech trees.

The paths at Leonardslee, steep and sometimes slippery, are unsuitable for the infirm of foot.

Deal and Walmer Kent H3
In 1538 King Henry VIII was excommunicated by the Pope because he had defied Rome, the Holy Roman Empire, and the Holy Roman Emperor, Charles V of Spain, by divorcing the Emperor's aunt, Catherine of Aragon, and by dissolving the monasteries and confiscating their goods. The Pope tried to persuade Charles V of Spain and Francis I of France, between whom there was no love lost, to invade England and throw down the upstart Henry. Henry, and therefore England, was in mortal danger; he responded with a show of strength, which included the construction of a number of forts round the coast to repel invasion.

Deal was a likely point of attack, and an important place to defend. Since the c. 13 the Cinque Ports had gone into decline; the sea had attacked and destroyed some, and deserted others. In the heyday of the ports Deal had thought itself fortunate to be a 'limb' or appendage of Sandwich, one of the original five. As the sea gradually deserted Sandwich, Deal grew in importance. Although it had no natural harbour, it is opposite the Goodwin Sands, and between them and the coast at Deal are the Downs, a roadstead where ships could anchor, protected to some extent by the presence of the sands to the E. and the coast to the W.

Henry built no less than three forts to defend this important anchorage, at Sandown (at the N. end of the modern town of Deal), at Deal, and at Walmer, now joined on to Deal on the S. side. Of these Sandown has itself succumbed to the eroding action of the sea and is little more than a heap of stones. Deal and Walmer remain, and today both are in the care of the D.O.E. Walmer is the official residence of the Warden of the Cinque Ports.

These so-called castles were really forts, the first in England to break away from the old conventions. Deal, the 'great castle', had a circular keep at the centre, rising above six attached bastions; round them was an outer ring of six larger bastions; then came a deep dry moat surrounded by an outer wall. All bastions were of stone, and were curved to deflect shot.

Revolutionary as these ideas were in England, the defensive castles at Deal and Walmer were already out of date by the time they were built. For by then a new kind of fort had been developed in Italy, based on angular as opposed to rounded bastions, and using earth rather than masonry as a shock-absorber, ideas that were incorporated in the castle at Yarmouth, Isle of Wight, built in about 1547.

It is interesting to speculate how Deal Castle, bristling with five tiers of guns, would have acquitted itself in the c. 16; but the old enmity between France and Spain soon re-asserted itself and the danger passed. Both Deal and Walmer were besieged in the Civil War, and eventually surrendered to the Parliamentarians. They were put in readiness during the Dutch wars of the c. 17, and again when an invasion by Napoleon seemed imminent. As a contemporary verse has it:

> Come the Consul whenever he will,
> 　And he means it when Neptune is calmer,
> Pitt will send him a damned bitter pill
> 　From his fortress, the castle of Walmer.

When this invasion threat, too, receded, military gave way to domestic needs, and Deal became the residence of the Captain – a purely honorary appointment. In 1941 the 'Governor's Lodgings', built over the seaward part of the castle and replacing an early-c. 18 construction, suffered a direct hit from a bomb; the ruins were later demolished.

Today the visitor to Deal enters by the original entrance on the landward side, crossing the moat on a modern wooden bridge, which replaces the original drawbridge, whose chains passed through the round holes on either side of the gate arch. Before the gate was a portcullis, and in the brick roof of the entrance passage may be seen the five holes through which missiles could be hurled upon intruders. Finally, if an attacker somehow succeeded in negotiating drawbridge, portcullis, overhead bombardment, and gate, he would receive a salvo from a cannon mounted in the gun port at the back of the entrance hall. All except the cannon were in fact relics of the Middle Ages.

Passing unscathed through the entrance hall, the modern visitor can walk on to the outer battlements, rebuilt in 1732, and explore the three floors of the keep. On the ground floor was the main living accommodation for the garrison; on the upper floor was the officers' accommodation, while in the basement the munitions and provisions were stored. Two of the basement rooms contain a well-arranged exhibition explaining the purpose, design, construction, garrisoning, and armaments of Henry VIII's castles, and their place in the history of England's defences against invasion.

From the basement it is possible to walk the complete 440yd circuit of 'The Rounds', the continuous gallery connecting the 53 hand-gun ports at the base of the outer bastions, which gave complete coverage of the moat; the sally-port at the end of the passage sloping down to this gallery from the basement of the keep gives access also to the moat itself.

Deal has other things to offer the visitor as well as the castle. Near the castle is the Royal Marines School of Music, formerly a naval hospital, a handsome brick building surmounted by a cupola; the Royal Marines depot and hospital are behind, in Gladstone Road. Just N. of the castle, beyond the monstrous Queen's Hotel, is the Royal Signal Tower, which now houses the Tourist Information Centre. The tower was built in 1795, and completed a chain of 13 stations giving direct communication by visual signal between the Channel and the Admiralty in Whitehall. It fell into disuse after the Napoleonic Wars, but from 1855 came to life again as the Time Ball Tower, a ball mounted at the top being lowered by electrical impulse from Greenwich Observatory at 1 p.m. every day, thus giving the correct time to the shipping in the Downs. This in its turn was discontinued in 1927.

A little further along we come to South Street, and to Carter House, once the home of Elizabeth Carter, c. 18 scholar-socialite admired by Dr Johnson. She was the daughter of the Perpetual Curate of St George's church here. A little further along is the dreary concrete pier that replaced the one knocked to bits by a wreck in the Second World War. Then comes the best part of Deal, N. of the Royal Hotel, where between the front and the High Street many of the houses date from about 1700. Through this narrow area Middle Street charmingly threads its way, crossed by a series of small streets running at right angles.

In the High Street at the w. end of one of these streets, Oak Street, is the attractive Town Hall of 1803, set curiously at an angle to the street. To the S. of it, across St George's Road, is St George's church, the civic church

Deal Castle   (Aerofilms)

of Deal, built in the early years of the c. 18 to meet the needs of the expanding town.

It was in 1699 that Deal finally ceased to be a 'limb' of Sandwich and was granted its own charter by William III. By this date it was growing rapidly – witness the houses built between the High Street and the sea. As the sea receded expansion took place seawards rather than landwards. The parish church of St Leonard's, up the hill to the w., was too far away to serve the growing town at the bottom and the seafaring folk on whom its prosperity depended, and the need for a new church became pressing. The moving spirit in urging this forward was Admiral Sir Cloudesley Shovel, the captor of Gibraltar, who owned property in the area and had often anchored his ships in the Downs. After his death by drowning off the Isles of Scilly in 1707, the work was held up through lack of funds, but was eventually completed in 1716. St George's is a fine example of a Georgian church. It

has a roof span of 80ft unsupported by any pillars. The galleries are later additions, including the topmost or pilots' gallery, built with a separate entrance so that the approach of the burly pilots should not disturb the other members of the congregation. The box pews and three-decker pulpit were removed in the c. 19, and in 1950 the present E. window replaced a Victorian window blown out by a bomb in 1942, which had represented Faith, Hope, and Charity. The new window incorporates the only fragment left, bearing the word 'HOPE', and now facing outwards.

In the churchyard is the grave of Captain Parker, one of Nelson's officers, mortally wounded in 1801. Nelson attended his funeral here and is said to have leaned against a tree in the churchyard and wept.

Although this is the civic church, used for ceremonial occasions and attended by the Mayor, the parish church is still St Leonard's, near the top of the town. The building

dates from the late c. 12. During the following century
the aisles were enlarged, and early in the c. 19 the
church was further enlarged northwards and the seating
turned through a right angle to face s. The result is one
of the most confusing interiors in the country, with
seats and galleries facing in various directions and the
altar, in its original position at the E. end, hidden from
view from many parts of the church; even when brought
down into the nave it is sideways on to most of the pews.

The 'Pilots' Gallery' over the w. entrance door was
erected by the pilots of Deal to replace the one destroyed
when the steeple fell down in 1658. On the front of it is a

painting of a man-o'-war, commemorating the great
storm of 1703. The artist has given a twist to the ship
in order to display both bow and stern. Altogether Deal
can offer no greater contrast than that between its
civic and its parish church, the one all spaciousness and
dignity, and the other a delightful muddle.

★

WALMER today is a district of Deal, to the s. Apart from
its c. 12 church – which, like the parish church of Deal,
stands well to the w. of the modern centre – there is only

Wings Place, Ditchling   (A. F. Kersting)

famous occupants: William Pitt and the Duke of Wellington. Pitt lived here during some of the time when he was primarily concerned with England's defence; the room he used as a study, little changed, can be seen. As for Wellington, who was Warden from 1829 to 1852, the room where he lived and died is shown, almost exactly as it was then, as well as a considerable collection of 'Wellingtoniana'. It is largely due to Lord Granville's successor, W. H. Smith, founder of the famous firm of that name, that so many important relics of these men have been preserved here.

Queen Victoria stayed at Walmer in 1835 when she was 16, and again with Prince Albert and their children in 1842 as guests of the Duke of Wellington; their rooms are also shown.

Outside, one can wander out on to the battlements, or round the garden, whose lawns and flowerbeds are kept immaculate in the usual D.O.E. style. From the battlements, and all along the front here, the coast of France is easily visible. Hovercraft are to be seen (but fortunately not heard) to N. and S., plying their way between the two countries, and the sea is busy with ships of every sort and size. The masts of the American ship *North Eastern Victory*, wrecked on the Goodwins in 1946, still stick forlornly up, another warning added to the three lightships and 15 buoys that mark the lurking menace of these sands.

Detillens Surrey *see* **Limpsfield**

Devil's Dyke W. Sussex *see* **Poynings**

Devil's Kneading Trough Kent *see* **Wye**

Ditchling E. Sussex C5
A village under the South Downs that has managed to avoid being swamped by the urbanization to N. and W. It has the misfortune to be situated at a busy crossroads, but apart from that it is a very pleasant place.

The mainly C. 13 church stands on high ground above West Street, a cruciform building, unusual in these parts, built of stone, chalk, and flint. The shafts of the windows in chancel and S. chapel have much stiff-leaf decoration in the capitals, and the label-stops to the hood-moulds portray heads of men and women, and are quite well preserved. Those at the E. window are larger than the rest, and are clearly a king and queen – possibly, it is thought, Henry III and Queen Eleanor. On the N. wall of the S. chapel is an Elizabethan monument to Henry Poole, d. 1580; and on the N. wall of the chancel, in a glass case, is an old pitch-pipe, for giving the note to the choir, last used in about 1877. The E. window is modern, as are the pulpit, the organ, and the screens to the S. chapel.

the castle to detain the traveller. It is much less forbidding than Deal's, for it has been domesticated. It was never as large in any case, having four bastions instead of six, but the arrangement was very similar. It owes its quite different character to having been, since the early C. 18, the residence of the Lord Warden of the Cinque Ports. The first resident Lord Warden, the 1st Duke of Dorset, built rooms out from the central keep on to the bastions. Lord Granville castellated the gatehouse and built 13 extra rooms above it in the 1860s. He also laid out much of the garden.

Inside, there are many relics of two of the castle's

DITCHLING

On the N. side of the chancel is a blending of ancient and modern, which can only be seen from the outside. Here a c. 13 priest's doorway is enclosed by a modern building that includes priest's and choir's vestries, toilet, kitchen, and boiler house. Access to the church is by steps leading from the priest's vestry into the N. transept beside the organ.

Across West Street, opposite the church gate, is Wings Place, formerly Anne of Cleves House; from 1541 until her death in 1557 Anne was the owner of the manor and patron of the church. The house is an attractive Tudor jumble of brick and timber. Further along to the w., past the white vicarage, is Cotterlings, faced with black and red mathematical tiles, a very good example.

Back at the crossroads, on the corner of West Street and South Street, is a Jacobean house, Crossways. On its wall in South Street is a stone head, and above it and to the left a charming memorial tablet to Dr. F. W. L. Bogle (d. 1964), with a French inscription considerably translated into English.

In East End Lane, the best street in Ditchling, there are good houses all the way along.

Up on the Downs to the s. is DITCHLING BEACON (N.T.), reached by a very steep road. From here there are tremendous views all round, including the sea to the s. Just w. of the car park are the remains of an Iron Age fort, dotted with hawthorn and other bushes.

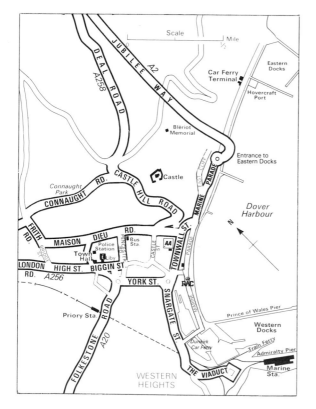

Dover Castle from the west

Dover Kent H4

This ancient place, one of the original Cinque Ports, has romantic associations for all Englishmen. Yet visually, but for the castle, there is really not much to admire – the romance of Dover is due to its history, and its history to its position at the gateway to England. It is built on two great chalk hills, the famous White Cliffs, on either side of the Dour valley, with the busy thriving harbour at the bottom, and houses climbing up the hills and the valley between. The E. hill's summit is occupied by the great castle, which overlooks town and harbour and frowns defiantly across the Channel at the coast of France.

Dover was a Roman town, Dubris. Of the fort built during the c. 2 little is known, but recent excavations in the vicinity of York Street have defined its extent as

(A. F. Kersting)

about three acres, and just outside it, in New Street, is the ROMAN PAINTED HOUSE, with its wall paintings and hypocausts well preserved. In the C. 3 a second fort was built nearer the harbour, replacing the first and overlapping it. Its precise extent has not yet been determined.

Near by, in Biggin Street, is Maison Dieu, built in the early C. 13 for pilgrims passing between Canterbury and the Continent, and Maison Dieu House, now the public library, dated 1665, with an attractive brick façade.

The parish and civic church of Dover is St Mary's in Cannon Street. It has a rather squat Norman w. tower and Norman arcades in the western half of the nave, giving way to Early English in the eastern half and in the chancel. The best thing in the church is the octagonal Norman font of Purbeck marble.

From the town it is a long walk up to the castle, but there is a car park at the top. The strategic possibilities of the site were early appreciated, and a large Iron Age fort was constructed here. The oldest building now standing is the Roman *pharos* or lighthouse, immediately w. of the Saxon church of St Mary in Castro. The lighthouse, which had a twin, long since lost, on the western hill, was probably erected in the C. 1 soon after the invasion in A.D. 43. It is octagonal outside but rectangular within, and was probably about 80ft high. It is now 62ft, but the top 19ft is medieval. The window openings are very narrow on the outside, no doubt to prevent the wind from blowing out the fire. The lighthouse was later used as the bell tower of the church beside it, which is thought to date from about the year 1000. It is a fine cruciform building, horribly restored by Scott in 1860–2 and by Butterfield in 1888; the latter decorated both nave and chancel with hideous mosaics.

As for the castle, its shape and extent have been determined by the outline of the Iron Age fort whose site it occupies. The Saxons certainly fortified the site, and William of Normandy extracted from Harold a promise to hand over Dover Castle intact when William came to claim his 'inheritance'. After the Battle of Hastings William hurried across to Dover and spent more than a week strengthening the fortifications. Whatever building he did, however, nothing remains of it. What we see today is largely the rebuilding, at vast expense, by Henry II in the 1180s, continued by Richard I after his father's death. During the civil strife of King John's reign the castle was subjected to determined attack by Louis, Dauphin of France, whom the barons who were opposed to King John had invited to take the throne. Louis tunnelled under the outer gate, bringing down one of its towers. But the defenders held out, John died, and Henry III became king. During the next half century more work was done on the castle: the damage done by Louis was repaired and the defences strengthened to prevent its repetition. This included the completion of the outer curtain walls and towers.

There have been additions and alterations ever since, notably by Henry VIII in the face of threatened invasion by the French, and again during the Napoleonic Wars for the same reason. During the Civil War the castle was held by Parliament, and thus avoided being 'slighted', but in the Napoleonic Wars nearly all the medieval towers were cut down to make gun emplacements. In the Second World War, although in 'Hellfire Corner' and a legitimate military target, the castle escaped almost unscathed, one theory being that Hitler intended to occupy it himself.

Today the castle is in the care of the D.O.E., and the visitor can explore the great square keep at the heart of the inner bailey. Built of Kentish ragstone dressed with Caen stone from Normandy, it rises to a height of 95ft, and covers an area of over 1,000 sq. yd. The walls are, on average, about 20ft thick. The well plummets down 400ft from the second floor through the keep into the natural chalk below. There are two stairways running from bottom to top, in opposite corners, connecting the three floors and continuing to the roof, from which there is a view over the town and across to France. At the N. end of the castle are the exciting underground works built in the c. 13 and altered, in brick, in Napoleonic times.

But Dover lives more in the present than in the past; it is a port (and hoverport) first and foremost. Here is a modern success story of continuous growth, for nowadays the docks handle in a year about 8m. passengers, nearly 2m. vehicles, and about 80m. gross tons of shipping.

Dungeness Kent *see* **Lydd**

Dunsfold Surrey B4

The village, mainly of brick and tile-hung houses, borders a huge, rough, rambling green near the southern edge of the county. To the N., Hascombe Hill provides the backdrop; to the s. the green degenerates imperceptibly into common. There is a pub called the Hawk and Harrier, with a picture of an aircraft on the inn sign, for an R.A.F. airfield lies to the E. It is out of sight, although the occasional roar overhead proclaims its presence. As for the church, it stands three quarters of a mile away to the w.

This church should not be missed, for it is not greatly altered since it was built towards the end of the c. 13 in Transitional style. The shingled tower and spire are c. 15, renewed last century. There have been other additions and alterations but they are not obtrusive, with one exception: after entering the churchyard through a lychgate of 1901 and a tunnel of yew, one is immediately struck by the galleting that covers the whole of the exterior of the church. This was done by restorers in 1882 when they removed the outer plastering, and looks just as inappropriate here as it does at Albury Park (*see* Albury).

Another most unusual feature of the exterior is the presence of three openings low down in the walls where the water that used to be sluiced over the brick floors to clean them was expelled. Nowadays the openings, no longer required, are blocked up on the inside, but on the outside the old wooden plugs and chains are still in position. One may be seen on the N. wall of the nave, another on the w. wall, and another on the w. wall of the s. transept.

Opposite the s. porch is a huge old yew tree, thought to be considerably older than the church. The porch is probably c. 13, although its own entrance doorway is obviously Tudor, and on its spandrels are vestiges of carved Tudor roses. The roof of the porch is lined with barge-boards, on which traces of the old painted decoration can still be seen. Then comes the massive oak door of the church itself, with Wealden ironwork.

Inside, there are several points of exceptional interest: the simple font of Sussex marble, probably of the same age as the church; the oak pews, some of which are also of the same age, although they have had the seats extended forward, and backs have been added; the string course which snakes its way round the entire church; the triple sedilia and double piscina in the chancel; and the tantalizingly indecipherable wall-painting w. of the doorway. Other bits of wall-painting were copied by the Victorians before being covered over; the copies, framed, hang on the walls where the paintings were found.

The floors of the transepts, which were evidently chapels, since both have piscinae, must once have been of different heights, the N. higher and the s. lower; this is clear from the positions of the windows and from the relative levels of the piscinae.

It is odd that the church should be at such a distance from the village, but it seems that this may have been holy ground even in pre-Christian times, and tradition dies hard. There is a holy well just below the church, reached by a public footpath. The water is said to possess miraculous properties for curing diseases of the eye.

Easebourne W. Sussex *see* **Midhurst**

Eastbourne E. Sussex E6

Some seaside resorts have their slightly dilapidated, down-at-heel aspects. Not so Eastbourne, which is all spick and span. Even the pier is in good condition, and hardly lowers the tone.

Sea air and sunshine are what Eastbourne has to offer. Make for the front, then start at its E. end and visit the Redoubt, near the Eastbourne Leisure Pool. It is a solid-looking fortification built as an important link in the chain of defences against Napoleon. In 1804 it was decided to build a series of martello towers on the E. and SE. coasts, supplemented by three heavily-armed circular redoubts, of which this is one. The other two were at Dymchurch and Harwich, but the Eastbourne redoubt is the best preserved. Building began in 1804 or 1805, and was probably not finished until about 1810, long after Nelson's great victory at Trafalgar had – although few fully realized it – made all these defences redundant.

The Redoubt is a circular, mainly brick, building sunk into the ground; at the top, just above ground level, and surrounding an area open to the sky, is a parapet for 11 24-pounder guns, and below it is a series of vaulted chambers, opening into the central area and used for accommodation, stores, and so on. Surrounding the building is a dry moat, over 20ft deep, formed by building another, outer, wall. Some of the material excavated to make the moat was banked up against the outside of this second wall as an additional defence against shell fire, and to disguise the outline of the redoubt. Across the bottom of the moat five 'caponiers' were constructed to provide positions from which penetration of the moat could be repelled by musket fire. The only entrance to the Redoubt was by a wooden bridge over the moat on the landward side; this bridge could be drawn up in the event of attack.

When the promenade was built here in about 1890, the moat and outer wall on that side had to be sacrificed. The present entrance, from the seaward side, was made through the outer and inner walls.

The inner area, into which one first enters today, was formerly used as a parade ground, but is now occupied by a 'model village', which somewhat surprisingly includes Fountains Abbey among its buildings. In four of the vaulted chambers of the Redoubt is a beautifully laid out exhibition that explains not only the function of the Redoubt but also, in imaginatively pictorial form,

the history of the coastal defences of England. One enters the exhibition by what was originally the guard-room. On the left are the detention cells, and on the right the stairway leading up to the parapet.

To the w., Royal Parade becomes Marine Parade, and, after the pier, Grand Parade. Here are some very fine flower-beds, leading up towards the bandstand, another – but very different – circular building, with Corinthian columns and a blue roof. No shops are allowed to desecrate with vulgar commercialism the elegance of Eastbourne's sea front – and no one who has experienced the sights and smells of parts of the front at Brighton, for example, can quarrel with Eastbourne's decision.

Opposite the bandstand is Devonshire Place, at whose seaward end, looking at the blue roof over another municipal flower-bed, is a statue of William Cavendish, wealthy landowner and 7th Duke of Devonshire, who had Eastbourne laid out as a resort in the middle of the c. 19.

At the end of Grand Parade, where it becomes King Edward's Parade, is the Wish Tower. This is yet another circular building, for it is Martello Tower No. 73 of the 74 similar towers erected between Folkestone and Seaford. Like the Redoubt, it is open to the public, and contains an exhibition of coastal defences, quite different from that in the Redoubt but equally fascinating. Here too it is possible to visit the parapet; but even more extensive alterations to the building as a whole have been carried out in recent times to ease the transition from military to touristic purposes.

The tower originally carried an armament of one 32-pounder gun; the gun now seen on the parapet, however, is a 68-pounder cast in 1858. From the tower there is a grand view of Eastbourne's imposing sea front running down past the Redoubt and along the coast to Hastings, while to the w. is the chalk cliff of Beachy Head – the lighthouse is just out of view round the corner. Inland, one looks along Wilmington Square to the modern Congress Theatre, behind which is Devonshire Park, formerly the marshy ground or 'wish' (Saxon *wisc*) that gave the Wish Tower its name.

On the sea-front we are almost entirely in the c. 19 – a notable exception being the T.G.W.U. Centre, the only really modern-looking building and the only one that is not white or cream. But away from the front we are at least partly in the c. 20, and there are excellent shops. A section of Terminus Road has been made into the now near-obligatory pedestrian precinct; one hopes there are more to come.

If from here we follow the signs for Brighton, we shall find ourselves going out on the A259 road, and after a mile we come to a church on the right with a massive tower. This is St Mary's, Eastbourne's parish church. The nave (except the w. bay) and the chancel belong to the c. 12; the chancel arch has late-Norman dogtooth moulding. The pillars of both nave and chancel are

alternately octagonal and circular. The last (w.) bay of the nave, however, and the great tower were added in the c. 14; the c. 14 font, below the tower arch, is plain and square, of Eastbourne greenstone like the tower arch itself.

The chancel is out of true with the nave. This is quite common, and usually thought to be a deliberate symbolization of the leaning head of Christ on the cross. A much rarer feature of the chancel in this church is the step down, instead of up, from the nave. This is presumably due to the pronounced slope of the ground on which the church is built.

There is modern glass in the windows of both N. and s. chapels, the former by Hugh Easton and the latter by Douglas Strachan, who designed the glass at Winchelsea (q.v.).

Immediately outside the N. door of the church is the c. 15 Old Parsonage, a good example of a stone Tudor house.

Back in the main road, and only a little way down, is the c. 12 Lamb Inn, and almost opposite is the Towner Art Gallery, in an c. 18 house. Here is a permanent collection of mainly modern works, frequently supplemented by temporary exhibitions. Forming part of the permanent collection is a group of sketches by Louisa C. Paris, a Victorian lady who visited Eastbourne in the 1850s. Her pictures give us a clear idea of how rural the environs of Eastbourne were then.

Now follow the Brighton road up on to the Downs, and turn left after about two miles along B2103 to Beachy Head, the grand climax to Eastbourne. This sheer white cliff, covered with green turf worn thin by countless visitors, stands over 500ft above the lighthouse perched on a ledge of Greensand at the cliff's foot. To build it, the stone and the men were lowered from Beachy Head by an overhead cable railway. The old lighthouse, known as Belle Tout, was built of Aberdeen granite in 1831 by Mad Jack Fuller (*see* Brightling). It still stands, minus the top part which housed the lantern, on the cliffs to the w.

Eastchurch Kent *see* **Sheppey**

East Clandon Surrey B3

A good village with a good unspoilt Early English church. There have been many additions to the church though: the shingled tower and spire, and the lean-to N. aisle, in 1900; the tomb and canopy of Lord Rendel in the same N. aisle by his grandson, H. S. Goodhart-Rendel; the c. 18 font. There are some Victorian-looking pews and choir stalls, but nothing is out of key.

Out of the village to the E. a drive leads across a large park to HATCHLANDS, the red-brick house built in the late 1750s by Admiral Boscawen 'at the expense of the enemies of his country', that is to say, with prize-money amassed in the French wars. It is thought probable that it was the ingenious admiral himself who devised a house with seven different floor levels cunningly interconnected and smoothly accommodated under one roof. The decoration was entrusted to Robert Adam, his first commission for a private house; and although the work lacks the assurance of his later style it shows unmistakable signs of it.

Admiral Boscawen died only 14 months after moving into his new house; during most of that time he was at sea. Nine years later his widow sold it to the Sumners, a family who were to own Hatchlands until 1889. The c. 18 Sumners consulted Repton and Bonomi about alterations. Repton appears to have strongly recommended plastering the exterior and painting it white.. As for Bonomi's proposals, most of them were fortunately not put into effect, either because the Sumners did not like them or because they could not afford them.

In 1889 the Sumner family sold Hatchlands to Lord Rendel, whose tomb we have seen in the church; he carried out some important alterations, including moving the entrance from the w. side to the E. and opening up the hall on the E. side of the stairs. In 1913 he left the property to his grandson. Goodhart-Rendel, himself an architect, made further minor alterations. He gave Hatchlands to the N.T. in 1945. The park is let for farming; the house is also let, and only a few of the ground floor rooms are shown to the public.

East Grinstead W. Sussex D4

A bustling town with a prosperous air and housing estates sprouting in all directions. The traffic along its High Street is heavy and continuous; nevertheless East Grinstead is a pleasant town with many attractive side streets. Moreover, the High Street itself is attractive, particularly the part near the parish church, where there are a number of Tudor timber-framed houses of outstanding merit.

The church, whose tall 'Perpendicular' tower is visible from a considerable distance and from many directions, was designed by James Wyatt when it had to be completely rebuilt after the collapse of the previous tower in 1785 had virtually destroyed the nave as well. The story of the tower is a chapter of accidents:

1683. 'The steeple was struck by lightning and the resultant fire caught the shingles of the spire. In a short time the bell lofts were all but burned to the ground and the bells melted; but by God's mercy and the industry of the people, with a Providential change of wind, the Church was preserved untouched by the fire and the surrounding houses in the Town were saved'.

1785. Rebuilt tower collapsed; nave damaged so badly that the walls had to be pulled down. Whole

church redesigned and rebuilt. It is said that Mr
Speaker Abbot, who lived at Kidbrooke Park to the
s., required the tower to be built 25ft higher than
before, to enable him to see the weathervane from
his house.

1836. Pinnacle blown off in a gale, damaging nave
roof.

1929. Flagstaff fell down and damaged one of the
pinnacles.

1930. Damaged pinnacle fell through church roof.
All pinnacles shortened and straightened.

The church is large and lofty within. It was much
altered in 1874. Just below the chancel steps, towards
the s. side, is the oldest dated iron tombslab in the
country (1570), which was for long used, upside down,
as the scullery doorstep in the old vicarage – hence its
good state of preservation. On the right side of the altar
is the figure of St Edmund, to whom the original parish
church is thought to have been dedicated, while on the
N. side is St Swithun, the patron saint of the present
church. At his feet are two ducks, symbolizing his association with rain. The figures are c. 20 carvings.

The tessellated mosaic pavement in the sanctuary is
the work of Constance Kent while she was imprisoned
at Portland. She was acquitted of the murder of her
brother in 1844, confessed to it in 1865, and was sen-
tenced to death but reprieved.

In the SE. corner of the churchyard, enclosed by
shrubs, is the tomb of the Revd John Mason Neale,
1818–66, famous Victorian 'liturgiologist, ecclesiologist,
church historian, author and translator of hymns',
to quote the memorial slab erected in 1966 to mark the
centenary of his death. For the last 20 years of his short
life he was Warden of Sackville College, just across
Church Lane.

Sackville College is a set of almshouses founded in
1609 by Robert Sackville and completed about 10 years
later, a beautiful example of Jacobean architecture
built round a quadrangle. On the entrance side, nearest
the High Street, were the sleeping quarters of the inmates, dormitories for 21 men and for 10 women. On
the left were the day living quarters, and on the right
was the chapel. The fourth side was built as a hunting-
lodge of the Sackvilles, and includes the hall, which
contains some of the original furnishings, but also an
accumulation of bits and pieces contributed by successive wardens.

When Neale took over he found things in a parlous
state; during his wardenship they improved out of all
recognition. Considering much of the work of restoration
was entrusted to William Butterfield it is a relief to find
that apart from the interior of the chapel, which is very
Victorian and by no means displeasing anyway, the
original Jacobean style was maintained.

Today, the hunting-lodge is a hunting-lodge no more.
The other three sides are still in use for their original
purposes, except that there are fewer than 31 inmates.

About a mile and a half s., off the road to Sharpthorne,
is STANDEN (N.T.) a late-Victorian house built by Philip
Webb for Mr and Mrs Beale in 1892–4, at a cost of
£12,000. Although it is strictly correct to describe it as
Victorian, it was in fact an *anti*-Victorian house, specifically designed as a protest against the accepted standards
and values of the age. Instead of being dark, flamboyant,
and fussy, it is light, modest, and restrained. William
Morris was closely associated with Webb in the design
of furniture and fittings, and everywhere his productions
are in evidence and his influence felt.

From the garden the house looks odd, to say the least,
but there is a lovely view over the Medway valley, with
an occasional glimpse of Weir Wood Reservoir through
the trees. On the other side of the reservoir, about two
miles SE. of Standen, is Michael Hall, a Rudolph
Steiner school partly housed in the early-c. 18 mansion
of KIDBROOKE PARK, which stands in beautiful grounds
laid out by Humphry Repton. The house seems to
have been much altered and added to in the early
c. 19 – an architectural puzzle as well as a prize.
Visitors can be shown round the ground floor rooms
on certain days during the summer on application to
the school bursar. The handsome stables, surmounted
by a cupola with a clock, are given over partly to class-
rooms and partly to flats.

A description of Kidbrooke Park that appeared in
1809, while Mr Abbot, its owner, was still Speaker,
begins: 'The rural retreat of the Speaker of the House
of Commons from the continual press of public business . . . is an object which will interest every lover of his
country'.

To the N. of Michael Hall a footpath leads down
through woods to a small bridge over the infant Medway.
Beyond this, alongside a jumble of farm buildings, are
the sad ruins of BRAMBLETYE, the mansion built for Sir
Henry Compton in 1631 and looking as if it could
be 100 years older. The gatehouse still stands, and the
porch with its coat-of-arms; to left and right are the two
corner towers, the right-hand tower still retaining its
large ogee cap.

Edenbridge Kent D3

This town is strung out along the old Roman road that
ran from London to the coast near the present town of
Seaford. The River Eden flows placidly under the main
street of Edenbridge about 100yd s. of the parish church.
Nowadays the town is not only strung out more than of
old – it stretches N. to the light industrial suburb of
Marlpit Hill – but it also straggles E. and w. into housing
estates. Only in a tiny area at the centre is there anything of much interest to the traveller.

The spacious parish church stands up a side street on
a piece of higher ground to the E. It is mainly Early
English and Decorated, built of sandstone. Its four-
square buttressed tower bears a clock, purchased second-
hand in 1796, with an hour hand only, and a convex

black face. On the top of the tower is a shingled spire. The church, including the porch, is roofed over with Horsham slates, very rustic-looking and, characteristically, having plenty of moss on them.

Inside there is a s. aisle that is almost as wide as the nave, and as its E. window is much larger than the E. window in the chancel one may be forgiven for thinking that here is a church with two naves. The E. window of the s. chapel is a Crucifixion scene by Burne-Jones, dated 1908 but entirely Victorian in feeling.

In the main street, where the street leading down from the church joins it, are some old timber-framed buildings, probably c. 15. To the N. is the c. 15 Old Crown Inn, with an overhead sign spanning the road across to Taylour House on the other side. On the door of the latter are the arms of Sir William Taylour, Lord Mayor of London in 1469. The house later became the Griffin Inn, but now bears once more its original name.

The Crown was at one time the haunt of smugglers, in particular of a gang called 'The Ramsey Gang'. In a secret passage upstairs casks were hidden, and pipes led off them to the tap-room below, the pipes being disconnected when the excise men were around.

Elham (*pron.* Eel'm)   Kent   G4

The Nail Bourne, which later flows so merrily through Patrixbourne and Wickhambreaux, is for much of the time dried up in its higher reaches, but the valley is very beautiful and very English. In these surroundings stands the village of Elham.

Elham has a square, which gives it an air of importance, almost that of a town, an impression reinforced by the large church with its solid battlemented c. 14 tower and recessed lead spire. The square stands well back from the main street and has no through traffic. It is surrounded on three sides by houses of varying materials and construction blending into a harmonious whole. The King's Arms, on the NE. side, has a Georgian tile-hung front but is timber-framed underneath. On the fourth side stands the church, a mixture of flint and other stones, not to mention brick and mortar. The tower has angled buttresses, which add to its massive proportions. One enters by the large N. porch, and just inside the church itself is a huge old chest of yew, made from the solid trunk.

The church is as impressive inside as out. The pillars of the arcades are square and huge, late-c. 12, contemporary with the font. Texts on c. 17 boards, high up, line the walls. Beside the pulpit is an old hour-glass, and there is a French gilded wooden lectern of the c. 17; on the wall behind it is a text from Ecclesiastes: 'Blessed art thou, O Lord, when thy king is the son of nobles', which is thought to refer to Charles II at the Restoration.

In the s. chapel is a c. 15 triptych. The central panel depicts the martyrdom of St Catherine, the one on the left shows Henry II and Becket confronting one another, while that on the right is of Becket's murder.

(N.M.R.)

The murder of Becket: the right-hand panel of the C15 triptych in Elham church

The chancel was all embellished early in the c. 20, and includes a huge and magnificent reredos, which partly obscures the 1896 window behind. There are two amusing Victorian windows on the s. side: one shows King David in his old age, and the other the young David playing the harp for Saul. The faces are those of Victorians: King David, in the first window, is the then vicar, the Revd Walker Wodehouse; in the second window, designed and made by the vicar's brother Frank, David is Madame Patti, the singer, Saul is Thomas Carlyle, and in attendance are Gladstone, Disraeli, and three of Queen Victoria's daughters.

Up on the main street of Elham, the Rose and Crown was the courthouse in the c. 15. It, too, like the King's Arms, was partly modernized in Georgian times, although one end of it has been left with its timbers exposed. Opposite is the Abbot's Fireside, which has been an inn ever since it was built in 1614. It has timbers with grotesque carvings, especially under the eaves, where housemartins build their nests.

The main street curves gently away to the NE., full of attractive buildings, while up the lane that climbs the hill beside the Abbot's Fireside is the old timber-framed manor house. Elham is naturally and deservedly popular, and has a sprinkling of antique shops and tea rooms, yet somehow remains unspoilt.

Etchingham   E. Sussex   E5
A village running up a gentle slope that rises from the floor of the Rother valley. At the bottom, near the river, is the Tudor-style railway station. Built in 1852, it stands more or less on the site of the medieval manor house, now vanished, of the de Etchyngham family. But if the manor house is lost, the nearby church still proudly stands, and is one of the great churches of the county, built in the C. 14 by Sir William de Etchyngham.

It is not very typical of these parts, with its massive central tower and high clerestory. It has an air of great solidity and strength, although the numerous metal cramps in the tower tell a different story, of major repairs, involving excavations and underpinnings, carried out in the C. 20.

The low timber porch is rather mean and out of proportion. Inside the church, the first impression is of severity, accentuated by the Victorian glass in the E. window, whose flowing tracery is best admired from the outside.

Yet this church has treasures; notice the sturdy Jacobean altar in the S. chapel, the misericords on the stalls in the chancel, and, on the chancel floor, the famous brasses: one of Sir William de Etchyngham himself, headless, and the other of his son, daughter-in-law, and grandson.

Apart from its church, Etchingham w. of the railway is undistinguished. But 500yd beyond the level-crossing to the E., on the right, is the entrance to Haremere Hall, a grand C. 17 manor house, occasionally open to the public.

Ewell   Surrey   C3
Start in Church Street, and enter the churchyard, where there stands the C. 15 tower of a church that apparently dates from the C. 11. It has a brick top, and a stair turret in one corner, and is now enclosed in iron railings and labelled a Building of Historic Interest. It looks forlorn and is inhabited by pigeons.

At the other end of the churchyard, beside the main road, is the parish church of 1848, to which mishaps and money have, on balance, been beneficial. The E. window replaces the one that was damaged in an air raid in the Second World War. There was a bad fire in 1973, which destroyed the Lady Chapel, organ, and N. aisle. By 1975 all was in order again, and the modern Lady Chapel, at the end of the N. aisle, is beautiful, especially the thanksgiving window by Lawrence Lee.

Holman Hunt painted *The Light of the World* in Ewell, and there is a copy of this famous picture at the foot of

the stairs leading to the gallery at the w. end. It narrowly escaped destruction in the 1973 fire.

Outside in the village (Ewell likes to think of itself as one), the imposing entrance to Bourne Hall leads off the High Street. The C. 18 house was demolished in 1962, to the disgust of the conservationists, and a large circular building in glass and concrete, completed in 1970, took its place. The small lake is still there, while outside, running along the roadside, is a stretch of the Hog's Mill River, beloved of the pre-Raphaelite painters; it rises in springs near by and flows N. into the Thames at Kingston.

In Spring Street there is a concave curve in the wall enclosing the grounds of Bourne Hall. This is where a former owner, Mr Barritt, generously set his wall back a little so that his neighbour across the way in Spring House could turn his coach at his own entrance.

There are some old buildings in the High Street. The C. 19 façade of No. 9 partially hides its early-C. 16 timber frame, which can easily be seen, however, from the side. It is the oldest house in Ewell. Now it is a shop, but in the C. 16 it was the 'Redde Lyon Inne'. The adjoining buildings, Nos. 11–15, are early-C. 17.

This brings us back to the other end of Church Street. Here on the right is the old lock-up of 1790, and next to it are two houses, Nos. 2 and 4, whose mathematical tiles conceal their timber-framed construction. After this comes the old malthouse, with a mill wheel set in the path leading up to it. From the brewing of ale it was turned in the C. 19 to use as a music room for the Glyn family, for whom Glyn House, further along the street, was built in 1839. Now the malthouse has undergone another metamorphosis, and is a church of the Brotherhood of Universal Truth.

Further along Church Street again is Ewell Castle, now a school, built as a private residence in 1814, Ewell's answer to Belvoir Castle in Leicestershire. (Nothing is left of Nonsuch Palace, Henry VIII's grandiose edifice to the NE.)

Roman remains have been found in Ewell, for it is on the line of Stane Street, the Roman road from Chichester to London. Indeed, this is really putting it the wrong way round; it was the small Romano-British station in Ewell with its abundant water supply that helped to decide the line of the road. A section of it has been unearthed in the churchyard itself, and behind the King William IV inn in the High Street the remains of a farmstead and a number of storage pits were found, together with Roman coins covering the whole period of the Roman occupation of Britain. Even these are not the oldest objects unearthed in Ewell: on the site of the post office Mesolithic flints were discovered, which would be something like 10,000 years old. Some of them can be seen in the museum at the modern Bourne Hall.

All these antiquities witness to the influence of geology on the distribution of population: the never-failing springs of Ewell (Old English *aewiell*, spring, source of a river) have ensured an abundant and reliable water supply, and their presence at this precise spot is due to their ability to escape to the surface through a bed of Thanet Sands interposed between the chalk of the Downs and the London Clay.

Ewhurst E. Sussex F5

This place would be worth visiting if only for the views N. and S. from the ridge along which it runs, particularly the northern view, in which Bodiam Castle is a prominent feature down in the valley below. Yet Ewhurst is itself beautiful, with its brightly painted weatherboarded houses and trim gardens.

The church has a shingled spire, oddly shaped, for it changes angle halfway up. The building is mostly C. 12 and C. 13, but inside the Victorians were active, filling and scraping. Recently the N. aisle chapel has been re-created and has a simple dignity. The most unusual feature, however, is the churchyard, which is dotted about with trees from N. America such as box elder, Colorado spruce, Indian bean, western red cedar, black walnut, Lawson's cypress from Oregon, and Bishop's pine from California, as well as the Pine with Five Leaves, from Mexico, and various trees from the Far East. There is even a monkey puzzle, dignified with the name of Chile Pine; with this one exception the trees look well, and the graveyard has become a garden, thanks largely to the enthusiasm of an American couple who fell in love with this place and made their home here.

Fairlight E. Sussex F5

The cliffs to the E. of Hastings are not white, like those of Eastbourne or of Dover; they are not chalk, but sandstone, and are overlaid with gorse and bracken. High up at the back of them is the old village of Fairlight, with its rugged Victorian church whose tower looks like a battlement. Here too is the coastguard station, which monitors the busy traffic in the Channel below.

These cliffs are known as the Fire Hills. The reason for this is obscure; the most probable is that when the gorse is in bloom, or when the bracken turns brown and the sun is upon it, especially the western sun, the whole area seems to be ablaze.

On a bright day the view from these cliffs is stupendous: to the W., the cliffs themselves mask Hastings, but Beachy Head, beyond it, is easily picked out; to the E. one sees the land curving gently round to the great power station at Dungeness, while to the S. the French coast is clearly visible. Even this, however, is nothing compared with the view from the tower of Fairlight church, from which in addition a great sweep of the land to the N. may be seen, stretching far into East Sussex and Kent.

On the sort of day when these views can be enjoyed, it would be vain to expect solitude. All this tract between

church and cliff has been designated a 'country park', and provided with car parks. Once away from the cars, however, there is plenty of room for all, with wide grass tracks between vast areas of gorse.

At the foot of the cliff to the W. is the Lovers' Seat, the secret trysting-place of Elizabeth Boys and her sailor-lover, who continued to meet in defiance of her parents' wishes. The parents eventually relented, however, and the young couple were duly married. Sad to tell, he was shortly afterwards drowned at sea, and Elizabeth died in childbirth. The footpath leading direct to the romantic spot is clearly signed from the road from Hastings to Fairlight.

At the other end of the Fire Hills is FAIRLIGHT COVE, where a genteel bungalow suburb has sprouted, served by the small modern church of St Peter's.

Farley Heath Surrey *see* **Albury**

Farnham Surrey A3

Farnham is a handsome Georgian town on the River Wey with a castle on the hill above. A glance at the map will show that it is also essentially a linear town, built along the river valley and on the line of the old E.–W. route followed by the Pilgrims' Way. In the Middle Ages, and until the C. 17, it was an important wool market; now it makes welding and pneumatic equipment, plastic coating, timber doors, machine-tool accessories.

The spine of Farnham, running E. and W. parallel to the river, is West Street and East Street, with a short narrow stretch in the middle called The Borough. Here are Georgian houses mingled with Victorian, and a good many neo-Georgian as well, the only discordant note being the Italianate National Westminster Bank, dating from 1865.

Down Church Passage, which leads S. off West Street, stands the very large parish church, mostly Perpendicular but vigorously restored in the mid C. 19 by Ferrey, witness the window tracery and fussy timber N. porch. The inside is better. There are beautiful late-C. 14 sedilia and piscina in the chancel. Under the tower is a bust of William Cobbett, 1763–1835, author and reformer, who was born in the town and is buried in the churchyard. In the N. transept, below the organ, is a brass memorial to Augustus Toplady, author of the famous hymn 'Rock of Ages'. He was born in West Street in 1740, and died in London at the age of 37.

Now out of the churchyard at the E. end and into the Church Lanes, Upper, Middle, and Lower – one of the most attractive corners of Farnham. Then up Downing Street and back to the 'spine', at the point where West Street narrows into The Borough. Here is the Italianate bank, and here too we can look up the length of Castle Street to the castle itself on its wooded eminence. On the corner of The Borough and Castle Street is the neo-Georgian Town Hall of 1930–4 replacing a Victorian one, and next to it along The Borough is the Bailiff's Hall, a c. 16 brick building rejuvenated in 1934 by Harold Faulkner, the architect of the adjoining Town Hall. The result is amusing. The tall chimney sprouting at the back belongs to a half-timbered bank of 1868 by Norman Shaw, as does also, presumably, the small portion of the building protruding from the side.

Soon the Borough widens into East Street, but there is nothing of great architectural moment here. The enterprising Redgrave Theatre is on the right, but the excitements are all inside. So back to Castle Street, whose charms are not individual but collective – and cumulative; good enough to seduce the eye from the castle itself. The period is mostly the second half of the c. 18 and the first half of the c. 19, the exceptions being the mid-Victorian Italianate stuccoed house not far up on the left (No. 8), and, on the right, the Town Hall, the tile-hung c. 17 Castle Coffee House, the early-c. 17 Windsor Almshouses, and the very good imitation-c. 18 house, No. 49, actually built in the c. 20 between the wars. The preservation of Castle Street and of much else of architectural value in the town is due to the efforts of Mr Borelli, a local landowner, from 1910 onwards.

At the top Castle Street curves gently and rises steeply to enwrap the castle. The wide pavement has six flights of seven steps each before a final flight of 17 steps. The distance between steps and between flights is regular, for the steps were built for Bishop Fox, the 'blind bishop' who lived in the castle in the early c. 16.

The castle itself dates from about 1138 and was built by Bishop de Blois, King Stephen's younger brother. The keep, built later in the c. 12, is in ruins, having been 'slighted' on Cromwell's orders after the Civil War and the stones used for repaving the town.

De Blois was Bishop of Winchester from 1129 to 1171, and Farnham Castle was the seat of the Bishops of Winchester from his time until 1927, when the diocese of Guildford was formed and the castle transferred to it. In 1956 the Bishop went to live in Guildford; the castle is now occupied by the Centre for International Briefing, which 'exists to prepare people for the experience of living and working abroad for the first time'. Some 2,000 students a year attend courses here. The Centre looks after the whole of the castle except the keep, which is in the care of the D.O.E.

The Great Hall, dates from about 1180, but has been so much altered over the years that it is difficult to see it as a Norman building at all. Its present shape is due to Bishop Morley, who was here during the reign of Charles II. The huge fireplace is his, and it was he who raised the walls to their present level and put on the flat ceiling. The Bishop's Chapel is also of his time, although the chandelier is c. 18, and the E. window is of 1894. The small candlesticks came from St George's Chapel, Windsor: when electricity was installed there, Bishop Randall Davidson (1895–1903), later Archbishop of Canterbury, obtained permission from Edward VII

Waverley Abbey: an C18 engraving

to transfer them to Farnham. There is in fact another chapel, which is Norman, as is the dining hall, formerly the kitchen.

The outer walls were rebuilt in the c. 14, with a small gatehouse, which since the early c. 19 has been capped with a curious Gothic cupola, and is now in use as a caretaker's dwelling. The great brick entrance tower is the work of Bishop Waynflete (1447–86), although it is known locally as Fox's Tower because Fox (1500–28) carried out certain modifications to it. Although it never had the slightest military purpose it nevertheless has false machicolations and a recess for a portcullis. The incongruous windows were added in the c. 18, as were the two sundials with their Latin inscriptions, meaning 'they [the hours] pass', 'they are counted'.

From the keep there is a fine view, not only of the rest of the castle buildings, but also of the town of Farnham and the surrounding countryside.

A corner of Farnham remains that is worth visiting, at the very bottom of the town on the s. side of the river. Here is the William Cobbett inn, facing N. at the s. end of Longbridge. In this pleasant c. 16–c. 17 building was born that indefatigable and self-opinionated complainer and reformer, a sort of latter-day Hampden. Near by, behind the attractive Bridge Square and be-

THIS first Cistercian Abby in England was founded by Wm Gifford B.^p of Winchester A.D: 1128, for an Abbot & 12 Monks. His Successors & others were Benefactors. A.D: 1189 Rich.^I con: firm'd their Possessions. The great Church now in Ruins was begun by Wm Bradewater A.D. 1203. In this ye Heart of Peter de Rupibus B.^p of Winchester was buried A.D. 1238 & about 6 years since dug up entire, inclos'd within a Lead Box containing a saline Liquid. The Abbot of this House was Superior of ye Order in England. At ye Dissolution it was val'at £143.3. Dugd. After that it was granted to Sr Wm Fitz Williams, from his Family it came to ye Oldhams, who sold it to Jo.^e Aislabie Esqr of whome it was purchas'd by ye present Proprietor Cha: Child Esqr

Sam & Nath. Buck del. & sculp. Publisht according to Act of Parliament March 2. 1737

(N.M.R.)

tween Red Lion Lane and the river, are The Maltings, and alongside them an old tannery now converted into a theatre and community centre.

Beyond this part of the town are two places that can conveniently be visited from Farnham: WAVERLEY ABBEY and Frensham Ponds. The ruins of Waverley (D.O.E.) stand beside the River Wey, across a field on the right of the B3001 road towards Elstead and a little under two miles from Farnham railway station. This was the first Cistercian abbey in England, founded by William Giffard, Bishop of Winchester, in 1128. A larger church was built in the following century. The abbey was dissolved in 1536. The chief remains today are part of the s. transept, an end wall and part of the side walls of the dorter, or monks' dormitory, and the vaulted cellarium. The ruins inspired Sir Walter Scott's novel *Waverley*, and the others that followed were given the same general name.

Close to the ruins across its own private lake stands Waverley House, an c. 18 house by Colen Campbell rebuilt after a fire in 1833. It is an important-looking house in yellowish brick with white window-casings, pilasters, and columns.

FRENSHAM PONDS can be reached from here without going back towards Farnham, by taking the next turning

to the right off the Elstead road and striking across country to Millbrook, where immediately after crossing the river one turns left for Frensham Little Pond. (Both Little and Great Ponds are N.T. property, and are best visited, incidentally, well out of season.) These sizeable lakes – the word 'pond' gives a false impression – are situated in one of the areas of sandy heathland so often found in Surrey and so appealing when found. Little Pond, being well away from a main road, is somewhat more secluded, but the sailing-boats on the Great Pond, which is on the w. side of the A287 road a little further s., are an attractive sight. Sailing, by the way, is for club members only; but there is good walking and riding in all this heathy area, much of which is N.T. property, including the largest of the low sandstone hills on Churt Common known as The Devil's Jumps.

Faversham Kent G3

Faversham is a town where past and present are in happy partnership. The splendours of the past have been preserved – yet the place is not a mere museum. There is modern industry – yet it has not overwhelmed the town. Even the 'traffic problem' seems to be under control.

The centre of Faversham is the Market Square, where, apart from vans delivering to shops during certain hours, road traffic has been eliminated. Here is the early-c. 19 guildhall, a rebuilding of the Elizabethan market hall still propped up by Elizabethan wooden pillars, although these have been much restored. Behind the hall is a fantastic Victorian pump in pink, white, and black, standing about 10ft high. Across the road in Middle Row is Tudor House, dated 1570, with decorated barge-boards; next to it is the truest piece of philistinism in Faversham: 'Tudor Bingo'.

On the s. side of the square stands Boots the Chemist. These premises were once occupied by the hostelry known as the Queen's Arms, and here King James II was brought captive in 1688. Some fishermen from the town found him on board a ship off the Isle of Sheppey, hiding from the forces of his Protestant foe, William of Orange. He was brought to the Queen's Arms and later transferred to the mayor's house, 18 Court Street. After three days he was allowed to return to London, but confronted with William's ultimatum he left England for ever, just one week after his arrival in Faversham.

Before going any further the traveller will be well advised, if the time is right, to visit the Heritage Centre in Preston Street, which runs s. from the Market Square. It is housed in a former pub, the Fleur-de-Lis, and is a little way up the street on the left. After hearing a 10-minute talk illustrated by coloured slides, the visitor can wander round a first-rate exhibition that will un-doubtedly whet his appetite for the architectural treasures in store. He will also learn much about the life of Faversham, which besides being a port is a centre of brewing and other industries, and was at one time much concerned with the manufacture of gunpowder. The Faversham Society has in fact restored one of the powder mills, which can be visited by appointment. Needless to say, there is not a grain of gunpowder there.

West Street runs from the Market Square westwards. It has several old houses, and is traffic-free, which means that the buildings can be properly looked at and enjoyed. Another of the streets radiating out from the Market Square is Court Street, running NE. Here is a true blending of domestic and industrial buildings. Many of the houses are c. 16 and timber-framed. On the right is the gigantic Whitbread-Fremlin brewery, emitting a strong odour of brewing over the surrounding area. Church Street runs along the far side of the brewery to the flint parish church behind, famous for its curious c. 18 openwork steeple, a copy of Wren's at St Dunstan's-in-the-East, London.

The interior is large and dark. The transepts and chancel are of the early c. 14, but the Norman nave was rebuilt in the middle of the c. 18, after the collapse of the central tower, with heavy Tuscan columns. There is much Victorian restoration both inside and out, the knapped flint of the exterior all dating from that period.

The most interesting features are the fine set of c. 15 misericords in the choir stalls, eight a side (perhaps the animal carvings on the s. side are the more amusing); and the paintings on the SE. column of the N. transept, depicting scenes from the life of the Virgin Mary. These date from the early c. 14, like the column on which they are painted.

The tomb in the s. chapel is traditionally supposed to contain the mortal remains of King Stephen, who was formerly buried in the nearby abbey, of which he was the founder. If this tradition is correct, Faversham's is the only parish church in England to contain the tomb of an English king.

Beyond Church Street, Court Street becomes Abbey Street, and leads between more lovely old houses to a timber-framed house on the right that was once the abbey guest house. Now it is called Arden's House, for it was here, in the mid c. 16, that Thomas Arden, former mayor of the town, was murdered by accomplices of his wife and her lover. His story is the subject of the Elizabethan play, *Arden of Faversham*. The house is joined on to the wall of the abbey gatehouse. Of the c. 12 abbey all that now remains are scraps of wall, such as may be seen in Abbey Close on the right.

At the very end of the street, Standard Quay leads down to Faversham Creek on the left of the Anchor Inn. Here is a long c. 15 building of brick and timber, which may have been a granary for the abbey; if so, its present use is similar, for it now provides storage for animal feeding stuffs. The creek itself is still used by small ships.

Back in Abbey Street, Quay Lane runs down into Conduit Street. Here on the right is a c. 16 timber-framed building now used by the local Sea Cadets. This

Arden's House, Abbey Street, Faversham

is the Training Ship *Hasarde*, named after a ship supplied by Faversham to help fight the Spanish Armada.

Further along the street is Faversham's own brewery, Shepherd Neame, while across the creek is the suburb of DAVINGTON, where the parish church is a former Norman priory, part of whose monastic buildings are incorporated in the house alongside.

Findon W. Sussex C5

Now a pleasant suburb of Worthing, under the Downs. A link with the past is the annual sheep fair, held on the second Saturday in September, which has been a regular event since 1790, although sheep fairs have taken place here from time to time for over 700 years.

The parish church is up a lane on the far side of the main road. It is Norman, all flint, even to the curious chimney in the NE. corner. Inside, a timber roof, probably c. 15, spanning both nave and N. aisle, its king-posts resting on the pillars of the arcade, gives the church an oddly lopsided appearance. The building was heavily restored in the c. 19 by Sir George Gilbert Scott. The old medieval font, a really rough thing, stands in the N. aisle, while the c. 19 replacement, evidently the one actually used, is on the s. side.

Findon Place, hard by, is a handsome c. 18 house, in complete contrast to the church. Yet church and house together form a charming unit; it is easy to forget, as one stands here in the tranquil past, that the bustling present is but two minutes' walk away.

Closer in to Worthing is the part of Findon known locally as 'The Valley', strung out along the main road; this is pure town. Here there is another church, All Saints, built in 1956 in a clean modern idiom.

Above Findon to the E. is the Iron Age fort of CISSBURY RING (N.T.), one of the largest in the country, on the site of a group of flint mines dating from much earlier times. The Roman occupation brought peace, and the fort fell into disuse; but after the Romans departed in the c. 5 the site was again fortified, perhaps for defence against the Saxons. Up on these breezy heights one may look E. along the coast to Beachy Head, nearly 30 miles away, while farther off to the sw., beyond Selsey Bill and the Solent, the Isle of Wight can often be seen.

Firle E. Sussex D5

The handsome village of Firle lies under the steep slope of the South Downs E. of Lewes. It is always marked on maps as 'West Firle', although 'East Firle' does not seem to have existed for the last 700 years. The buildings are mainly of brick and flint. The church, predominantly flint, is of the c. 13 to c. 15, apart from the Norman N. doorway. The N. chapel, now the vestry, was added in the c. 16 and contains three tombs of members of the Gage family, owners of Firle Place from then until the present day.

The Gages came from Gloucestershire, and acquired their Sussex property when John Gage married Eleanor St Clere, a local heiress, in the c. 15. The most ambitious of the three tombs is that of his grandson, Sir John Gage (d. 1556 – the date 1557 in the brass inscription is incorrect), and his wife Philippa. Sir John is the probable builder of the house, although its history is not well documented. He appears to have steered a skilful course between the Scylla of Rome and the Charybdis of the Reformed Church; he remained faithful to Rome yet retained the favour of Henry VIII, and indeed was a commissioner for the Dissolution of the Monasteries. Later, however, he also enjoyed the patronage of Mary Tudor, and as Constable of the Tower of London presided over the execution of Lady Jane Grey.

The other tombs are of Sir John's son Edward, and grandson John. Edward, as High Sheriff during the Marian persecutions, supervised the burning of the Lewes Martyrs, and in 1580, during Elizabeth I's reign, his son John was committed to the Fleet prison for 'obstinacy in popery'. The family remained Roman Catholic until the c. 18, when the 7th Baronet, Sir William (1695–1744), 'the Father of Sussex Cricket', became a member of the Church of England.

Firle Place stands .E. of the village in a large park. At first sight it appears to be Georgian, and so it is, but encased within it is Sir John's Tudor house (assuming it to be his). The Georgian rebuilding was probably carried out by Sir William, or possibly by his cousin Thomas, the 1st Viscount, who succeeded him at Firle. (The Gages are a distinguished family, but it was surely Thomas's brother Joseph whose career was the most eccentric: having amassed a vast fortune by investing in Mississippi stock, and having used the money to make, in turn, unsuccessful bids to become King of Poland and of Sardinia, he eventually went to Spain, where he acquired a silver mine, was made a grandee, and was given command of the Spanish army in Italy, where he waged war against the Austrians and was awarded a pension of 4,000 ducats by the King of Naples.)

Thomas, like William, became a Church of England man and a firm supporter of the House of Hanover – no wonder he became the 1st Viscount. His younger son, also Thomas, was commander-in-chief of the British Army in America during part of the American War of Independence; his direct descendants down to the present day have in turn been Viscounts Gage and owners of Firle Place.

The house is a handome and elegant building faced with creamy Caen stone. One enters through the Georgian entrance arch, under the Long Gallery, a rare example of a Long Gallery built, rather than converted, in the c. 18. From the entrance arch one crosses a courtyard into the Great Hall, whose Tudor hammer-beams are concealed within the Georgian plasterwork. Thereafter one sees in turn the fine staircase hall and the drawing room leading out of it, and then, upstairs, another drawing room, an ante-room, and the Long Gallery – a series of rooms containing a magnificent collection of pictures, furniture, and, perhaps especially, china.

From the Long Gallery a corridor leads downstairs again. On its walls are an address to General Thomas Gage from the city of New York, and a plan of the city dated 1775. There is also a painting of Firle in 1837, showing a game of quintain in progress (see Offham), after which, according to a contemporary account, 'a cold collation of upwards of 300 dishes' was served.

On the Downs above Firle is their highest point E. of Lewes: Firle Beacon, 713ft/217m. above sea-level. A road runs up to the ridge from the village, and from the car park there it is an easy walk of just over a mile, past a number of ancient burial mounds, to the summit.

Fishbourne W. Sussex A6

This place is famed for the Roman palace discovered in 1960 by workmen laying a water main. It is one of the most thrilling Roman sites in Britain, and one of the largest; even so what has been excavated is only a fraction of the original, much of which is buried irretrievably under the A27 Chichester–Portsmouth road

Fishbourne Roman Palace: Boy Riding a Dolphin (A. F. Kersting)

and a modern housing development immediately to the s. Once Roman sailors tied up their ships here (the sea has receded since the C. I), Roman gardeners tended plants imported from their sunnier homeland, and Roman dignitaries discussed politics and sipped wine. For whom this magnificent residence was built is a matter of speculation, the strongest probability being Cogidubnus, King of the Regni and vassal of Rome (*see* Chichester).

What we see is the N. wing of the palace and the formal gardens, both of which could accommodate several cricket pitches. The N. wing is entirely enclosed in a pleasing modern hangar-like structure of wood and glass; the remains consist chiefly of mosaic and tessellated floors and of hypocausts, the mosaics of exquisite and sophisticated design and workmanship, some remarkably complete. The garden lay-out follows exactly the Roman planting plan, the C. I and C. 2 bedding trenches having been clearly traceable by the different colour and consistency of their soil. The plants – box for the intricately patterned hedges, rosemary, acanthus, lilies, roses, flowering trees – are all of varieties known from contemporary writings and wall-paintings to have been popular among well-to-do Romans.

A superbly imaginative museum, which should be first port of call, brings the whole site vividly alive, and by means of photographs, diagrams, and reconstructions explains its development from the first military supply base of about A.D. 43, through its heyday as a palace to its final destruction by fire in about A.D. 300. Models help you to keep your grip on the story at each stage, while comparative plans and pictures demonstrate both the superiority of Fishbourne over other Romano-British villas so far discovered, and its similarity to contemporary buildings in Italy.

Folkestone Kent H4

Unlike Dover, which is primarily a port and only secondarily a resort, Folkestone, flanked by steep chalk cliffs and backed by lumpy chalk hills, is undecided. The smart Sealink cross-Channel ships slide in and out of the harbour with surprising frequency, yet the town is out to waylay the tourist, and many retired folk live there.

On the left down Wear Bay Road, below the Dover road, are the stumps of two martello towers, the second standing in the middle of a miniature golf course on the East Cliff. From here there is a fine view of the harbour.

Tontine Street, one of the busy main streets of the town centre, climbs up the hill from Harbour Street, but the explorer on foot will bear left up the narrow Old High Street, traffic-free and little more than an alley; at the top he will turn left into Bayle Street, then right into The Bayle, where in 637 St Eanswythe, grand-daughter of King Ethelbert, founded a nunnery. (The name 'Bayle' came later, and is said to be connected with the word 'bailey', the enclosure of a castle.)

The bones of the saint rest where they were discovered in 1885, in the sanctuary of the parish church of St Mary and St Eanswythe at the far end of The Bayle. This church was founded in 1138, but the French burned it down in 1216 and it had to be almost entirely rebuilt. The E. end of the chancel contains the best of the c. 13 architecture, and dates from c. 1236. The fine central tower was rebuilt c. 1400. Over all this early work are vast Victorian accretions: stained glass (the best by Kempe), altar, wall-paintings. Curiously enough it all blends in remarkably well, and the whole effect is magnificent.

From the churchyard a footpath leads w. to the town war memorial at the w. end of the Road of Remembrance. (At No. 3 Albion Villas near by, Dickens lived in 1855 and wrote part of *Little Dorrit*.) From here westwards runs Folkestone's most famous street, The Leas, a cliff-top promenade containing a mixture of mid-c. 19 and modern buildings. Below, the cliff is wooded, and there are many pine trees whose scent, in an onshore breeze, mingles seductively with that of the sea.

Half-way along The Leas is a large statue of William Harvey (1578–1657), the town's illustrious son whose discovery of the circulation of the blood was an important milestone in the development of medicine. The western half of The Leas is a footpath only; at the far end of it is another martello tower, and above SANDGATE, the small town at the foot of the cliffs to the w., there are no fewer than five more, while huddled between beach and High Street are the remains of Sandgate Castle, one of Henry VIII's coastal forts. This one was partly demolished in 1806 and effectively turned into yet another martello tower. It is now privately owned and not open to the public.

Frensham Ponds Surrey *see* **Farnham**

Glynde E. Sussex D5
Below the E. side of the chalk hill crowned by Mount Caburn, an Iron Age fort near Lewes, lies the village of Glynde, running down the slope to Glynde Reach, tidal arm of the River Ouse. At the top of the village is Glynde Place, a Tudor house turned back to front by its c. 18 owner, Richard Trevor, Bishop of Durham, in the reign of George II.

The house one sees today, although much altered, still largely retains, externally, the Tudor character it had when first built by William Morley in the reign of

Elizabeth I. Since then it has remained in the same family, although it has not always passed in direct male line of descent; hence from the Morleys the property passed to the Trevors, and from them to the Brands.

William Morley's Elizabethan house of flint and Caen stone faced w., and was built round a courtyard. At that time the road passed close to the front of the house. Richard Trevor turned the house round the other way, converting three rooms on the E. side of the courtyard into one large front hall and moving the road back from the w. side of the house to its present line.

When the house is open the parts shown are this hall, the courtyard and the old Tudor gateway on its w. side, the drawing room, the main staircase and landing, the Long Gallery, and the 'Red Room', used as the dining room in Victorian times.

It would be foolish to compile here a catalogue of treasures; each visitor will have different preferences. There are three very fine bronze reliefs by Francesco Bertos, two in the hall and one above the fireplace in the Long Gallery, depicting biblical scenes. There was once a fourth at Glynde, but it found its way – nobody knows how or when – to America, and it is now in the Museum of Fine Arts in Chicago. Its subject is the Massacre of the Innocents.

In the drawing room the Rubens cartoon for the ceiling of the banqueting room in Whitehall Place is outstanding; it depicts the Apotheosis of James I, an event about which modern historians have reservations. On the landing the needlework counterpane and matching pillows worked by the nine daughters of John Trevor in about 1720 compel admiration tinged with sympathy, while the Trevor portraits in the panelled Long Gallery are both interesting and amusing. Another Trevor portrait, on the N. wall of the hall, is of Sir John Trevor with his wife and five children, all looking very serious in their severe c. 17 garb, and indubitably Welsh.

Next to the house is Glynde church, a delightful Georgian church built by Richard Trevor, Bishop of Durham, which even the alterations to the chancel carried out in the 1890s do little to mar. Up the road in the opposite direction is GLYNDEBOURNE, famous for its opera, which it owes to the vision of its former owner John Christie, who started opera here in the 1930s. Glyndebourne formed part of the Glynde estate until 1589, when it was given to one of the Morleys as a wedding present. The Victorian house still contains considerable Tudor portions.

Godalming Surrey B4
The parish church here is dedicated to St Peter and St Paul; a Godalming joke is that a third saint is urgently needed – to look after the people who have to cross the road. The little town is certainly traffic-torn, and because its charms, though considerable, are not obvious, it demonstrates the importance of walking; virtually nothing can be seen here from car or coach.

The key building of Godalming is the Old Town Hall, known locally as the Pepperpot. Standing at the junction of the High Street and Church Street, it is a white stuccoed building with an open arcade on the ground floor and the old council chamber, now a museum, above. It was built in 1814 on the site of the former market hall, which had become unsafe. Since Godalming lacks a central open space of any kind, the Pepperpot provides a much needed focal point.

From here one may stroll round the town and savour its intimate delights. Down Church Street there are several houses of interest, apart from the church itself, with its Norman tower topped by a huge lead spire, probably c. 13, and various additions through the centuries; one of them is Church House, which must go back at least to the c. 15, although the fancy barge-boards under the eaves are Victorian; the significance of the date over the door, 1086, is uncertain.

Mint Street, leading out of Church Street, contains the wholly Georgian Brook House – many of the apparently Georgian buildings in the town, as elsewhere, are in fact much older. What a pity the bricks of Brook House have been covered with ugly pebbledash! One of the many charming corners of Godalming is at the bottom of nearby Mill Lane, where a causeway on the left rises to The Mint. Here the tiny c. 18 Friends' Meeting House stands close to a row of c. 16–c. 17 timber-framed cottages; behind them, through an archway, is an equally attractive early-c. 19 house. At the bottom of the hill is an old mill by a stream, the mill race still to be seen though no longer in use.

The High Street itself is a medley of building styles, with alleys and courts leading off, and ending with the grand climax of the King's Arms Royal Hotel on the left, its brick front dated 1753 although the building behind is much older. This is the only one of Godalming's old coaching inns that is still a hostelry; the town had several, as it was formerly on the main road from London to Portsmouth.

The visitor who walks down Bridge Street from here to the River Wey will be able to return along the riverside walk, which brings him back just below the parish church, at the Phillips Memorial Cloister, in memory of Jack Phillips, the local man who was the wireless operator on the *Titanic* on her ill-fated maiden voyage in 1912. The inscription on the wall inside starts with the letters s.o.s., the message he continued to tap out, in vain, until the ship went down.

This is only a fraction of what should be seen in Godalming. The visitor with a couple of hours to spare would do well to buy a copy of the town guide *A Godalming Walk*, by David Coombs, an outstandingly good example of the genre, to which I gladly acknowledge my debt.

Godalming is a hilly town and a wooded one. From various points near the centre, over the tops of the trees on the hill to the N., may be seen the tips of spires. Even their tips proclaim them to be Victorian. They are in fact the spires of CHARTERHOUSE, the famous public school moved from London in 1872 into entirely new buildings designed by P. C. Hardwick. These still form the nucleus of the school, a splendid and majestic group in yellow-brown Bargate stone, displaying the passion for asymmetry so prevalent among certain Victorian architects, and the self-confidence seemingly shared by them all. The Great Hall, however, is by Sir A. W. Blomfield, 1885, the chapel by Sir Giles Gilbert Scott, 1922–7, and the Art School by J. Dartford, 1958; and there is a good set of more modern buildings on the other side of the playing-fields.

For a complete change go two miles along the B2130 road towards Hascombe and visit WINKWORTH ARBORETUM (N.T.), 99 acres of trees and shrubs running down the side of a steep valley to two large lakes. At the right time in the spring the carpets of bluebells are so thick you cannot see the green of the grass beneath; later on, the azaleas set the valley on fire, while in their turn the softer browns, reds, and golds of autumn are no less appealing.

Goodwood   W. Sussex   B5

Goodwood, between the South Downs and the sea near Chichester, is unique among the great houses of England, for it is nearly all faced with flint, a very rustic material for such a grand building. The grand building would have been grandiose if the designs of James Wyatt, hatched at the end of the c. 18, had been brought to completion.

Originally the house was a modest one of 1720. This was enlarged by Sir William Chambers c. 1760 for the 3rd Duke of Richmond, who at the end of the century employed Wyatt to build him a very much larger house, insisting that the walls should be faced with flint, the local stone. Wyatt's design was for a huge octagon, with saucer-shaped domes at the corners, and incorporating the end of the old house in one of its sides. This side and one other were completed, but then the money ran out, the Duke died, and the plan died with him. The half-completed third side was finished in 1838, so that the Goodwood we see today is three sides of Wyatt's proposed octagon, with the old house, rebuilt by Chambers, at the back.

We enter the main house at the NE. end, and we very soon realize that if Goodwood is largely the creation of the 3rd Duke, its presiding genius is Charles II, whose favourite favourite, Louise de Queroualle, Duchess of Portsmouth, bore him a son Charles, who was created 1st Duke of Richmond, and from whom all subsequent Dukes of Richmond are directly descended.

The first room entered is the Round Reception Room, which is under one of Wyatt's saucer domes. Among several interesting pictures here is one by Lely of Frances Theresa Stewart, or 'La Belle Stewart'. The King himself was one of her many admirers; she managed, however, to ward off his advances, ran away from court and married. This portrait of her as Minerva was the inspiration for the figure of Britannia on the coinage.

After this comes the ballroom, planned by the 3rd Duke to be a picture gallery as well. Here as he intended the portrait by Van Dyck of Charles I and his family takes pride of place. This picture has a curious history, for after Charles's execution it found its way into the Orléans collection, and when the Duc d'Orléans was executed during the French Revolution it was bought by an English banker and in 1804 sold to the 3rd Duke of Richmond for £1,100.

There are numerous portraits and other pictures in this and the other state rooms, such as Van Dyck's *Five Children of Charles I*, Lely's portrait of Charles II, and Kneller's of the Duchess of Portsmouth, and of their son, the 1st Duke, who looks remarkably like both his parents. The Sèvres china and Louis XV furniture were collected by the 3rd Duke when he was Ambassador Extraordinary at Versailles in 1765. There is some good English furniture too, its simple, clean lines restful to the eye compared with the ornateness of the French.

After the grandeur of the Yellow Drawing Room, the dining room, and Wyatt's entrance hall, with its pillars of pink marble, it is almost a relief to go across to the 'old' house, where the Long Hall, created by Chambers, seems quite modest in comparison. Here are sporting pictures by Stubbs, a delightful little four-octave conductor's piano made in Edinburgh in 1786, and an indescribable object known as 'The Trophy', a huge silver table-piece presented to the 5th Duke by the veterans of the Peninsula War in gratitude for his having obtained for them the right to wear campaign medals, despite the opposition of the Duke of Wellington. Leading off this room is the Tapestry Drawing Room, rebuilt, probably by Wyatt, to accommodate the tapestries acquired by the 3rd Duke during his sojourn in France. The four Louis XV Gobelin tapestries by Michael Audran and Pierre François Cozette, in specially designed frames, depict scenes from Cervantes's *Don Quixote*. The ceiling of this room is particularly beautiful, done in the style of Adam, but rather more ornate; its colours – pink, green, gold – do not sound very promising, but they are handled so surely that they are in fact highly successful.

This is only a tiny fraction of what can be seen at Goodwood, where, incidentally, the visitor is permitted to wander freely round the rooms that are open – there are no roped off sections.

Goodwood Racecourse, laid out by the 3rd Duke, is high up on the Downs to the N., on the E. side of a hill known as The Trundle, the site of an Iron Age fort enclosing a Neolithic causewayed camp. There has always been a close connexion between the course and the great house, and members of the Royal Family are wont to stay at Goodwood when attending the race meetings. Racing now takes place on 11 days in the year, on a racecourse that is the most beautiful in England.

Goudhurst Kent E4
Seen from afar, crowning a hill, this of all Kent's villages is the most reminiscent of Italy or Spain. Yet on closer inspection it is very English: a mixture of styles, much weatherboarding and tile-hanging, a pond at the bottom of the main street and the church at the top providing focal points. And all around there are glorious views of the Weald.

The church looks Perpendicular, but there are older parts inside. The stumpy c. 17 tower was built to replace the original tower burnt down in 1637; it has a Classical doorway, ill-suited to the Wealden sandstone it is made of, but has great strength and solidity.

Inside, the church is spacious and light; much of the stained glass was blown out by a land mine in 1940 – not an unmitigated disaster – and replaced by clear glass. But the pride of the church is its monuments. In the s. chapel is the oldest: a brass on the floor commemorating John Bedgebury, d. 1424. His home was Bedgebury Park, one of the oldest manors in England, having a deed of gift dated 815. After his death the property passed to the Culpepers, because his widow, Agnes, married Walter Culpeper. There is a brass commemorating them too, but all that is left of it is three shields on the slab next to the Bedgebury brass. (The third brass, of an unknown man in armour, is of later date, probably c. 1520.)

In this same chapel is a large monument, carved in 1599, portraying four generations of the Culpepers. In a niche at the top is the half-figure of Sir Thomas Culpeper; below are his son and daughter-in-law, Sir Alexander and his wife Mary, together with their son Anthony; and below that again are Sir Anthony and his wife Ann, with a number of their children. The monument in a bay window just outside the chapel is of the 'old' Sir Alexander, Sir Thomas's father. His iron foundries at Bedgebury cast guns for the fleet that fought the Spanish Armada, long after his death. The monument is of painted wood, and portrays Sir Alexander and his wife, recumbent figures confidently awaiting the Judgement Day. On the E. jamb of the window is a small stone relief dated 1537, depicting God in Majesty, the Virgin and Child, St George slaying the dragon, his foot poised somewhat tentatively on the dragon's head, and the kneeling figures of Sir Anthony Culpeper and his wife, with four sons and seven daughters.

There are also two monuments in the Classical manner, both in marble. One of them, perhaps the most delightful of all the monuments in the church, is of William Campion, d. 1702; this is on the wall on the N. side of the altar in the s. chapel. The other is on the s. wall of the sanctuary, and is of an earlier William Campion, d. 1615, with his wife and nine children.

(A. F. Kersting)

Goudhurst church: the effigies of Sir Alexander and Lady Culpeper, 1537

The Campions lived at COMBWELL PRIORY, a house near the southern edge of the parish, from the Dissolution of the Monasteries until the c. 20. It is still a private house, though no longer in the Campion family.

Another interesting house, about a mile and a half sw. of the village, is FINCHCOCKS, a red-brick house built in 1725 in the Baroque style for William Bathurst. Despite its grand appearance it is only the width of one large room from front to back. It now contains an interesting collection of historical keyboard instruments.

PATTENDEN, or Pattyndenne, on the B2079 road leading s. from Goudhurst, is a half-timbered manor house of 1470.

Further along this same road, on the left about two miles from Goudhurst, is BEDGEBURY PARK (*see also* Kilndown), the estate of the Bedgeburys in the Middle Ages, and of the Culpepers from the c. 15 to the c. 17, and today a girls' boarding school. It owes its present general appearance to Viscount Beresford, who bought the existing c. 17 brick house in 1836, and to his stepson,

Alexander Beresford Hope. Beresford encased the old house in sandstone and added another floor, two wings, and a parapet; Hope replaced the parapet by a pavilion roof in the French style in 1854–5, and put up the Bavarian-looking spire over the stable block, the architect of both being R. C. Carpenter. The result, to modern eyes, is a fascinating c. 19 curiosity of vast proportions. There is a good view of it from the public footpath that leaves the road about 400yd N. of the drive entrance and runs, undefined, through the field N. of the park.

On the other side of the park is BEDGEBURY PINETUM, a large wooded area belonging to the Royal Botanic Gardens and containing many rare trees and shrubs.

Great Dixter E. Sussex *see* **Northiam**

Guildford Surrey B3

Guildford, the county town of Surrey and worthy of its title, owes its origins to its situation at the point where the prehistoric E.–W. route, known now as the Pilgrims' Way, crosses the River Wey where it has worn down and broken through the chalk wall of the North Downs. Its name is thought to mean the ford over the Gil (or Gilon), the old name for the river; theories involving golden sands or flowers, although more romantic, are less probable. Only a few prehistoric or Roman remains have been found, perhaps because the river banks have been raised and re-aligned subsequently, and it was here, down by the river, that the earliest settlements were established.

The place grew in importance in Saxon times, but the growth was slow. When the Normans arrived the town had hardly begun to climb up from the river. The Normans built a castle to guard the natural route between London and the coast, and from now on Guildford's importance and growth were assured. In the Middle Ages it began to prosper as a centre for dyeing and finishing wool cloth woven in the surrounding villages. The district specialized in a blue kersey, which became famous at home and abroad, and to this day the arms of Guildford contain woolsacks and the Guildford colour is blue.

Another reason for the town's growing prosperity was its geographical situation at the crossroads already mentioned, particularly as it was a convenient day's ride from London. The many innkeepers, merchants, and shopkeepers did a roaring trade with the travellers.

In the C. 17 the prosperity of the wool trade began to wane, but fortunately another source of wealth was found, which at least helped to alleviate the loss: in 1653 the canal called the River Wey Navigation was opened, connecting Guildford with the Thames and London. In 1763 it was extended to Godalming. Traffic on the Wey Navigation reached its peak towards the middle of the C. 19, but the coming of the railway in 1845 brought the usual decline and eventual demise of the canal, although it remained in commercial use for over 100 years more. Finally in 1963 it was acquired by the N.T. and is now busy again – with pleasure-craft.

The population of Guildford at the beginning of the C. 19 was about 2,500; now it is about 60,000, although the population of the borough, much enlarged by the local government reorganization of 1974, is about double that figure. The town is an important railway junction and a commercial and shopping centre. There is little manufacturing industry, although Dennis Motors is famous: starting in the High Street in 1895 as a cycle shop, the firm produced its first motor vehicle in 1901. Now at its Woodbridge site in the northern part of the town it makes fire engines, ambulances, refuse collection vehicles, and a variety of other things.

Guildford is a cathedral and university town; the modern University of Surrey occupies the N. side of Stag Hill – part of a Norman hunting ground – at the top of which is the C. 20 cathedral designed by the late Sir Edward Maufe. The separation of Guildford from the diocese of Winchester had been mooted even in the C. 16, but came about only in 1927, some 400 years later. The first bishop was enthroned in the parish church of Holy Trinity, but this soon proved too small to play the part of a cathedral and it was decided to build a new one away from the town centre. The foundation stone was laid in 1936, but the Second World War put a stop to the work, so that the building was not consecrated until 1961, by which time it was at last almost complete. It occupies as good a site as any English cathedral, a little apart without being too remote, and commanding a fine view of the town and of distant countryside. Physically and otherwise it is closely associated with its neighbour the university.

The Cathedral of the Holy Spirit, built in a style which might be termed C. 20 Gothic, gives an immediate impression of mass and space, owing mainly to the height of the side aisles, which provides support for the nave and avoids the need for buttresses; it also allows high lancet windows to flood the nave with light. There is remarkably little stained glass, which adds to the feeling of space within. The exterior of warm brick, mostly made from the clay on which the building stands, is simple without being too austere, while the interior of pale Doulting stone from Somerset enhances the impression of light and clean lines. The roof is of reinforced concrete covered with copper, to avoid the twofold danger of fire and death-watch beetle.

From the w. end there is a view all the way to the High Altar, uninterrupted by any screen, and there is no clutter of choir stalls as at Coventry to distract the eye; only the somewhat domestic-looking lampshades in the nave might be said to intrude a little. Although the building is cruciform, the transepts are short. The 'dorsal curtain', or backdrop to the High Altar, also invites comparison with Coventry, where the famous Sutherland tapestry of Christ in Glory dominates the eastward view. Guildford's tall Lurex curtain in blue and gold *suffuses* rather than dominates.

All the chapels and vestries are in a close group round the chancel. The baptistry is at the w. end on the s. side; the font, of Travertine stone from Italy, is placed at the intersection of a green cross of Swedish marble, and the effect is so beautiful that it seems a pity the baptistry is in such an inconspicuous corner.

The engraved angels on the glass doors of the narthex at the w. end, designed by John Hutton, are beautiful too – and, incidentally, distinctly female. Outstanding among the sculptures of the interior are the stone carving by John Cobbett of the Virgin and Child, on the first pier of the nave on the N. side, and the wooden statue by Douglas Stephen of the same subject in the Lady Chapel at the far E. end. There are a number of sculptures round the soaringly solid exterior; the most exciting is the golden angel above the tower, his outstretched hand (this angel is certainly male) pointing imperiously into the wind.

OPPOSITE: *Guildford Cathedral: the nave*
(A. F. Kersting)

Guildford Cathedral is a most estimable and lovable building, with an open, welcoming atmosphere. It lacks any air of mystery, such as is found in the medieval cathedrals.

As for the town itself, the traveller's best plan is to stroll down the length of the High Street from E. to W. to the river at its foot, turning off to left or right as mood dictates. The High Street is one of the most satisfying streets in the South-East, and that is a large claim. It is also the focal point, or rather line, of the town, which has no market place or other natural centre and whose river is normally modest and retiring, although given to fairly frequent outbursts of muddy self-assertion and flooding of its banks.

At the very top of the street, then, is the Civic Hall – really in London Road, the eastward extension of the High Street; this is on the right (N.) side, and is a handsome building of the early 1960s. After that, the High Street proper begins, and the first building of particular interest, on the left, is the Royal Grammar School, or, as the legend over the entrance arch has it, 'Schola Regia Grammaticalis 1552'. This refers to the year when it received a royal charter from Edward VI, for it was founded in 1509 by Roger Beckingham, a London grocer. The present building dates from 1553–86, and is still a grammar school. Through the entrance arch is a small Elizabethan quadrangle, all of stone except the side next to the street, whose inside has half-timbering. There is a library containing chained books. On the opposite side of the street are the c. 20 buildings of the same school, not very exciting but doubtless more convenient.

Next on the right, beyond Chertsey Street, comes the Hospital of the Blessed Trinity, commonly known as Abbot's Hospital after its founder George Abbot, Archbishop of Canterbury from 1611 to 1633, a native of Guildford who was himself a pupil of the Royal Grammar School. He founded the hospital in 1619 to house a master, 12 men, and eight (later increased to 10) women. The massive gatehouse with its four cupolas is entirely Tudor in style; it opens out into a charming courtyard very like that of an Oxford or Cambridge college. Abbot himself was an Oxford man, a scholar of Balliol and later Master of University College and vice-chancellor of the university.

The side of the courtyard now facing one has its own bell-turret and cupola behind a stepped brick gable. The clock face was erected in 1742, replacing a sundial. In the SE. corner of the courtyard is the staircase leading to the Large Board Room, which is immediately above the entrance arch. It has fine oak panelling, and an elaborate mantel over the fireplace depicting Adam and Eve. The table is Tudor, and there is a set of mahogany

Chippendale chairs. The room above this is the Muniment Room, or Treasury, now called the Monmouth Room, for it was here that the captive Duke of Monmouth spent the last night of his journey to the Tower of London after the Battle of Sedgemoor in 1685.

On either side of the courtyard are the lodgings for the inmates; there are still about 20 of them, although nowadays the women outnumber the men. On the ground floor on the N. side is the so-called Common Room, once a communal dining hall; it has good oak panelling, and round the walls are fixed benches of excruciating discomfort. On the first floor above is the Banqueting Room, with a splendid carved oak mantelpiece. In the corner of the landing outside is the mechanism of the clock already mentioned. The works are much older than the clockface, and indeed are said to date from the c. 14.

The chapel is on the ground floor in the NE. corner of the courtyard, its chief feature the windows of Flemish painted glass depicting the story of Jacob.

Across the High Street directly opposite Abbot's Hospital is Holy Trinity, the parish church. It is an c. 18 brick building replacing a Norman one whose central tower collapsed in 1740. Abbot's tomb, which survived from the earlier church, is in the s. chapel.

A little way down from Abbot's Hospital is Guildford House, formerly known as Child House, after John Child, a lawyer, for whom it was built in 1660. From 1844 to 1929 it was used as a shop, and from 1929 to 1956 as a restaurant. In 1957 it was bought by the Corporation and is now, after restoration, used as a centre for exhibitions, meetings, and adult education. It is of timber-frame construction and has oversailing on the front elevation and on the side overlooking the courtyard. The richly carved staircase of elm and oak is outstanding; when the Corporation took over the house the carvings were found to be coated in several layers of paint, which had to be laboriously stripped off. The best rooms upstairs are the Powell Room, originally the main drawing room, with a plaster ceiling, and the Pine Room, which retains its original fireplace and was probably the principal bedroom.

A little further down the High Street on the same side is the Guildhall, generally acclaimed the finest building in the street. The front dates from 1683 and was put up by public subscription; the justly famous clock overhanging the road is of the same year, given, so it is said, by its maker John Aylward in exchange for the freedom of the town. Inside, the building turns out to be Tudor. The Courtroom, on the ground floor, has c. 17 panelling, and contains portraits of Charles II, James II, and William and Mary, while upstairs in the Council Chamber (still so called, although the few council meetings held in the building all take place in the Courtroom) are portraits of James I and of Elizabeth II, among others.

Opposite the Guildhall is Tunsgate, a gateway in

Abbot's Hospital, Guildford: the gatehouse

(A. F. Kersting)

the classical style. It was built in 1818 on the site of the old Tuns Inn as the entrance to a corn market; before that the market, which dated from Tudor times, projected into the High Street and obstructed traffic. In 1933 the central columns were moved apart to allow vehicles to pass through, which they still do. Beyond them, however, is a haven for pedestrians, the shopping precinct of Tunsgate Square.

Further down the High Street on the right is the Angel Hotel. The front is early-c. 19, but parts of the building are much older; the back is early-c. 17, and there is a c. 13 vault, which may have been the wine store of a prosperous medieval merchant.

Near the bottom of the street, Quarry Street goes off to the left; here on the right is Guildford's oldest church, St Mary's which boasts a Saxon tower and a Norman-to-c. 13 interior rising by steps from nave to crossing to chancel to sanctuary.

Castle Street, steep and narrow, climbs out of Quarry Street to the remains of the Norman castle. Only fragments are left, apart from the grim and sturdy c. 12 keep on its even earlier man-made motte of chalk. It looks NW. across the town to the cathedral on its answering eminence, and s. up the Wey valley to distant wooded hills; below are outlying bits of walls and bastions. The castle grounds, bought by the municipality in 1885 from Lord Grantley for the sum of £4,490, are open to the public daily without charge, their formal flower beds contrasting strangely with the gaunt old ruin in their midst; a wild garden would be much more appropriate but doubtless also more difficult to achieve.

Back to Quarry Street and turn left: here on the left is the Guildford Museum, containing exhibits illustrating the archaeology and history of the district and of the county, including Wealden ironwork. There are also relics of Lewis Carroll, who often visited his sisters' house near by and died there in 1898.

Next, Quarry Street curves round to the right and down the hill to Millbrook, by the river; a right turn here brings one back towards the bottom of the High Street. On the left, on a spit of land jutting out into the Wey, is the Yvonne Arnaud Theatre, an attractive building of the 1960s. If time allows, one may walk down the left side of the theatre and so across the river on a footbridge to Millmead, which leads back along the riverside to St Nicholas's church. The medieval church here, which had always been subject to flooding, was rebuilt on higher ground in 1837, and again on even higher ground in 1870–5 by S. S. Teulon in a blatant style. (All this part of the town is still liable to be flooded; in the disastrous floods of September 1968 the floor of the church was under 6ft of water, the bus station inundated, Millmead and Millbrook awash, and the theatre surrounded.) Another right turn on to the old Town Bridge, now reserved for pedestrians, brings one back across the river and up into the High Street.

Two buildings in the vicinity of Guildford should be visited if possible: Loseley House and Shalford Mill.

LOSELEY HOUSE, about three miles sw. off the A3100 road, is an Elizabethan mansion built in the 1560s for Sir William More; it contains panelling which may have come from Henry VIII's Nonsuch Palace near Ewell, and a good collection of furniture and pictures. The present house, which is only the N. wing of the original, is a restrained and dignified piece of architecture, subtly proportioned.

SHALFORD is sandwiched between the River Wey and the Tilling Bourne s. of Guildford. It was once a village but is now a traffic-torn suburb. However, down an inconspicuous turning to the left about 300yd s. of the church is the c. 18 water-mill (N.T.) on the Tilling Bourne, a timber-framed building with brick walls to the first floor and tile-hung side walls. It was working as a corn mill until 1914, and then was disused. In 1932 it was given by the owner, Major Godwin Austen, to the Ferguson Gang, a 'saintly mafia' who worked secretly and pseudonymously to preserve Old England, handing over properties and considerable sums of money – no questions asked – to the National Trust. Shalford Mill was one of these properties; here the secret meetings of the gang were held.

The storage area, about half the building, has been converted into a dwelling. There is a large overhanging projection from the second floor, from which the mill hoist used to be suspended. For the rest, there are four floors, all open to the public. From the ground floor the water-wheel, almost 14ft in diameter, can be inspected. On this floor the meal from the millstones was collected in bins or sacks; here too is the machinery for driving the millstones on the first floor. On the second floor is the auxiliary machinery of the mill: sack hoist, oat crusher, and two wire machines for separating the bran from the flour. On the third floor are the bins for storing the corn before grinding.

Hadlow Kent E3

A village in the low-lying clay lands NE. of Tonbridge, a land of orchards and hop-fields. Its fame rests on a folly, the octagonal Gothic tower soaring to a height of 170ft in a flurry of gables, pinnacles, and crockets, and dominating the flat landscape. As these words are written, the whole fantastic edifice is encased in scaffolding; the tower is undergoing a thorough restoration, which was long overdue.

The tower is a monument to man's overweening ambition, built by W. B. May in 1838–40 as an appendage to Hadlow Court Castle, a vast Gothic mansion built by his father and completed by himself a few years before the tower. The house was pulled down in 1951, all that remains being a few outbuildings now converted into private houses, and a monstrous gatehouse, largely covered in ivy, fronting the main street at the end of Castle Terrace. The gatehouse, like the tower, is of brick, concrete-rendered. In places the concrete has peeled off, exposing the brick; it all looks dilapidated and forlorn, but perhaps it, too, awaits restoration. May's object in building the tower, apparently, was to outdo William Beckford, whose tower at Fonthill in Wiltshire, although higher, had fallen down in 1825. Stories that May built in order to see the sea, or spy on his estranged wife, are unfounded.

The rest of Hadlow is pleasant but not outstanding. Church Street leads off the main street on a sharp bend. May's folly is straight ahead, whereas the tower of the church is almost hidden behind a roof on the left. This is the most attractive corner of Hadlow; on the left of Church Street are a couple of weatherboarded houses, then a tile-hung house on each side; at the end on the right, opposite the entrance to the churchyard, are George House and Chancel House, joined together in one medieval building with a Georgian front.

Enter the church by the w. door under the tower, built in Saxon times, heightened in Norman. The w. doorway is Early English, replacing a previous one whose outline can be clearly seen. The door itself is dated 1637. The arch connecting the tower and nave is late-Saxon or early-Norman; from here there is an uninterrupted view through the wide c. 13 chancel arch to the E. end of the church.

For the rest, the N. aisle and porch were built, and the chancel rebuilt, in the c. 19, and there are only two excitements. One is the c. 16 wall monument to Sir John Rivers on the s. wall of the chancel: the original inscription is lost. The other is the 'Coverdale Chair', now in the Lady Chapel. This chair was presented to the church in 1919, and is supposed to have been used by Miles Coverdale, c. 16 Bishop of Exeter and translator of the Bible. Unfortunately it seems more probable that it is a c. 19 reconstruction made from various bits and pieces of carved wood, which, although old, are not old enough to be contemporary with Coverdale. Whatever the truth of the matter, it is a good piece of work, with various allegorical carvings round the base and a front panel depicting the Expulsion – Adam and Eve being expelled by God from the Garden of Eden.

In the sw. corner of the churchyard is a sad sight: W. B. May's mausoleum, another Gothic monster, surrounded by nettles and covered in brambles. A pity to remember Hadlow by this; better to leave along the Tonbridge road and see, on the right, the modern buildings of the Hadlow College of Agriculture and Horticulture. The college owns considerable lands here and towards W. Peckham, and is alive and well.

Halnaker (*pron.* Hanneker)   W. Sussex   B5
A pleasant straggle of houses lining the A285 road three miles NE. of Chichester, where it follows the line of Stane Street, the Roman road from Chichester to London. No outstanding buildings here; even Halnaker House, built by Lutyens in 1938, standing well back and largely hidden from view, looks comfortable rather than exciting.

A public footpath continuing N. from the end of Park Lane takes one to within sight of the old Halnaker House, a great Tudor mansion built by the 9th Earl de la Warr, incorporating parts of an earlier house built by the de Haye family. It is now a ruin sadder even than Cowdray (*see* Midhurst). In 1765 it passed into the possession of the 3rd Duke of Richmond, who, having built Goodwood, had no need of Halnaker, and thereafter it was quite neglected. Even today, however, there are considerable remains of the c. 14 gatehouse and of the c. 13 chapel behind and to the E.

On top of a hill nearly a mile NE. of the ruins stands Halnaker Mill, an c. 18 brick tower mill complete with sails. It was restored in 1934 and again in 1955. This well-known landmark can be approached by the footpath that leads up from the main road at Warehead Farm. The track follows the line of Stane Street between hedges, then leaves it, turning left on to the open hill. The walk from Warehead Farm to the mill takes about 15 minutes, and there are two stiles to climb.

The brick base of the mill was formerly clad in tiles, but many of these have peeled off; the fantail is missing, but the sails are in good repair. All the windows have been bricked up, and the inside walls are covered with names.

There is, of course, a fine view from this hill: Chichester Cathedral to the sw., Bognor to the SE., The Trundles to the NW. Surely one can feel exhilaration here rather than the depression of Belloc's poem:

> Spirits that call and no one answers;
> Ha'nacker's down and England's done.

But that was written before the restoration of 1934.

Hastings   E. Sussex   F5
This may not be the smartest, but it is arguably the most exciting, of the SE. coast resorts.

A good starting-place is the castle, perched on the edge of the cliff between the old and the modern towns. This was the first Norman castle to be built in all England. When William set sail from Normandy in 1066 he intended to land at Hastings, but his fleet was blown off course and he found himself at Pevensey instead. Luckily for him his great adversary, Harold, was busy repelling another invasion in the North, and William was able to land and make his way to Hastings unmolested. Here was an excellent harbour, protected on the E. side by a steep hill. On this hill he dug a deep ditch to prevent unwelcome access from the E., and the excavated earth was thrown up on to the top of the hill to form a mound; and on this mound he built his castle.

It was not a very grand affair. In fact it was a prefabricated wooden castle, brought over in sections from

Old Hastings

(A. F. Kersting)

Normandy. It was only later, after William had been crowned King on Christmas Day, that the Normans set about building a permanent castle of stone.

The conformation of Hastings is very different today. Half the cliff on which the castle stood has disappeared. By the end of the c. 13 the proud Cinque Port of Hastings was humbled, for the harbour had silted up; the centre of the modern town now occupies its site.

Yet what is left of the castle is immensely impressive. From here one looks down upon the town of Hastings, and beyond it to St Leonards, Bexhill, and round to Beachy Head, whilst to the E. is Old Hastings – though even this was once a 'new' town built in the c. 10 to replace the original Hastings, which had disappeared under the sea – and the modern 'harbour', which is really no more than the beach, inadequately protected by a breakwater, itself broken. (Nevertheless, there is a busy little fishing industry here, and it is often possible to buy fish on the spot, fresh-caught and tasting utterly different from the frozen sort.)

The stone castle built to replace the temporary wooden structure was completed within a few years of 1066. It was, and remained until 1216, an important link in the chain of Norman coastal defences, as well as the point of departure and return for cross-Channel journeys. It also, from the earliest times, contained a collegiate church, which was endowed in 1070. In 1216 the castle was dismantled by King John, who feared an invasion by the French and decided to deny its use

to the enemy rather than use it himself; and although it was refortified about 10 years later by Henry III, the terrible storms that swept the SE. coast in the second half of the c. 13 finally put paid to Hastings as a port, and with the extinction of the harbour the castle, as a fortification, was a white elephant. Only as an ecclesiastical centre did it survive, until dissolved by Henry VIII. Despite the castle's strategic position and importance, it was never put to the test of assault or siege.

The approach to the castle today takes one past the great ditch dug by the Conqueror's troops when they first arrived. To the w. of it is the mound on which the prefabricated castle was placed, now surmounted by a flag pole, and always known as the Mount; to the E. of the ditch is a level piece of ground with a heaped-up, crescent-shaped portion at its northern end. This is known as 'The Ladies' Parlour', probably because it was the tournament ground of the castle; by tradition the tournaments were always presided over by a lady, who was saluted by the champion knight.

The modern visitor enters the castle through the main gateway. The Mount is on the left. From its summit one can see the whole lay-out of the castle area, or what is left of it, for about half of it has gone over the cliff. If one faces straight out to sea, behind and to the left are the remains of the curtain wall. To the left was the eastern gateway, which had a bridge across the ditch to the tiltyard or tournament ground. The stumps of the two towers that flanked it can still be seen. Immediately in front of the Mount is the central lawn, while to the right are the remains of the collegiate church. Of the college itself nothing is left.

There is also nothing left of the castle keep, and it is not even known where it was sited. It was probably intended to put it on the Mount, in place of the wooden structure, but this plan was not carried out. It is thought that the keep may have been at the s. end of the castle, overlooking the cliff; if so, it has of course long ago toppled over.

Compared with the rest, there is quite a lot left of the church; indeed the central tower, added about 100 years after the Conquest, is the most conspicuous part of the castle. The chancel arch was also built at this time, and is therefore pointed rather than rounded.

Near the main gateway is the entrance to a series of passages hewn out of the sandstone rock, which can be visited on application to a member of the staff looking after the castle. The purpose of this underground complex is not known; some say it was to serve as dungeons. It possesses the property of magnifying sound, so that the merest whisper is audible throughout the whole system.

After the castle, the best plan is to explore the eastern part of Hastings, including the Old Town. To the e. of the castle is a large grass-covered area called West Hill. Below the far side of the hill are St Clement's Caves, natural underground chambers in the sandstone, deep down. Formerly used by smugglers, the caves were much extended in the c. 19 by a Mr Golding, who, with his family, spent years tunnelling and burrowing and sculpting, until he had produced a veritable money-spinner of a tourist attraction. Now it belongs to Hastings Corporation, and there are conducted tours. The main chamber can be hired for parties; it makes an exciting place for a dance or a dinner. The caves were used as a huge air-raid shelter during the Second World War, and besides the sculptures by Mr Golding, the figures of Churchill and Montgomery have been carved out of the rock.

From the caves there is a way down the side of the hill to the Old Town, situated in a valley between West Hill and East Hill. Old Hastings has three large churches: St Clement's, the first that one comes to from the caves, and the borough church of Hastings; All Saints, across the way under the slope of East Hill; and the Roman Catholic church, St Mary Star of the Sea, with walls of unknapped flint. This church was founded by Coventry Patmore, the c. 19 poet, who lived for a time at Old Hastings House near by, the stables of which are now the Stables Theatre.

St Clement's was built at the end of the c. 14 in the Perpendicular style, or rather rebuilt after French raids. It suffered severe damage from bombs in the Second World War, but has been gallantly restored. Specially interesting are the medieval font, the c. 18 brass chandeliers in the nave, a modern carving in yew wood

of the Adoration of the Magi by John Reid, which is in the Lady Chapel at the e. end of the s. aisle, and a very small modern window, on the e. side of the porch, in memory of Mr F. H. Smith. In the s. aisle is a framed picture and sonnet in memory of Dante Gabriel Rossetti, who was married here in 1860. The sonnet, by M. Ambler, describes the Virgin as 'an angel-watered lily'.

All Saints was also rebuilt after the French raids at the end of the c. 14. It dates from about 1436, and is also in the Perpendicular style, but was savagely restored by Butterfield in 1870. Entrance is by the w. door, and owing to the severe slope of the ground there are steps up from the w. tower into the nave, and more steps up from the nave into the chancel. On entering one is immediately confronted by the e. window, at the top of the hill, so to speak, a lurid rendering of the Crucifixion, impossible to ignore. It was put up in 1861.

The tower is mercifully unspoilt. Its roof is a delight – as is the rhyming encouragement to bell-ringers on its N. wall, dated 1756. But the most dramatic feature of the church is, no doubt, the Doom, or representation of the Last Judgement, on the wall above the chancel arch. In this medieval painting Christ is shown sitting on a rainbow; from his wounds spring the stems of flowers, presumably lilies, emblems of the Resurrection. In the bottom right-hand corner the Damned are being hanged rather than roasted or boiled, as is more customary. The Devil appears to be acting as hangman. On either side of Christ are Mary his mother and St John, in an attitude of supplication.

A path leads up through the churchyard on the s. side of the church into a quaint street called Tackleway. The first part of the name derives from the Old French *tegill*, or tile. On the right are the houses, on the left the slope of East Hill, and at the far end of the street is the sea, although when we get there we find that the harbour intervenes, and that Tamarisk Steps lead down to the 'Stade', where stand the tall weatherboarded and tarred wooden huts in which nets and tackle are stored. A turn to the left here takes us along Rock A Nore Road to the Fisherman's Museum, housed in a former church, beyond which is the eastern end of Hastings: the road peters out and there is nothing except shingle and cliffs ahead.

At the other end of Old Hastings, George Street merges into the modern town. Pelham Crescent comes first, immediately below the castle – in fact yet another chunk of the castle's cliff had to be sliced off to make room for it. The crescent is a beautifully shaped row of houses built by Joseph Kay for the 1st Earl of Chichester in 1824, with a church at the centre and apex, St Mary-in-the-Castle; this is now a temple of a sect known as The Assemblies of God. Although handsome, the grey houses look rather dour.

In the Town Hall, in Queen's Road, is the Hastings Embroidery, which the visitor to the town should try not to miss. This wonderful piece of *appliqué* work was done by the Royal School of Needlework to mark the 900th anniversary of the Battle of Hastings. It is a pictorial history of England from 1066 onwards, and consists of 27 panels, each separately framed; its total length is over 240ft.

Next, the pier. This got off to a bad start: it was found that the site chosen was on a submerged forest, which made the task of driving in the piles difficult, and slowed up the work considerably. It was finally opened on August Bank Holiday 1872, a day of ceaseless rain. Thereafter, the history of the pier has not been without incident: it suffered severe damage by fire in 1917; and it was deliberately cut in two in the Second World War as a discouragement to would-be invaders – until the outbreak of war, steamers had called regularly. Now it is restored to a modicum of its former glory.

Opposite the pier is the White Rock Pavilion, a low white building that recalls Spain or Italy. It contains a good theatre and concert hall. Here, too, just after Christmas every year the leading competitors in the Hastings Chess Congress are to be seen locked in combat. Less exalted competitors play at the Falaise Hall, further up the hill. The congress is an important event in the international chess calendar, attracting top-class players from all over the world.

The White Rock Pavilion is named after the rock that once stood near the site, on the w. side of the old harbour entrance. Found to be in the way of a proposed promenade along the front, it was blown up in 1834 and the pieces removed.

Westward of the pavilion Hastings merges imperceptibly into ST LEONARDS, originally intended to be a select residential town on its own. With this in mind, James Burton, and his even more distinguished son Decimus, fired by the example of Brighton, laid out the beginnings of St Leonards from 1828 onwards.

The centre-piece is the Royal Victoria Hotel, down on the front, flanked by colonnaded terraces. This composition, even today, has a certain faded dignity – but it is all ruined by the huge bulging bulk of Marina Court, the 1930s horror adjoining it to the E.

Behind the Royal Victoria Hotel lurks Burton's Assembly Rooms, now the Masonic Hall, and rising up the hill beyond are attractive oval-shaped gardens with lawns, trees, shrubs, and winding paths. This was a quarry when the Burtons found it. At the bottom is a large pond. On either side are Maze Hill (E.) and Quarry Hill (w.). There are Burton houses here, and in Quarry Hill an ugly block of modern flats spoiling the view across the gardens from the other side.

At the top of Maze Hill is an archway, marking the northern entrance to the 'estate'. Beyond, St Leonards sprawls hugely; the little nucleus that started it all could easily be missed altogether by the traveller of today.

Hatchlands Surrey *see* **East Clandon**

Herstmonceux (*pron.* Hersmnsue)   E. Sussex   E5
This 'wooded hill of the Monceux family', who came from Normandy and acquired the manor here in the late c. 12, straggles along a busy road for three quarters of a mile, a mixture of ancient and modern: old brick and weatherboarded houses rub shoulders with modern houses, 'farm shops', cafés, and places selling Sussex trugs (sturdy wooden garden baskets made here for generations). Most of what is interesting lies almost two miles E. and s. of the main village, beyond the hamlet of Flowers Green, charming in appearance as in name. Here are the church and the castle.

The church is Early English and Decorated: compare the leaf-carving on the capitals of the N. and s. aisle pillars, the former bold, strong, and simple, the latter tight, formal, fussy. They and the Norman font, both of peculiarly Sussex design, look curiously modern.

The glories of the church are the Fiennes brass (1402) in the chancel floor, and the spectacular canopied tomb (1534) of Thomas, Lord Dacre, and his son Sir Thomas Fiennes. It is almost certain that the effigies don't belong to another family and were bought as job lots by the Dacres from Battle Abbey at the Dissolution. The whole monument was restored in 1970, and now glows with colour.

Other things to notice are the slender wooden wands on the pew-ends, each holding a single candle, and the Victorian dormer windows, which would look more appropriate on a seaside villa.

Opposite the church is the entrance to the castle, since 1948 the home of the Royal Greenwich Observatory. Boundary stones at the gate and elsewhere are carved with the device of a foul anchor, for the Observatory was formerly administered by the Admiralty. It is now run by the Science Research Council.

Built of rose-red brick, and set in greenly undulating parkland, Herstmonceux Castle rises perfect and complete from the waters of a wide, duck-dotted moat. Beyond it, past a number of huge and ancient sweet-chestnut trees, said to be older even than the castle, lie the formal Elizabethan gardens with clipped yews and intricate flower-beds, and walled gardens containing shrubs and herbaceous borders. Here in the upper rose garden is the Reclining Equiangular Sundial, erected in 1975 to mark the Observatory's 300th anniversary. Beyond these gardens, broad grass rides lead one seductively through clumps of flowering trees and, in spring daffodils, to a stream, lakes, and woods. A pretty folly – a miniature house in Queen Anne style – completes the view.

The castle was built by Sir Roger Fiennes in 1440, when brick was just coming into fashion. It must always have been more domestic than military, despite its turrets, battlements, and machicolations. In 1777 it was largely dismantled, the materials being used for Herstmonceux Place, a gloomy-looking mansion just s. of Flowers Green. Many legends of ghosts grew up

ABOVE: *Herstmonceux Castle* (A. F. Kersting)

BELOW: *Hever Castle* (A. F. Kersting)

about the ruins, encouraged no doubt by smugglers who found them a convenient hiding-place for contraband. The buildings were faithfully restored by two successive owners between 1913 and 1933.

The Observatory is a sympathetic and welcoming custodian. Its lesser buildings are screened by trees, while the six telescopes comprising the Equatorial Group on the hill to the E., with their bee-hive shapes and blue-green copper domes, positively enhance the view. Only the silo-like Isaac Newton telescope, its eighty-eight spiral stairs providing a laborious and ill-rewarded climb, strikes a discordant note. The two rooms in the castle open to the public contain an exhibition that tells the story of the castle and of the Royal Greenwich Observatory, and explains, simply and clearly, the development of astronomy. And almost everybody enjoys the map of the current night sky at the entrance, and the telescope lens in the room on the left, which plays strange tricks with your image as you approach.

Hever Kent D4

A hamlet hidden among lanes. The Early English church incorporates fragments of a Norman one. It has a Jacobean pulpit, and a matrix, or outline, of a priest brass at the w. end of the chapel behind the organ, the brass itself having disappeared. Its probable date was *c.* 1320. There are other brasses, including one in the chancel to Margaret Cheyne, d. 1419; Richard Clarke, date unknown but probably a little earlier; and Thomas Bullen, d. 1538, the father of Anne, Henry VIII's second wife, showing him in the robes of the Order of the Garter.

The Henry VIII Inn across the road was originally called the Bull. Later it became the Bull and Butcher, thus renamed, according to legend, by the local people

A Roman sarcophagus in the gardens of Hever Castle
(A. F. Kersting)

after Anne's execution. The legend, however, is certainly false.

Finally, the castle, where Henry pursued his sensational courtship of Anne. Built as a fortified farmhouse at the end of the C. 13 by William de Hever, it passed to the de Cobhams, and was further fortified at the end of the C. 14. In the following century it passed to Sir Geoffrey Bullen, or Boleyn, a wealthy London merchant; Thomas, Anne's father, was his grandson. Thomas's son and royal daughter were executed in 1536, and after his own death two years later the castle was seized by the King and bestowed upon his divorced fourth wife, Anne of Cleves. After various other changes of ownership it was eventually purchased in 1903 by an American, William Waldorf Astor, later 1st Baron Astor of Hever, whose descendants are still there.

Today the moated castle is externally much as it was in the C. 16, with its massive gatehouse, drawbridge, portcullis, and courtyard. Inside, however, most of the woodwork is of 1903–7, in skilful reproduction of the early-C. 16 style. There are also many interesting portraits, and touching Tudor relics such as the set of baby clothes made by the Princess Elizabeth, later Elizabeth I, for her half-sister Mary's unborn child, conceived only in that unhappy queen's imagination.

As for the C. 20, not only did Mr Astor carry out, through his architect F. L. (son of J. L.) Pearson, a major restoration of the castle; he also built a Tudor-style 'village' on the N. side, with access from the castle by a bridge over the moat; ornamental gardens, including an Italian garden containing statuary of a high quality; and a large lake formed by diverting and damming the River Eden, which passes close by.

In 1968 the river wreaked terrible vengeance by overflowing its banks and flooding the castle to a depth of over 6ft, causing it to be closed to the public for an entire season.

Hindhead Surrey A4

If one cannot entirely agree with the verdict of Cobbett – 'the most villainous spot that God ever made' – one can at least sympathize. Yet Cobbett's reasons and ours are quite different: to him, Hindhead was a wild and desolate place, abhorrent to one who liked his land fat and prosperous; to us, it is the wildness that is so desirable and the evidence of man's interference that is abhorrent.

Here, surely, the former amply compensates for the latter. The direfully-named Gibbet Hill to the N., and the vast horseshoe-shaped valley called The Devil's Punchbowl (both N.T.), comprise one of the most enthralling landscapes in the region. The hill, a mere 894ft/272m. high, nothing at all compared to the giants of the North and West, commands a view more immense than does many a Dartmoor tor or Pennine peak. In the distance are downs, while in the middle distance and foreground are wooded hills. Tracks lead off in all directions across the heaths. A clear day in autumn may be the best for this landscape, when the colours – gold, green, red, and the blue of the distance, accentuated perhaps by a recent shower – come close to perfection.

Horne's Place Kent *see* **Appledore**

Hove E. Sussex C6
This seaside town, adjoining Brighton (q.v.) to the w., is less brash and self-confident than its larger neighbour. It has an air of faded gentility. Standing on the enormously wide promenade at the top of the shingle beach, and turning one's back on the sea, one looks across a large green to a row of solid buildings in a mixture of styles and periods, including the modern: Embassy Court, a block of flats built, surprisingly, as long ago as the 1930s, lacks the elegance of its Regency neighbours, but looks more comfortable to live in. Brunswick Terrace and Brunswick Square were built in the 1820s, and mark the full flowering of Regency architecture; Adelaide Crescent, leading up to Palmeira Square, marks the transition from Regency to Italianate.

The town really comes to life further inland, where Regency gives way to Victorian and later. Pearson's splendid All Saints' church in Eaton Road, with its lofty columns and clean lines, raises the spirits; so, on the right day, can the Sussex County Cricket Ground just to the E. of it, where present-day Hove begins.

Hythe Kent G4
Like all the Cinque Ports except Dover, Hythe has been badly let down by the sea. Its proud church up on the hill, though parts of it are older, owes its most ambitious architecture to the prosperity of the Cinque Ports, which reached its height in the c. 13. At this time the sea came up to the very foot of the Greensand ridge on the slope of which the older part of the town is situated; now the town has to straggle across a third of a mile of flat land to reach the 'sea front', and there is no harbour.

The parish church grew with the early prosperity of the port. To begin with, it had a simple nave and chancel; this was in about 1100. In about 1165 N. and s. transepts and aisles were added, and a new chancel. But it was in the next century that the present magnificent chancel and s. porch were built, the tower erected, the arcading rebuilt, and the clerestory windows inserted in a heightened nave. The church we see today is of almost cathedral proportions and splendour. The chancel is well above the nave and seems to soar upwards to the gate of heaven. The s. porch, too, owing to the slope of the ground, has a many-stepped approach, so that by the time we reach the truly High Altar we are feeling humbled indeed.

The tower fell down in 1739 and the present tower is a mid-c. 18 replacement. The remarkable 'crypt' – more correctly the ambulatory or processional path, for it is a

vaulted passageway under the E. end and cannot be reached from the interior – contains 8,000 thigh bones and about 2,000 skulls. Their date and origin are the subject of learned discussion, and although no firm conclusions have been reached it seems most probable that they are medieval, and were at some stage dug up from the churchyard.

If Hythe was abandoned by the sea that had brought it prosperity, it was later rescued and redeemed by the Royal Military Canal, built in the early C. 19 as a defence against Napoleon; it bisects the lower town and gives it character, forming a sort of linear recreation area much appreciated by the townspeople and visitors. The shingle beach, when finally one gets to it, is pleasant enough on a fine summer's day, and the spluttering of rifles on the firing ranges to the E. (where there are two well-preserved martello towers) can hardly be heard above the noise of traffic and the sucking of the sea on the pebbles.

The lower town is undistinguished, but up the hill, where the church is, things improve; there are pleasant houses and gardens. Some of the narrow streets up and down have been closed to wheeled traffic, so that one can walk about in peace.

Further up still, in the former village, now superior suburb, of Saltwood, stand the beautiful ruins of SALTWOOD CASTLE, hidden from view behind trees and by the folds of the ground. Visitors enter by the barbican, then weave their way in and out of turrets, along sections of ramparts, and up and down innumerable steps. The gatehouse, with its massive flanking towers, built by Archbishop Courtenay at the end of the C. 14, is private, and indeed the whole castle is privately owned.

In the C. 12 Saltwood was the seat of Henry d'Essex, Warden of the Cinque Ports and Constable of England. He was also Henry II's standard bearer, but in a battle on the Welsh border he disgraced himself by throwing down the standard and running away. Saltwood was then given to Sir Ranulf de Broc, enemy of Becket. After Henry's impetuous outburst against Becket in 1170, the Archbishop's would-be murderers came to Saltwood to confer with de Broc about ways and means. The result of their conference is part of English history.

The castle nevertheless became the property of the Church, and remained such until the time of Henry VIII. In 1580 an earthquake did considerable damage, and thereafter the castle gradually diminished in importance and fell into disrepair. There was no major attempt at restoration until the C. 20, when Sir Phillip Tilden, the architect, was asked to supervise the work of restoring some of the buildings to the original medieval design. Much of the castle, however, is still in

Skulls in the crypt of Hythe church
(A. F. Kersting)

Ightham Mote: the moat and gatehouse
(Eric Chalker)

Ightham Mote: the courtyard
(A. F. Kersting)

ruins; one feels that just the right amount has been restored.

In the 'Motor House' several old cars are exhibited, including a 1923 Rolls Royce Silver Ghost, and a 1933 3½-litre Bentley.

Ightham (*pron.* Eye-tm)   Kent   E3

A bypass, still too close for comfort, has rescued this village from death by strangulation. A stream wanders slowly through the village centre; here are houses with half-timbering, much restored. A good example is Town House, while the c. 16 house opposite is a motor repair shop. One end of it sticks out awkwardly into the road; the man who built it in 1555 was rightly fined for thus obstructing the highway.

The church is up the hill to the N. It goes back to Norman times – witness the two small round-headed window-openings in the E. wall; but it was almost entirely rebuilt in the c. 14 and c. 15. The N. aisle was reconstructed in brick in 1639; it should be viewed from the outside, where the long, flat, mellow bricks can be appreciated.

Inside, the nave has a tremendous timber roof. There are four Jacobean box pews on the N. side of the aisle, the pews of the James family, who lived at Ightham Court and were lords of the manor for 300 years.

The monuments in the chancel are outstanding. Sir Thomas Cawne, d. about 1374, lies under the N. window, a full-length figure in armour. The window was provided for in his will, and has curious cork-shaped decorations in the tracery. The severe simplicity of this monument is in complete contrast with the ornateness of those on the s. side to the Selbys of Ightham Mote. There is a double monument to Sir William Selby, d. 1611, and his nephew, also Sir William, d. 1638. Near by, against the E. wall, is the prodigious monument to his wife, Dame Dorothy, d. 1641. She was an expert needlewoman, and two of her needlework pictures, 'The Golden Age' and 'The Gunpowder Plot', are themselves depicted in stone on the monument. There is a photograph of 'The Gunpowder Plot' on the w. wall of the church.

Beyond the church, the bypass, and the railway stands the substantial Ightham Court, where the James family lived. It has been much altered over the years since the c. 16, and even its impressive forest of 'Tudor' chimneys is in fact all c. 20 imitation.

Some two and a half miles s. of Ightham, past the hamlet of Ivy Hatch, is the moated fortified medieval manor house, IGHTHAM MOTE, in a secluded dell below the road. The oldest part was built by Sir Thomas Cawne in about 1340, and the word 'mote' almost certainly signifies that it was on the site of the meeting place of the Saxon moot, or council.

There have been various owners of Ightham Mote down the centuries, but the Selbys retained it the longest, from 1591 to 1868. In 1953 it was bought by

Mr C. H. Robinson, an American, in fulfilment of a boyhood dream.

Iron gates mark the entrance to the first 'courtyard', with a mounting block on the left, and the half-timbered stable block, now cottages, lining the roadway to the w. A bridge over the moat leads through the c. 15 gatehouse into the enclosed courtyard within. (On the outside of the gatehouse is a vertical opening in the wall; this is the 'parley-hole', with a right-angled bend in it, through which strangers could be required to establish their identity without being able to reply by hostile action.) The gatehouse door has linenfold decoration, unusual on an outer door.

Across the courtyard opposite the gatehouse is the oldest part of the house: the c. 14 Great Hall and solar, and behind the solar, the chapel with crypt below. The part to the right (s.) is c. 15, much altered over the years and now private. To the left (N.) is the timber-framed Tudor part added in the c. 16, containing a second chapel.

Visitors first pass through the entrance hall, where a painting of Ightham Mote by Sir Winston Churchill adorns one of the walls, into the Great Hall, a lofty room with its original oak roof timbers and a large c. 15 window facing back into the courtyard.

Below is the crypt, which has stone vaulting and double doors with more linenfold carving; from here a Jacobean stairway leads to the c. 14 chapel, with a timbered wagon roof.

Beyond the w. end of the chapel is the solar, which has the usual window through which the lord could see what was going on in the hall below, and a squint giving a view on to the altar in the chapel. The solar has oak timbers carried on a king-post, and an oriel window overlooking the courtyard.

A passage room leads from the solar into the Tudor chapel with lovely linenfold panelling and a painted barrel roof. It is not known why anyone felt the need to build this second chapel.

The door at the w. end of the chapel, which has five keyholes to ensure protection against surprise intrusion – the owners of the house adhered to the Roman faith after the Reformation – leads across the head of a stairway into the drawing room. The beautifully painted paper arras here is late-c. 17 work. Below this room is the so-called Billiard Room, formerly workshops, with a small doorway leading directly out to the moat.

Visitors are free to stroll round the garden and lawn. One of the two magnificent cedar trees here was unfortunately uprooted in the gales of January 1978; its sweet-smelling wood was pressed into service in the huge fireplace of the Great Hall.

Isle of Harty Kent *see* **Sheppey**

Jevington   E. Sussex   D6

A downland village near Eastbourne, once frequented

by smugglers coming up from Birling Gap. There are some picturesque houses, and, up a narrow dead-end lane, a church with a Saxon tower, dating from the first half of the c. 10. The old Saxon windows are now blocked up, but their outlines on the N. and s. sides about 12ft above ground can be clearly traced.

Inside the rather musty building there is a Saxon sculpture on the N. wall of the nave, near the tower, depicting Christ slaying the dragon of Evil. All periods of medieval architecture except the Perpendicular are represented in this church, and the c. 19 restorers were not idle – their straightening of the squints between nave and chancel was a particularly, and literally, misdirected effort.

Jullieberries Graves Kent *see* **Chilham**

Kidbrooke Park E. Sussex *see* **East Grinstead**

Kilndown Kent E4
This village, set on a ridge in beautiful Wealden countryside, is unremarkable in itself, but boasts a church that is unique, and yet comparatively little known. It was built in 1840 by Viscount Beresford of Bedgebury Park – in a fit of pique, it is said, because things were not done to his liking at Goudhurst, in which parish he resided. The church he built was a sandstone box, plain and unpretentious.

But Beresford's stepson, Alexander Beresford Hope, then an undergraduate at Trinity College, Cambridge, was cast in a different mould. Possessed of ample means, high ideals, and an inordinate admiration of c. 13 Gothic architecture, he was one of the founders of the Cambridge Camden Society, which stood, in architecture, for what the Oxford Movement stood for in theology. It was in the forefront of the trend now called the Victorian Gothic Revival. Hope was determined to transform Kilndown church into a fine demonstration of all its ideals, within the limits imposed upon him by the rather squat and discouraging pile erected by his stepfather.

The squatness was cleverly disguised by erecting a parapet round the roof. The spire was given crockets to add distinction. But this was nothing to what was done inside. The glass probably makes the strongest impact, and produces the strongest reaction, for or against. It is by Franz Eggert, of Munich, because Hope could find no one in England capable of giving him what he wanted. The windows on the s. side were all blown out by a bomb in the Second World War – glass by one German destroyed by another. The one window to St Jerome, a copy of the original, but quite different in style, was put in in memory of Margaret Ann Carwithen, who lived

in the parish and died in 1956 at the age of 15. Her faith and courage inspired her brother-in-law, James Davidson Ross, to write a book, *Margaret*, which was a bestseller for many years and brought many pilgrims to Kilndown.

Other remarkable features of the church are the brightly painted pulpit (to reach its dizzy heights the preacher has to climb steps leading up from the vestry), R. C. Carpenter's colourful screen, the brass chandeliers and lectern, both by Butterfield, Salvin's fixed stone altar (a copy of William of Wykeham's tomb in Winchester Cathedral), and the handsome reredos designed by Carpenter's partner, Slater. The tarsia, or mosaic woodwork, panels on display at the back of the church were originally presented by Beresford Hope to his old college at Cambridge, where they adorned the chapel; they are now on indefinite loan to Kilndown.

Bedgebury Park (*see* Goudhurst), where Beresford Hope's family lived, is a large mansion to the SE., now a girls' school, and is quite as extraordinary a building as Kilndown church.

Kits Coty House Kent *see* **Aylesford**

Knole Kent *see* **Sevenoaks**

Lamberhurst Kent E4
Once a centre of the Wealden iron industry, and famous as the place where the railings for St Paul's Cathedral were made, Lamberhurst is now a busy village on the A21 London–Hastings road. The traffic in the main street, all the noisier for having to climb a hill running up from the River Teise, is tiresome, yet the village remains remarkably unspoilt. On the E. side of the street are two old coaching inns, the Chequers and the George and Dragon. Next to the latter is Crown Chemicals, a thriving factory making veterinary products, of international repute despite its small size.

On the other side of the street is Coggers Hall, a timber-framed house of the c. 16, while all about are a number of tile-hung and weatherboarded houses and cottages. Then at the bottom the road forks: to the right it climbs in a series of attractive bends up the hill to Lamberhurst· Down, where there is a large green; to the left it continues towards Hastings and after half a mile reaches, on the left, the drive entrance to SCOTNEY CASTLE (N.T.).

Here are buildings of three periods. The earliest is the moated castle in the River Bewl valley, built by Robert Ashburnham during the Hundred Years' War in about 1378–80, only a few years earlier than Bodiam (q.v.), which has many structural similarities with it. Only one of the four original corner turrets is still standing at Scotney. Like Bodiam, Scotney was never put to the test of attack by the French.

In the early c. 15 Scotney passed to the Darell family, who lived there for 350 years. In the c. 17 they rebuilt much of it, and some of the new house still adjoins the

Scotney Castle nr Lamberhurst, showing the surviving turret (Janet & Colin Bord)

old castle ruins. Partly as a result of their rebuilding, the Darell family sank into debt, until finally in 1778 Scotney was sold to Edward Hussey, whose grandfather had moved to Sussex from Staffordshire in about 1700 and had acquired the house called Rampyndene at Burwash (q.v.), and an interest in the forge that supplied the famous railings.

It was Edward Hussey's grandson, also Edward, who in 1836 decided to build yet another home at Scotney.

This is the imposing building at the top of the hill, a Tudor-style house by Anthony Salvin, made from stone quarried out of the hillside between it and the castle. This house is still private, while in the outbuildings are the offices of the Kent and East Sussex Region of the N.T.

Apart from the buildings, Scotney has a beautifully landscaped garden. Most visitors start at the bastion on the edge of the lawn of the present house, where one looks down over the 'quarry' to the ruins of the old castle, glimpsed through trees, before walking down the paths through the well-planned mixture of deciduous and evergreen trees and shrubs that makes Scotney 'a place for all seasons'.

For the energetic there is a public footpath leading N. through delightful countryside from Scotney to Lamberhurst church, two miles away (and E. to Kilndown, q.v., a similar distance). Lamberhurst church is C. 14 and Decorated, with a Perpendicular SW. tower and a shingled spire. Inside, there is a pulpit dated 1630, with a sounding-board. The furniture has been turned round through 90 degrees in an attempt to overcome the liturgical problems set by the medieval plan.

Near by, on the edge of the golf course, stands Court Lodge, a plain Georgian-looking mansion, which may have been built from stones taken from the old Scotney Castle.

Lancing   W. Sussex   C6

This is a suburb E. of Worthing, between Sompting and Shoreham Airport, and extending from N. of the main coast road, the A27, to the sea. In the northern strip is the austere flint parish church, a Norman building originally but much altered in the C. 14.

Lancing would be an unexciting place were it not for the College, standing high up on a breezy hillside, the last spur of the Downs. The buildings look out across the valley of the River Adur and the harbour of Shoreham to the power station at Portslade and to Brighton beyond. Sometimes even the Seven Sisters can be seen, over 25 miles away. This view is to the SE. Then the eye travels round to the bare chalk hills above Shoreham, and on again to the dominant chimney of the huge cement works to the N. Due S. is Shoreham Airport, and beyond that the sea; not a beautiful but a satisfying landscape.

There is excitement in the view of the college buildings themselves as one approaches them from the road below, the soaring majesty of the immense chapel by R. H. Carpenter blending well with the quiet dignity of the adjacent school buildings, designed by his father, R. C. Carpenter. Here is Victorian Gothic architecture at its best.

The college was founded in 1848 by Nathaniel Woodard, then curate of New Shoreham, and is the first of the Woodard Schools, of which there are now 25. Woodard's lofty purpose was nothing less than 'the union of classes by a common system of education' – a form of comprehensive education, in fact, based firmly on the Christian faith, so that the dominance of the chapel is wholly appropriate. Inside, the promise of the exterior is fulfilled: its height, its confidence, its single-mindedness, take the breath away. It is, of course, all of a piece: C. 14 Gothic faithfully reproduced in the C. 19. Here is none of that variety, that jumble of periods, so characteristic of many English churches. Indeed for

all its magnificence the interior does display a degree of uniformity verging on monotony. Yet, take it all in all, this is an architectural experience it would be a pity to miss.

Leeds   Kent   F3

A pleasant if not very exciting village with an unusual and handsome church – unusual owing to its exceptionally massive Norman tower, surmounted by a comical wooden cap. The interior is very wide, with generous N. and S. arcades whose piers are C. 15. There are notable Meredith monuments in the N. chapel and an C. 18 candelabrum in the aisle. Across the entire width of the church is a glorious C. 15 screen.

Near the junction of the road that goes through the village with the A20 road to the N. is the entrance to the grounds of Leeds Castle. From the car park visitors must walk a considerable distance before they gain entrance to the castle itself, unless they are 'senior citizens' or disabled. The walkers make a wide detour by the 'duckery' and woods, in order to avoid the golf course, which lies across the more direct route.

A stone castle was first built at Leeds by Robert de Crèvecoeur, a Norman baron, during the reign of Henry I, on the site of a wooden Saxon castle built at the end of the C. 9. It occupied two 'islands' rising out of the marshy ground of the valley of the River Len, later dammed to form a large lake. The de Crèvecoeurs held Leeds Castle until after the Battle of Evesham in 1265, when Robert's great-great-grandson, another Robert, who had supported Simon de Montfort against Henry III, was forced to hand over Leeds Castle to the King's friend and supporter Sir Roger de Leyburn, whose son William conveyed the castle to Edward I in 1272.

At this time the defences of the castle were as follows: an outer and an inner barbican, a drawbridge, and a gatehouse at the southern end of the larger of the two islands; then an inner bailey surrounded by walls and leading to the main castle at the other end of the island; then another drawbridge leading to a fort, known as the Gloriette, on the smaller island to the N. Edward considered there was a danger of attackers crossing the moat direct to the inner bailey, bypassing the barbicans and the gatehouse; he therefore constructed an outer bailey surrounded by a high curtain wall rising sheer from the water, and placed five bastions at strategic intervals along its circuit.

Henry VIII was the next monarch to carry out important alterations. He added an upper floor to the Gloriette and thoroughly repaired all the rooms; he also built the Maidens' Tower to house the maids of honour, on the E. side of the inner bailey halfway between the gatehouse and the main castle. He was the last monarch to own the castle, for he gave it to Sir Anthony St Leger as a reward for services rendered. Later it passed to Sir John Culpeper, created Lord Culpeper by Charles I in 1644. He remained the faithful

mpanion of Charles II throughout the days of exile, nd at the Restoration Leeds Castle became his once ore. The 2nd Lord Culpeper's daughter and heiress arried the 5th Lord Fairfax, who thus acquired the astle. Later it passed, through the female line, to the ykeham-Martins. In 1822 Fiennes Wykeham-Martin odernized the main castle, at the same time restoring visually to its medieval appearance. He also put attlements on the Maidens' Tower.

The castle remained in the possession of the Wykeham-Martin family until 1926, when it was bought by Lady aillie. When she took it over the castle was in a bad ate of repair. Over the years she restored it to the state which is is now seen; most of the things in it, too, were ollected by her. She also set up the Leeds Castle oundation, to whom the property passed on her death 1974. The castle was first opened to the public in 976.

Having at last arrived, the visitor enters the castle by e gatehouse – the barbicans are ruined – and faces the ain building across the inner bailey, where there is ow a croquet lawn. At this closer view it can be seen at the 1822 rebuilding is, after all, distinctly of its me. The visitor is next directed to the right, through water gate to the Lower Walk, between the outer

bailey and the lake, passing under the walls of the Maidens' Tower. He then enters the castle proper by the vaults below the kitchen area, whence stairs lead up to the 'Heraldry Room'. From here he passes into the Gloriette by the enclosed bridge on the site of the old second drawbridge.

Several rooms are on view, and a variety of objects: tapestries, furniture, pictures, statues. The Seminar Room is used for medical research conferences, and has also been used for meetings of heads of state and foreign ministers. Impressive as the contents of the castle undoubtedly are, they do add up to rather a hotch-potch. But then the same might perhaps be said of the castle itself. It cannot be denied, however, that it has its thousands of devoted admirers, drawn chiefly no doubt by its romantic setting.

Leonardslee W. Sussex *see* **Cuckfield**

Lewes E. Sussex D5
This is the county town of East Sussex. Start at the castle: you command the whole Ouse valley down to Newhaven. Immediately below you (so it seems) is the High Street, a thin slit between the buildings. To your E. is Cliffe Hill, pitted with chalk quarries; half-way up

PPOSITE: *Lancing College chapel: the W end*
A. F. Kersting)

BELOW: *Leeds Castle*
(Leeds Castle Foundation)

The barbican, Lewes Castle

(A. F. Kersting)

is the monument commemorating the 17 Lewes Martyrs, burnt at the stake in Mary Tudor's reign. To your w. is the square tower of Lewes gaol. To your N. is Offham Hill, where Simon de Montfort defeated Henry III in 1264.

The castle itself was built by William de Warenne, who was given the town of Lewes by William the Conqueror. Originally it stood on two artificial mounds, one where the keep is now, the other on the far side of the bowling green to the E. The barbican, or gatehouse, is a c. 14 addition. The castle was never put to the test of a siege. In the c. 17 it was largely dismantled and the stone sold. Now it is looked after by the Sussex Archaeological Society, which has an interesting museum in the Elizabethan Barbican House.

Before the Normans came, Lewes had grown up as a settlement on the E.–w. route along the line of the Downs, where the river had to be crossed, compelling the traveller to descend momentarily from the easily traversed hills to the tiresome bogs and forests of the valley. Only later did it acquire importance as a stronghold commanding the approaches from the sea against the potential invader sailing up the estuary of the Ouse. Thus it became a crossroads; and a crossroads it remains to this day, although at last the longed-for bypass has arrived.

Lewes is a medieval town, much altered in Georgian times. The High Street, climbing the long steep hill westwards from the river, is picturesque and full of character. At the top, on the left, is St Anne's church, a large Norman building of flint, with a Norman font, restored in 1925, directly in front of you as you enter.

Below St Anne's to the s. are the large modern blocks of the County Council buildings. Although they are below the top of the hill, they still break the skyline from the valley, and must be accounted a visual disaster. Down the High Street on the other side of the road is Shelleys Hotel, an Elizabethan building with a Georgian front. The porch bears the date 1577. It used to be called The Vine, but from 1663 it was the residence of the

shelley family. Further down again, on the same side
as Shelleys, is the Grammar School, founded in 1512.
The present building, of knapped flint, dates only from
1851.

There are several buildings displaying mathematical
tiles. Shelleys Hotel has them, on the E. side of the building towards the back; so has St Michael's Old Rectory
(No. 120), Bartholomew House in Castle Gate, and the
house occupied by the offices of the Electricity Board,
on the S. side of the High Street.

St Michael's church, on the same side of the High
Street as the castle, is famous as one of the three round-
towered churches of Sussex, the other two being at
Piddinghoe (*pron.* Piddinghoo) and Southease, both in
the Ouse valley below Lewes. Inside is a monument
commemorating Sir Nicholas Pelham and his family.
He defeated a force of French raiders who in 1545 had
attempted to land at Seaford, then at the mouth of the
river. The punning inscription reads:

> What time the French sought to have sack't
>   Sea-Foord,
> This Pelham did repel 'em back aboord.

Across the High Street once more, we come to the
Bull Inn, c. 15 with late-c. 16 additions. Note the satyrs,
dating from about 1600. Here Tom Paine, the radical
reformer who later wrote *The Rights of Man*, lived from
1768 to 1774. Further up on the same side is The Bookshop, housed in a quaint timber-framed building also
dating from the c. 15.

At the bottom of the steep hill to the S. is the part of
Lewes called Southover. Here is Southover Grange,
built in 1572; John Evelyn, the c. 17 diarist, lived here
as a boy, and attended the grammar school up the hill.
The property is now municipally owned, its pleasant
lawns and gardens open to the public without charge.

In Southover High Street is Anne of Cleves House,
so called because that unlucky lady received it, along
with the rest of the property of Lewes Priory, as part of
the compensation she was paid for granting Henry VIII
a divorce. The front half of the building is early-c. 16;
the back is Elizabethan. It now houses a museum containing, among other exhibits, some interesting examples
of Sussex ironwork, including firebacks.

In 1077 William de Warenne and his wife Gundreda
had pulled down the wooden Saxon church of Southover
and built a stone church in its place. This is the church
of St John the Baptist, altered almost beyond recognition in Victorian times. They also gave a parcel of
land near by to Cluny Abbey in Burgundy, whose monks
proceeded to build the great priory of St Pancras, with
a church of cathedral proportions and monastic buildings
to match; all were almost totally destroyed at the
Dissolution in 1537, and now what little is left is sandwiched humiliatingly between the railway and the
bypass.

Limpsfield Surrey D3

A long village under the North Downs whose High
Street climbs the slope of the Greensand ridge to the S.
The church has a c. 12 tower and a chancel rebuilt in
the c. 13, and was much enlarged in the c. 19 by the
addition of a N. aisle by J. L. Pearson. Inside, the
building has an airy freshness in complete contrast to
the rugged austerity of the exterior.

To the S. of the church is a mixture of ancient and
modern buildings, the former well represented by
DETILLENS, a mid-c. 15 Wealden hall house encased in
Georgian brick in about 1725. The original hall has
been divided up ever since Tudor times, and now its
tie-beam and king-post are to be seen in the main bedroom upstairs. The visitor is shown this room and seven
others, as well as a unique collection of British and
foreign orders and decorations, and is also permitted to
wander round the pleasant garden. The house takes its
curious name from a Mr Detillins (the second 'i' later
changed to 'e'), who lived there in about 1700.

Further on again, beyond the golf course, is the village
of LIMPSFIELD CHART, with a church beside the common.
It is a late-c. 19 building; the tower was added in 1902,
and is spoilt by being surmounted by an absurd shingled
spire. There is a wooden painted reredos, in relief,
depicting the Adoration of the Magi – unashamedly
sentimental yet oddly moving. On the S. wall of the
chancel is a framed silk altar frontal apparently made
by Japanese Christians for one of their mission stations,
full of symbolism and very Japanese-looking indeed.

The houses lining the common give an impression of
a country village, but behind them suburbia takes over.

Lingfield Surrey D4

People who enjoy looking at churches will not wish to
miss Lingfield, a sprawling village that boasts, as well
as a popular racecourse, the county's only large Perpendicular church, built (except the c. 14 tower) by
Sir Reginald Cobham to go with the college he founded
here in 1431. Inside is a spacious nave with large chancel
arch, spacious N. aisle and shorter S. aisle. The bulge
half-way along the outside of the N. wall was for the
stairs to the rood.

There is a Royal Arms of Queen Anne on the S. wall
of the nave, a good Perpendicular font, a two-sided
lectern of uncertain date, some good choir stalls with
misericords, and, on the N. side of them, a c. 16 bench
with carved panelling – the choir stalls were evidently
cut out along this side to make way for it. But what
most people come to see are the monuments and
brasses.

The grandest monument is of Sir Reginald Cobham,
d. 1446, and his wife Anne, d. 1453, and they are in the
grandest position, in the middle of the chancel (cf. the
tomb of his kinsman at Cobham, Kent). Their alabaster
figures lie upon the tomb; his head rests on a Moor's
head, his feet on a 'sea-wolf', while hers rest on a wyvern,

LITLINGTON

or winged dragon. Sir Reginald's grandfather, the 1st Baron Cobham, d. 1361, lies on the other side of the screen in the N. chapel, an impressive figure in red, black, and gold. His son the 2nd Baron, d. 1403, is on the N. side of this chapel, depicted by a magnificent brass on the top of his tomb. Immediately E. of this is another tomb, with nothing to tell us whose it is, although it is probably that of Sir Thomas Cobham, d. 1471, and his wife Anne, great grand-daughter of Edward III.

There are also two very fine wall-monuments on the s. wall of the chancel, to Francis Howard, d. 1695, and his wife Mary, d. 1718, ornate yet restrained; her inscription contains a eulogistic catalogue of her virtues.

Sir Reginald Cobham's college was seized by the rapacious Henry VIII in 1544, and the buildings demolished in the C. 18, the only one spared being the Guest House, N. of the churchyard. It is now the public library. On the site of the college proper, W. of the church, is a fine brick and tile-hung house of c. 1700; the Horsham slates on the roof were probably taken from the old building, and the stone wall between the house and the churchyard is part of the original E. wall of the college.

The group of houses forming a miniature square at the s. approach to the church is the most attractive corner of Lingfield. There is little else to see – only The Cage and Cross at Plaistow Street. They stand under an oak tree with a hollowed-out trunk, opposite Gun Pit Road. The 'Cross' is a pillar said to have been built c. 1473 to mark manor boundaries, and the 'Cage' is the village lock-up stuck on to it in 1773 and last used in 1882, for the incarceration of poachers.

Litlington E. Sussex D6

This village under the Downs is smaller and less famous than its upstream neighbour Alfriston, but equally picturesque. To its E. the hills rise steeply; to its W. the Cuckmere river, tidal here, saunters muddily through the water meadows. From the footbridge near the s. end of the village one looks sw. across to the White Horse below High and Over, the charmingly named summit of the road from Seaford to Alfriston, or N. to Alfriston church spire peeping over the surrounding trees.

Litlington's small Norman church has a white weatherboarded bell-tower and shingled cap. There are Norman windows on the N. side of the chancel and a Norman s. doorway. Inside, the nave has a floor with a pronounced slope, and roof timbers that look extremely old. The rudimentary brownish-grey font is early-C. 16 but looks older. In the chancel, the Easter Sepulchre is of the same date, but the piscina is C. 13 and the double sedilia C. 15; both are so high that it is clear the floor must have been lowered at some later date.

Church Farm, next to the church, is very ancient. There is Caen stone in the walls of the house, which

Lullington's tiny church   (Janet & Colin Bord)

suggests that part of it may have been a Priest's House, since Caen stone was seldom used for secular buildings owing to its cost.

On the left as one goes s. through the village is the old rectory, a flint house with stone facings. From its cellars there is said to have been an underground passage leading to other houses in the village and used by smugglers. Certainly Litlington was on one of the smugglers' routes from Cuckmere Haven. Also on the left are nurseries and tea gardens, while on the right are the post office and shop, and the old inn, the Plough and Harrow, sensibly modernized.

The grand house of Litlington is Clapham House, among trees up the hill at the s. end. Mrs Fitzherbert, the Prince Regent's mistress, is said to have lived there for a time and been visited by him when he was staying at Brighton.

On the road from Litlington to Wilmington, where it climbs a spur of the Downs, a finger-post points to 'Lullington Church' on the left. A narrow path paved with bricks leads past two cottages; these and the church are the totality of LULLINGTON.

The tiny church turns out to be the chancel – or rather, part of the chancel – of a medieval church. It was restored in 1893; a photograph on the w. wall, taken to mark the occasion, shows a group of the local bigwigs, looking pretty pleased with themselves.

There are traces of the old nave on the ground in the churchyard, from the edge of which there is a view across the Cuckmere valley to Berwick, with the ridge of Ashdown Forest in the far distance.

Loseley House Surrey *see* Guildford

Luddesdown Kent E3

Here is a good example of the violent contrasts of Kent: Luddesdown is but four miles from, say, Strood, but what a difference! Reached by exceedingly narrow lanes with exceedingly high hedges, it is no more than a bare quorum of houses, a pub, and a church. The church is a Victorian rebuilding of a medieval one, high and handsome. Next door to it is Luddesdown Court, a house that has been continuously occupied for at least 900 years, since Odo, Bishop of Bayeux, who came over with the Conqueror, lived in it. And in spite of later additions and alterations the basic elements of the medieval manor house survive.

About a mile and a half s. in the same parish is the hamlet of Great Buckland, and beyond that at the side of a dead-end lane is Dode church, a tiny Norman building restored at the beginning of the c. 20. The village it served was wiped out by the Black Death in 1349.

Between here and Vigo Village, a vast housing estate ('a new concept in living') two miles sw., the lanes are, if possible, even narrower and more twisted, and the thick woods are infested with squirrels.

Lullingstone Kent D3

There is not even a village here in the beautiful Darent valley s. of Eynsford (in Eynsford itself see the remains of the Norman castle, the most complete example in England of the ring-work alternative to a keep castle); just a house or two, a farm or two, one of the most important Roman sites in the South of England, and one of the most intriguing – and deceptive – of Tudor manor houses, in whose grounds stands a small Norman church updated at various times from the c. 14 to the c. 18.

Owing to a perhaps merciful lack of bridges over the river from the busy road opposite, access by car is along a narrow lane from Eynsford, further down the valley, passing under an immense and rather handsome brick railway viaduct.

The Roman villa comes first, in place as well as time. It is hard by the river, over which a footbridge leads back on to the main road. These remains, in the care of the D.O.E., are roofed over, and walkways have been constructed to enable the visitor to view them from all sides and from above. Five distinct periods of building are evident: about A.D. 80–90, when the first small villa was built on or near the site of an Iron Age farmhouse; towards the end of the c. 2, when the modest villa was converted by a new owner into a luxury residence, being re-roofed with red and yellow tiles instead of thatch and provided with a bathing suite complete with under-floor heating; then about 280 (after being abandoned about 200), when the villa reverted to being a farmhouse, although on a much grander scale than before; in the c. 4, when the owners made many alterations, notably the laying of two mosaic floors; and about

370, when the then owners became Christian and built a chapel and ante-room, the only example in Britain of a chapel inside a Roman villa. Finally the villa was destroyed by fire early in the c. 5. This is a mere outline of the story, which can all be read in what is left today.

The c. 4 mosaic floors are among the best so far discovered in Britain. One of them shows Jupiter disguised as a bull and abducting Europa, who is riding on his back. Two cupids stand by; one of them is playfully pulling Jupiter's tail, while the other gestures with his arm. The other mosaic depicts Bellerophon mounted on the winged horse Pegasus and slaying the Chimera with his spear.

Arranged in cases beside the upper walkway, or balcony, are various objects found in or around the villa: two busts of the owner's ancestors – these are plaster casts of the marble originals, which are now in the British Museum; pottery; implements; and a sandal, the leather of which is entirely worn away by the centuries, leaving only the iron nails.

A few hundred yards further on to the s. stands Lullingstone Castle, which looks at first sight like a Queen Anne mansion, but which in fact dates from the reign of Henry VII. It was built by Sir John Peche, friend to both Henry VII and his son Henry VIII – the latter often visited him here. The massive brick gatehouse is clearly Tudor, but the rest of Peche's manor house is concealed behind a Queen Anne façade.

Lullingstone Castle has been in the same family ever since it was built. It passed from Sir John Peche to his nephew Sir Percyval Hart, and then by direct descent down the male line until the death of Percival Hart in 1738, when it passed to his son-in-law, Sir Thomas Dyke, from whom the property has passed ever since in direct line of succession in the Hart Dyke family.

Percival Hart was a fervent supporter of the Jacobites and friend of Queen Anne. It was he who built the beautiful Queen Anne façade seen today. Until the time of his successor there was an inner gatehouse and a moat round the house; but Sir Thomas Dyke pulled down this second gatehouse and filled in the moat.

From the front door one passes immediately through the porch into the Great Hall, a Queen Anne room containing family portraits and a painting of the house as it was before the alterations carried out by Sir Thomas Dyke, showing the two gatehouses and the moat.

Leading off the Great Hall is the State Dining Room, with Queen Anne panelling and more family portraits; there is also a jousting helmet of Sir John Peche's, used by him at tournaments held in the time of Henry VII and Henry VIII, at which he excelled. Above a massive and elaborate Jacobean sideboard is a French bracket clock in the style of Louis XV.

One next passes through a recess forming a small dining room furnished in c. 18 style to the Grand Staircase, the treads of which were made specially shallow to enable the corpulent Queen Anne to mount them. The State Drawing Room at the top of the stairs dates from Elizabethan times – witness the barrel ceiling. The panelling was added during Queen Anne's reign, and her portrait hangs on the E. wall, reminding us that she was certainly no beauty. Among many interesting things in this room is a doll that belonged to her in her childhood.

Leading off the State Drawing Room is the Queen's State Bedroom, with an exquisitely carved four-poster bed. The Woman of the Bedchamber's room and the Queen's tiny powder closet lead off the main room, on the N. side. A short passage leads back through an ante-room, containing various c. 17–c. 19 relics, to the Grand Staircase.

Outside there is a vast lake to the s. of the house, while on the N. side of the lawn is the little Norman parish church of Lullingstone. There is little left that is Norman, although the ground plan is the original one except for the N. chapel added in the c. 16 by Sir John Peche to accommodate his own tomb. He also erected the screen, which incorporates the motifs of the Tudor rose for Henry VIII, the pomegranate for Catherine of Aragon, and the peach stone representing his own name. On the s. side of the altar is the tomb of his nephew Sir Percyval Hart and his wife, beneath a canopy reaching almost to the ceiling, while the whole of the w. wall of the N. chapel is a memorial to Percival Hart, 1666–1738, 'the munificent repairer and beautifier of this church'.

Lullington E. Sussex *see* **Litlington**

Lydd Kent G5

A name associated in most people's minds with the cross-Channel airport that lurks almost unnoticed to the E. of the little town. The borough of Lydd itself, which, like New Romney, gradually declined after the course of the River Rother was diverted by the violent storm of 1287, is now little more than a village separated from the sea by the ever-lengthening bank of shingle known as Dungeness. Even the fields between are shingly.

Lydd, however, is like the curate's egg – excellent in parts. The High Street, for instance, has a number of good buildings, and the handsome c. 18 Town Hall puts New Romney's entirely in the shade. At the very w. end of the street Tourney Hall, early-c. 18 and rather grand, is better looking than its rather drab surroundings.

Then there is Coronation Square, s. of the church, really just a small triangle, but attractive; out of it runs Skinner Road, leading past The Rectory, dated 1695, to The Ripe, a huge triangle of grass with houses round the edges. But the jewel of Lydd's crown is the immensely long church, the 'Cathedral of the Marsh'. Not only is it immensely long; its Perpendicular tower is immensely tall. It was raised to its present height of

132ft early in the c. 16, when Thomas Wolsey was rector here.

One enters by the w. door, or, to be more precise, by one of the w. doors, for the tower has two doorways under a single arch. From here one looks straight up to the three bright lancets at the E. end, with no screen to interrupt the view. Nave, aisles, chancel: all quite un-cluttered. Some of the nave piers lean outwards, but what is chiefly noticeable is their fine proportions. The church is mainly Early English, but the variety of window traceries confuses the issue, many of the windows having been inserted, or altered, at later dates. Of the pillars of the arcades only the four pairs at the eastern end are Early English; w. of that they are Perpendicular, and have much larger, square, bases.

The chancel was destroyed by a bomb in the Second World War. Here at last the opportunity this disaster afforded to do something worthwhile has been seized. The modern chancel by Anthony Swaine is spacious and beautiful, and the glass by Leonard Walker in the three lancets really exciting.

The fluted bowls in the double piscina in the s. chapel should be noticed, and the tomb in the N. chapel of Clement Stuppeny, d. 1608, which was used for just the same purpose as that of Richard Stuppeny at New Romney, Kent, that is, as a council table. Those of a literary turn of mind will surely enjoy the touching if leaden verses on the wall monument in the vestry, commemorating Anne Russell and her four-year-old son.

No one must leave the church without seeing the unmistakable fragment of the old Saxon church, at the w. end of the N. aisle, its rough wall and the modern font below it combining well.

DUNGENESS, four miles SE., a dreary waste of shacks and shingle, has its own forlorn fascination. After the bird sanctuary the road forks right for the grey bulks of the power stations; Dungeness 'B', by far the larger and more powerful, can be visited – on Wednesday after-noons, at the time of writing.

The road that goes straight on leads to Dungeness itself, the beach, the huts, the lifeboat, the fish stalls, and the two lighthouses: the concrete modern one (1960), with black and white bands, looks as slim as a pocket torch; the old one (1904), brick, all black and tapering, is open daily, and from its top there is a good view of the sweeping coastline. The stump of the even older one (1792) stands near by, now turned into staff dwellings.

Lympne (*pron.* Lim) Kent G4

A nice blend of ancient and modern, on a hill over-looking Romney Marsh and the English Channel, and a view, if the light is right, of the French coast.

Among the more ancient things is the church, with a square Norman tower of *c.* 1100. The present chancel, built in the c. 13, occupies the site of the Norman nave. The present nave and N. aisle in the Early English style

The modern lighthouse at Dungeness nr Lydd   (A. F. Kersting)

were added in the same century, and the tower is roughly midway between the E. and w. ends.

In the tower is a steep iron staircase of 32 steps that goes spiralling up to the belfry, a journey that those subject to vertigo may prefer not to make. There were entirely necessary restorations in both the c. 19 and c. 20, which have done no visual damage. A lovable church this – but the large empty tower space intervening between the nave and the quite long chancel, and a N. aisle very much out at the side, must make it liturgically awkward at times.

Lympne Castle, hard by, is both ancient and modern. The oldest part is a section of the square tower next to the church, which is thought to date from the c. 13. (The former castle on the site was a residence built by Archbishop Lanfranc at the end of the c. 11 for the Archdeacons of Canterbury.) The kitchens below and the Great Hall alongside them are part of the 'modernization' of c. 1360. The Great Hall will at that time have had a central fireplace, the present one at the end of the room being a Tudor innovation. The Great Tower at the w. end of the building is partly c. 14 and partly c. 15.

The castle was completely restored at the beginning of the c. 20 by Sir Robert Lorimer, who also built on a new wing N. of the Great Tower. During the restoration traces of old buildings, such as a c. 13 hall, came to light, but unfortunately no records were kept. Lympne Castle is just a trifle dull, but amply makes up for it with the view from the Great Tower.

Below the castle the ground drops steeply, through woods, to the Royal Military Canal at the bottom. Between woods and canal is the most ancient part of Lympne, the remnants of the Roman Fort of the Saxon Shore, now known as STUTFALL CASTLE, a name, ironically enough, derived from the Saxons. This large fort covered 10 acres; now all that can be seen are a few lumps of masonry. A footpath leading down on the E. side of the castle approaches close to them; it is steep, rough, somewhat overgrown in places, and has stiles.

Modern Lympne is N. of the village, and includes an airport now known as Ashford Airport, which sounds more important.

Maidstone Kent E3

This is the county town, on the River Medway, a large and still growing place. Here is hustle and bustle; here accents approaching those of London are heard. Yet for all that Maidstone is unmistakably a provincial town.

The parish church of All Saints, the Archbishop's Palace and Stables, and the College, make a pleasing group of Kentish ragstone buildings in Mill Street, where the River Len runs into the Medway. All Saints is a huge and impressive building all in the Perpendicular style, with an exceptionally wide nave, and wide, rather squat, Perpendicular windows filled with undistinguished Victorian glass. The tower is only 8oft high, although it once had a wooden spire of 100ft, destroyed by lightning in 1730. The church was built as a collegiate church; chancel and nave were separated by a great rood screen, beyond which the canons sang their services. The nave was for the people. The impression of spaciousness is enhanced by the uniformity of the architectural style, and by the removal in the c. 19 of a good deal of c. 18 clutter.

The present rood screen is, of course, Victorian (Pearson, 1886). The font is Jacobean; the marks of the original iron hinges of the lid can still be seen. Some of the most interesting things are concentrated in the chancel: the four c. 15 sedilia, all on one level, which is unusual; the huge brass, almost entirely worn away, of the founder, Archbishop Courtenay; and the 20 late-c. 14 misericords of the choir stalls, one of which – in the back row on the N. side – portrays the college cook, holding a meat hook and a ladle. The early-c. 20 murals, however, are rather weak.

The remains of the college for secular canons founded by Archbishop Courtenay in 1395 are opposite the s. side of the church, and include a very fine gatehouse, while on the N. side is the Archbishop's Palace, a medieval building with Elizabethan additions. This now belongs to the Borough of Maidstone, and members of the public can wander round it at will, provided it is not being used for a function of some sort. From the back there is a good view across the River Medway.

On the other side of Mill Street are the palace stables, a long low c. 15 building in Kentish ragstone, behind which are some gardens with seats. The building itself was bought by the town in 1913, and now houses the Tyrwhitt-Drake Museum of Carriages, which is well worth a visit. Its founder, Sir Garrard Tyrwhitt-Drake, limited the collection to vehicles that are not mechanically propelled and were, preferably, made by a recognized coachbuilder. Within these limitations, however, a wide variety of vehicles is displayed, from dress coaches such as that built for the Duke of Buccleuch in 1830 to the humble 'growler' or the Irish 'jaunting car'.

The centre of Maidstone, once the river is left behind, is not exciting, and has been rendered even less so by the modern incursion of glass and concrete, which reduces all towns to a dull uniformity. The museum, badly and deliberately damaged by fire in 1977, should be visited, as it houses a collection of more than average interest. So should Mote Park, a vast green open space on the E. side of the town, not far from the centre. It was once the private park of Mote House, now a Cheshire Home, and contains a large artificial lake made by widening the River Len.

The college cook, Maidstone (N.M.R.

Modern Maidstone has also spread out far enough to include ALLINGTON CASTLE within its boundaries. This is situated in a bend of the Medway to the N., and i approached off London Road (A20). Fortified in 128 by Sir Stephen Penchester, it later belonged to Si Henry Wyatt, who at the end of the c. 15 partially converted it into a Tudor manor house. Here his son Sir Thomas Wyatt, the poet and courtier, was born i 1503. Sir Thomas was a close friend of Henry VIII an often entertained him at Allington; in the Great Hal is the table at which they will have shared many a meal It was he, too, who introduced the handsome brown pigeons whose descendants still flutter and strut about

Sir Thomas's son, Sir Thomas Wyatt the Younger led the rebellion against Queen Mary in 1554 tha ended in ignominious defeat and his own execution on Tower Hill. The downfall of its owner signalled the demise of the castle, which gradually became more and more ruinous, until in 1905 Lord Conway bought it together with the estate, for what even then was the paltry sum of £4,800. Over the years, however, he spent some £70,000 restoring it. Finally his daughter sold it in 1951 to the Carmelites, the present owners.

The Mardens (E., N., W., Up) W. Sussex A5
The Mardens are all in deep South Downs country between Chichester and Petersfield. In the days when people went about on foot and used footpaths, the Mardens were grouped reasonably close together; bu now that we seem to need roads, one covers a considerable distance to see all four of them.

E. MARDEN is thought by some to be the 'prettiest' Perhaps it is, with its small church perched above a little green and a few cottages. The thatched well-head on the green itself adds picturesqueness to the scene

Mayfield: the chapel of the Convent (A. F. Kersting)

But despite this idyllic core, the village has its less attractive perimeter: stuccoed houses with woodwork painted the wrong colour, some unsightly farm sheds and pylons. However, the brick and flint predominate. The exterior of the mainly c. 13 church is of flint, apart from the dumpy weatherboarded 'tower', and so is the attractive St Peter's Cottage opposite, dated 1728. The interior of the church is of chalk, plastered over. There is a chubby, robust font of chalk with a lead lining, perhaps of the c. 12 but with a modern base; and a pretty little organ that once belonged to Prince Albert, who used to play it at St James's Palace.

At N. MARDEN there is no village – just church and farm. The church is approached along a fenced-off footpath beside the muddy farmyard, and is a tiny Norman building with nave and apsidal chancel rolled into one. The best feature is the s. doorway, made of Caen stone and elaborately carved in the late-Norman manner. It must have been a laborious business to get the stone up here from the coast. The lancets at the E. end were fussily restored by the Victorians on the outside and look quite absurd. However, this church, although clearly 'redundant', is well cared for; will its mute but strong appeal continue to be heeded?

UP MARDEN, also church and farm only, is if anything even more remote. This time the church is c. 13, and more purely so than N. Marden's is Norman. The Early English lancet windows are refreshingly simple.

Only the pulpit jars, and the white paint on the tie-beams. This church, and the churchyard, is well cared for. It was not always so: we read that in the c. 17 the chancel was 'indecently and beastly kept' and that 'the pigeon dung and other filth' gave off such an 'ill and noysome smell' that people were 'inforced to stop their noses or carry flowers in their hands'.

W. MARDEN is the largest of the Mardens, and, despite its lack of a church, really the best. There is no discordant note; even the petrol pumps are discreetly hidden away, with just an arrow at the roadside to indicate their presence. The village, mostly of flint and brick, runs up a slope at right angles to the Chichester–Petersfield road. One row of cottages is thatched. Near the top the slope becomes a hill and the road is shaded by beech trees until it emerges on to a plateau of the Downs. Here is the hamlet of Forestside, and soon after that comes the London to Portsmouth railway and the Hampshire border.

Margate Kent *see* **Thanet**

Mayfield E. Sussex E4
This hilltop village of the Weald commands splendid views, and is itself good to look upon. It stands on a ridge, and the spire of its parish church can be seen from many points in the surrounding countryside. On closer inspection the village fulfills all expectations: there is

weatherboarding, half-timbering, tile-hanging – buildings of almost every period and material are represented, all blending into a harmonious whole.

The building of outstanding interest is undoubtedly the Old Palace. This is at the E. end of the High Street, on the N. side, and has a Tudor gatehouse. It is open to inspection by visitors on request, and preferably by appointment.

This was once a residence of the Archbishops of Canterbury. It was founded in the C. 10 by St Dunstan, and it is here that he is supposed to have been visited by the Devil and to have seized a pair of tongs and pinched the Devil's nose, to such good effect that the Devil took one mighty leap to the site of the present town of Tunbridge Wells, where he plunged his face into water; hence, they say, the chalybeate springs that have since been discovered there.

Nothing remains from the days of the great saint: a pair of tongs is shown to visitors, but no extravagant claims are made for them. The oldest part of the present buildings is the courtyard, round which the palace was built and which dates from the C. 13. This unfortunately has been roofed in with a rather low and oppressive ceiling in recent times, and given a fireplace to match. But most of the original C. 13 walls are intact. In this room are a C. 13 Madonna and Child, an almanack of 1705, which was found folded up in the mortar of the wall during C. 19 restoration work, and a Spanish wooden altar with elaborate carving, now a sideboard, which it is thought may have been washed ashore from the Spanish Armada. It is an exquisite piece of work, but immensely heavy, and surely an unsuitable object to take to sea. Here also is a bench that once belonged to William Pitt, and bears his initials.

Thomas Cranmer was the last Archbishop of Canterbury to own the Palace. In 1545 he made it over to Henry VIII. Later it became the property of Sir Thomas Gresham, the founder of the Royal Exchange. His crest, a grasshopper, appears on the fireplace in the Visitors' Dining Room. The sword with which he is supposed to have been knighted by Elizabeth I lies beside St Dunstan's tongs. Whether or not this is really the actual sword, it is at least of the right period.

After Sir Thomas's time, the palace gradually went into a decline. By the second half of the C. 18 it was a ruin, and so it remained until 1863. In that year it was purchased by the Duchess of Leeds and given to Mother Connelly, founder of the Convent of the Holy Child Jesus at St Leonards-on-Sea, on condition that the buildings at Mayfield should be restored. It must have been a daunting task, but Mother Connelly and her nuns were equal to it. By their enthusiasm, and the support of Roman Catholics here and on the Continent, the necessary money was raised within two years. Meanwhile much work was already proceeding, under the direction of E. W. Pugin, and by 1865 the restoration was nearing completion.

Until then, apart from the removal of some beautiful stone stairs in the entrance hall and their replacement by some clumsy pillars, Pugin's work had been sympathetic and even sensitive, but during the succeeding years he could not resist making a lot of fussy additions to the great C. 14 hall, which had been turned into the chapel of the convent. Mercifully these have now been removed, and either not replaced at all or replaced with modern work that blends harmoniously with the medieval and the best of the Victorian restoration. The result is impressive. There is a great feeling of space, enhanced by the 40ft span of the three tremendous arches, which were intact even when the buildings were at their most ruinous. They spring from corbels supported by grotesque figures.

Beside the convent itself, and connected with it, is the Roman Catholic girls' boarding school of St Leonard's, housed in undistinguished Victorian buildings with many modern additions.

Near the Tudor gatehouse in the High Street is the convent guest-house, a grey stone building with a handsome doorway. Opposite is Walnut Tree House, C. 14, half-timbered and close-studded. Next to it is the Middle House Hotel, an Elizabethan half-timbered house built by Sir Thomas Gresham for his retinue. Back on the N. side of the street is the village sign; an inscription on its pillar tells us that Mayfield was a centre of the Sussex iron industry, and quotes a local rhyme:

> Master Huggett and his man John
> They did cast the first cannon.

The parish church is a little further along on the same side of the street, standing back. It is really very close to the Old Palace, an ironic comment on denominational differences. Above the doorway of the porch is an old scratch-dial. The porch itself is C. 15, with rib vaulting and amusing bosses. Within, we are struck by the great size of the church. On both sides the nave has four bays, and at its eastern end a fifth that comes to an abrupt stop before it is completed; was this the result of simple miscalculation?

On the S. wall near the door is a C. 17 monument to Thomas Ainscombe, who died in 1620. There is a rustic-looking octagonal font of 1666, a Jacobean pulpit with arabesque carving, and an elegant C. 18 communion rail.

In the nave are C. 18 candelabra, while on the floor are two contrasting iron grave slabs. The name of the deceased on both slabs is Thomas Sands, but the slabs themselves are very different: the one dated 1668 is crude in the extreme – it must surely have been done by some apprentice; the other, dated 1708, is very grand and is embellished with an elaborate coat-of-arms. It is pleasing to imagine they were both done by the same hand.

Mereworth (*pron.* Merryworth)   Kent   E3

In the 1720s John Fane, later 7th Earl of Westmorland, replaced the medieval manor house at Mereworth with a brand new castle. The architect was Colen Campbell, who designed it as a copy of Palladio's Villa Rotunda at Vicenza in Italy. As the hamlet of Mereworth and its medieval church were inconveniently near, Fane had them knocked down and removed to a new site at a respectful distance to the N. The old church was replaced by an up-to-date building based on St Paul's, Covent Garden, and St Martin-in-the-Fields, with a Palladian interior.

Nowadays, the 'Castle', an Italian villa in mid Kent, may be seen through firmly shut gates beside the A26 road. On the other side of the road are two large lodges, which were separated from the rest of the drive by a later re-alignment of the road – a tiny revenge for the high-handedness of the 7th Earl.

It is possible to make a circuit of the park by continuing past the gates towards Wateringbury and taking the next turn to the right, then right again along Park Road, a country lane, which runs up a hill with the woods of the park on the right. At the top of the hill,

behind a tangle of barbed wire, nettles, and brambles, stands a ruined triumphal arch with huge columns and ornate Corinthian capitals. The park of Mereworth Castle behind it shows signs of considerable neglect.

Further along on the left is the large C. 13 church of EAST PECKHAM, now redundant, closed, and standing in an overgrown churchyard. On the far (S.) side is an old wooden stable once used for the horses of the church-goers; this also is locked. More right turns lead back to the A26 road, from which it is easy to find the village of Mereworth.

Here things are in better order. There are, naturally, no very old houses, and there are several new ones: bottom half brick, top half weatherboarding. A group of these stands opposite the C. 18 church already mentioned. This is an interesting building, quite as incongruous in these surroundings as the 'Castle' itself. The identity of the architect is not known. The steeple at the w. end consists of a tower supporting a lantern supporting a spire, a most imposing structure. The body of the church has immense overhanging eaves, and a large semi-circular porch with Ionic columns extending from the w. end.

Mereworth Castle, designed by Colen Campbell after Palladio   (A. F. Kersting)

Michelham Priory seen across the lake

(A. F. Kersting)

Inside, the church has columns painted to look like marble, continuing all the way round; at the E. and W. ends they are incorporated in the walls. The gallery was once the 'Castle pew'; part of the wall above has sham organ pipes painted on it. High up at the E. end is some golden C. 16 glass brought from the castle that Fane's replaced.

On the S. side there is an elegant C. 18 font, and W. of it a chapel containing monuments brought over from the old church: the huge, ornate, brash tomb of Sir Thomas Fane and his widow; the C. 16 tomb of Sir Thomas Nevell, by no means self-effacing but quite over-shadowed by Sir Thomas Fane; the C. 15 effigy of a knight; the badly damaged brass to Sir John de Mereworth (d. 1366) on the floor towards the E. end of the chapel, with legs missing and much of the Norman-French inscription defaced; and, most notable of all because most rare, an early-C. 16 'heart shrine', built to contain an embalmed heart – on the floor of its recess is a carving of a heart held by an angel's hands.

Michelham Priory E. Sussex E5

In the unexciting plain N. of the Downs near Hailsham, on the banks of the Cuckmere river, stand the remains of this C. 13–C. 14 priory, administered with great

expertise by the Sussex Archaeological Society.

When the Augustinian canons acquired the property in the C. 13 the river had already been used to form an island site. This may have been occupied by a Norman manor house: during recent excavations some remains were found that may have belonged to such a building. Of the priory church itself nothing whatever is left above ground.

We enter the grounds by the gatehouse, built by Prior Leem in about 1395; its upper rooms have hearths now furnished with Sussex ironwork, and the walls display brass rubbings from Sussex churches. In the dove-cote near by, built in about 1800, there is a shop selling guide-books and postcards, as well as pottery, examples of Sussex craftwork, and so on.

Facing us is a long building. To grasp the lay-out of the original priory it is first necessary to identify the site of the cloister. This is a square space on one's left as one faces the entrance to the building, and has a yew hedge enclosing it on two sides, while within it is a C. 13 well. To the N., that is, beyond the yew hedge that runs parallel to the building, is the site of the church, the plan of which is clearly marked out on the ground; beyond the other hedge was the chapter house, with dorter, or dormitory, above. The part of the building n the left of the entrance still has its original medieval walls, and was the refectory or dining hall, while on the fourth side, immediately in front of the present entrance, would be the store rooms, with guest rooms over. The present entrance leads into a vaulted room that completes the ground floor part of this western range – it may have been the parlour, where guests were first admitted, or possibly the buttery or food store; over it is the prior's chamber. To the right of the entrance is the purely Tudor wing, standing on the site of the original prior's lodging, with cellarage below.

After the Dissolution of the Monasteries the buildings passed into lay hands, and the former refectory was turned into a farmhouse. Whereas the refectory had reached from ground to ceiling without a break, the farmhouse consisted of three floors. The main Tudor wing, on the right, was built about 1595 by Herbert Pelham, who also took over the farmhouse and incorporated it into his new home.

Inside, the lay-out of the existing building is clearly explained. It contains a full and fascinating collection of exhibits of all sorts. Indeed, if one had a criticism it might be that there is almost too much to see, and that the variety of periods from which the exhibits are drawn tends to compound the bewilderment caused by the architectural confusion of the buildings.

Outside again, there is more to see. Beyond the E. end of the vanished church is a fish stew, the pond where the canons stored the fish they had caught in river or moat. In the barn yard are Kent and Sussex wagons; there is a small museum of blacksmith's implements; and in the great Tudor barn itself is a continuous exhibition of pictures, which, incidentally, are for sale. There is a well-equipped restaurant. Finally, one can wander round the spacious lawns and inspect the moat and the various water-birds, and visit the water-mill, now back in operation and producing flour, also for sale.

Midhurst W. Sussex A5

This is a small town in the valley of the River Rother, which cuts a way between the Upper Greensand hills around Haslemere to the N. and the chalk Downs to the s. Running alongside the huge car park at the N. end of North Street is a causeway leading across a marshy field and over the river to the ruins of Cowdray, built from the 1520s onwards on the site of an earlier house. The new house was started by Sir David Owen, continued by Sir William Fitzwilliam, and completed by Sir Anthony Browne (*see* Battle), Sir William's half-brother, who took over in 1542. Sir Anthony's son, also Sir Anthony, succeeded on his father's death in 1548, and was created 1st Viscount Montague in 1554. Thereafter the Montagues lived at Cowdray until the disastrous year 1793, when the last of the line, the young 8th Viscount, was drowned whilst attempting to shoot the Laufenberg Falls on the Rhine, only about a week after Cowdray itself was gutted by fire; almost all the

contents were destroyed and the building was left a shell. Thus was fulfilled, although tardily, the dire curse pronounced by an irate monk on being turned out of Battle Abbey, that Sir Anthony's house should perish by fire and water.

After the death of the 8th Viscount the estate passed to his only sister, who married William Poyntz. Their two young sons were drowned before their very eyes at Bognor in 1815, and their daughters eventually sold the estate to the 6th Earl of Egmont, whose nephew, the 7th Earl, built the Victorian mansion that is the present Cowdray Park. In 1908 the 8th Earl sold the house and estate to Sir Weetman Dickinson Pearson, who carefully restored the ruins of the old Cowdray. In 1927 he was created Viscount Cowdray; his grandson, the 3rd Viscount, is the present owner of Cowdray Park and the estate.

The A272 road from Petworth approaches Midhurst through Cowdray Park, with the Victorian mansion hidden from view away to the left. Polo is played here in the summer, and is a great public attraction. The park is also large enough to accommodate a golf course; and there is plenty of room for motorists to pull off the road and picnic. Much of the park is under cultivation nowadays, which makes it less visually attractive.

The old Cowdray is a recognizably typical Tudor building: tall gatehouse, courtyard, entrance porch, hall and chapel, in brick partly faced with stone. Over the porch doorway, near the s. end of the E. range, are the arms of Henry VIII; he came here in 1538 on a visit to Sir William Fitzwilliam, who had been created Earl of Southampton the previous year. The stone ceiling of the porch is elaborately carved, with fan vaulting, and with the Tudor rose at the centre.

It is this eastern range that is the most complete. The N. and s. ranges have almost entirely disappeared, and on the w. side there is not much except the great gatehouse, which, although only a shell, still reaches to its full height.

The porch in the eastern range led into a passage known as The Screens, two openings from the left of which led into the hall. At the far end of The Screens was another porch, giving access to the chapel, whose apsidal E. end, probably a later addition to the original, still sticks out beyond the rest of the east range. To the N. of the hall was the parlour, under the Great Chamber. Both these rooms contained numerous valuable pictures which at the time of the fire were being stored in the North Gallery, where the fire started, and were all lost. The fire itself was caused by workmen who left some rubbish smouldering overnight, and was aggravated by high winds. The last straw was that the key to the fire-engine house was nowhere to be found.

On the other, or s., side of The Screens were openings into the buttery and the passage leading to the kitchen, in a hexagonal tower in the far sE. corner of the ruins. This is part of the original house, and the only one untouched by the fire. In the kitchen itself are the old iron range, a large iron hotplate, and a table that is almost certainly even older than the house. Above the kitchen is a museum, where there are sketches of the house done before the fire. From here one can climb another flight of stairs out on to the tower, where there is a grand view over the remainder of the ruins, and of the town of Midhurst and the surrounding countryside.

The town is worth exploring. In North Street, near its N. end, is the Grammar School, founded in 1672 for the education of 12 boys 'in Latinn and Greek and in writing and arithmetic'. Among famous pupils were Richard Cobden, the 'apostle of Free Trade', H. G. Wells, and Sir Charles Lyle, the geologist. Now the school incorporates the former secondary modern schools and is a Comprehensive co-educational school for day pupils and boarders. There are about 1,000 pupils, and modern blocks and playing fields behind the old building.

Across the street and a little further s. is the Angel Hotel, where the Pilgrim Fathers stayed on their way from Southampton to Plymouth. To every inn that accommodated them on their journey they gave the name 'Angel'.

The old centre of Midhurst is the Market Square, just below the church on the left. In it stands the old Town Hall, which now houses the church's parish room; below the outside steps leading up to the first floor, in a roofed recess, are the old stocks and pillory.

The church itself is dull. The lower half of the tower is late-Norman, but the church as a whole is a Victorian rebuilding of the 1880s. The E. window was destroyed by an enemy bomb in the Second World War, affording an opportunity, which was not taken, to replace it with something exciting.

Every evening the curfew is rung from the church at eight o'clock. Legend has it that this custom originated when a 'London rider' (the commercial traveller of former times), being lost on North Heath, was guided by the sound of a bell to Midhurst; in gratitude he gave a parcel of land to provide for the ringing of a bell in the town each evening at the same time.

Also in the Market Square is a fine half-timbered Elizabethan house, now a restaurant called the Tudor Rose but formerly known as Elizabeth House; the old name still appears over the door. Lower down, at the junction of West Street and South Street, is another island building of the C. 16, timber-framed with brick infilling. This was once the Market Hall, and is where the Grammar School was first housed. It is now an annexe of the Spread Eagle Hotel, the main part of which is on the w. side of South Street. The old timber-framed portion dates from the first half of the C. 15, while the newer portion below has a front of c. 1700. Beyond that again is the stretch of water known as South Pond, where municipal ducks take their ease.

South Street crosses the lower end of South Pond on

Midhurst: South Pond

an old bridge spanning the former Midhurst Canal. On the far side of the bridge is a road still known as The Wharf. The canal was cut in the C. 18, and was the chief means of getting heavy goods to Midhurst until the railway arrived; now, alas, both have gone.

At the other end of The Wharf a footpath leads to the top of the wooded St Ann's Hill, where there are traces of the old castle of the Bohuns, medieval lords of the manor of Midhurst. Their 'castle' here, really no more than a fortified house, is thought to have been built in the latter half of the C. 12. From this elevated position one can look through the trees and see the ruins of Cowdray below. Another footpath takes one back to the Market Square.

From the Market Square one can now go straight on along West Street, where on the left, opposite the end of Wool Lane, is the old doorway of the Commandery of the Knights Hospitallers of St John, which stood here until 1811. The Knights were here from the reign of Edward II until the Dissolution of the Monasteries over 200 years later, when the order was suppressed. The property was then given to the Earl of Southampton, and has formed part of the Cowdray estate ever since.

In Bepton Road (turn left at the traffic lights at the end of West Street) is the Roman Catholic church, a striking modern building in the shape of a segment, with a main front which is nearly all window, and a detached campanile.

Finally to EASEBOURNE (*pron.* Ezbourne), a Cowdray

(A. F. Kersting)

estate village one mile N., which was once bigger and more important than Midhurst; the old and the new Cowdray are in the parish. In the church, thoroughly and insensitively restored in 1876 by A. W. Blomfield, is a monument to Sir Anthony Browne, 1st Viscount Montague, removed here from Midhurst church in 1852. He stands against the window of the S. chapel, towering above his two wives. To the side are the very different C. 19 monuments to William and Elizabeth Poyntz, with discursive but touching inscriptions, while all by himself on the other side of the church is Sir David Owen, the first builder of Cowdray, recumbent in alabaster.

Minster-In-Sheppey Kent *see* **Sheppey**

Newtimber W. Sussex C5
A few houses dotted about, a church, and Newtimber Place, under the Downs N. of Hove. The church of knapped flint, much of it covered with plaster and pebbledash, is C. 13, thoroughly restored in 1875. The roof is tiled, except for a fringe of Horsham slates all round, left over from the old church. The tower replaced a weatherboarded steeple in 1839.

Inside, there is a Jacobean pulpit, and several interesting monuments, especially those to the Buxtons of Newtimber Place: a tablet on the N. wall of the nave commemorates Sydney Charles, 1st Earl Buxton, 1853–1934, statesman, friend of Gladstone; an incised slate

monument on the W. wall above the font commemorates his wife, Mildred Anne, Countess Buxton; there is a carving above the pulpit of St George, in memory of their son Denis Sydney Buxton, killed in action in the First World War shortly before his 20th birthday, and a statue of a mother and child at the entrance to the nave in memory of his twin sister Doreen Fitzroy, who died in childbirth in 1923.

The house where the Buxtons lived from 1901 onwards, Newtimber Place, is up the lane to the N. The first sight of it the visitor has is of the E. front, across the moat that completely encircles the house. It is one of the most immediately appealing façades one could imagine. The house has walls of flint with brick surrounds to the windows, a modest building, yet having a quiet dignity and beauty. It was built for the Osbornes in 1681. The porch is a later addition and slightly spoils the effect, but it is at least in flint and brick too and could be so much worse, and must have been so obviously desirable, that one can readily forgive it.

In the entrance hall are some remarkable Etruscan-style murals with furniture coverings to match, put in by a Mr Newman after he bought the house in the mid C. 18; the artist's identity is a matter of expert debate. Mr Newman also built the elegant doors on either side of the W. wall of the room. The dining-room furniture is nearly all C. 18, including the dining table, still used by the owners. The drawing room also contains superb furniture, including a Louis XIV escritoire, and a small cabinet of 1680 in tortoise-shell and silver, thought to be one of the only pair in existence; its doors are wafer-thin and incredibly light.

In the passage leading to the library is Tudor panelling found in an attic and reassembled by Lord Buxton. (There was a Tudor house here, parts of which still remain.) The library itself is part of the 1681 house, but was extended by Lord Buxton to the W. and overhangs the moat slightly. In this room and in the passage outside are interesting mementos of his public life, particularly in South Africa, where he was Governor-General from 1914 to 1921, mementos that recall a culture and a political background that seem a thousand years removed from today's.

Northiam E. Sussex F5
A long, rather straggly village, with many weatherboarded houses. One of them, overlooking the green, is of three storeys, which is unusual. On the green itself is the famous oak tree in whose shade Elizabeth I is said to have dined and danced on her way to Rye in August 1573. She took off her shoes, and gave them to the people of Northiam. Meanwhile the tree has suffered the ravages of time, and now has to be held together with clamps and chains.

The church lurks behind and above the green. The tower was probably built early in the C. 12, but the great buttress and the octagonal stair turret are C. 15

additions. The old part is in a dark-brown sandstone, but the later additions are grey, and the contrast gives a curious effect. The c. 16 stone spire was rebuilt in the c. 19 and was raised by 10ft.

On the N. side of the church is the Frewen family chapel, built in 1846 by Sydney Smirke. The Frewens first came to Northiam from Worcestershire in 1583 in the person of John Frewen; he was presented to the living by his father, who had bought it from Viscount Montague of Battle. John was a Puritan, and two of his sons were named Thankful and Accepted. The latter was chaplain to Charles II in exile, and at the Restoration became Archbishop of York. One wonders to what extent his Puritan upbringing survived his association with the emancipated Charles.

There are two famous houses in Northiam, Brickwall and Great Dixter. BRICKWALL belonged to the Frewens from 1666, when Stephen, brother of Thankful and Accepted, bought it from William White, until 1972. As the White family had been there since 1491, it was in the possession of only two families during a period of nearly 500 years. Today it is a boys' boarding school. It is here that Queen Elizabeth's shoes are kept and shown to anyone who asks, when the house is open.

The visitor to the house passes through the imposing c. 19 gateway, also built by Sydney Smirke, and is confronted by a three-gabled timber-framed building of the early c. 17. It was William White who enlarged the original building and put on three gables. The right-hand gable is dated 1617, and the centre gable 1633; the left-hand gable is a c. 19 replacement, and is dated 1835. There seems to be no trace of the pre-c. 17 building.

Inside, the drawing room has a superb plaster ceiling of 1685. In 1967–8 it was discovered to be on the point of collapse and had to be restored; the oak timbers on which it was originally hung could no longer bear the great weight of five tons, now suspended from a steel grid. The ceiling is probably English work, but under strong Continental influence: Sir Edward Frewen had it constructed after his travels abroad. His portrait hangs above the door; he was a Baron of the Cinque Ports and represented Rye at the coronation of James II.

The chandelier in this room was once at Marlborough House, having been made for William IV when Duke of Clarence. The sedan chair in the corner, in black leather and brass, was used by Martha Frewen (1694–1752) on her journeys to church. She met a tragic end, being burnt to death in her bedroom.

The plaster ceiling above the grand staircase is perhaps even more magnificent than the one in the drawing room; if it, too, could be restored, it would be possible to make a fair comparison.

The dining room is Victorian, and contains a number of Frewen portraits of that period.

Northiam's other famous house is at the other end of the village. GREAT DIXTER is a c. 15 hall house, restored and extended by Lutyens in the early part of the present century. One of the additions is in fact a c. 16 hall house, which was seen by Mr Lloyd, the then owner of Great Dixter, at Benenden in Kent. It was in a derelict condition and was about to be pulled down. Mr Lloyd bought it there and then; its timbers were all carefully numbered, transported to Northiam, and re-assembled on the SE. side of Great Dixter, forming part of the enlarged house.

Only the c. 15 parts of the house are open to the public: hall, parlour, and solar. The hall is one of the largest timber halls in the country; it measures 40ft by 25ft, and is 31ft high. Evidence provided by the armorial bearings on the hammerbeams suggests that the hall was built some time between 1450 and 1464.

A door in the NW. corner of the hall leads into the parlour, now two-thirds its original length. On one of the beams in this room is an inscription which reads:

JOHN HARRISON DWELT ATT DIXTERN
XXXVI YERS AN VI MONTHES.
CAME THE FERST OF ELISABETHE RAIN.

John Harrison was only the tenant, the owner being the 3rd Lord Windsor, but perhaps after such a long tenancy the perpetration of this purely factual graffito was justified.

From the SW. corner of the hall a modern staircase leads up to the solar. The stone fireplace here is the original one, but the oriel windows are part of the restoration by Lutyens, as also is the squint through which the hall may be seen, although there may very well have been one in the old house. Altogether Lutyens's restoration is conscientious and quietly effective, and his modern additions blend remarkably well with the old. The same is true of the furniture, collected by Mr Lloyd over the years, and coming from a variety of places and periods.

Many people visit Great Dixter as much for the gardens as for the house. Except the Sunk Garden, which was designed and constructed by Mr Nathaniel Lloyd in 1923, all the gardens were laid out by Lutyens. They are divided into separate compartments, in the Renaissance tradition, but lead out of one another. The planting has been carefully planned to give an informal effect, a counterpoint to the more or less formal lay-out.

Nymans W. Sussex *see* **Cuckfield**

Offham Kent E3
Offham has a long green, with houses ranged round the edges in a rather East Anglian fashion. On the green is something unique in England: a quintain. This is a relic of the Middle Ages, and is actually derived from a Roman pastime. The quintain itself consists of an upright post, about 10ft high, with a swivelling cross-piece at the top. One arm of the cross-piece broadens

at its extremity, and at the far end of the other is a hook from which a sandbag or similar object is suspended. The contestant's aim is to ride at the quintain and pierce the broad arm, getting out of the way before the sandbag can swing round and deliver him a smart blow behind. It was never considered a fitting pursuit for the elderly, and certainly not for females.

At the N. end of the village is the church, which is of quite unusual interest. It is Norman, with c. 13–c. 15 additions and alterations. The original Norman building consisted of nave and square chancel, with a wide rounded arch between the two. Then, as often happened, in the c. 13 the chancel was lengthened, and the tower, which is on the N. side of the chancel, was added. The really unusual feature here is that the new pointed chancel arch was built *inside* the Norman rounded arch, and the gap filled in with rather rough masonry. The narrower arch gave a much more restricted view of the sanctuary and to compensate for this two squints were knocked through the wall on either side.

In the following century two further alterations were made: the E. window was put in, and a S. aisle constructed. The tracery of the E. window has lovely flowing lines. It is in fact a copy made in the early c. 20, necessitated by the parlous state of the original stonework. As for the S. aisle, it was demolished in the c. 15 and the arches connecting it with the nave filled in. Also in the c. 15, the nave windows were remodelled and a S. porch added. The corbels for the rood, which was probably knocked down at the Reformation, can still be seen.

In this church it is fairly easy to see where alterations were made at every stage. There have been none of a structural kind since the c. 15. Recently the clutter accumulated in the chancel by the Victorians has all been cleared away, and the modern pulpit, severely plain, looks exactly right.

Old Romney Kent *see* **Romney**

Old Soar Kent *see* **Plaxtol**

Otford Kent D3
The centre of the village is the duck pond, flanked by two weeping willows. No matter that this is really no more than a busy roundabout; it still makes a pretty picture.

Standing at the green and looking S. the traveller will see the ruins of the palace of the Archbishops, built by Archbishop Warham in the early c. 16. What is left is the western half of the N. range of a large courtyard house, of Tudor brick dressed with stone. At the right

The unique quintain on Offham green
(A. F. Kersting)

The Great Hall of Parham (A. F. Kersting)

(w.) end stands a tall tower, which closer inspection shows to have contained three rooms, one above the other. At the other end is a shorter tower, which once stood beside the gateway. Between the two, and making one continuous block running E. and w., are three cottages, whose lower halves are built into the walls of the old palace. To the s. there is an open field where a stream, no doubt below ground in Warham's day, gurgles past the ruins of his palace. The whole scene is bizarre. But then Otford Palace must always have been unnecessary, for surely Warham could have managed with nearby Knole, enlarged and dignified by Archbishop Bourchier and bequeathed to his successors.

The parish church of St Bartholomew lurks modestly E. of the green. It is difficult to realize that going from the palace to the church we are going back in time, for the palace is dead and the church is not. In fact we are going back over 400 years, for the N. and w. walls of the nave date from about the time of the Conquest. The tower, now rendered in nasty stucco, was added about 1180–90, and the chancel is c. 14. The s. aisle is early c. 16, probably a little later than Warham's palace. A thorough restoration was carried out by G. E. Street in 1863; the arcades and the pulpit are his work.

Dominating the chancel is the monument commemorating Charles Polhill and his wife Martha, by the c. 18 sculptor Sir Henry Cheeve. Martha died in 1742 and Charles in 1755. Charles, dressed in a voluminous toga and leaning on an urn, is flanked by two female allegorical figures; one of them is holding an anchor and the other is reading the Bible. Martha is relegated to a relief medallion at the top. The inscription tells us that 'their Life was a state of Friendship and mutual Affection'.

Charles's elder brother David, d. 1754, is commemorated in a wall monument by the same sculptor in the s. aisle. It is less ambitious but has a longer inscription. The brothers were great-grandsons, through the female line, of Oliver Cromwell.

Owletts Kent *see* **Cobham**

Parham   W. Sussex   B5
Parham consists of a small church and a great house, standing back from the South Downs near Storrington in a vast park where a herd of about 250 fallow deer roams. There was once a village too, but in the latter half of the c. 18, being considered a source of infection,

A Kangaroo *by George Stubbs (1724–1806)*   (From the collection at Parham Park)

it was demolished and its inhabitants moved to nearby Rackham.

The manor of Parham was given by Henry VIII at the Dissolution of the Monasteries to the Palmers, who during the reign of Elizabeth I decided to build themselves a new house. The foundation stone was laid in 1577 by the 2½-year-old Robert Palmer, who, however, in 1601 sold the house to Thomas Bysshop of Henfield. The Bysshops and their descendants lived at Parham until 1922, when it was sold to the Hon. Clive Pearson, younger son of the 1st Viscount Cowdray (*see* Midhurst). Today it is the home of his daughter, Mrs Tritton, and her husband.

Parham is a large but simple Elizabethan house in grey stone, roofed with Horsham slates, without frills or fuss, in an incomparable setting. The entrance was originally on the s. side, but was moved to the N. in about 1800. Visitors are first shown the Great Hall, which faces s. This room is structurally much as it was

when the house was first built. There are important portraits on the walls, including one of Elizabeth I, which has always been at Parham. Painted late in her life, it shows not a line or a wrinkle on her face, for such a thing was not allowed. Throughout the house there is a fine collection of pictures, mainly portraits, and of needlework. Not much china is displayed, but what there is is of high quality.

The Great Parlour, which was the Elizabethan family's private sitting room, had its ceiling raised in the c. 19; this destroyed the Great Chamber above. The ceiling was put back to its original level after the Pearsons took over, and the fine plasterwork now seen dates only from 1935. Here there is a Van Dyck portrait of Madam Kirke, dresser to Charles I's queen, Henrietta Maria, and one by David Mytens of Charles I when Prince of Wales, aged 18.

The Adam-style 'Saloon', the height of elegance, was, until about 1790, a wood store. Upstairs, the Great

149

Chamber contains a four-poster bed, with a spectacular tester and canopy and a superb needlework bedspread. This bears the letter M in the pattern, with a royal crown and three fleurs-de-lis of the French coat-of-arms, and was once thought to be the work of Mary Queen of Scots, who was married to the Dauphin, but it is now considered more likely to be that of Marie de' Medici, another French queen.

The West Room contains a number of interesting portraits, including that of Sir Ralph Assheton and his wife Elizabeth. She had run away from him, but he pursued her, fetched her back, and had this picture painted, in which he is shown grasping her hair and with a foot on her dress. Both here and in the next room, the Ante-room, are notable wall hangings. In the Ante-room perhaps the most interesting portrait is that of Charles II, painted by the Dutch artist Simon Verelst. Verelst was famous as a painter of still life, but when he came to England he found that nobody was interested in anything but portraits. He has certainly succeeded here in bringing out the sensual side of Charles's character.

The Green Room, where the furniture is all of mahogany, centres round the personality of Sir Joseph Banks, the botanist and explorer who accompanied Cook to Australia, and who was married to a member of the family from which Mrs Tritton is descended. There is an inlaid box containing three silver tea caddies bearing his arms, one of his specimen boxes, and two terrestrial globes, one of which is dated 1807 and dedicated to him. There are also portraits of Banks: a full-length portrait shows him at the age of 15, another as a young man, by Reynolds, and another with Omiah, a South Sea Islander brought back by Cook from his second voyage round the world. Omiah and his impeccable manners were a source of great interest and admiration in English c. 18 society.

Also in the Green Room is a painting by Stubbs of a kangaroo, the first representation of such a creature to be seen in Europe. Banks brought the skin of this animal from Australia; Stubbs inflated the skin to give himself a model, and drew a kangaroo, although naturally he had never seen one. The result must be adjudged a creditable effort by this great artist.

The Long Gallery (160ft) is filled with such a variety of things that even the excellent guides give up: one is left to wander round on one's own – there is a guide available to answer questions. The modern design by Oliver Messel on the ceiling has its critics as well as its admirers.

In an adjoining bedroom there is an Elizabethan four-poster, a collection of Stuart needlework pictures, and a Jacobean painted wooden font with a carving of the Garden of Eden: Adam and Eve stand beside a tree in which a serpent is entwined; they have already resorted to fig-leaves, but do not look much ashamed of themselves.

OPPOSITE: *Penshurst Place: the Great Hall*
(A. F. Kersting)

A short distance across the park to the s. is the church of Parham, with a c. 14 lead font, c. 19 box pews, and a drawing room complete with fireplace for the squire's family. Not to be missed.

Pegwell Bay Kent *see* **Thanet**

Penhurst E. Sussex E5
A little gem, about three miles w. of Battle: church, farm, manor house, and pond. The small church has a Perpendicular tower truncated and topped off with tile-hanging and a pyramidal roof. The interior, too, is simple Perpendicular, with old roof timbers and two king-posts. The church has been spared any unsympathetic restoration: the Jacobean pulpit and box pews – the pews were probably higher at one time – are still there, and the much older (c. 14?) screen. The N. chapel is c. 17. Only the lighting is modern, replacing the former gas lamps; but it blends in.

The manor house next door is Jacobean, or perhaps Elizabethan. It presents a handsome if somewhat severe stone front to the s., but on the other side (which has become the front now) there is a bit of a jumble – stone, tiles, brick, and Georgian-style porch and portico.

The farm buildings are well above average: there is a large wooden barn with tiled roof, and a merciful absence of concrete and asbestos.

Penshurst Kent D4
This pretty, and largely c. 19, village on the Medway has a church that is a mixture of periods and styles, and a famous manor house. Approached from the N., Penshurst Place bursts upon the view, a venerable pile of mellow brick and stone. At its heart is the original stone house of c. 1340, built by Sir John de Pulteney, a London wool merchant. The visitor today enters by way of the large walled garden, and thence up steps into the hall of the original house; this hall survives almost intact, with its splendid chestnut roof, its dais, and its central hearth.

A small doorway in the sw. corner leads to the vaulted undercroft of the solar, and a large door leads up stone stairs to the solar itself, where a small squint enabled the lord, or members of his family, to see what was going on in the hall below. This solar, too, belongs to the original building; it is now the State Dining Room.

On the other side of the hall, past the minstrels' gallery, is the rest of what still remains of the c. 14 house: the pantry and buttery. Behind them was the kitchen, but this was demolished in about 1836.

In 1430 Penshurst was bought by Henry V's brother, the Duke of Bedford. He added the part later known as

Penshurst Place from the S (A. F. Kersting)

the Buckingham Building, after the Duke of Buckingham, who became the owner in 1447. The principal rooms of this part are now those known as Queen Elizabeth's Room, reached from the State Dining Room, and the Tapestry Room, with a small panelled room, the Pages' Room, leading off it.

The part of the house running N. from the Buckingham Building is Elizabethan, added by Sir Henry Sidney, father of the famous Sir Philip, poet and courtier, who died of wounds in the ill-starred campaign in the Netherlands against Spain. Philip's younger brother, Robert (from whom the present owner, Viscount De L'Isle, is directly descended), added the part running s. to the sw. tower, including the Long Gallery. The panelling here dates from c. 1620, but the Jacobean-style ceiling is of the present century. Below this room are the Panelled Room and Nether Gallery, which leads into the Tea Room. This was the main family kitchen until after the Second World War, when the kitchen equipment there, which looks so old-fashioned today, was still in use.

During the c. 18 Penshurst suffered neglect, and it was not until his father's death in 1815 that John Shelley – in direct descent from the Sidneys, but through the female line – set about repairing the ravages of time and extravagance. Almost the whole of the N. front of the house, except the tower at the w. end and the King's Tower in the centre, which are Elizabethan, is of this early-c. 19 period, although in Tudor style. The part w. of the King's Tower is not open to the public, but the E. side contains a fascinating toy museum. The archway of the King's Tower leads into the courtyard, on the far side of which is the c. 14 hall.

After Penshurst Place, the village comes as an anticlimax, but it deserves more than a cursory glance.

The church, with its spiky Perpendicular tower, has a c. 13 N. arcade and a c. 14 s. arcade, but there is much c. 19 rebuilding: chancel arch and E. wall, N. aisle, screen. The Sidney chapel was rebuilt in 1820 by J. B. Rebecca, the architect employed by Sir John Shelley on the house.

At the s. entrance to the churchyard is a charming group of half-timbered cottages, some Tudor, some designed in the mid c. 19 by George Devey, who also laid out the gardens of Penshurst Place. Past these cottages, where the wall of Penshurst Place begins, are the Tudor-style gateway and lodge, also by Devey. Then the road dips down to his bridge over the Medway.

Peper Harow Surrey B4

This was doubtless a rowdy spot when it was *Pipera hearg*, 'the heathen temple of the pipers', but now it is a haven of peace a mere two miles w. of Godalming as the crow flies, hiding down a private road giving public access to church and farm only. It has, however, been 'rediscovered'.

The church is of no great interest; it has Norman bits, a plain Gothic early-c. 19 tower, and considerable additions by Pugin done in 1843. Past the church stands the grand house, built in yellowish brick by Sir William Chambers (*see* Goodwood) in 1765–8, in a park laid out by Capability Brown. The house has also been much added to: a porch with over-elaborate pinnacles, a third storey, and a N. wing, so that it now looks rather clumsy. But the original house cannot have been very grand – too small, one might think, for its park. It is now a boys' school. The stables, also by Chambers, are much more attractive, ranged round three sides of a quadrangle, the fourth side closed by a low convex wall. At first glance these outbuildings appear to be done in the same bricks as the house, but on closer inspection they turn out to be partly of Bargate stone, cut to look like bricks – an almost perfect match.

As for the farm, this actually comes first, on the left before you reach the church. The farmhouse is a handsome c. 17 building, bottom part stone, top part hung with pretty scallop tiles. Adjoining the farmhouse is a superb set of farm buildings, consisting of large wooden barns and a row of stone cottages ranged, like the stables of Peper Harow House, round a quadrangle, but a much larger one. A square c. 18 dovecote stands by the farm entrance. In the middle of the quadrangle is a granary probably built c. 1600, famous throughout the county. It is a tile-hung square building on two floors supported by 25 oak pillars, five rows of five. Picturesque as it is, the granary is not at present in good condition and needs a few thousand pounds spending on it. Farm machinery is kept under it, but the floors are not safe for the storage of grain.

At the other end of Capability Brown's park, beside the road from Milford to Farnham, is a fantastic group of buildings, known collectively as Oxenford. First, chronologically, there is a ruined abbey, an offshoot of Waverley (see Farnham), adjoining the site of the old Peper Harow House before the new house was built by Chambers. Next comes the c. 17 farmhouse, then Oxenford Lodge, probably by Chambers too. Finally there are farm buildings by Pugin of all people, including a large 'medieval' barn and a grandiose gatehouse, both with strong ecclesiastical overtones. A large pond between the road and the buildings completes the whole extraordinary picture.

Petworth   W. Sussex   B5

On a low hill on the N. side of the valley of the Rother stands the little town, full of narrow streets and right-angled bends choked with traffic. Petworth has learnt to live with it; schemes for bypasses come and go, and still the traffic rumbles on. One of the more recent schemes, and probably the most hare-brained, involved the digging of a cutting about 50yd from the w. front of Petworth House and continuing across the park laid out by Capability Brown.

Petworth House (N.T.) was built at the end of the c. 17 by the 6th Duke of Somerset on the site of a former residence of the Percys. The N. front was altered in the late c. 18 when Lord Egremont added the North Gallery to accommodate his father's collection of antique sculpture, and the SE. part of the house was sympathetically rebuilt in 1869–72 by Anthony Salvin. The front that matters most, the w. front, is the one that has suffered most. Originally it was given a dome, and the roofs at its N. and S. ends were raised above the rest. A bad fire in 1714 destroyed the dome; and since that date the roofs at the ends have been lowered, with the result that this front, which was originally designed as the entrance front, now appears somewhat squat, monotonous, and

unimpressive. The monotony is all the greater since the demolition of the church spire in the town behind, which used to provide a much-needed vertical feature, as is shown in W. F. Witherington's charming picture, *Fête in Petworth Park*, painted in 1835 and now in the North Gallery.

Nevertheless the very plainness of the w. front, relieved to some extent by the subtle use of local green sandstone for most of the walls and of Portland stone for the dressings, serves to accentuate the striking contrast between the two sides of Petworth House, which to the traveller who visits it for the first time comes as a delightful surprise. For on the E., which is now the entrance side, the house is in the town, or separated from it only by its own stables, which are very close to the house itself, the whole effect being of an untidy huddle; whereas on the w. side it is all clean lines and well-mannered understatement, and the town has disappeared from view and from thought, to be replaced by the sweep of the enormous park, with a low wooded hill and a lake to provide focal points in the picture.

Until the house and part of the estate were made over to the N.T. in 1947, Petworth was owned by the direct descendants of the Percys, Earls of Northumberland from 1377. On two occasions descent was through the female line: the first was when Lady Elizabeth Percy (1667–1722) married Charles Seymour, 6th Duke of Somerset, who was known as the 'Proud Duke'; it was he who rebuilt the house between 1688 and 1693, and, despite the fire of 1714 and the alterations already referred to, this is, essentially, the house we see today. The second occasion was when the Proud Duke's son, the 7th Duke, who was created Earl of Northumberland and Earl of Egremont, died without a male heir, the Earldom of Northumberland and certain estates going to his son-in-law, while Petworth, and the Earldom of Egremont, passed to his sister's son, Charles Wyndham, who became the 2nd Earl of Egremont.

The 2nd Earl's son, the 3rd Earl (1751–1837), was a great patron of the arts, and collected many of the best pictures that now hang in the house, including those by Turner, who was a close friend and spent much time at Petworth. It was also the 3rd Earl who built the North Gallery. For some reason he postponed his marriage to the lady with whom he had lived for several years until she had borne him six children, and on his death the Earldom of Egremont passed to a nephew and later became extinct, although the Petworth estate passed to his eldest son, George Wyndham, who in 1859 was created Baron Leconfield. The 6th Lord Leconfield, whose father made over Petworth to the N.T., was created 1st Baron Egremont in 1963, so that his son, the present Lord Leconfield, also enjoys the revived title of Lord Egremont. He still lives at Petworth.

One enters the house through the stables on the E. side, where in a long corridor is a display of beautiful Sussex firebacks; then, across an open-ended courtyard,

Petworth House, the W front   (A. F. Kersting)

with Salvin's restoration on the left and the 'pleasure grounds' to the right, is the entrance to the house itself. Only the downstairs rooms are shown, together with the Grand Staircase, which it is necessary to climb in order to appreciate the murals, put up after the fire of 1714 had destroyed the old staircase. On the ceiling here is a portrayal of the Assembly of the Gods, on the landing are the Muses, on the s. wall is the Duchess of Somerset riding in a triumphal chariot attended by her children and dog, and at the bottom are scenes from the story of Prometheus. All these murals are by Laguerre. The Grand Staircase is ostentatious, even vulgar – and magnificent.

Most people's favourite room is the so-called Carved Room, with its gorgeous decorative carvings by Grinling Gibbons and the hardly less splendid work of John Selden – not to mention the view across the park through the large windows in the w. wall. At the N. end of this wall is a small water-colour by Mrs Percy Wyndham done in about 1860, showing what the room looked like then.

The North Gallery added by the 3rd Duke is also shown, and the chapel, the only part of the medieval manor house, apart from the cellars, to survive intact.

Except the lectern, which is c. 14, all the furnishings of the chapel were commissioned by the 6th Duke of Somerset and date from the years 1685 to 1692. There is a very grand family pew at the w. end, while the arms of Percy are in the s. windows and those of Seymour in the blocked up N. windows. The whole chapel seems a tribute in praise of the Proud Duke rather than of anyone else; it is, however, in complete contrast with the rest of the house.

Visitors to Petworth House can also walk in the pleasure grounds and the great park; the latter they share with a herd of about 400 fallow deer.

The town itself is worth wandering round. The church has a rather odd-looking but not unattractive tower; its parapet and low tiled roof were built in 1953 to replace the spire by Barry (architect of the Houses of Parliament) that had been there since 1827, and that had to be demolished in 1947 because it was deemed unsafe. Barry's spire was itself a replacement of an earlier wooden one with a pronounced slant. Thus Barry's spire had only been up for a few years when Witherington's picture was painted. Inside the church, the hand of Barry has again been busy; indeed he virtually rebuilt it, and very little of the original c. 14 edifice is discernible.

PEVENSEY

Opposite the church a narrow cobbled street called Lombard Street, which in medieval times carried the town's main drain in its open central gulley, leads down to Market Square. This is the centre of the town, and contains the island building of the stone Market Hall, built in 1793 by the 3rd Earl. Below it is Golden Square, the old cattle market. From here turn left into the High Street, then left again up Middle Street and across to East Street; there are pleasant buildings all the way. In East Street, on the right, is Daintrey House, a c. 16 timber-framed house with a fine Queen Anne front; Stringer's Hall, next door, is also Elizabethan. Further along on the left, just beyond the post office, is a close-studded c. 16 house with a gateway bearing the Percy badges, the crescent and the rose, recently repainted.

In Grove Lane, on the sw. edge of Petworth, is New Grove, a good c. 17 stone house where several distinguished men have lived, including Grinling Gibbons, who must have derived pleasure from the view over the little town, and the great house that he had been commissioned to adorn.

Pevensey   E. Sussex   E6

When William set out from Normandy in 1066 he meant to land at Hastings, but his invasion fleet was blown off course. Luckily for him, however, the winds deposited him at Pevensey. For here was a convenient and sheltered harbour with flat beaches where his men and horses could simply wade ashore; here too was a ready-made fort, built by the Romans, which was in surprisingly good order considering it was about 700 years old.

As things turned out he had no need to defend the Roman fort immediately, but was able to press on towards Hastings, skirting the s. side of the all but impenetrable Weald, until finally confronted by Harold, breathless after his lightning march from the north.

After the battle William began to organize his new kingdom. Sussex was divided into wedges called 'rapes', running N. from the coast, each responsible for its own defence. He gave the Rape of Pevensey to his half-brother, Robert de Mortain, who built his own castle within the walls of the Roman fort. Thus Pevensey became, as it were, a castle within a castle.

Today, the harbour William found so convenient has disappeared, and the arm of the sea of which it formed part is the flat and marshy but well-drained area called Pevensey Levels, surrounding Pevensey on the landward side. Here cattle graze, and a few sheep. The Roman fort, built in the c. 4 to try to keep out the marauding Saxons (it was one of the 'Forts of the Saxon Shore', like Richborough and Reculver), and the Norman castle within it, are still there, looked after by the D.O.E.

It seems sensible to examine the Roman fort first. This is best done by walking round the outside from the E. gate to the w. For safety's sake one should walk on the

Grinling Gibbons carving in the Carved Room at Petworth
(A. F. Kersting)

pavement beside the road, even though it is on the side away from the walls, for there is an incessant stream of traffic here.

This Roman fort, which they named Anderida, was the last of the Forts of the Saxon Shore to be built. It differed from the others in two ways: its walls were higher, nearly 30ft, and it was oval in shape instead of straight-sided, because it followed the shape of the un-inhabited peninsula on which it was built. Its E. gate, where we start, is quite small. It merely led down to the harbour which surrounded the fort to E. and N. Its arch is a modern rebuilding of a Norman rebuilding of the original Roman arch.

As we follow the road round to the right (N.), we notice that the wall is roughly made, consisting of flint and sandstone rubble faced with green sandstone and ironstone, which with the addition of red brick form also the bonding courses. The walls were built in sections by different gangs of workers, and in some places the join can be seen, where the courses are out of alignment.

We notice also the bastions on this part of the wall; there are three within the space of about 100yd. They were carefully sited so that no part of the wall was left hidden from view, and as this is one of the sections where the angle of the wall is sharpest, the bastions occur more frequently. We see no bastions along the straight section that follows.

Soon after the third bastion is a section where the wall has collapsed; here is a well-disguised machine-gun post from the Second World War, during which Pevensey Castle was occupied by British, Canadian, and U.S. troops, and by the Home Guard. There are other similar relics of the 1939–45 period in various parts of the Roman and Norman remains.

At the end of this collapsed section – there is another longer length on the seaward-facing side of the fort – are parts of a small postern about 7ft wide, approached by a curved passage of which one side survives, and blocked by another gun position from the Second World War. After passing three more bastions we come to the main, or W., gate of the fort. This is the only direction from which the fort could be approached by land. The Romans dug a ditch about 16ft wide, across which the road was carried on a wooden bridge. Part of this ditch can be seen on the right. They also built a gatehouse, standing back between the two bastions; fragments of the base of the gatehouse can still be seen. Originally it was probably three storeys high, and reached well above the level of the bastions on either side. After the departure of the Romans it was occupied for a time by the Britons, but was finally overrun with terrible slaughter by Ella the Saxon in about 477.

When the Normans took over, they found the Roman ditch silted up and the gate in ruins. They dug a new ditch (which has silted up in its turn, leaving no trace on the ground), and built a new gate between the bastions, a little in front of the Roman one; of this Norman

gate only fragments of the jambs now remain. As we walk from here to the gatehouse of the Norman castle itself we traverse a distance of about 200yd, and over three times as many years.

Robert de Mortain regarded the Roman wall merely as outer defences, and after carrying out repairs to the W. and E. gates and at a few other points he set about building the inner bailey, which we now enter. He threw up defence works consisting of a series of palisaded banks and ditches. It was not until about 1100 that the first stone construction within the inner bailey was erected: the great keep above the eastern length of Roman wall. This may have been the work of de Mortain, or of his successor, Richer de Aquila, who is familiar to some as the chief character in Kipling's story 'The Old Men of Pevensey' in *Puck of Pook's Hill*. At about this time, too, the block containing a postern gateway, further round to the s., was built.

The present gatehouse was built about 1200, as the first step in replacing Robert de Mortain's earthwork defences, and in the middle of the c. 13 the remaining walls of the inner bailey and their towers were constructed. In 1940 these towers were adapted for military occupation once more: they were lined with brick, wooden floors were inserted, the windows were glazed, and roofs put on.

At various points on the inside of the walls the remains of fireplaces can be seen. These suggest the existence of living rooms, but there is no trace of any masonry, and they must have been built of wood, if at all.

It is known that a wooden hall was built in 1302, presumably up against the N. wall, as well as a chapel, which probably occupied the site of the earlier Norman chapel whose remains can be seen not far from the N. tower. The well dates from Robert de Mortain's time. The cannon, on the other hand, is one of two that were available here for the defence of England against Spain at the time of the Armada, and which fortunately were not required. It is a product of the Sussex iron industry, and on it is a Tudor rose and the letters E.R. (Elizabeth Regina). The other one of the pair is now in the Tower of London.

Pevensey Castle has had a history of ups and downs since the Conquest. William Rufus took it by siege in 1088; King Stephen did the same in 1147. It was besieged again by Simon de Montfort the younger in 1264–5, when the supporters of Henry III took refuge in it after their defeat at Lewes; this time the castle held out, as it did again in 1399 when besieged by the troops of Richard II against the supporters of the future Henry IV. From then on, apart from the brief scare at the time of the Armada, and the more prolonged one of the 1940s, the castle has fulfilled no military function.

Before leaving Pevensey the visitor should have a look at the Mint House and the parish church. The Mint House, on the street corner just outside the E. gate of the castle, is a half-timbered, tile-hung building of the c. 14, and is so called because it is on the site of the Norman mint, where coins were produced until about 1154. The inside of the building was much altered in the c. 16, and it is now essentially a Tudor house. Here its owner, Andrew Borde, entertained the young Edward VI in 1547. It is now an antique shop, but open to the non-buying visitor.

The large parish church is early-c. 13. On the inside of the doorway arch, on the left-hand side, are some pilgrim crosses, cut in the stone by pilgrims on their way to Canterbury. The church interior, with side aisles and clerestory, is all of a piece architecturally, but there is a grand alabaster memorial to John Wheatley, d. 1616, to the right of the door as one enters, and a delightful wrought iron screen of 1968–9 opposite the organ console.

Plaxtol Kent E3
A village set on a hill, on the Greensand E. of Sevenoaks, and commanding tremendous views, especially to N., E., and SE. – rolling hills, covered with woods and orchards.

The church stands near the top of the village. It is mainly c. 17, much enlarged in the c. 19, but may incorporate bits of an earlier chapel that stood on the same site. In the nave are two beautiful brass chandeliers given in 1785 by a Miss Hannah Baldwin of Broadfield. The pulpit is c. 17, with incongruous figures. The reredos consists of scenes from the Passion, in carved oak – Crucifixion, Deposition, Entombment – all enclosed in heavy c. 19 frames of stone. The E. window and others replace those destroyed by enemy action in 1940, for here we are in Battle of Britain country.

Down the hill to the E. are the more modern houses, and at the bottom is a factory where art metal work is made. An exceedingly old house, probably c. 14, is used as the showroom. Over the tiny stream and up the hill beyond is a house on the right bearing the date 1700 in enormous, bold figures. This is Broadfield, where Hannah Baldwin lived. Soon afterwards, on the left, we come to the manor house called OLD SOAR (N.T., in the guardianship of the D.O.E.).

At first glance Old Soar is an attractive c. 18 house in red brick. But attached to its NE. side is a humble but remarkably unspoilt example of part of a medieval manor house. Built c. 1290 in Kentish ragstone, it stands in dramatic contrast with its more sophisticated neighbour.

In 1290 the most important and by far the largest room in any manor house was the hall, where all took their meals, and all except the lord and his family slept. Kitchen and pantry were often alongside it, separated from it by a passage. Above and to the side of the hall, usually at the 'top' end, would be the solar, the 'bed-sitting room' of the lord and his family, leading out of which would, typically, be a *garde-robe* or privy, and a private chapel which often also served as the lord's study

or office. The ground floor below these private apartments would be taken up with storerooms.

Such was the arrangement at Old Soar, but the main room, the hall, with its kitchen and pantry, was absorbed into the new brick house built about 1740. Only slight traces of it remain, but today in any case the c. 18 house is private, and only the solar, chapel, another chamber on one side of which was the *garde-robe*, and the undercrofts or storerooms, are open to the public. Why the c. 18 builder left all this part intact is a puzzle – was it respect for the past, or simple expediency, or did the money run out? We can only wonder, and be grateful.

The visitor to Old Soar enters by the wide doorway into the vaulted undercroft below the solar. In the far left-hand corner is the stairway to the solar, whose stark emptiness comes almost as a shock. Of course this is only a shell; yet it will never have been anything but severely simple. Even the brick flooring is a later 're-finement', probably dating from the c. 16; originally it was of stone. But the timber roof, with its tie-beams and king-posts, is the original one.

The opening in the N. corner of the solar, across from the stairs, leads into the 'spare bedroom', the chamber on whose far side is the pit of the privy. The opening in the other corner of the solar leads into the chapel. The window in the far wall of the chapel was at some time extended downwards to form a doorway and its top cut off; it has now been restored. On the left of it is a corbel for a statue, or perhaps a candle. The piscina beside the window in the right-hand wall is a c. 14 insertion.

Back in the solar, in the middle of the opposite, SW., wall, are traces of an opening, now blocked. This may have been the window, common in medieval manor houses, that enabled the lord to look down into the hall and keep an eye on what was going on.

Plumpton E. Sussex D5
A village under the steep northern escarpment of the South Downs, four miles NW. of Lewes. The old Norman church stands to the W., beyond the Agricultural College. Its key is kept at the post office.

The building dates from about 1100. A church here is mentioned in Domesday (1086), so that the present structure must be on the site of an earlier Saxon one. Outside, the venerable walls, mainly of flint, seem to epitomize Norman strength and solidity, although in fact the tower, and the shingled broach spire, are of the c. 13. Within, the Victorian restorers have laid about with heavy hand. Some wall-paintings on the N. wall, uncovered in 1955 by Mr E. Clive Rouse FSA, are, with the aid of a lively imagination, dimly recognizable. The paintings above the chancel arch, however, were totally obliterated in 1868; they are described by A. S. Cooke in *Off the Beaten Track in Sussex* as having been 'infinitely brighter and more complete than those at Preston and Clayton'.

Polesden Lacey: ABOVE: *the E front*
BELOW: *the Library*   (A. F. Kersting)

The East Sussex County Agricultural College is housed in pleasantly grouped brick buildings on the E. side of the church. Beyond them stands Plumpton Park (private), by Lutyens. A public footpath skirts the S. side of the grounds, where innumerable daffodils and a lake (the domain of a pair of black swans) recall Wordsworth.

A footpath on the opposite, or S., side of the main road rises steeply to a Bronze Age settlement high up on an area of the Downs known as Plumpton Plain. This is one of the best-known Bronze Age settlements in the country, and consists of two main sites, each containing embanked enclosures linked by tracks. To the S. is a well-defined field system, which may have been associated in some way with the settlement. The track that brings us here continues across the Downs until it drops away to the main Lewes–Brighton road at Falmer.

Plumpton railway station is two miles N. of Plumpton, beyond the racecourse. The village of PLUMPTON GREEN runs N. from the railway whose coming brought it into existence. Here is another church, All Saints, consecrated in 1893, complete with pitch pine pews and encaustic tiles. Its octagonal tower-cum-spire is a good joke, probably unintentional. The rectory next door serves both churches.

Polesden Lacey   Surrey C3

This is the headquarters of the N.T.'s Surrey and W. Sussex region. Its position is superb, in the deep, wooded country of the North Downs NW. of Dorking.

The presiding genius of the place is the spirit of Mrs Greville (1867–1942), only child of William McEwan, the brewing millionaire. In 1891 she married Capt. Ronald Greville, elder son of the second Lord Greville, and in 1906 the Grevilles bought Polesden Lacey for £100,000. Capt. Greville died only two years later.

Mrs Greville was a well-known society hostess, and numbered the royal family among her friends, many of whom she entertained here and at her London house. King George VI and his wife, when Duke and Duchess of York, spent part of their honeymoon at Polesden Lacey.

William McEwan had the nucleus of a fine collection of pictures, furniture, and other works of art, which his daughter inherited and added to throughout her lifetime. This collection, and this house, garden, and large estate, she left to the N.T. on her death.

The house has no long history. There has been one on the site for centuries, but the present building dates only from the early C. 19. Nor has the property belonged to one family for any great length of time. Even the name Polesden Lacey only became attached to it at the end of the C. 18.

Richard Brinsley Sheridan, the playwright, owned Polesden Lacey from 1797 until his death in 1816; on acquiring it he wrote to his wife: 'we shall have the nicest place, within a prudent distance of town, in England'. Within two years of his death the house had been pulled down, the only buildings left standing being a stable converted into a cottage and 'a barn and hovel, boarded and tiled'. There were also 318 acres of land. This property was sold at auction to Joseph Bonsor, who paid £10,000 for it, built a Regency villa designed by Thomas Cubitt, and considerably enlarged the estate.

Bonsor died in 1835, whereupon the property underwent several more changes of ownership, and, during that of Sir Clinton Dawkins at the turn of the century, substantial alterations and extensions, until bought by the Grevilles in 1906. The Grevilles added the two bows to the projecting wings on the entrance front and remodelled much of the interior.

The splendid pictures and furniture are described in some detail in the guidebook on sale in the house. The dominant feature of the entrance hall is the panelling surrounding the fireplace, which was originally in Wren's City church of St Matthew, Friday Street, demolished in 1881. The carving is by Edward Pearce. The large round-headed panels were designed to display the Ten Commandments.

The dining room, library, and study are furnished in sober good taste: so is the tea room, which contains several exquisite small pieces, and the billiard room. The drawing room, however, stands out in contrast to the rest. Not that it is in bad taste; but its good taste can hardly be described as sober. Sumptuous, opulent, flamboyant, are adjectives that seem more appropriate here. The panelling is thought to be Italian and much of the furniture is French. This room was seriously damaged by a fire in 1961, which broke out in one of the upstairs flats, but now all is restored, except a small corner, which has been deliberately left to show the seriousness of the damage.

One must confess that the house of Polesden Lacey, although attractive, is not of much architectural interest. But it contains great treasures, and stands in beautiful grounds; plenty of time should be left to explore the gardens.

Poynings   W. Sussex C5

A village much photographed from the Downs. It stands at the very foot of the steep escarpment. The place itself is nothing much, just a village stretched along a twisty road. Its church, however, is a proud flint building of the late C. 14 in the Perpendicular style, with an embattled fortress of a tower and a simple cruciform interior. The simplicity appeals to modern taste. The large E. window has clear glass; the Perpendicular font, octagonal, has little ornamentation. The Jacobean pulpit has more, with carved panels and back-board; the communion rails, however, also Jacobean, are crudely – and charmingly – rustic.

In the E. window of the N. transept are two small

RANMORE

panes of c. 14 glass depicting the Annunciation, in soft yellow tones, and at the entrance to this transept, on the E. side of the organ, is a thurible, or censer for burning incense, probably imported from the Continent; it has elaborate carving, and bears the date 1760 on the top.

On the hilltop immediately above the village is an Iron Age fort, and inside it a hotel and a large car park. The approach road has double yellow lines, which tells all. On the way up is a golf course. The whole hill is nowadays called the DEVIL's DYKE, taking its name from the deep, steep re-entrant on the E. side. Here, legend has it, the Devil attempted to flood the Sussex plain by cutting a way through the chalk of the Downs and letting the sea in. An old woman in her cottage below, hearing sounds of digging, lit a candle to see what was afoot, and the cocks (thinking the candle was the rising sun) began to crow. This frightened the Devil, the Prince of Darkness, who promptly stopped digging and ran off.

The Downs have changed character greatly in recent years. Now, instead of bare grass and sheep there is considerable cultivation on the tops, and on the steep slopes where cultivation is impracticable there is much scrub; hawthorn is everywhere, but there are several other kinds of tree, including ash and beech.

Quebec House Kent *see* **Westerham**

Queenborough Kent *see* **Sheppey**

Ramsgate Kent *see* **Thanet**

Ranmore Surrey C3
No more than a hamlet scattered about the grassy top of the North Downs scarp above Dorking, with woods on either side. There was once a big house, Denbies, built for himself in 1849 by Thomas Cubitt, whose son, 10 years later, employed George Gilbert Scott to build him a church near by.

The house no longer exists, or only fragments of it. The church of St Barnabas, however, still stands beside the road that runs along the ridge. It has a fine octagonal tower surmounted by a spire. The unknapped flint of the walls gives the building a severe appearance. Inside, the fittings include a font in maroon and black marble, and an alabaster pulpit with white marble columns. The whole church breathes Victorian self-confidence. Now in the last decades of the c. 20 the confidence has withered a little: there are two services a month, and the church school next door is converted into a private dwelling.

In the winter the traveller who stumbles upon Ranmore may be forgiven for imagining that he has reached the outer limits of civilization; but in fact, as the frequent 'no parking' and 'strictly private' notices testify, on a fine summer weekend this is a place of recreation.

Reculver Kent H3
Twin towers on the edge of a cliff three miles E. of Herne Bay proclaim the site of something older than themselves. For the towers are c. 12 additions to a Saxon church now ruined, standing within the site of the Roman fort of Regulbium, built early in the c. 3, the first of the Forts of the Saxon Shore.

Reculver is romantic when seen from along the coast or from out to sea, but the romance evaporates on closer inspection, for these piquant ruins, looked after by the D.O.E., are flanked on three sides by caravans, and would no doubt be entirely surrounded by them if the sea had not claimed the fourth side, and indeed more than a third of the fort itself.

In Roman times Thanet was an island, separated from the mainland by a wide tidal channel. Reculver was built to guard the northern entrance to the channel and Richborough the southern. Since then the channel has silted up, while the sea has encroached upon the land on the N. side and receded on the s., so that the fort at Reculver, which was built over half a mile from the shore, is now on the sea's edge, whereas the fort at Richborough, built right on the coast, is now about two miles from it.

The defences of the fort of Regulbium consisted primarily of a massive stone wall about 15ft high, surmounted by a parapet. Its shape was a square, each side being about 200yd long. There were two ditches running right round the outside of the wall, the distance from the wall to the outer edge of the outer ditch being about 25yd. Inside the wall was an earth bank, some 15yd wide, which facilitated access to the wall for the defenders, and a road running all the way round the inner edge of the bank.

Of these defences, all that now remain are parts of the inner core of the stone wall, which can be followed along the side of the path which runs E. from behind the King Ethelbert Inn round to the E. side of the fort. There is very little trace of the headquarters building, the barracks, or other buildings that once stood within the walls, many of their stones having been used to build the church.

At one time the fort was occupied, and it may have been built, by the First Cohort of Baetasians, the Baetasii being a Gaulish tribe from Brabant in present-day Belgium. The garrison is thought to have been about 500 strong. The fort was finally abandoned in about the year 360.

Three hundred years later Egbert, king of Kent, founded a minster at Reculver. Additions to the original church were made in the c. 8, and in the c. 12 the w. façade, with its two great towers, was built. In the following century the chancel was enlarged.

In those days it was still an important church and Reculver a sizeable village. By the early c. 19, however, the sea had reached almost to its present line, and the then vicar, egged on by his mother, prevailed upon the parishioners to dismantle the church and build a new one a mile inland. Naturally there was an outcry; meanwhile steps were immediately taken to build up the sea defences, and encroachment by the waves was stayed. But by that time the act of vandalism was almost complete, and today little remains of the old church except the w. end. In order to preserve what had long been a landmark for shipping, Trinity House took over the w. towers and their leaded wooden spires. The spires were blown down in 1819 and replaced by wind vanes, now in their turn removed. The philistine vicar's new church has itself been replaced by the present church of St Mary, over a mile up the road, a flint building of 1876. It is we of the c. 20, however, with our caravans, our shanty shops, and our bingo, who have perpetrated the ultimate philistinism at Reculver.

Richborough Castle Kent H3
This great fort, the Roman Rutupiae, lasted as long as the Roman occupation of Britain itself, for it was built at their landing-place by the Roman invasion army in A.D. 43 and was the last of the Forts of the Saxon Shore to be abandoned in the c. 5. Fragments of Iron Age pottery found on the site suggest that it was inhabited much earlier, but there is no evidence of a specifically military purpose. In A.D. 43 the site was on a small peninsula sticking out into the River Wantsum, which separated Thanet from the mainland of Britain.

The walls we see belong to the last period of building, the construction of the Fort of the Saxon Shore towards the end of the c. 3. The walls, which on the eastern or seaward side have long ago been washed away by the tides, stand inside a ring of ditches dug at the same time, whereas the ditches inside were dug about 30 or 40 years earlier. The cruciform mass of masonry at the centre is the remains of a huge monument built about A.D. 85, which towered above the river and the sea and celebrated the final conquest of southern Britain.

At the E. end of the N. wall are the remains of a house first built at the same time as the monument, and rebuilt in the following century. It was knocked down when the walled fort was erected, but soon afterwards a bath-house with hypocausts was built on the same site, and this was probably in use until the end. To the s. of it are the remains of the chapel of St Augustine, put up in Saxon times to enclose a stone said to bear the saint's footprint.

Today the ruins of Rutupiae, which are in the care of the D.O.E., and are most easily reached from Sandwich, stand in rather forlorn surroundings. Immediately E. is the railway and the muddy Stour; then across the marshes is the road from Ramsgate to Sandwich and the clutter of an industrial estate; beyond that is the Stour again, doubling back on itself, more flat land, golf courses, and the sea. Better perhaps to look through the postern in the middle of the N. wall to Richborough Power Station: if not beautiful it is at least impressive, and provides a dramatic contrast to these venerable remains.

Ringmer E. Sussex D5

This village, under the Downs E. of Lewes, where the chalk meets the clay, is growing. 'Ringmer is so rapidly becoming urbanized that it is as well to remind ourselves of its history before that is completely buried under pavements and houses'. So, alarmingly, says the guide-book on sale in the church.

The flint church itself is very large and solid, and unlikely, one feels, to suffer burial at the hands of pave-ments and houses. Its four-square tower is late-c. 19, an extension to the w. end, but the rest of the structure is medieval, a happy medley of styles and materials, blending well together, both inside and out. The walls, for instance, contain flint, brick, sandstone, and Isle of Wight greenstone; the roof is covered partly with tiles and partly with enormous Horsham slates. Within, the bases of the nave pillars are Norman, but the nave arches are c. 13 or Early English. The chancel and side chapels are Perpendicular. The c. 18 gallery was taken down in 1865; the present gallery, the gift of the late John Christie of the well-known Glyndebourne family, was erected in 1932. John Christie also gave the magnificent organ, which, however, unfortunately blocks the c. 15 stained glass window in the w. wall of the tower.

The church contains two curiosities: in the s. chapel is a lurid red and white candelabrum of the present century; and on the s. wall of this chapel are a flute and bassoon from the old orchestra that until 1865 provided the music for the services.

The chapel is known as the Springett Chapel, after the Springetts of Broyle Place, a house two miles E. of Ringmer on the left of the road to Hailsham. The prop-erty has a very long history. From the time of King John to that of Elizabeth I it was a palace of the Archbishops of Canterbury. It passed to the Springett family in 1639. One of them, Gulielma Springett, married William Penn, the founder of Pennsylvania.

Vicarage Way leads s. from the church. First comes the attractive modern vicarage, then Vicarage Close, a group of homes for elderly people that includes the former vicarage, built in 1671. Like the church, the whole blends well together. At the far end is Little Manor, an old house well restored in this century.

Here at the junction of Vicarage Way and the main road from Lewes is the village sign. On it appear the names of William Penn and Gulielma Springett, and of John Harvard, the founder of the American univer-sity, and Ann Sadler, who were married in 1636, when Ann's father was vicar here. Thus the village has a double connexion with America.

Pride of place on the village sign is, however, reserved

for Timothy the tortoise, coupled with the name of the naturalist Gilbert White. Timothy was the property of White's aunt, Mrs Rebecca Snooke of Delves House, N. of the church. Gilbert White was a frequent visitor there, and on the death of his aunt in 1780 he took Timothy back to his own home. He has some amusing observations about him in *The Natural History of Selborne*.

There are many new houses in Ringmer. There is, for instance, a large estate on the right as one comes from Lewes, behind the post office, breathing new life into the village. The past is preserved in the names of the roads in the estate, such as Springett Avenue, Harvard Road, Penn Crescent. Despite all this 'urbanization' there is a feeling of spaciousness about Ringmer, partly due, no doubt, to the presence of the large recreation field beside the main road.

Robertsbridge E. Sussex E5

Robertsbridge is a village of graceful curves winding up a gentle hill, with many old houses in a pleasing mixture of styles – and a steady stream of traffic, much of it, during the week, consisting of heavy lorries.

Like Etchingham, Robertsbridge climbs a hill from the Rother valley. Unlike Etchingham, however, it can boast no grand church; indeed, although originally an appendage of a Cistercian abbey, it now has no church of its own at all, being in the parish of nearby Salehurst. It makes up for this deficiency by the charm of its houses, and it is worth walking the whole length of the street from bottom to top; there is a wealth of weather-boarding, half-timbering, and tile-hanging. The Georgian tile-hung inn called the George Hotel, on the right at the top, brings the varied but harmonious street to a quiet climax.

Now a different world can be explored, by turning off the High Street to the E. If at the George Hotel and on foot, cross the road and take the footpath; otherwise turn up Fair Lane, which leaves the High Street lower down. Here, too, are some pleasant houses and cottages, climbing up a hill. Robertsbridge and the thunder of traffic are soon left behind. Across the Rother valley, now on the left, is the village of Salehurst, with its c. 13–c. 14 church. Vehicles are not allowed on our road beyond Rodlands Farm, but the road itself, now a bridleway and footpath, continues due E. and leads, after another half mile, to the ruins of Robertsbridge Abbey.

This Cistercian abbey was founded in 1176, and originally erected at Salehurst, near the site of the present village sign, by Robert de St Martin, after whom the bridge over the Rother, and thus the place by the bridge, was named. In the c. 17 an attempt was made to associate Robertsbridge with the river rather than with the abbey by renaming it Rotherbridge, but the old name stuck.

Now the abbey is incorporated into Abbey Farm.

as we round a bend in the track we see ahead of us a building that appears to be half church half house, for the w. wall contains a large ecclesiastical-looking window; this was the w. window of the abbot's house. In the garden beyond are the ruins of the refectory, with climbing plants and creeper breaking its stark lines.

A short distance back towards Robertsbridge a footpath leads off to the right, crosses the Rother by a footbridge, and continues up to Salehurst across the track of the old Kent and East Sussex Railway that used to run between Robertsbridge and Headcorn (*see* Tenterden). Thus if you have come out from Robertsbridge on foot and do not want to return by the same route, you can get back by following the lane from Salehurst or by walking along the old railway – the tracks have been taken up and the path cleared of undergrowth.

Rochester   Kent   F2

An industrial city, forming part of the Medway towns conurbation (Chatham, Gillingham, Rochester, Strood). It owes its existence and historical importance to its position at the lowest practical crossing of the River Medway, as with London and the Thames. It was a Belgic settlement before the time of Christ. Then the Romans came, and built the first bridge, and a fort to guard it, for it carried the imperial route, later known as Watling Street, from the coast to London and beyond. The Saxons and the Danes knew it; and in their turn the Normans refortified it.

Rochester is a centre of tourism, a fact it owes preeminently to two very diverse characters, the Norman bishop Gundulph, and the English novelist Charles Dickens.

Gundulph was appointed bishop here in 1077, and started the building of the castle and the cathedral. For some of the outer wall of the castle he followed the line of the old Roman wall, but there is little that can confidently be attributed to him. The massive keep of ragstone rubble was built after his time, in the reign of Henry I. It is worth climbing the rough steps to the top of this, the highest tower keep in England, for the view it affords of river, city, cathedral, and the hills that ring them round. The keep has a tower at each of the four corners. Three of them are square, but that in the SE. corner is rounded: it was held by rebellious barons in 1215 against King John, whose engineers eventually managed to undermine the tower and destroy it. Later it was rebuilt in rounded form.

The keep stands in the s. corner of the encircling walls, which extend on the NW. side almost to the river's edge. Between wall and river is the road known as the Esplanade, where there stands a bridge chapel built in 1387; it was last restored in 1937 and is now the boardroom of the Bridge Wardens, who administer a trust set up in 1391 for the protection and maintenance of Rochester Bridge. The trust has certainly carried out

its task, even providing in 1970 a second road bridge alongside to relieve the press of traffic, which is still heavy despite the M2 carried over the valley on its high bridge a mile and a half upstream. On the river itself, below the Esplanade and opposite the middle of the NW. wall of the castle, lies the Cambria, the last existing Thames barge to be propelled by sail alone. Her masts can be seen rising up beyond the walls from within the castle grounds, where there are lawns, paths, and seats – for all is now tamed and organized by the D.O.E.

On the s. side of the castle, across Baker's Walk, is Satis House, a c. 16 house that has been given a Georgian front. It is now a school. Over the portico is a bust of Richard Watts, who owned the house in 1573 when he entertained Elizabeth I. It is called Satis House because Her Majesty is reputed to have expressed her thanks on departure with the one word 'satis'. The Old Hall next door is said to be the place where Henry VIII first met the unfortunate Anne of Cleves on her arrival in England in 1540.

As for the cathedral, it should appeal to those who like a bit of everything, for almost every style and period of church architecture is represented, and the result is a complete and rather splendid muddle. Here again, there is little of Bishop Gundulph's own work to be seen from the outside, except the rugged tower embedded, as it were, in the angle of the choir and N. transept, and known as Gundulph's Tower. This dates from about 1080, and originally served the wily bishop as watch-tower and potential fortress in case of trouble from rebellious Saxons.

The w. front is famous, and the view of it intimate, for this cathedral has no grand approach, or even a close. Its own dimensions are not great, and it is huddled and cramped by its surroundings; to the w. it cowers below the castle. Yet here is one of the finest Norman w. doorways in the country, with its rich carvings and figures, dating from the mid c. 12. The two main figures at the sides are so badly mutilated – probably by Cromwell's soldiers – that their identity is in question: they are thought to be either Solomon and the Queen of Sheba or Henry I and his queen, Matilda. Above the doorway is a huge Perpendicular window, flanked by two tall turrets with blind arcading and conical caps. On either side of these turrets, and recessed, are two large turrets at the ends of the N. and s. aisles. These turrets are all Norman work, although much restored by J. L. Pearson in the late c. 19. Doorway, turrets, and c. 15 window make a harmonious whole.

On the left as one faces the w. door is the church of St Nicholas, built in 1423 for the use of the citizens of Rochester after one of the numerous quarrels between them and the monks of the cathedral. The church was rebuilt in the c. 17, and in 1964 was converted into diocesan offices, except the centre, which was retained as a church. The S.P.C.K. bookshop is also in the building. In the churchyard outside is a catalpa tree, or American

The cathedral and castle at Rochester

Indian bean tree, which is rare in Britain. This specimen, over 100 years old, is propped up by wooden poles.

Beyond St Nicholas's church is the C. 15 Chertsey's Gate (or College Gate), which is the 'Jasper's Gate House' of Dickens's *Edwin Drood*.

The cathedral is entered by the small door on the left of the great w. door, and is revealed as a typical monastic church, with a solid stone screen (and now an organ above it) completely separating choir from nave. On the floor at the w. end are curved lines marking the apse of the Saxon church built here at the beginning of the C. 7. The work of Gundulph nearly 500 years later can be seen again in the s. aisle, where the arcade arches are plain and unadorned. Forty years afterwards the columns were encased and the inner or nave sides of the arches enriched with mouldings. The w. wall of the nave has double arcading, which has unfortunately been filled with incongruous mosaic lettering.

Facing E. and looking up the nave we see a fine, solid piece of Norman architecture. Each pillar matches its fellow on the opposite side, but differs from all the others. Then at the E. end of the nave comes a surprise: a sudden change into the C. 14, with pointed arches and Purbeck marble columns. The monks had decided to rebuild the entire nave in the current style; but the money ran out and the work was abandoned. Nowadays most people think this was a blessing in disguise.

The clerestory and nave roof are of the C. 15. The N. transept dates from about 1240, whereas the s. transept was built forty years later, and was the original Lady

Chapel. (The present Lady Chapel, extending westwards from this transept, was added in the late C. 15.) The central tower was completed in the mid C. 14, but the top part, above the roofline of the transepts, and its squat spire, were built in 1904. There is no homogeneity about Rochester.

Passing through the C. 13 stone screen with late-C. 19 figures, we come to the choir, a mixture of Norman, Early English, and C. 19 restoration by Sir George Gilbert Scott, who also designed the reredos. The choir has its own N. and s. transepts, the latter being considerably out of the perpendicular. An unusual feature of this end of the church is that the N. and s. aisles are, for some reason, unconnected with the choir, being separated from it by Gundulph's massive Norman walls with blind arcading.

In the s. choir transept is a superb, richly carved C. 14 doorway leading into the chapter room, beyond which is the ruined Norman chapter house. On either side of this doorway are female figures representing the Old and New Testaments (Synagoga and Ecclesia). The persons above them are unidentified; they might be the four evangelists. Higher still are angels rising from flames, and at the top is a naked figure representing the soul of the donor being received into heaven.

In the western part of the choir, on the N. side, is a C. 13 wall-painting of the Wheel of Fortune; Fortune, depicted as a queen, turns the wheel, on which three men are revolving, willy-nilly.

The choir is raised on a magnificent crypt, entered

from the s. choir aisle. The two western bays are Gundulph's early Norman work, but the rest is Early English; its avenues of columns and fine vaulting make this crypt one of the best in England.

If we leave the cathedral by the s. door, passing on our left the remains of the Norman cloisters, we come out on to College Green, where the old Bishop's Palace is. Here Erasmus stayed with Bishop Fisher, later beheaded by Henry VIII for refusing to acknowledge the King as Supreme Head of the Church.

The traveller to Rochester is fortunate in that all the places of historical interest are concentrated within a fairly small area and can easily be visited on foot. Past the Old Bishop's Palace on the left is the c. 18 Minor Canon Row, while straight ahead is Prior's Gate, another c. 15 monastic gate and an even better example than Chertsey's Gate. Round the corner to the right past the King's School, once a monastic school and refounded by Henry VIII after the Dissolution, is the Archdeaconry, an old house enlarged in 1661; opposite is Oriel House, 1758, at the entrance to The Vines, a park where once the medieval monks had their vineyard.

In The Vines is an avenue of plane trees. Taking the path that diverges to the left from this, one comes out into Maidstone Road opposite Restoration House, a large house in fuzzy brick where Charles II is reputed to have stayed on 28 May 1660 on his return to England after his enforced exile. Here, too, Pepys stayed in 1667 when investigating how the Dutch admiral De Ruyter had managed to sail into the Medway and inflict severe damage upon the English fleet. The seriousness of his task, however, did not prevent Pepys from acting true to form: he records that he 'went into the Cherry Garden and here met a pretty young woman and did kiss her'. The house was the model for the home of Miss Havisham in *Great Expectations*.

At the bottom of Maidstone Road is the High Street. To the right, and across the road, is Eastgate House, so called because a short distance back along the street was the medieval e. gate of the city, its site now marked by sections of the city wall – part Roman, part medieval – on either side of the street. Eastgate House, therefore, is outside the old city boundary. It was built in 1591, and is timber-framed with brick-nogging. It is now the city museum. In the garden is Dickens's Swiss chalet from nearby Gad's Hill.

Dickens's links with Rochester are very close. Although born in Portsmouth in 1812, he lived in Chatham for four years from the age of five and knew all this district intimately. On one of the walks he used to take with his father he saw a large country house at Gad's Hill, Higham, near Strood, and dreamed that one day it might be his. After a youth of grinding poverty, he became a successful and famous man, and his boyhood dream was realized: he bought the house in 1856 and lived there from 1860 until his death in 1870. He had expressed a wish to be buried in Rochester, but although there is a memorial to him in the cathedral, he was not allowed to be buried in any less illustrious place than Westminster Abbey.

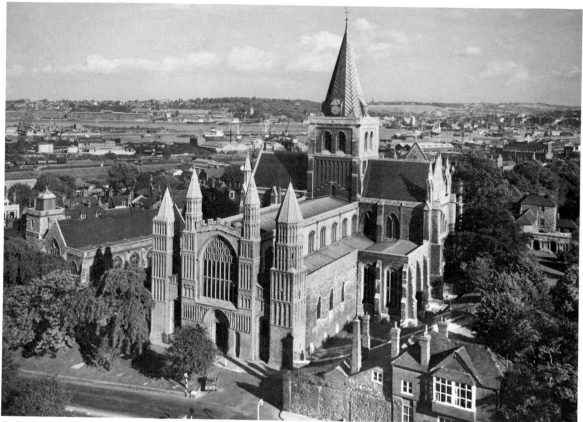

Rochester Cathedral　　　　　　　　　　　　　　　　　　　　(A. F. Kersting)

This chalet in the garden of Eastgate House was given to Dickens by Fechter, the actor. It came in separate parts and was a puzzle to assemble. It was eventually erected in the grounds at Gad's Hill, and in it Dickens did much of his subsequent writing. After his death the chalet had a chequered career, which there is not space to relate here; visitors to Eastgate House, however, can, on inserting a coin in the appropriate slot, hear a recorded account of the whole story.

Continuing NW. along the High Street the traveller comes to the site of the East Gate already mentioned. Road traffic has to bear right, but pedestrians can go straight on into the next section of the street. Here on the right, standing back, is La Providence, a square of almshouses for those of Huguenot descent, rebuilt in 1960. The original 'hospital' was founded in the C. 18. Next, on the same side, comes Watts' Charity, founded in 1579 under the will of Richard Watts to provide accommodation for 'six poor travellers'.

Soon, across the street, is the Pilgrims' Passage leading to the C. 15 Deanery Gate and the N. side of the cathedral.

The passage derives its name from the pilgrims who took this route to the shrine, in the cathedral, of William of Perth, a saintly Scottish baker providentially murdered just outside Rochester in 1201 whilst on a visit to Canterbury. His body was promptly brought back by the monks of Rochester and buried in the cathedral. Miracles were attested almost at once, and pilgrims began to appear. Ever since the murder of Becket in 1170 the Rochester monks had had to endure the sight of crowds of pilgrims to Canterbury passing along Watling Street under their very noses. Now they had their own martyr, and if St William of Perth and Rochester had not quite the status of St Thomas of Canterbury, his pilgrims nevertheless contributed enough to finance the rebuilding of much of Gundulph's cathedral during the C. 13.

Back in the High Street, and on the other side, is a building with a large clock jutting out over the street. This is the Corn Exchange, given to the city in 1706 by Sir Cloudesley Shovel, M.P. for Rochester, and the admiral who, with Sir George Rooke, captured Gibraltar in 1704. He also gave the plaster ceiling in the Guildhall, further along the street near the bridge. The Guildhall was built in 1687, and is surmounted by a ship weather-vane added in 1780.

Across the street from the Guildhall is the Royal Victoria and Bull Hotel, an c. 18 hostelry known, before a visit from Princess Victoria in 1836, simply as the Bull Inn, where Pickwick and his companions, in the second chapter of *Pickwick Papers*, got tipsy and went to a ball. Rochester was the first place the members of the Pickwick Club made for on their travels, and the first building they remarked upon there was the castle – Mr Snodgrass with 'poetic fervour', Mr Pickwick with the profound reflection, 'What a study for an antiquarian!', and Mr Jingle in his usual staccato fashion. Now we too find ourselves back at the Esplanade, below the 'glorious pile – frowning walls – tottering arches – dark nooks – crumbling staircases'. There is no escaping Gundulph or Dickens in Rochester.

Yet there is another Rochester, the Rochester not of tourism but of commerce. Walk down Blue Boar Lane under the railway to the river at Blue Boar Pier. Here are ships, boats, cement works, and the muddy river sliding round in great loops to the sea. Not a tourist to be seen.

Rolvenden Kent F4

This is a beautiful village, with a wide street of tile-hung and weatherboarded houses leading to the old church of St Mary the Virgin at its s. end.

Approach the church past enormous yew trees, and pass through the glass swing doors at the w. end. Here is an interior funny but lovable. A good c. 14 nave leads past a clutter of unfortunate woodwork to a rather specially horrible E. window. Occupying most of the s. chapel is the family pew of the Monypennys, a large drawing room of a pew, reached by steps leading from the chancel and containing, at the last count, 11 chairs. Looking back one is alarmed to see a w. gallery apparently on the point of collapsing under the weight of the organ; however it is some comfort to know that they have co-existed since 1825.

Safe outside again, we see a pleasant housing estate across the road to the N., and another on the s. side just below the church – the latter is called, with a certain inevitability, Monypennys. (The family originated in Fife, Scotland, and came to Rolvenden in the c. 17.) Further down on the same side of the road, and standing back, is GREAT MAYTHAM HALL, an enormous neo-Georgian house built by Lutyens in 1909; it is now divided into flats and managed by the Mutual Households Association. The earlier house on the same site was once the home of Frances Hodgson Burnett, and may have been the setting of *The Secret Garden*.

Romney Kent G5

In the c. 13 the River Rother still flowed out to sea here instead of at Rye; yet already the sea was retreating and Romney was growing seawards in pursuit. The important part was round the harbour there, at the apex of the bay, and became known as NEW ROMNEY. This was the prestigious Cinque Port of medieval times. But the famous storm of 1287, which diverted the course of the river, was the writing on the wall for New Romney. Now in the c. 20 the defection of the sea is even more complete than at Rye, where at least the boats are moored below the old town walls; you cannot even *feel* the sea here. It is in fact over a mile away at Littlestone.

Yet New Romney, a small town barely more than a village, is still the capital of the Marsh. On the s. side of its attractive High Street stands the c. 19 grey Town Hall, trying to look important. On the other side are several old timber-framed shops whose floors are below street level: it is thought that the roads here have been raised at some time, or even at various times, such as after the 1287 storm. On the corner of St John's Road stands Priory House, a beautiful c. 18 building of mellow brick, with two large slightly bowed windows facing on to the High Street. Behind it in St John's Road is a medieval stone building, all that remains of St John's Priory, with worn stone embellishments, including several heads. One of them, the largest, has its mouth wide open in astonishment.

Back on the other side of the High Street, Church Approach leads to the parish church of St Nicholas, the pride of New Romney. On the way one passes the c. 18 Assembly Rooms, another pleasing brick building, tacked on to the end of the older School Room, dated 1676. Then comes the grand Norman tower of the church, its floor well below street level, its w. door a splendid Norman extravagance.

Here for a change is a church whose architecture is easy to follow. It consists of tower, nave, N. and s. aisles, and chancel. The w. half is Norman, the E. half being added in the c. 14, when the Cinque Ports were still flourishing, and the existing church was obviously considered unworthy of such an important town. At the same time the aisles were widened. The dividing line between Norman and Decorated is quite easy to spot. Structurally, apart from a little Victorian tinkering in the N. aisle, the church is still much the same today, and a very impressive and satisfying building it is.

In the s. aisle is the tomb of Richard Stuppeny, jurat (councillor) of New Romney, who died in 1527. His great-grandson had the tomb 'new erected' in 1622 for the convenience, if that is the right word, of the jurats of his own time: they would sit round it to hold council and elect the bailiff or mayor (*see also* Lydd).

Inland from here is the tiny scattered hamlet of OLD ROMNEY, the northern part of the old town whose southern half deserted it in pursuit of the sea. The church is the sole survivor from the former days of glory, standing back from the main road across a field and approached by a lane from the other side. It is a predominantly c. 13 church, with a NW. tower and small

St Nicholas's church, New Romney

(A. F. Kersting)

shingled spire, and with many C. 18 fittings inside, including box pews and a w. gallery.

Rye E. Sussex F5

In the Middle Ages Rye was an important port surrounded on three sides by the sea; it early became a member of the Confederation of the Cinque Ports, and like Winchelsea was at the receiving end of some particularly fierce French raids. It was fortified in the C. 14 against the twin enemies, the French and the sea. As a result of the storms at the end of the C. 13 the ports of Winchelsea and Hastings were virtually finished, although they both struggled on for a time. For Rye, however, the results were a little less disastrous: the River Rother altered course, and now flowed past Rye instead of out to sea at Romney, and the retreat of Rye's harbour was more gradual and less complete than in the case of the other two. Now it is some two miles away; but it still exists.

Attacks by the French were catastrophic in their immediate effects, but less dire in the long run. The town was sacked in 1339. In 1377 it was visited again

and burnt; all the wooden buildings were destroyed and only those made of stone survived, and by no means all of them. The church bells were stolen and carried off to France. Much of the church itself was damaged: the tower collapsed and some of the roof fell in; the tower brought down with it some of the chancel, and the arches of the transept and of the N. chapel. Apparently Rye put up rather a feeble resistance, and some of the leading citizens were hanged as traitors. However, the following year due vengeance was exacted on the French: two Norman towns were raided and much of the loot which had been taken from Rye, including the bells, was recovered. Raids and counter-raids continued. Much damage was done in another French raid in 1448, but the C. 16 seems finally to have brought peace of a sort to Rye. It was visited by Frenchmen again after 1572, but this was by Huguenots seeking refuge after the St Bartholomew's Day massacre in their own country. Many of them settled permanently in Rye.

Today Rye has friendly relations with the French, but the battle with the other enemy, the sea, is still being fought out at the distant harbour mouth. Here the

The Landgate, Rye   (A. F. Kersting)

shingle that the sea deposits so relentlessly is scooped up on to lorries, carted off westwards whence it came, and dumped on the shore at Pett Level, just E. of Hastings. This seemingly futile, but in fact necessary, exercise goes on day after day for about eight months of the year, four lorries making 15 journeys a day each. This preserves not only the harbour at Rye but also the coast at Pett.

To explore the town of Rye, start at the Landgate. This gate, and the town walls, were built in about 1340. There are remnants of the old walls on the s. side of Cinque Ports Street. There were originally three gates, but the Landgate is the only one left. This was the only approach to Rye from the landward side – hence the name of the gate – and even on this side there was an artificial ditch crossed by a drawbridge. Above the gate the machicolations can still be seen, and in the archway the grooves where the portcullis fitted. It is curious that the two arches of the gate are of different shapes, the outer pointed and the inner elliptical. The clock, incidentally, is a peaceful addition of 1863, in memory of Prince Albert.

Through the gate the street curves round to the right. This is Hinder's Cliff, from which there is a view across the marshes and out to sea. Below are recreation grounds, in an area known as The Salts, so called because in former times it was enclosed to allow the sea alternately to cover and uncover it, leaving deposits of salt. Beyond The Salts is the river, where quite sizeable boats are anchored.

After Hinder's Cliff, the street becomes the High Street. On the left at the first crossroads is the Apothecary's Shop, with a remarkable bow window. On the right a cobbled street descends, and in it, on the right, is the chapel of a C. 14 friary; this building, usually called the Monastery, dates from about 1379. Now it contains the showroom of a firm of pottery manufacturers. At the top of this street, and extending round the corner into the High Street, is a stationer's shop, in a building hung with mathematical tiles. These are tiles intended to simulate the appearance of bricks, at a time when bricks were expensive. There are good examples in Rye, such as No. 5 Landgate and No. 60 Church Square (the Old Customs House). One can usually spot them by looking at the corners of the building in question; any damaged tiles are also apt to give the game away. But it is not always very easy.

Further along the High Street is the Old Grammar School, founded by Thomas Peacock in the early c. 17. The building is of brick, and was used as a school until 1908. Opposite is the George Hotel, which despite its name and appearance is about 500 years old.

The George Hotel is on the corner of Lion Street,· called after the Red Lion Inn, which used to be in the building on the right at the top of the street, now occupied by tearooms. At the house next door John Fletcher the dramatist was born in 1579.

Also at the top of the street is the c. 12 parish church. Its most famous feature is doubtless its clock, which has claims to being the oldest clock in England with the original works still going. The enormous pendulum swings to and fro under the tower. As famous as the clock itself are the jacks, or Quarter Boys, on the outside of the church above the clock face, who strike the quarters but not the hours. They and the clock face were added in the c. 18. Those now seen are not the originals, but modern replicas made of fibre-glass; the originals are in the N. chapel inside.

This is a very large church, and there is much to see. Of special interest, perhaps, are the magnificent mahogany communion table in the St Nicholas, or N., chapel, the Burne-Jones window of 1897 in the N. aisle, and the c. 20 windows in the s. transept and at the w. and E. ends. The E. window replaces a Victorian one destroyed in the Second World War.

The nave was built after the chancel and completed the cruciform design. It is a good example of the Transitional period of architecture, between Norman and Early English: the arches between nave and aisles became more and more pointed as the building progressed westwards from the crossing. The church once had a w. door, but this was blocked up by the Victorian restorers.

On the left of the entrance to the church as one faces it is the Town Hall. This dates from 1743, a handsome brick building faced with stone. Here may be seen Rye's four maces, and other exhibits, including the gibbet cage in which the dead body of the murderer Breads, the butcher, was displayed to public view in 1743. In this year the mayor was James Lamb, who lived in the house now called Lamb House, and against whom Breads bore a grudge. One dark night Lamb was due to attend a party, and Breads concealed himself in the churchyard, which lay on the route. When he saw a man approach wearing the mayoral cloak, he leapt out from behind a tomb and stabbed him to death. His victim, however, was not Lamb, who was ill and had stayed at home, but Lamb's brother-in-law, who had agreed to go to the party in the mayor's place and had borrowed his cloak for the occasion. Later, Breads's bloodstained knife was found near the scene of the crime, bearing his

OPPOSITE: *Mermaid Street, Rye*
(A. F. Kersting)

name. In any case he admitted his guilt, although quite unrepentant. He was tried by his intended victim, condemned, and hanged on The Salts, his body afterwards being exhibited in the gibbet cage, in a field w. of the town still known as Gibbets Marsh.

Across the road is the Olde Tucke Shoppe; it has been a bakery for over 200 years. The building itself is late-c. 14. Beyond the Town Hall is the Flushing Inn, which dates in part from the c. 13. It was behind this inn that Breads had his butcher's shop. Along the side of the Flushing Inn runs Church Square. Here on the right is the E. side of the churchyard, in which stands a curious brick reservoir or water tank, oval in shape and built in 1735.

At the end of the street, down a slope, is the Ypres Tower. This square stone building, with round towers at the four corners, dates from the middle of the c. 13; it is therefore older than the town walls and the Landgate. At first it was called Baddings Tower, and stood on a cliff whose foot was lapped by the sea. It was built as a defensive castle against the French, and as such was singularly unsuccessful. In 1430 it was sold by the town to John de Ypres, which is how it acquired its present name. In 1518 it was sold back to the town and used as a prison until the second half of the c. 19. It now contains a museum, open in the summer, displaying exhibits of local interest.

The street running w. from here is the s. side of Church Square. Here on the left is a small house called Friars of the Sack. This c. 13 house was once part of a friary; the friars were 'Friars of the Sack' because they wore sackcloth. On the right, where Church Square becomes Watchbell Street, is a lovely timber-framed house called St Anthony.

At the end of Watchbell Street, after passing the Roman Catholic church, which resembles some Spanish basilica (built in 1929, it has a black-and-white marble altar and pulpit), one comes to a sort of platform called The Look-out. Below is the Strand Quay, with boats and ancient warehouses; beyond, across the marsh, is Rye's sister town of Winchelsea.

A turn to the right brings one down Traders Passage to Mermaid Street, the most famous street in Rye. Another of the gates of the old town, the Strand Gate, which used to stand at the bottom of this street, leading straight up from the river, was pulled down in the early c. 19. Up the street on the left is Hartshorne House. This dates from the c. 15, but it was much altered in the c. 16. In the c. 17 it was the home of Samuel Jeake, who acquired it as part of his wife's dowry; her maiden name was Hartshorne, hence the name of the house. It is also known as the Old Hospital, from its use as a hospital in the Napoleonic Wars. The house opposite is

The Barbican or town gate of Sandwich   (A. F. Kersting)

Jeake's Storehouse, 1689. Jeake was a prosperous merchant who was also a keen astrologer; a plaque on the wall of the house shows the position of the constellations at the time when the foundation stone was laid.

Near the top of the street is the Mermaid Inn, a picturesque c. 15 half-timbered building that is probably Rye's best-known hostelry.

Turning right at the top of Mermaid Street into West Street one sees on the right the fine Georgian Lamb House. We have already met the mayor whose residence it once was. Another famous incumbent was Henry James, who lived there from 1898 until his death in 1916. It is now N.T. property.

After the glories of Rye itself, RYE HARBOUR, two miles s., may seem a come-down, but it is worth seeing, if only by way of contrast. Turn left a short distance along the Winchelsea road. Opposite this turning, on the right, are the remains of a martello tower, and across the River Brede is the start of the track leading to CAMBER CASTLE (D.O.E.), one of the forts run up by Henry VIII for defence against the French.

Rye Harbour itself is, frankly, a bit of a mess. There is a jumble of factories and warehouses, a Victorian church, and then the end of the road: boats, harbour office, and the old Watch House, its bricks painted black and its tower truncated. There is also a pub, with the unusual name of William the Conqueror. On the right is yet another martello tower, ruinous, ivy-clad on its N. side, and guarding the entrance to a caravan

park. It is unique in one respect: it has a name – Enchantress. Did it, perhaps, once call to sailors like the Syrens of old?

Nowadays even Rye Harbour is not on the sea, which is still another mile away. To reach it it is necessary to walk, on a narrow road used by the Southern Water Authority, who are responsible for all such coastal defences (against the sea) on the coasts of Kent and Sussex, and whose lorries ply between the harbour mouth and Pett Level, as already described. A walk out to the bar, across the saltings, is pleasant enough: on the left, if the tide is up, ships and boats glide past, while on the right is a nature reserve where sea birds abound. Then at last comes the shingle beach and the sweep of the bay.

St Leonards E. Sussex *see* **Hastings**

Saltwood Castle Kent *see* **Hythe**

Sandwich Kent H3
This beautiful place beside the murky Stour is, after Canterbury, the finest medieval town in Kent. It was one of the original Cinque Ports, and seems never to have got over the shock of losing its trade as a result of the silting up of the river. This process began in the c. 15 and by the following century it was complete. Now the town itself is choked – by motor traffic. And yet it is still a good place to walk about in if one is able to avoid the obviously busy times.

In its heyday it was of sufficient importance to have three large churches. Now only St Clement's, in Knight-rider Street, is in full use; it has a good Norman central tower, an Early English chancel, and a nave rebuilt in the c. 15. St Mary's, in Strand Street, has fallen on evil days. The central tower collapsed in 1668 and brought the rest of the interior down with it. Now it is just a shell – but services are held there from time to time.

St Peter's, in Market Street, is the church one sees from a distance. Here, too, the central tower fell in, a few years before St Mary's, but less disastrously. The present brick tower is capped by a lead cupola that looks like a squashed onion. The church has been de-clared 'redundant' and is maintained by the Redundant Churches Fund, although occasional services are held. The c. 13 interior looks all the loftier and more impressive for being bereft of pews.

A walk round Sandwich seems to start naturally from The Quay, alongside the Stour at the N. entrance to the town. Here a narrow bridge, until recently a toll bridge, carries the Ramsgate road over the river. Here, too, is the Barbican, or town gate, partly c. 16 and partly c. 20, a picturesque start. Behind the Barbican is the High Street, and an immediate right turn out of it is Strand Street. Here on the left is the Three Kings Inn, on the far side of which is an archway between it and the next house, The Sandwich Weavers. Through the archway and on the right is a ruined medieval flint building, patched with the local yellowish brick; orig-inally Strand Street was further back and no doubt this building was on it.

Past the half-timbered Sandwich Weavers and another half-timbered house, The Pilgrims, which has been well restored, is The Old House, on the other side of the street, where Elizabeth I once stayed. She was wined and dined – and petitioned to authorize funds for harbour clearance; she enjoyed the entertainment, but appears to have ignored the petition.

After St Mary's church, on the left, comes the King's Arms. The plaster conceals timber-framing, and the building is dated 1592. A lively carving of a satyr adorns the corner. Further on on the same side is Manwood Court, a handsome brick building with six stepped gables built as a grammar school by Sir Roger Manwood in Elizabeth I's reign.

Soon, on the left, a path leads along the line of the old town walls, between an avenue of trees, a haven from traffic. It is possible to make a complete circuit back to The Quay by this path, crossing only three roads on the way. But there is more of the town to explore, and it is better to turn left at the first of these roads, Moat Sole. Here on the left are some almshouses, looking thoroughly Victorian, which they are. But this is St Thomas's Hospital, founded in 1392; the entrance arch of the gateway survives from the original buildings.

Past the Guildhall, rebuilt outside in 1910–12 but retaining some of the original Elizabethan interior, is the Cattle Market, leading to Delf Street; here a right and then left turn leads into Market Street, whence Seven Posts Alley, on the far side of St Peter's church, leads back to the High Street.

It would be a pity to miss Upper Strand Street, which runs SE. from the High Street, parallel with The Quay. Here on the left is the Old Customs House, whose casing of brick and general c. 18 appearance conceals a medieval timber frame. Inside, on the ground floor room where business was conducted, is a large Royal Arms of James I. The house is on the corner of Quay Lane, which leads down to The Quay through Fisher Gate, the only medieval town gate left – the Barbican came later. Fisher Gate was built in 1384, during the Hundred Years' War, and has a groove for a portcullis.

Upper Strand Street finally comes out into Knight-rider Street; turn right for St Clement's church, and for the three famous golf courses lining Sandwich Bay; turn left for The Quay, once the hub of a busy port, but now chiefly a car park. To the sensitive traveller, nostalgia is the mood of Sandwich.

Scotney Castle Kent *see* **Lamberhurst**

Seaford   E. Sussex   D6
The sea appears to be winning its running battle against the town of Seaford, which has received such a ham-mering over the years that most of its front teeth have been knocked out. The martello tower, in the forefront of the fight against a different enemy from that which it was designed to repel, was until recently a café, but this display of defiance only drove the sea to greater fury, and yet another outpost had to be abandoned.

But at a respectful distance further back, Seaford is a pleasant enough place to retire to – in both senses. The large Norman and Victorian church of St Leonard proclaims the former importance of the place, when it was at the mouth of the River Ouse. Within, the browny-pink colour of some of the nave pillars is said to be due to scorching from fires started by French raiders in the Hundred Years' War. On one of the s. side pillars there is a devil putting his tongue out, a most un-Seafordlike gesture.

There are the remains of an Iron Age fort at Seaford Head, on the cliffs to the E., domain of gulls and golfers. It is a large, roughly triangular area enclosed by a bank, and containing about three greens of the golf course as well as parts of fairways. Here is a splendid view: W. to Newhaven, Brighton, Shoreham, and Worthing; E. to Friston Forest, East Dean, and the Seven Sisters; N. to the empty Downs. To the s. is the sea, the scourge of Seaford.

Sevenoaks   Kent   D3
This is a commuter's town *par excellence*: half an hour or so to London by fast train. It sprawls around its hills

ABOVE: *the Seven Sisters*
(A. F. Kersting)

OPPOSITE: *Knole House, Sevenoaks:
a view across Green Court*
(A. F. Kersting)

and down into the plain to the N., where there are also gravel works and industry. No one can say why the place came to be identified by seven oak trees. As this has always been, and still is, heavily wooded country, surely a group of seven oaks would have been hard to find. However, the derivation seems indisputable.

The centre of Sevenoaks is unremarkable. This is the fork where London Road and the High Street divide. Nearly all the buildings of any interest are in the High Street to the s. of it. As one approaches from the direction of Tonbridge, the town proper seems to begin at Sevenoaks School, on the right. First comes a dull, flat-roofed modern block, but then an attractive range of buildings in ragstone, with galleting, originally two low rows of almshouses flanking a taller central building, which was the school, the whole designed by Lord Burlington in the 1720s. (The school itself was founded in 1418, and endowed in 1432 by Sir William Sennocke.) Past this, on the same side of the street, are the Manor House, of about 1800, with a pretty fanlight over the front door to relieve the building's otherwise austere appearance; Old House, of about 1700, on a bend in the road; and the Red House, 1686, which was once the home of Francis Austen, uncle of Jane. Its stables, now of course put to other uses, stand across a side street on the right. The Manor House is now owned by Sevenoaks School, while Old House and The Red House are offices.

On the other side of the street, Oak End is an c. 18 house; the Royal Oak Antique Galleries (formerly the Royal Oak Hotel) are in an early-c. 19 building, and The Chantry was built in about 1700 on land that originally formed part of the endowment of the chantry established in 1257 in St Nicholas' church.

Next to The Chantry is the parish church of St Nicholas, of which John Donne, poet and Dean of St Paul's, was absentee curate from 1616 to 1631. There is evidence that there was a Norman church here on the site of the present chancel, but the church we see today is c. 13, with a number of alterations and additions down the centuries. The roof is modern; the previous one, part of an early-c. 19 rebuilding, was accidentally destroyed by fire in 1947.

On the outside wall of the s. chapel, below the window at its E. end, is a stone commemorating John Braithwaite, head coachman to the 1st Duke of Dorset, who died as a result of falling off his coach in 1723. 'His loss was Greatly lamented, and by none more, than By his Lord and Master'.

The 'Lord and Master', the 1st Duke of Dorset, was Lionel Sackville, member of the illustrious family who have lived in the same great house at Sevenoaks for about four hundred years. KNOLE (N.T.) – so called because it stands on a piece of high ground or knoll on the E. side of the town – was bought in 1456 by Thomas Bourchier, Archbishop of Canterbury, for £266 13s. 4d.

It thus became a seat of the archbishops, and was retained by Bourchier's successors, Morton, Deane, Warham, and Cranmer. Thomas Cranmer, after he had fallen out of favour with Henry VIII, was reluctantly forced to hand over Knole to the King. Then after several more rapid changes of ownership it was presented, subject to lease, by Elizabeth I to her second cousin, Thomas Sackville, who in 1603 was able to buy the freehold and thus became the outright owner of Knole; it remained in the family until 1946, when it passed into the keeping of the N.T.

The reason why the family name of recent owners of Knole is Sackville-West can be explained as follows. Thomas Sackville was created 1st Earl of Dorset. The 7th Earl was created 1st Duke of Dorset by George I. The 4th Duke, 1793–1815, was killed in a hunting accident, leaving no issue, and the title passed to his cousin. When he died without a male heir, the title died with him, and the ownership of Knole passed to the 4th Duke's two sisters. On the death of the elder in 1864 it passed to the younger, who was married to George John West, 5th Earl de la Warr. Their offspring assumed the double surname of Sackville-West. Thereafter the title of successive owners of Knole was Lord Sackville, the family name being Sackville-West. Victoria Sackville-West, who, with her husband Harold Nicolson, bought Sissinghurst Castle in 1930, was 'returning' to the home of her ancestors, for she was a direct descendant of Thomas Sackville and his wife Cicely, daughter of Sir John Baker of Sissinghurst.

As one approaches Knole across its park, where numerous fallow deer roam, it looks more like some medieval city than a house; a huge complex of buildings, on which vast sums of money were spent in the past. One enters through the main gate into the first of the Oxbridge-type courtyards which transformed what was little more than a jumble of medieval buildings into a palace fit for an archbishop – or a king. This court is known as the Green Court. (It is not certain whether Bourchier built it, or Morton, or even Henry VIII.) One passes from this into another court, the Stone Court, so called because it is paved with stone flags, under which there are large reservoirs of water. This court is certainly the creation of Bourchier, but its gables were added by Thomas Sackville. The balcony is of the time of the 1st Duke of Dorset in the c. 18, although the stone wreath surmounting it was brought by the bride of the 5th Earl from her home in Essex in the time of Charles II.

A detailed description of the interior of Knole would quickly become tedious. Most of the rooms shown date from Bourchier's time, but were embellished by the Sackvilles. Thomas Sackville himself spent huge sums on his improvements, such as the extraordinarily elaborate screen and minstrel gallery in the Great Hall. There is a very large collection of pictures, furniture, silver, pottery – and even a Charles I billiard-table with contemporary cues and billiard-balls.

Some people are particularly interested in these possessions, others in the people who possessed them. The

The S front of Knole (A. F. Kersting)

Sackvilles are a fascinating family, and pretty varied. According to Victoria Sackville-West they were 'a race too prodigal, too amorous, too weak, too indolent, and too melancholy' (*Knole and the Sackvilles*). But they were not dull. There is Richard Sackville, Thomas's father, so wealthy that he was nicknamed 'Fillsack'; Thomas himself, poet and statesman; the 3rd Earl, spendthrift and gambler; the 6th Earl, a rakish, witty Restoration character; the 3rd Duke, lover of cricket and women (including the Italian dancer, Giannetta Baccelli, whom he brought to Knole and who lived happily with him there for several years – her nude figure reclines at the bottom of the Great Staircase built by the 1st Earl). Sevenoaks has reason to be grateful to the 3rd Duke, for in 1774 he presented the townspeople with the Vine cricket-ground, on the right of the Dartford Road. It was out in the country in those days, and even now it is part of an open area with something of a village atmosphere. Indeed the town is beholden to all the Sackvilles, who, with their great house, add distinction to a pleasant but not otherwise exciting place.

Shalford Surrey *see* **Guildford**

Sheerness Kent *see* **Sheppey**

Sheffield Park E. Sussex D5
Sheffield Park (Sifelle in Domesday, gradually changing through Shifeld to Sheffield) is famous for a superb garden and a steam railway. For connoisseurs of architecture the recently opened mansion is also an attraction.

The interest of Sheffield Park dates from 1769, when the estate was bought by a Yorkshireman, John Baker Holroyd, afterwards Lord Sheffield. He engaged James Wyatt to rebuild the house, and Capability Brown and Humphry Repton to lay out the grounds. The house is in the neo-Gothic style, complete with turrets, battlements, pinnacles, and a huge ecclesiastical-looking window giving the illusion of a private chapel within. It is in the process of restoration, and the redecorated rooms have the lightness and elegance of much of Wyatt's early work. Among its many distinguished visitors was Edward Gibbon, a life-long friend of the 1st Earl. He is buried in the Sheffield mausoleum in the parish church at Fletching.

The gardens belong to the N.T. They were much altered by the 3rd Earl in the late C. 19; he added the upper lakes and bridge, and planted many magnificent exotic trees. On his private cricket ground (now a small arboretum) the Australian touring team for many years played the opening match of their tour, against his Eleven.

Today the glory of the gardens is the display of rhododendrons, azaleas, acers, and conifers, skilfully grouped to enhance each other's beauty both of shape and colour. In spring their flowers and in autumn their foliage set the lakes aflame with their reflected scarlet, tawny, and palest gold. The creator of this splendour was Mr A. G. Soames, who bought the estate in 1909.

Between Sheffield Park station and Horsted Keynes, 5 miles N., the story-book steam locomotives of the Bluebell Railway (all that is left of the East Grinstead–Lewes line) chug their leafy way through the countryside, hauling coaches packed with delighted children and nostalgic adults, who can also enjoy the collection of vintage engines pensioned off in the station museum.

Sheppey Kent F2/G2
Sheppey, the Isle of Sheep off Kent's N. coast, seems at first sight a dreary pylon-bestridden waste. A single swing bridge carries all the road and rail traffic on and off the island. Most of the traffic going on to it is bound for the docks or the car ferry terminal at Sheerness, at the NW. corner. Shake that traffic off, and Sheppey begins to acquire some individuality. Its N. coast, fronting the Thames estuary from the mouth of the Medway eastwards, has crumbling cliffs of London clay, backed by a hill ridge that drops quite steeply to the s. on to a flat plain reminiscent of Romney Marsh.

During the Hundred Years' War Edward III built a castle beside the Medway to defend it against French raids. The place was called QUEENBOROUGH, after his queen, Philippa. The castle was razed to the ground by Cromwell after the Civil War and now not one stone stands upon another. The High Street is almost the only presentable piece of townscape on the island; it curves, then straightens, and has an end open to the estuary. The c. 14 church stands back from it on the N. side, the churchyard so cluttered with gravestones that it looks like some over-stocked antique shop. The ragstone tower is exceptionally rugged, while the dormer windows – one on each side of the church – look, by contrast, curiously domestic. Inside, the roof and E. wall have late-c. 17 paintings, now very much faded. Next come the two oldest houses: Church House, dated 1703, and Nos. 72 and 74, formerly one house, dated 1706. A little further on is the handsome if modest c. 18 Guildhall, projecting over the pavement on pillars.

SHEERNESS lies a short distance N. of Queenborough, at the very tip of the estuary. Naval docks were laid out here in 1665, and remained in the hands of the Navy until 1960. New docks were built in 1813. As early as 1667 Sheerness and Queenborough were attacked by the Dutch, who occupied Sheppey for some weeks – the last time that any part of the United Kingdom was occupied by an enemy until the Germans took over the Channel Islands in 1940. The part of Sheerness around the docks is known as Blue Town, because, it is supposed, many of the houses used to be painted with blue paint stolen from the naval stores. Further E., Sheerness has an esplanade and pretends to be a resort. Considerable damage was done during the January gales of 1978.

The road next climbs the hill to Minster, or MINSTER-IN-SHEPPEY, where there is a church of outstanding interest. Actually it is two churches standing side by side and joined together: the one on the N. side is the abbey church of the nunnery founded by Queen Sexburgha in 674; it was burnt by the Danes in 835. The nunnery was rebuilt but it was again devastated in 1052, this time by the followers of Earl Godwin. From the following century onwards the church was gradually rebuilt, and the parochial church was added to the s. side, probably in the c. 13.

Today perhaps the chief interest of the church is in its monuments. In the s. wall of the choir is the effigy of Sir Robert de Shurland, about 1310; near his feet is the head of a horse rising from the waves – there is a story that he was rescued by his horse from drowning. In the eastern arch of the arcade lies Sir Thomas Cheyne, d. 1559, while in the NE. corner of the N. or Nun's Chapel is a c. 15 knight supposed by some, almost certainly wrongly, to be the Duke of Clarence, brother of Edward IV, who was drowned in a butt of malmsey wine. To the w. of this is the effigy of an unknown knight, discovered in 1833 buried deep in the churchyard. There are two fine early brasses, of c. 1330, on the floor of the choir: these commemorate Sir John de Northwode and his wife. The lower part of the former, from the knees downward, is a replacement carried out in 1511.

Outside the w. end of the church at the entrance to the car park is the c. 15 gatehouse of the nunnery, the only part of the nunnery buildings still standing. Cars go to the side of it, but it is much used by pedestrians as a passage.

Next along the road eastwards is the village of EASTCHURCH, where the church has a good Perpendicular rood screen running the whole width of the building, and a window on the s. side commemorating C. S. Rolls (of Rolls Royce) and C. S. Grace, killed in a flying accident here in 1910. To the NE. of the village is the house called Shurland, having an impressive façade of brick with stone dressings, and a courtyard. It was visited in 1532 by Henry VIII and Anne Boleyn; there was much junketing, and the bill exceeded £50.

WARDEN and LEYSDOWN, both at the E. end of Sheppey facing the open sea, are not beautiful; the latter is a caravan-cum-shanty town of considerable proportions, which also suffered severe flooding in January 1978. To the s. of it, on the flat part of the island, is a complete contrast: the ISLE OF HARTY. Now at last one can appreciate why Sheppey is so named. Here in the SE. corner is Harty's remote church, with traces of Norman work. It has a lovely Decorated niche in the E. wall, a fine old rood screen, and, in the s. chapel, a c. 14 chest with a carving of two jousting knights. As they are wearing leg-guards, which English knights never did, it is thought that the chest must be Flemish or German.

Near here, and looking across the narrow strait of the Swale towards Faversham Creek, is the Ferry Inn – but there is no ferry.

Shere Surrey B3

A pretty village astride the Tilling Bourne between the North Downs and the hills of the Lower Greensand.

The best way to approach any village for the first time is on foot – a counsel of perfection admittedly – and this applies with greater force than usual in the case of Shere, which in the summer at any rate is apt to be jammed with traffic despite the bypass. An approach to be recommended is from Gomshall Road; turn off it on to a footpath where there is a sign 'To the Swimming Baths', which crosses a field (the swimming pool is on the right) to a wooden bridge over the river leading straight into the churchyard.

There is a paucity of first-class building stone in Surrey compared with some other parts of England, and it is interesting to note that, according to the guidebook to Shere church, 'the fabric is a mixture of Bargate stone and rubble, ironstone, Caen stone, re-used Roman tiles, clunch from the chalk pits of the North Downs, Horsham slab on part of the roof, Purbeck and Petworth marble . . ., English oak, and Tudor brick'.

As we make our way round the side of the church to the w. end, where the entrance is, we can see that the tower is Norman, surmounted by a c. 13 shingled spire. The shingles are Canadian cedar, put on in the restoration carried out after the Second World War. The arch of the s. doorway has Norman zig-zag carving, but entering by the w. doorway and through the beautiful Jacobean door has the advantage of an immediate view of the entire length of the church, right up to the altar and the Decorated E. window (the chancel was lengthened in the c. 14).

Of special interest in the interior are the medieval glass in the E. window, and in the windows of the N. chapel and the s. aisle; the brasses; and the c. 13 font restored in 1955. The quatrefoil and squint in the N. wall of the chancel provided communication with the church from the anchoress's cell built out on this side in the c. 14. In this cell Christine, daughter of William the Carpenter, was 'enclosed' in 1329. She apparently broke out a few years later but was duly 're-enclosed'. She would see the altar through the squint, and receive the sacrament through the quatrefoil.

Much necessary restoration work was carried out between 1956 and 1968, and at the same time the chancel was cleared of all the clutter that had accumulated there during the first half of the century.

In the village itself there are several old timber-framed houses; in Middle Street, for instance, Manor Cottage dates from the c. 15 and Forge Cottage and Bodryn from the c. 16. Another old building, across the street, contains the post office and the N. end of Forrest Stores; the post office part dates from about 1550, and the other from about 1400. The White Horse inn on the s. side of the river is said to date from about 1500. There is a genuine blacksmith's in this street, although the building is un-genuine Tudor of 1914. Mixed up with all the old buildings are a number dating from the c. 19 and early c. 20.

Shere has been dismissed by some as 'overrated'. Perhaps it is best for each to make his own assessment. It is certainly a village much visited and much admired.

Shipley W. Sussex C5

Shipley lies a little way s. of the A272, but in a different world, a world of quiet, pastoral fields and the infant River Adur. The small village itself has some pleasant houses, including a village stores hung with tiles of various shapes and sizes, and the two glories of the place: the Norman church, early c. 12, and the large smock mill, early c. 19, which seem to be talking to each other across the centuries – and over the top of the modern vicarage which stands between them; all three are ranged in a line above the N. bank of the river, which is the southern limit of the village.

The church was built by the Knights Templars, probably about 1125, a surprisingly late date considering the narrowness and Saxon-like appearance of the s. doorway. The immensely strong Norman arches of the tower probably impress one most; even the weak N. aisle, added in the 1890s by J. L. Pearson, cannot detract much from that. Yet the tiny blue and gold reliquary dating from the c. 13, in a niche in the N. wall of the chancel, makes its own peculiar appeal.

Once upon a time the river was navigable to Shipley, which explains the mooring stone now standing within the well-restored Tudor s. porch; the marks round the base of the stone were made by chains and ropes.

The smock mill to the w. is as impressive as the church. It bears a memorial tablet to its former owner, Hilaire Belloc, that lover of Sussex, 'who garnered a harvest of wisdom and sympathy for young and old'.

Village, church, and mill look s. across the river and the level fields to Chanctonbury Ring, high up on the Downs.

Shoreham Kent D3

In this pretty village in the charming Darenth valley Samuel Palmer, famous c. 19 artist, lived and worked at Water House, from 1827 to 1834. The clear waters of the Darent flow under a pleasant brick bridge in mid village, and close by is the white-stuccoed house where the artist resided. A riverside footpath leads past it to an open space where on fine summer days the local families play. The footpath continues N. towards Lullingstone (q.v.).

At the entrance to the short drive of Water House is Flint Cottage, a most curious small house of large unbroken flints and brick, with a roundel on the front wall and a head-and-shoulders bust of a man dressed, perhaps, in a toga.

Further up the slope to the E. is the old George Inn, on a corner, and making, with the houses opposite, and the lychgate of the church, an attractive group. Through the lychgate is a long avenue of clipped yew trees planted in the c. 19 and leading past the s. side of the church, whose c. 18 tower is another curious mixture of flint and brick. The early-Tudor porch has an entrance carved out of the upturned trunk of a single oak tree.

The special glory of the church interior is the c. 16 oak rood screen that spans the entire width of nave and s. aisle, like the best of the Devon screens, although less elaborate. A staircase in the wall on the N. side leads up to the top of it. Its carving includes the pomegranate emblem of Catherine of Aragon, which may have some connexion with Henry VIII's visits to nearby Otford. In the N. chapel is an c. 18 organ which was once in Westminster Abbey, and is thought to have been played at the coronation of George II. If this is true, it was probably played by Handel. Its case is exquisitely carved. The early-c. 19 pulpit is also from Westminster Abbey; the living of Shoreham is in the gift of the Dean and Chapter.

During the Second World War all the windows of the church were blown out by bomb blast except one, the Burne-Jones window in the s. aisle, just w. of the screen. It was made by William Morris & Co. in 1903.

On the w. wall near the entrance is a highly coloured c. 19 picture by C. W. Cope that portrays a dramatic moment in the life of the village, the homecoming in 1875 of the vicar's son, Verney Cameron, leader of the second relief expedition sent to Africa to try to find Livingstone. When he found some of Livingstone's party he learnt that the explorer himself was dead, but Cameron pressed on, and he and his companions were the first white men to cross the continent of Africa from coast to coast. The picture depicts his return to Shoreham, and shows him approaching his father, surrounded by an excited crowd of villagers.

On the hillside above Shoreham is a cross cut in the chalk of the North Downs, commemorating the fallen in two world wars.

Shoreham by the Sea W. Sussex C6

Set at the mouth of the River Adur and flanked by resorts, Shoreham sticks out like a sore thumb, for it is a busy port, with three miles of docks, a group of oil storage tanks, and a massive power station with two huge chimneys.

There has been a port here since Roman times, but there are few really old buildings in Shoreham. One of them, Marlipins, is in the High Street on the corner of Middle Street, with a chequerboard front of stone and flint. It was probably a warehouse of some sort, and dates in part from the c. 12, although its front is c. 14. It is now owned by the Sussex Archaeological Society and houses a museum open in the summer. Across the otherwise undistinguished High Street is the river, where hundreds of sailing boats are moored.

Leading off the N. side of the High Street are several small streets with pleasant houses, many of them having

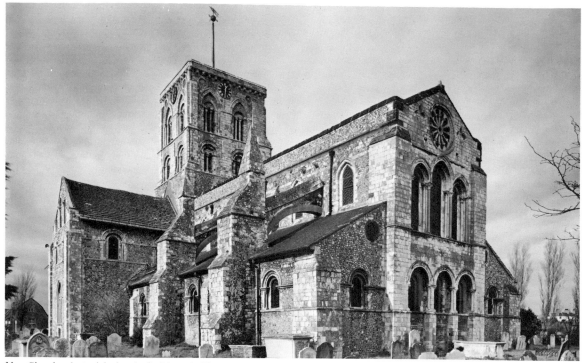

New Shoreham's parish church, St Mary de Haura (A. F. Kersting)

walls of flint. One such street is Church Street, at the far end of which, on the right, is a flint house that was once St Saviour's School, founded in 1858 by the Revd Nathaniel Woodard when he was curate of the parish church. The school was moved by him in 1870 to Ardingly (q.v.) and became Ardingly College (*see also* Lancing).

The parish church of St Mary de Haura is just past the old school. (The 'de Haura' means 'of the harbour'.) It is Norman and Transitional, and one of the grandest churches in Sussex, despite having lost all but one of its nave bays. In this and other respects it resembles Boxgrove Priory, although it was never a collegiate church.

When and how the church lost the other five bays of the nave and its aisles is not known. They were certainly all there at the beginning of the c. 17; it is thought that this part of the building became ruinous either after a French raid in 1628 or during the Civil War. The destruction that the French or the Cromwellians began may, it is surmised, have been completed by a violent storm in 1703, which demolished much of the town.

Be that as it may, the existing w. end is clearly a patching-up job done in the early c. 18, in which a Norman doorway was re-used to provide the w. entrance. Entering through this, the visitor finds himself in the

only part left of the original church, that is, the stump of the nave, the transepts, and the lower stage of the 'central' tower. All this was built in the early part of the c. 12. To the E. of this the purely Norman building was replaced from the end of the century with a grander choir and aisles in the Transitional style, the aisles extending right up to the E. end of the church. The upper part of the tower was probably built at about the same time.

Before the destruction of most of the nave, this church must have been impressive indeed. Its total length was 205ft, immense for what was only a parochial church. It is sad that so much of it is lost; but perhaps the parishioners of today are thankful not to have to maintain such a huge building.

All this part of Shoreham is known as New Shoreham, to distinguish it from OLD SHOREHAM upstream. In former times the river was navigable to Old Shoreham and beyond it to Bramber, but when the river silted up these places declined and New Shoreham surpassed them in importance. Nowadays Old Shoreham is a northern suburb, joined on to its upstart neighbour by housing, but retaining, somehow, its village atmosphere. Here is yet another Norman church, less splendid than St Mary de Haura, but imposing all the same. In truth

The Hangleton Cottage in the Weald & Downland Open Air Museum   (Gerd Franklin)

much of the nave is Saxon, the w. end of it having once formed the base of the Saxon tower. What gives the church such a Norman appearance is the central tower, and particularly the tower arches. The tie-beam at the E. end of the nave may also be Norman. The chancel was lengthened in the C. 14, and considerably restored in the C. 19.

The old wooden toll bridge across the river, which used to exasperate even the most patient of motorists when it carried the main E.–W. road along the Sussex coast, has been replaced by a modern concrete bridge a little further upstream, over the top of which the tall chimney of the cement works can be seen, while on the hillside across the valley to the NW. is Lancing College, providing a startling architectural contrast with its surroundings.

Singleton W. Sussex A5

Mercifully most of this brick and flint village under the Downs is just off the busy A286 road from Midhurst to Chichester. The houses are not picturesquely grouped, but they add up to a satisfying whole, though possibly rather a dour one.

If the village stands back from the road, the church stands back from the village. It is an ancient building

with a four-square Saxon tower. It is thought that the nave too was originally Saxon, and that there was an upper room over it, witness the window above the chancel arch and the doorway above the tower arch.

Many of the pews in the nave are Tudor. In the tower is an C. 18 gallery, reserved, one would guess, for those of lower rank. In the C. 13 openings were punched in the walls of the nave to make the aisles. At the same time, probably, the Saxon chancel arch was replaced by the arch we see today. Two wall monuments in the s. aisle should be noted: the C. 17 monument to Daniel Court, crude and endearing; and the much more sophisticated one to Tom Johnson, the huntsman, with its turgid and condescending inscription, which ends, however, with a lively rhyme, reminding us that 'Men, like Foxes, take to Earth'.

The Victorian reredos designed by Slater is worth a glance: a deeply incised representation of the Last Supper, with Judas Iscariot looking particularly guilty and alone.

Singleton's chief attraction for most visitors, however, is the WEALD AND DOWNLAND OPEN AIR MUSEUM, situated on the right of the road which leads to Goodwood Racecourse. Its main purpose is 'to rescue good examples of vernacular architecture', and this it does by acquiring old buildings that would otherwise be condemned to extinction and re-erecting them here. The beautiful site of fields and woodland makes an ideal setting for the buildings, which visitors can enter and look round for themselves.

Everything is well done. The car and coach parks are sited near the entrance, hidden from view by the trees. An explanatory display is housed in a nearby barn, which itself serves as an example of an 'aisled' barn common in West Sussex and East Hampshire but rare elsewhere.

The museum occupies some 35 acres, and contains a fascinating collection of old buildings, gradually increasing in number as the availability of funds and labour permits. There is, for instance, the small c. 14 Winkhurst House, moved from a valley drowned by Bough Beech Reservoir near Edenbridge, and the c. 15 Bayleaf Farmhouse from the same locality. Both these have fires going inside, tended by volunteer helpers, the smoke going out through the roof in accordance with medieval practice. Titchfield Market Hall, from Hampshire, condemned as a dangerous structure by the local authorities and due to be demolished, was, instead, carefully dismantled and re-erected here in the early 1970s. The plan is that it should eventually form the centre of a group of buildings simulating a market square. There is an c. 18 granary from Littlehampton, supported on stone piers or 'staddles', which look like toadstools; a charcoal burners' camp up in the woods above Pendean Farmhouse, a c. 16 house that used to be situated just s. of Midhurst and was about to be demolished to make way for sand-quarrying when it was rescued; and the very primitive c. 13 flint and rubble cottage whose reconstruction is based on remains found in the deserted medieval village of Hangleton, now a suburb of Hove. The Littlehampton granary contains a well-stocked and well-patronized shop.

The museum has several buildings 'in store', ready for assembling when funds permit. One of the most exciting projects – as well as the most difficult and expensive – is the erection of a water-mill from Lurgashall, W. Sussex, which involves the construction of two lakes at different levels, to provide sufficient head of water to turn the large wheel.

The museum directors are careful to emphasize that it is 'primarily a preservationist body and in the first instance will always fight to keep buildings in situ'.

Sissinghurst Castle   Kent   F4

'The story of Sissinghurst can be summed up in a sentence: a great Tudor and Elizabethan mansion slowly fell to pieces because there was nobody left to care for it, until in 1930 it came into the hands of two gifted people, V. Sackville-West and Harold Nicolson, who repaired the surviving buildings and created among them one of the loveliest gardens in England'. (N.T. Guidebook)

This 'castle' is no fortress, with battlements, barbicans, and drawbridges, but a peaceful brick manor house. The earliest manor house here was built in the c. 12, but only three arms of its moat survive. The house itself was pulled down at the end of the c. 15 by a new owner, Sir John Baker, who built the house whose long entrance range still stands. He inserted the present gatehouse in about 1535. This house was in its turn demolished (except the entrance range and gatehouse) in Elizabeth I's reign, probably by Sir John's son, Sir Richard, who built a truly vast mansion round a courtyard running SE. from the tower, which, with the so-called South Cottage in the far s. corner, is all that is now left of it. The rest was pulled down in 1800, when it was already in ruins; its ruin was accelerated by its occupation by French prisoners during the Seven Years' War (1756–63), at the end of which Sissinghurst and its contents were valued at £300, a paltry sum even in those days.

After the demolition of 1800 the buildings that were still standing became the parish workhouse, and remained such until 1855. From then until 1930 it was lived in by farm labourers. Then the Nicolsons arrived. She, Victoria Sackville-West (to give her her maiden name, by which she was known as a writer), was a direct descendant of Sir John Baker, whose daughter married Thomas Sackville, 1st Earl of Dorset (*see also* Sevenoaks). Over the years she and Harold Nicolson – later Sir Harold – designed and created the garden the visitor sees today, which she herself described as 'profusion . . . within the confines of the utmost linear severity'; elsewhere she wrote of their intention that there should be 'the strictest formality of design, with the maximum informality in planting'. The visitor of today can judge how far they succeeded, and how far the N.T. has remained faithful to the original intention.

Apart from the garden itself, which is of quite outstanding interest and beauty, and of which there is a detailed description in the N.T. guidebook, there is not a great deal to see, since such a small part of the original buildings is standing – the entrance range with gatehouse, the tower, the South Cottage, and the Priest's House, a small building to the N. of the tower, built for his private chaplain by one of the Bakers in the c. 16. In the Nicolsons' time, we are told, 'Sissinghurst was never luxurious, nor even very comfortable'. One finds that easy to believe.

But if there is not much to see, only the tower and the library in the northern wing of the entrance range being open to visitors, yet what there is is of great interest. The library, stacked from floor to ceiling along two of its walls with 4,000 books, occupies what was from earliest times the stables. On the first floor of the tower's N. turret is Victoria Sackville-West's sitting room and writing room. On the second floor is a small museum illustrating the history of the house and the making of the garden. There are photographs of both house and garden at various stages of dilapidation and renovation, diaries and correspondence by the Nicolsons concerning Sissinghurst, and a rather poignant photograph of their wedding at Knole in 1913. In the middle of the room is the extremely antiquated-looking printing-press on which Virginia and Leonard Woolf printed the first edition of *The Waste Land* by T. S. Eliot, and other early products of the Hogarth Press; Virginia set up the type and Leonard worked the machine.

In the third-floor room of the tower is a collection of photographs of N.T. gardens. Finally the visitor reaches the top, whence there is an exhilarating view of the garden and the Kentish countryside.

Smallhythe Kent *see* **Tenterden**

Smarden Kent F4
This must be a serious contender for the title of the perfect village: compact – no sprawl – and possessing a splendid church, plenty of half-timbered, weather-boarded and tile-hung houses, nothing unsightly, nothing self-consciously pretty. Only the fearsome traffic jars.

The main approach to the church is under part of a weatherboarded house at the w. end of the main street. This forms a kind of lychgate. The church itself is c. 14, except the c. 15 tower, and is built of a mixture of rubble and Bethersden marble, with a small amount of Kentish ragstone. In the NE. corner of the tower is the stair turret so characteristic of this part of the country.

Inside, you will catch your breath at the vast span of the roof, the widest in the county and earning the church the proud title of 'The Barn of Kent'. The intricate arrangement of the timbers is understandable, considering the thrust they have to bear. The same arrangement is in fact repeated in the much narrower, though by no means narrow, chancel.

The severity of the interior, looking E., is relieved by the painted wall panels on both sides of the chancel arch. These were reredoses for the N. and s. side-altars. Between the stonework were medieval paintings, but these were whitewashed over, and when the whitewash was removed at the beginning of this century what was left of them fell away. The present paintings date from the time of this restoration.

In the cross-aisle opposite the battered old c. 14 font is a long oak chest, possibly c. 16, and an oak alms-box, on top of which is an enamelled copper plate, which probably came from Limoges and dates from the c. 13. The design is thought to be either a baptism or the Presentation of Christ in the Temple.

The windows of the church are a mixture, some Decorated, some Perpendicular. In the nave, all the windows except the easternmost on the N. side are filled with clumsy square panes of clear glass. The glass in the E. window is unmistakably Victorian. The s. window of the chancel is the most curious: a medley of coloured fragments, some old, some looking Victorian, with bits of heads, arms, clothing, plants and animals, right way up, sideways, and upside down. Result: the best window of the lot.

There are so many things to admire in this church,

Smarden's Cloth Hall   (A. F. Kersting)

and one or two to puzzle over. The rood loft stairs on the
s. side, for instance: how did they connect with the rood
loft without more or less completely obscuring the
reredos in the s. chapel?

In the chancel are some elegant altar rails, late-c. 17
or early-c. 18; sedilia of unusual design, piscina and
credences, low-side window, Easter sepulchre, and what
was almost certainly a wafer-oven next to the piscina.
Then in the E. wall are two more puzzles: the large
arched recess behind the present altar, and the piscina,
if such it be, to the s. of it and very low down, having
the usual drain in its floor but also an iron hook suspended from its 'ceiling', purpose unknown and hard
to imagine.

On the s. wall of the nave is a framed copy of the
charter granted in 1576 by Elizabeth I, confirming an
earlier one granted by Edward III, which allows
Smarden to hold a weekly market and an annual fair.
One such fair was held in 1976, to celebrate the charter's
quatercentenary.

Smarden has some glorious houses. The c. 16 Chequers
Inn, the half-timbered Old School House, and Gillets, an
early-c. 19 house, standing back, are in the main street.
So is Chessenden, a beautiful c. 15 hall house; the two-
storeyed canted bay in the middle and the gable over
it were later additions, made after the central hall had a
floor put across it half-way up. This building, now so
much and so rightly prized, was at one time used as the
village poor house. Next to it is the Zion Baptist chapel,
a handsome building of 1841 – there has been a Baptist
community in the parish since 1603.

A little further on comes the Dragon House, dating
from 1331, built by the Pell family from Flanders, the
first of those Flemish weavers who brought such prosperity to Smarden that Edward III was moved to grant
the place its first charter. The Pells' weaving shed still
stands behind the house, which takes its name from the
row of white-painted dragons, probably of later date,
carved on its front.

Down Water Lane, leading past the left side of the
Chequers, a bend to the left and another to the right
brings one to Hartnup House, the oldest part of which,
the half-timbered N. end, dates from the middle of the
c. 15. The central, brick, portion is dated 1671, and the
house takes its name from the then owner, Matthew
Hartnup, the village apothecary.

Past Hartnup House is the Cloth Hall, a splendid
half-timbered house of about 1430. It was built as a
farm, but it became the main warehouse for the local
cloth industry, and at its N. end is a hoist and loft. The
infilling between the timber studs, or uprights, is ochre-
coloured, as it mostly was at first in such houses, instead
of the white more commonly seen today.

Yet another house testifying to the importance of the
old cloth trade of Smarden is The Thatched House, an
early-c. 16 weaver's house on the right of the road to
Biddenden, just beyond the bridge over the river Beult.

Sompting   W. Sussex   C6

Sompting is now an eastern suburb of Worthing. Yet it
has by no means entirely lost its village character, and
there are still fields where cattle graze. The traffic, it
must be admitted, is heavy, despite the bypass to the N.,
which separates Sompting from its church.

And what a church! It is perhaps the most famous in
the county, with its Saxon tower and Rhenish helm,
unique in England. Here is no primitive crudity, but
rather a kind of quiet self-confidence. The church stands
in the country, on a slope leading up to the Downs; to
the s., the main road is the boundary between country
and town. On the N. side of the church stands a farm,
up against the churchyard; while across the lane that
climbs to the Downs stands Sompting Abbotts, a Victorian mansion, now a boys' preparatory school, worth
a glance if only for the contrast with the church.

The church tower has a pyramidal cap of shingles,
called 'Rhenish' because such shapes are frequently
found among the towers of the Rhine valley in Germany.
Apart from the tower, the church is mainly Norman;
Saxon and Norman meet in a sculptured slab of stone
now placed on the N. side of the nave: the front is an
early-c. 13 portrayal of Christ in Majesty, while on the
back are two stones with interlaced decoration done in
Saxon times.

Towards the end of the c. 13 the church was taken over
by the Knights Templars, who added a N. transept,
and a separate chapel on the s. side, somewhat below
the level of the nave; this was converted into a s. transept
by the Victorians, who inserted an arch opening into the
nave. The original Norman s. doorway of the Knights
Templars' chapel now forms the main entrance into
the church.

Southease   E. Sussex   D6

One of the three round-towered churches of Sussex, the
other two being Piddinghoe (pronounced Piddinghoo),
just down the Ouse valley towards Newhaven, and
St Michael's, Lewes. Southease is no more than a
hamlet, grouped round a green. On one side stands the
church, and beside it a small house with a thatched
roof; opposite stands Southease Place, a house of modest
proportions with large banks of heather growing outside. On the other side of the church, across the small
by-road, is the Old Rectory. Some farm buildings complete the scene. The whole makes a satisfying group,
and the main road is just far enough away.

In 966 King Edgar issued a charter granting the church and manor of Southease to Hyde Abbey, Winchester, in whose hands they remained until the Reformation. The church pre-dates the Conquest, though the surviving portions of the Saxon church are scant: the nave walls, a blocked-up window high up in the N. wall, and a short length of cornice just to the right of it. There were also side aisles in existence in Saxon times, evidenced now only by the piscina on the outside of the N. wall. The tower is Norman. The altar is Elizabethan, now standing on chocks to give it much needed extra height, and with a modern top to enlarge the 'working surface'. There are c. 13 wall-paintings on the N. and W. walls, but these, even with the help of the framed sketches provided, require considerable imagination to interpret. At the back is an exquisite little late-c. 18 organ, with a mahogany case and gilded pipes.

Fortunately there is no through road from Southease across the Ouse valley; only those in possession of a key can unlock the level-crossing gates at Southease station.

Squerryes Court Kent *see* **Westerham**

Standen W. Sussex *see* **East Grinstead**

Stopham   W. Sussex   B5
A delightful place: very small, and up a cul-de-sac. It consists of church, manor-house farm, another farm, a cottage or two; Stopham House, down by the river and across the main road, hardly seems part of it.

The church, with the unspoilt c. 17 manor house on its N. side, is early-Norman. The low tower and simple nave and chancel make a pretty picture, and the roof of Horsham slate enhances it. Inside, the rounded chancel arch and N. and S. doorways remain, mercifully, as they have always been, simple and austere. The font, although probably c. 15, looks as rugged as the rest. Even the Victorian additions, such as the pulpit, give no offence. There is a good collection of brasses on the nave floor. The Norman W. doorway is blocked up, and the tower arch is crudely pointed – it must be an early example of the style.

Yet the famous building of Stopham is not the church but the bridge to the S., which carries a busy road over the River Arun. Built in stone in 1423, it has seven low rounded arches with refuges on both sides over the piers. The middle arch was heightened, with bricks, in 1822. Traffic is controlled by lights, but the parapet still gets badly knocked about. A good view of the bridge can be obtained by those prepared to use the muddy path through the nettles beside the river bank to the N.

Stutfall Castle Kent *see* **Lympne**

Telscombe   E. Sussex   D6
A village in a dip of the Downs, approached from the Lewes–Newhaven road near Southease. There are stupendous views across the Downs on the way up. The village itself, at the right season of the year, late March or early April, is adorned with bank upon bank of daffodils; a notice asks the visitor not to pick them. The flint church is mainly Norman. At the top of the hill beyond the village the road peters out into rough tracks, by which one may descend on foot, horse, or bicycle to the coast at Saltdean or Telscombe Cliffs, at the W. edge of Peacehaven; but it is better to stay on the heights.

Tenterden   Kent   F4
Tenterden was once a port, with a quay at Smallhythe to the S.; it was a member of the league of Cinque Ports, which at one time numbered over 30 towns. It was also an important centre of the cloth trade. The church was rebuilt in the town's heyday, a reflection of its local

Smallhythe Place, nr Tenterden (once Ellen Terry's home)

pre-eminence and an expression of civic pride. The cloth trade has long since departed; but Tenterden is still a sizeable town, of considerable local importance. To be honest, it is a bit of a sprawl; the neighbouring village of St Michael, for instance, with its large housing estates, is now absorbed. But the old town, with its wide main street and substantial houses, remains intact, a busy shopping centre and a place of character still.

The sheer size of Tenterden church is breathtaking. The noble c. 15 tower (containing what is generally considered the finest ring of bells of any parish church in the South-East) can be seen from a long way off, and on close acquaintance it does not disappoint. The soaring tower arch at the w. end of the nave is also very impressive.

The chancel is c. 13, the nave c. 14. Much of the tracery of the windows was replaced in 1864–6, and the chancel arch was rebuilt; the screen, choir stalls, lectern, and pulpit were all put up in 1899. There is much earnest Victorian glass about, and the whole effect is heavy and dark.

The N. chancel aisle was converted into a Lady Chapel in 1930. Its flat ceiling was removed, revealing the original timbers. Its E. window was inserted in 1930, replacing a window put up in memory of the Revd Philip Ward, who was vicar here from 1830 until his death in 1859, and was married to Nelson's daughter, Horatia. This window was considered unsuitable for a Lady Chapel; it is now in the church at Woodton in Norfolk, between Norwich and Bungay, the 'unsuitable' bits having been replaced.

On the N. wall of the chapel is the Jacobean memorial to the Whitfields, with large figures kneeling at a prayer desk. And on the w. wall is one of the most moving

(Gerd Franklin)

objects in the church: a small alabaster relief, badly damaged, depicting the Resurrection; Christ is shown emerging from the tomb, one foot placed rather tentatively on the body of a sleeping Roman soldier.

On the N. wall of the chancel is a memorial to the Revd Matthew Wallace, b. 28 October 1728, d. 14 November 1771 'aged 43 years and 6 days'. The apparent miscalculation is in fact correct, owing to the change from the Julian to the Gregorian calendar in 1752. Wallace was a Scot, and his memorial refers to 'the National Prejudices . . . between the Northern and Southern Divisions of Great Britain' – in other words, Stuarts versus Hanoverians.

The white-fronted Town Hall, dated 1790, on the left as one comes down to the High Street from the church, is particularly attractive, with its balcony carried across the pavement and resting on elegant pillars. Opposite, the half-timbered Tudor Rose café catches the eye, whilst a little further along is a car showroom housed in a handsome c. 18 building, incorporating, at its E. end, a warehouse door and hoist. Further on again, at the end of the street on that side, a couple of modern shops conceal the bottom half of what must have been a good early-Georgian house of brick, Eastwell House. Its portico has been removed and tacked on to the front of the modern shops – a rather macabre architectural joke.

Lovers of old railways should not miss Tenterden Town Station, the headquarters of the Kent & East Sussex Railway, which used to run from Headcorn, on the London–Ashford line, to Robertsbridge, on the London–Hastings line. This is now a private company, which is gradually re-opening the line from Tenterden towards Robertsbridge, and which runs trains throughout the year. Further information can be obtained by writing to the General Manager, Kent & East Sussex Railway, Town Station, Tenterden, Kent.

SMALLHYTHE, already mentioned, is a hamlet two and a half miles away on the road to Rye. It has a small brick church rebuilt in 1516–17, and two half-timbered houses, close-studded and with overhanging upper storeys. One is the Priest's House, early-c. 16, and the other, Smallhythe Place (N.T.), was the country home of the actress Ellen Terry from 1899 until she died there in 1928. It dates from about 1480, and served originally as the port house. Both building and contents – mementoes of the theatrical profession and of a much admired and much loved member of it – are sensitively preserved and displayed.

Thanet Kent H2/3
(The towns of Margate, Broadstairs, Ramsgate)
Although each of these three towns has its separate identity and civic pride, they are physically so close, packed on to the blob of chalk at the far eastern edge of the region, that it seems convenient to group them under one heading.

'Dreamland' (B.T.A.)

MARGATE claims its citizen Benjamin Beale as the mid-c. 18 inventor of the bathing machine, which boosted the new fashion of sea-bathing. The village soon became a town, the resort of 'the nobility'. Development since those early days has been intense, and now the 'nobs' tend to stay away.

The town faces N., and the air is bracing, especially when a nor'easter blows. The cliffs are low but vertical. As one approaches from the W., one first crosses the alluvial flat lands where vegetables are grown in enormous fields. Then Margate begins, with BIRCHINGTON, a pleasant place with a flinty church, partly Norman, restored in the c. 19. Dante Gabriel Rossetti died at Birchington in 1882; there is a memorial window in the S. aisle of the church, and a monument outside the S. door designed by his fellow pre-Raphaelite Ford Madox Brown.

Next comes WESTGATE-ON-SEA, which has two bays and low chalk headlands, and it is worth turning left off the main road to approach Margate by the coast road or the promenade. Unfortunately towards the end the skyline ahead is dominated by a huge block of flats, which also dominates the whole of this part of the coast when viewed from out to sea. On closer inspection it turns out to be standing ankle deep in Bingoland, while behind that is a large amusement park known appropriately as Dreamland.

Storm damage to Margate Pier, 1978   (Press Association)

Ramsgate harbour and yacht marina   (A. F. Kersting)

The ornate clock tower at the E. end of Marine Terrace marks the end of Dreamland and the beginning of the town centre. Ahead is the small harbour. Behind it was the pier, torn apart in the January gales of 1978; it was decided to demolish what little remained. Beyond the harbour is Fort Crescent and the Winter Gardens, gateway to the select district of Cliftonville, and easy walking along the cliffs that will take you to the very edge of Thanet, two and a half miles away.

Behind Fort Crescent is Trinity Square, and at the bottom of Trinity Hill, in King Street, is Margate's Tudor house, restored in 1952 after Second World War damage. This pretty timber-framed building stands opposite a large car park, and somehow looks rather pathetic, a fish out of water. Inside is a small museum. Across King Street is Hawley Street, whence Love Lane leads off to the right to an area of narrow streets in which stands the Old Town Hall of 1820.

Further up Hawley Street is Cecil Square, first laid out in 1769 but now almost entirely modern; its upper half contains the municipal buildings and public library, and a shopping precinct.

Beyond Charlotte Square is the flint parish church of St John the Baptist, one of the longest churches in Kent (150ft), and possessing a tall Victorian broach spire. The interior goes back to the C. 11 with additions and alterations being made down the centuries, not least in Georgian times, when box pews and galleries were fitted, only to be removed by the Victorians, who also stripped all the plaster off the outside walls, exposing the flint.

Down to the N., on Grotto Hill, is the famous shell grotto, about which its proud owner of the mid C. 19, a Mr Newlove, wrote some enthusiastic verses, beginning:

Enter; the scene that greets you here,
No common scrutiny demands:

and ending on a note of bathos:

Mark well the harmony, and taste
Shown in the various quaint designs.

In fact, these underground chambers covered with shells are fascinating. Theories about the date of their decoration vary, incredibly, from 2000 B.C. to A.D. 1800.

Better documented is Salmestone Grange, in Nash Road, a restored grange of c. 1280, with monks' kitchen, refectory, and dormitory. The chapel, dating from 1324, has good modern stained glass in all the windows. The Grange is used by the adjacent boys' primary school run by Benedictine monks, but is open to the public in the summer holidays.

After the heady wine of Margate, BROADSTAIRS, three and a half miles SE. on the other side of the peninsula, is like a cup of cold water. First comes ST PETER'S, part of Broadstairs yet seeming an independent village, with its own church and High Street. The church is a large flint and brick building, Norman but much restored in the C. 19. The villagey impression vanishes at the other end of the High Street, where St Peter's starts to merge into Broadstairs.

Broadstairs itself is charmingly grouped round Viking Bay, a sandy bay backed by low chalk cliffs, on top of which are the promenade and C. 19 houses. Nothing exciting architecturally, but also nothing offensive – except Grand Mansions, large, looming, and out of scale. At the N. end of the bay the small harbour provides the focal point, and beyond it are more white cliffs, with a wide promenade at their foot. The North Foreland Lighthouse can be seen, high up above the cliffs, and actually on the landward side of N. Foreland Road, the main road running up the coast.

Over Harbour Street is a flint arch of about 1540 called York Gate, with a groove for a portcullis. Further up on the right, Fort Road, for pedestrians only, curves round under an archway. This is Archway House, where Dickens wrote part of *Barnaby Rudge*. Further up is Bleak House, yellowish brown, castellated, and well named, although when Dickens lived in it it was called Fort House. Here he wrote *David Copperfield*. Indeed, Dickens, who kept returning to Broadstairs and stayed in various houses in the town, has been turned into a tourist attraction and there is an annual Dickens festival in October.

After Bleak House, Church Road leads back inland to Nelson Place and Holy Trinity church, widened in the early C. 20 by the addition of N. and S. aisles in Norman style. Within, the enormous width combines with the flattish roof to give a most unusual effect.

Refreshed by Broadstairs, the cup of cold water, one is perhaps ready to move S. for another draught of heady wine, RAMSGATE. The flavour is different from Margate's. Ramsgate is a little more serious and business-like; a little less intent on keeping up the fun pressure. The harbour is much bigger, and has two parts, the outer harbour, which is tidal, and the inner, which is not. Together they form a great splodge of colour and movement that is the heart of Ramsgate. Wide sands run NE. from here, while to the W. are yet more chalk cliffs. The road at the back of the inner harbour climbs up an arched red ramp, above which are solid-looking c. 19 houses and hotels. From up here, from the Paragon or West Cliff Promenade, the view looking back to the harbour, and across the town climbing up from it, is dramatic. Indeed this is the best side from which to approach, except that as at Margate there is one huge block of flats throwing all else out of scale.

Students of unusual church architecture will want to see St George's on Church Hill, a spectacular building of the 1820s designed by the little-known Henry Hemsley, with a soaring tower reminiscent of Boston Stump, and a soaring interior too. Then, at the western end of St Augustine's Road is St Augustine's (Roman

Catholic), Pugin's masterpiece, now the church of St Augustine's Abbey, also by Pugin, across the road. Next to the church is The Grange, Pugin's own house.

A little further on is the end of the town, with a view across Pegwell Bay to Richborough Power Station at Ebbsfleet, with its three great cooling towers.

Much has happened at PEGWELL BAY; much happens still. Here is the busy hoverport and, a short distance inland, Manston Airport. Here or hereabouts the Romans landed in A.D. 43, the Saxons in 449, and in 597 St Augustine landed with 40 companions, and sent a message to King Ethelbert 'saying that they came from Rome bearing very glad news'. A cross near the entrance to the golf club commemorates this event; the replica of a Viking ship, sailed across the sea by a Danish crew in 1949 and now resting beside the road above the hoverport, commemorates the landing of 449; the Romans, in Richborough Castle (q.v.), have left their own memorial.

Tonbridge   Kent E4

Start, perhaps, by climbing up the winding path that scales the motte of Tonbridge Castle. The River Medway was fordable here for centuries, and the high ground beside it made the ford easy to defend; these two factors explain the siting of Tonbridge. The name, incidentally, is thought to derive from 'dun burgh' or 'hill fort' – there are traces of an Iron Age fort by the castle.

The castle was built soon after the Norman Conquest. It was destroyed by fire in 1087 but was rebuilt at once. The motte survives to its full height; it is a huge conical mound of earth, about 270yd in circumference at the bottom and tapering to 83yd at the top. A sandstone keep was built on top of it, probably in the c. 13, and there are bits of the wall still standing; the well sunk straight down through the motte can also be seen. From the motte, when the leaves are off the trees, there is a good view over the town; immediately below, on the s. side, is the River Medway, here split up into several channels and flowing through attractive gardens, not too formally laid out. To the NW. are the hills of the Lower Greensand.

On the E. side of the motte is the massive gatehouse, erected late in the c. 13 on the N. side of the bailey, itself enclosed by stone walls, of which there are some remains. This rendered the motte redundant and it quickly fell into disuse. The gatehouse has arrow-slits and concealed machicolations, and once had two portcullises and two pairs of folding gates. It was also built as a *residential* gatehouse, with the great hall on top. The castle was slighted at the end of the Civil War, but even so the actual edifice of the gatehouse was left largely intact except for the top storey. At the end of the c. 18 a Gothic mansion was built on to the E. side of it, and now serves as offices of the Tonbridge and Malling District Council.

From here descend to the High Street at the point where it crosses the main stream of the river, and turn left. Almost at once on the left is the timber-framed c. 16 Chequers Hotel, and next to it a similar building of the same period now occupied by an outfitter's; both have almost a forest of timbers inside, and oversailing outside.

Next, on the right, and in complete contrast, comes the Rose and Crown Hotel, a most attractive brick building of the c. 18, although there was a hostelry here at least a hundred years before. The pillared porch stretches right over the pavement. Soon after comes a c. 15 house, now a pub, called The Ivy House, on the corner of Bordyke, a street so named because it ran beside the town ditch or dyke, constructed along with the castle gatehouse as part of the strengthening of the town's defences in the c. 13.

Next on the right is the handsome c. 18 front of Ferox Hall, and then on the left Tonbridge School, with its Victorian buildings forming an E-shaped group with the street at the open end of the E. But its foundation dates from 1553, when Sir Andrew Judde, Master of the Skinners' Company, founded a 'Free Grammar School'. The original School House was pulled down in 1864. Tonbridge became a boarding school in the c. 19; nowadays there are both boarding and day boys. When it became a public school the Skinner's Company founded Judd School – the name had now shed its 'e' – to cater for the needs of local boys. This stands opposite the West Kent College at the s. end of the town, in Brook Street.

Go back down the High Street and turn left along Bordyke, where there are several handsome houses, including The Priory, a sandstone building, probably of the late c. 16. Soon a backhanded right turn brings one into East Street, where on the left is the splendid Portreeve's House, an Elizabethan building with two oriel windows and oversailing. Opposite is New Court, modern flats by no means displeasing to look at.

Leading off East Street is Church Lane, at the end of which is the parish church, a building of Norman origins although mainly c. 14, thoroughly renewed and enlarged in 1877–9. The c. 15 E. window was destroyed by a bomb in 1944 and replaced by a window of modern design by Leonard Walker 10 years later.

Tonbridge's commercial prosperity really started in the 1740s, when the Medway was made navigable up to the town. This meant that timber, hops, and fruit could be sent down to the Thames and thence to London. From the 1780s, with the advent of Government mail coaches, the town became a communications centre, but, as with so many places, it was the coming of the railway that revolutionized it. It had been intended that the main line from London to Dover should go through Maidstone, but owing to objections it was re-routed in 1842 by Redhill, Tonbridge, and Ashford. In 1852 St Stephen's church in Quarry Hill Road had to be built to serve the growing population in the southern part of the town, where the railway was. Finally in 1868 the line from London by Sevenoaks was opened, shortening the journey considerably. Thereafter the population increased fairly rapidly, from some 8,000 a hundred years ago to about 32,000 today. There is a variety of industries, including printing, plastics, chemicals, fellmongering, electrical engineering, and the manufacture of chemical metering plant. The ancient 'dun burgh' has moved with the times.

Tunbridge Wells   Kent   E4

This town, unlike its near neighbour Tonbridge, is quite young. There was nothing here except a cottage in the woods until Lord North by chance discovered the chalybeate, or iron-bearing, springs early in the c. 17. Iron being good for the body if not for the soul, the fame of the springs grew, more were uncovered, and in 1630 Charles I's queen, Henrietta Maria, hastened her recovery after the birth of the future Charles II by camping on the common and taking the waters. In the second half of the century permanent buildings began to go up, and the independent identity of Tunbridge Wells was established. The prefix 'Royal' was granted by Edward VII in 1909.

Today the chief charm of the town lies in its numerous parks and commons. 'The Common' itself, sloping down from Mount Ephraim – so named, like Mount Sion on the other side of the valley, by Dissenters who disapproved of the loose morals of the Restoration – reaches almost to the middle of the town at London Road, and is a properly unkempt area of trees, bracken, and outcrops of sandstone rock. More formal, but also attractive, are Calverley Grounds and The Grove, while further out are Rusthall Common and Dunorlan Park.

Tunbridge Wells has sobered up since the euphoria of the Restoration and the arrival from Bath of Beau Nash in 1735 to supervise the festivities of the Georgian era. The town grew in higgledy-piggledy fashion and in a northerly direction, until in the 1820s Decimus Burton came, to impose some order upon the scene. With order came respectability, encouraged by the patronage of Queen Victoria. In 1846 the railway arrived, and, in the words of a contemporary advertisement, 'placed the lovely scenery, the waters and healthful breezes of Tunbridge Wells within the attainment of all classes'. And, one might add today, many nationalities, for here language schools have sprouted, and during the season numerous young foreigners roam the town, imparting a cosmopolitan air.

The traveller who wishes to explore it should start, logically, at the beginning, or southern end. Here is the most famous street, The Pantiles, so called because it was once paved with square tiles or 'pantiles', replaced in 1793 by flagstones, which are still there. The Pantiles is a c. 17 pedestrian precinct, with a wide raised pave-

The Pantiles, Royal Tunbridge Wells   (Janet & Colin Bord)

Church of King Charles the Martyr, Royal Tunbridge Wells   (A. F. Kersting)

ment, a row of trees, and a line of colonnaded shops. The buildings are of various periods and of no great distinction, but the total effect is pleasing. Beside this raised portion of the street is another, lower level, with a pub near one end, and then a third, lowest level, where traffic – but not through traffic – is allowed. At the NW. corner of The Pantiles are the springs, with a chained drinking cup; they say you get used to the taste.

A passage leads out of the N. end of the street across Nevill Street into another pedestrian area, Chapel Place. Here is the church of King Charles the Martyr, built in the 1670s and 1680s, the dedication being a counter-blast to the Dissenters. It has a white-painted timber belfry, and, inside, a stupendous plaster ceiling upheld by two great columns with ornate capitals; by way of contrast there are plain wooden galleries round three sides.

Chapel Place leads into the lower end of the High Street, where Mount Sion runs steeply up to the right. Then three more streets climb up out of the High Street, all exceedingly narrow: Frog Lane, Little Mount Sion, and Warwick Road, Next, South Grove leads up to the small park called The Grove. At the far end the High Street, which climbs and curves gently, widens out into Mount Pleasant. Here on the left is the Central Station, which is certainly well named but does nothing to enhance the appearance of the town. Mount Pleasant, tree-lined, is also well named, after the station has been left behind, but the Town Hall complex at the top,

which includes Public Library, Assembly Hall, and Police Station, is an uninspired hunk of 1930s brick. On the left is Church Road, and Decimus Burton's Holy Trinity church. Built, in a rather dreary Gothic style, in 1827–9 because the church of King Charles the Martyr was proving too small for the growing town, it is now, ironically, threatened with demolition. Close to it, with an entrance arch facing on to Mount Pleasant Road, the continuation of Mount Pleasant, is The Priory, in a Tudor style, also by Burton. The Priory is now offices.

This is, in fact, Burtonland, into which the Town Hall complex already mentioned unfeelingly intrudes. Originally the church and The Priory formed the western end of a continuous line of planned townscape extending eastwards along Crescent Road to Calverley Park Crescent and Calverley Park. All the buildings are of sandstone. First, in Crescent Road, come two houses on the left, past the police station; and on the right, the Calverley Hotel, built by Burton as a private house, where Queen Victoria stayed, but soon enlarged by him and opened as a hotel in 1840. (Beyond and behind it is the Roman Catholic church of St Augustine, opened in 1975 and providing a refreshingly light touch.) Then comes the entrance to Calverley Park, Burton's wonderfully spacious lay-out of solid town houses arranged in a great sweeping arc round the top of Calverley Grounds, which slope westwards back to Mount Pleasant. Just past the entrance to Calverley Park in Crescent Road, and

UPPARK

almost opposite the multi-storey car park (not as obtrusive as it sounds, for it stands well back), is the entrance to Burton's Calverley Park Crescent, an arc of houses fronted by a raised colonnade originally intended to have shops on the ground floor, and facing across gardens. The slender columns of the colonnade support the elegant balcony running the length of the crescent, which, after The Pantiles, is the pride of Tunbridge Wells.

Going back now along Crescent Road and Church Road one reaches Mount Ephraim, the road running along the top of the Common. From opposite the Wellington Hotel, tracks lead down past a large outcrop of sandstone rocks, across The Common and so back to The Pantiles.

The most remarkable rock formation in the area is HIGH ROCKS, a mile and a half w., which can be approached via Major York's Road, Hungershall Park, and High Rocks Lane. High Rocks, which is just over the county border in E. Sussex, is a huge sandstone block, standing among trees, where rock climbers from all over the country come to practise their sport.

Uppark (N.T.) W. Sussex A5

Uppark stands near the top of a hill of the South Downs on the seaward side of S. Harting. No large house could have been built on such an elevated site until after 1650, the year when Sir Edward Ford, who owned the modest house here, of which very little trace remains, invented a pump that would enable water to be supplied in sufficient quantity to a large establishment. The original waterwheel for Uppark can still be seen beside the road running down into S. Harting.

Sir Edward's house and estate passed to his grandson, Lord Grey, who became involved in Monmouth's Rebellion, and commanded the rebel cavalry at Sedgemoor with disastrous results for Monmouth. Although taken prisoner by James II, he contrived somehow to get off with a fine, and returned to Uppark. When William of Orange arrived in England in 1688, Lord Grey excused himself from helping James II on the grounds that he had a severe attack of gout; thus when William became King he was restored to royal favour: he was soon made Lord Privy Seal and created Earl of Tankerville. It was probably after William's rise to power that the building of the great house at Uppark was begun. Designed by William Talman, it was certainly finished by 1694.

In 1747 the house was sold by Lord Tankerville's great-grandson to Matthew Fetherstonhaugh, who had been left an immense fortune by a relative who had no heir – on two conditions: that he should buy himself a baronetcy, and a country estate in the South of England. Matthew quickly complied: he became Sir Matthew and bought Uppark. He also married the talented and charming Sarah Lethieullier from Middlesex.

Although the house they found was already very

Uppark

attractive, they made four important changes: they built the Saloon on the s. side, which meant raising the level of the first floor; they redecorated some of the state rooms, putting in fine plaster ceilings and replacing the old panelling with wallpaper; they moved the outbuildings from the E. to the N. side; and they assembled a great collection of carpets and furniture, and works of art. When all this had been done the house, except for the N. entrance, must have looked much as it does today.

The only son of the careful and prudent Sir Matthew was a very different kind of man. Sir Harry inherited Uppark at the age of 21 on his father's death in 1774. Gay and dissolute, but possessed of good taste, he later became a close friend of the Prince Regent, and entertained him and a host of others regardless of expense. In 1780 he had brought back to Uppark a 15-year-old girl from Cheshire called Emma. Uneducated, and already encumbered with a baby, she was of such surpassing beauty that these defects paled into insignificance. So, at any rate, thought Sir Harry, who kept her at Uppark for a year (by which time she was expecting her second child) before tiring of her and unceremoniously bundling her out; so, too, thought Charles Greville, who befriended her; so thought Sir William Hamilton, who married her; and so thought Nelson, whose mistress she became and whose daughter she bore.

In about 1810 Sir Harry fell out with 'Prinny', and retired from high society. Perhaps even he was running short of money. It was at this stage that he became friendly with Humphry Repton, and they discussed together various possible improvements to the house and grounds. The chief alteration actually carried out was the addition of the N. portico, which looks out of keeping with the rest. It was during this period, too, that negotiations took place between Sir Harry and the Duke of Wellington, to whom a grateful nation wished to present a country house of suitable magnificence. Uppark was

(A. F. Kersting)

ne of the houses suggested. At first the Duke was charmed with the idea, but no sooner had he clapped eyes on the place at the top of its steep hill than the canny soldier calculated that he would have to replace his horses, worn out by the climb, at impossibly frequent intervals. The negotiations were broken off.

In 1825, at the age of 71, Sir Harry married for the first time, the lady of his choice being his head dairy-maid, Mary Ann Bullock. Not long afterwards, Mary Ann's sister Frances came to live with them at Uppark.

The marriage was evidently a happy one. Sir Harry left Uppark and all its contents to his wife. He died in 1846 at the age of 92. Mary Ann lived on until 1874, when her sister, who had continued to live at Uppark, succeeded to the estate and assumed the name of Fetherstonhaugh. For 13 years of the period between 1874 and Frances's death in 1895, the housekeeper was Mrs Wells, mother of H. G. Wells; so it came about that the great writer has left us some vivid descriptions of 'life below stairs' here.

Under Frances's will the property then passed to Colonel the Hon. Keith Turnour, and after him, in 1931, to Admiral the Hon. Herbert Meade; both added the name of Fetherstonhaugh to their own, as this was a condition of inheritance. In 1954 the admiral gave the house and part of the estate to the N.T.

The visitor to Uppark today approaches it from the . and enters it by the portico designed by Repton. This is a pity, because it gives a false impression. If time allows, the visitor is well advised first to view the exterior from the s. or SE., when the dignity and simple elegance of the house, a two-storeyed building of brick with stone dressings, will become apparent. It will also be seen that the original entrance was on the E. side, but that the grand frontage is on the s., where there is a large pediment over the Saloon constructed by the Fetherstonhaughs after 1747.

Inside, an arcaded corridor designed by Repton leads from the front door to the Staircase Hall, where two large pictures of Uppark, probably by Tillemans, show the house as it was in Lord Tankerville's time. The large side-table here was originally decorated in white and gold, but is thought to have been repainted in black in mourning for Sir Harry after his death in 1846.

Beyond a small panelled room containing various personal possessions of successive owners of Uppark, and the Porcelain Room, once Sir Harry's bedroom, is the Small Drawing Room, in which stands the bed used by the Prince Regent and referred to by him in a letter to Sir Harry in 1795 as 'my old Bed'. It dates from the 1740s, and according to tradition was brought to Uppark by Sarah Lethieullier.

After the Red Drawing Room, so characteristic of the mid c. 18, comes the Saloon, the finest room in the house. Its date and its architect are, curiously, unknown; in manner it marks the transition from the Palladian to the Adam style. Passing from here to the Little Parlour, and thence to the Stone Hall, originally the principal entrance hall, the visitor next comes to the Dining Room, on whose table Emma is traditionally supposed to have danced for the amusement of Sir Harry and his guests. In all these rooms there are beautiful pictures and furniture, for most of which we have to thank Sir Matthew and his lady, and also Sir Harry, who added to their collection.

After seeing the splendours of the state rooms it is amusing to come down to earth, so to speak, in the kitchen and the housekeeper's room. The kitchen was moved here from its c. 18 position only in 1895, which is almost incredible when one considers that the distance from the old kitchen (which one passes on the way out) to the dining room is about 100yd or more, and involves negotiating two flights of steps. The food was carried from the kitchen down the first flight of steps, and loaded into trolleys heated by charcoal. It was then trundled across to the house by an underground passage, at the end of which it was unloaded and carried up the second flight of steps into the service lobby adjoining the dining room. Here it was kept on hot plates until ready for serving.

The kitchen now shown is, by comparison with the old, the height of modernity – although cooking was of course done at the open range, and the food kept hot in brick-built warmers fired by charcoal.

The housekeeper's room is much as in Mrs Wells's time, which was from 1880 to 1893, when she was finally discharged by her exasperated mistress; apparently she was not a very good housekeeper, lacking the necessary training for such a responsible job. She also became very deaf; her son tells us (H. G. Wells, *Experiment in Autobiography*, 1934) that she and Miss Fetherstonhaugh 'were two deaf old women at cross purposes'. It is hard to imagine that they were separated by only a couple of hundred years from the beginning of Uppark's colourful history.

Wakehurst Place W. Sussex *see* **Ardingly**

Walmer Kent *see* **Deal and Walmer**

Wanborough Surrey B3
The tiny, untidy hamlet of Wanborough is one of the oldest settlements in Surrey. It lies under the N. slope of the Hog's Back, close to the line of the ancient route from the Channel to the West. There are springs in the area, a fact discovered by early man, who settled here about 10,000 years ago. The Saxons named it *Wenberge* or 'bump barrow', referring to a Bronze Age burial chamber that used to crown the hill above until the C. 20 bulldozers flattened it to make way for a road.

The Saxons built a church at Wenberge shortly before the Conquest; it is mentioned in Domesday. The manor was acquired in 1130 by the monks of Waverley Abbey (*see* Farnham), who eventually rebuilt the church and erected the great barn to store wool; it later became the tithe barn and now houses agricultural machinery.

When Waverley Abbey was dissolved in 1536 the manor of Wanborough passed into the hands of a series of lay owners, and down the years the fortunes of the church fluctuated; at times it was used mainly for secular purposes. Eventually it was sympathetically repaired and returned to purely religious use in 1861. It is exceptionally small. The walls are of flint and rubble – and Roman tiles; the w. wall, however, was rebuilt in brick in the late C. 17. Inside, there are bits and pieces of various dates: the original C. 13 church survives in the lancets in the N. wall, and in parts of an old piscina built into the s. wall at the E. end. The C. 15 screen was well restored in the C. 19.

The C. 17 manor house alongside has seen better days. At the end of the C. 19 it was let to Sir Algernon West, private secretary to Gladstone, and had several distinguished visitors, including Queen Victoria. In the Second World War it was used as a training centre by the Special Operations Executive, concerned with sabotage and secret armies in enemy-occupied countries.

Washington W. Sussex C5
This pleasant village stands at the N. edge of the Downs and the s. edge of the Weald, a fact reflected in the variety of building materials used: flint, sandstone, timber, tiles, and brick. Washington is most fortunate in being bypassed by the A24 to the w. and the A283 to the N.; the only jarring note is the huge sand quarry beyond the latter road. The houses are trim and well cared for, the gardens well tended.

The main street of the village runs w. up quite a steep hill to the church at the top; from here there is a fine view back down the street and across to Chanctonbury Ring with its clump of beech trees, only a mile away.

The church itself, a hard, flint building (except the tower, which has almost a Cornish look about it), was largely rebuilt in Victorian times. The massive solidity

of the columns and arches of the arcade, which date from the C. 13, is impressive.

Beyond the church there is a bridge over the A24 which runs, a river of traffic, in a cutting far below beyond the bridge the Downs roll on towards the distant west.

Waverley Abbey Surrey *see* **Farnham**

Weald and Downland Open Air Museum W. Sussex *see* **Singleton**

Westerham Kent D3
This attractive small town stands on a gentle hill above the infant river Darent. There are houses of various periods, but the general impression is Georgian, with considerable C. 20 additions round the edges.

In the middle is a triangular green, with statues of two famous men. The first is of a native, General James Wolfe, whose defeat of the French on the Heights of Abraham, near Quebec, in 1759, won Canada for the British. He fell in the moment of victory. His statue shows him with drawn sword, as though leading his troops into action. The second statue is of Winston Churchill, who made his home nearby at Chartwell. He is shown seated, a brooding bulldog.

Behind a corner of the green stands the church, parts of which date from the C. 13. There is a shingled spire and the roof is covered with Horsham slates. All the windows were restored in Victorian times, and many of them are filled with stained glass by Kempe. The w. window in the N. aisle, however, is a memorial window to Wolfe designed by Burne-Jones. There is also a tablet to Wolfe over the s. doorway, which commemorates him in typically C. 18 verse:

Proud of thy Birth, we boast th' auspicious year,
Struck with thy Fall, we shed a general tear.

The font, in which Wolfe was baptized, is C. 14. In the tower is a curious and rather splendid wooden spiral staircase, medieval although much restored, leading to the belfry. Also in the tower, on the N. wall, are the Royal Arms of Edward VI; only one other example exists, at Hemel Hempstead.

At the bottom of the town is QUEBEC HOUSE (N.T.), Wolfe's boyhood home, although not his birthplace, which was the vicarage.

Quebec House is a modest building, which has undergone considerable changes. When the Wolfes lived there it had already been standing for some 200 years, and was called Spiers. In its present form it is probably much the same as in Wolfe's time. It now contains several portraits of Wolfe, and various 'Wolfiana', such as the travelling canteen made for his use during the Quebec campaign, and his dressing-gown, in which his body was wrapped to be brought back to England. Perhaps

Squerryes Court   (Country Life)

most fascinating of all is the copy of the letter written to his own father by Lieutenant the Hon. Henry Browne, in whose arms Wolfe died.

In 1968 the River Darent overflowed its banks and poured into the house up to a height of over 4ft. The damage took 18 months to repair. The river rises in the grounds of another of Westerham's famous houses: SQUERRYES COURT, whose drive entrance is on the A25 at the w. end of the town.

This house was built in 1681, in what is now known as the William and Mary style, on the site of a much earlier house; the de Squeries, who took their name from it, are known to have been living here during the reign of Henry III (1216–72). In 1731 the house and estate were bought by John Warde, and the Warde family have lived there ever since.

In front of the house, which is built of brick and is beautifully proportioned, there is a smallish lake; above it is a gazebo, built by John Warde in about 1740 as a shelter from which he could watch his racehorses in training.

Behind and beside the house are formal terraced gardens, laid out when the house was built; at the top of the terraces is an ornate urn marking the spot where Wolfe was standing when he received his first commission – he was a friend of the Warde family. He is thought to have been 14 at the time.

Inside, the visitor sees the entrance hall, dining room, drawing room, tapestry room, Wolfe room, picture gallery, and the regimental room of the Kent and County of London Yeomanry (Sharpshooters).

There is some beautiful furniture, much of it of English design and manufacture, and a most interesting collection of pictures. The collection of Dutch pictures in the dining room is specially fascinating. Although far from the best from an artistic point of view, the picture of Christ driving the Money Changers from the Temple, in the corner by the entrance door, is amusingly anachronistic, as it depicts the event as taking place in a Christian cathedral, complete with crucifix, pulpit, and sounding-board. The picture of John Warde, 'the father of foxhunting', in the drawing room is much admired, and rightly; his punchbowl beneath the picture is a lovely piece of work, and surely equally amusing, with its inscription 'WOO HOOP'.

Amusing, too, is the iron fireback in the entrance hall. On it are depicted scenes from the Bible: Abraham about to sacrifice Isaac, Isaac blessing Jacob, Joseph being cast into the pit, Joseph being shown Joseph's coat (and remarking 'AH IT IS MY SONES COT'), and Joseph's brethren, dressed in c. 17 Puritan costume.

There is a friendly, intimate atmosphere about Squerryes Court, partly because it is not very large, but more, perhaps, because the owners still live there.

CHARTWELL (N.T.), a mile and a half s. along the road to Four Elms, is another famous house in the district, having been the home of Sir Winston Churchill for some 40 years. Architecturally, with its rather ugly red brick and its rambling, indeterminate shape, it is nothing, but its position on a hillside, commanding grand Wealden views, is superb, and its contents full of interest.

The house is arranged to capture as far as possible the flavour of the 1930s, at the same time displaying many mementoes of Churchill's war and post-war years. It still has the atmosphere of a family home. The garden too is popular, particularly the Golden Rose Walk given by their children to Sir Winston and Lady Churchill for their golden wedding in 1958, and, of course, the famous wall built by Sir Winston's own hands between 1925 and 1932.

Westgate-on-Sea Kent *see* **Thanet**

West Malling (*pron.* Mawling)　Kent　E3
A most attractive small town in the fruit-growing district w. of Maidstone. Approaching from the N., where the A20 road effectively marks the limit of the town, one soon comes to the High Street proper. On the left is Swan Street, near the bottom of which, on the right, is St Mary's Abbey, on the site of a Benedictine nunnery founded by Bishop Gundulph of Rochester at the beginning of the C. 12. Now it is occupied by an Anglican Benedictine community. The gatehouse, beside the road, looks C. 15; over the wall one can glimpse the great tower, which survives from the original Norman buildings. Further along is the rather daunting modern chapel, a high box rounded at the ends, whose roof appears as a lid too small for it. Through an arch in the wall by the road a cascade falls, from the little stream that runs

through the abbey grounds. On the opposite side of the road, on the corner of Frog Street, stands a most attractive house of mellow brick, early-C. 18.

Back to the High Street and turn left. The street widens out, with Arundel House, a rather gaunt but handsome C. 18 house, on the right at the bus stop. Further up is another Georgian house, Street House, also on the right; then soon, set back on the right, is the church, with chunky medieval tower surmounted by a soaring spindly shingled spire of 1837. Inside, it turns out to be almost entirely a rebuilding of 1901, at least so far as the nave and side aisles are concerned. Up in the chancel, on the s. side, is a C. 17 monument to Sir Robert Brett, his wife Frances, only daughter of Sir Thomas Fane and Mary, Lady Delaspencer (*see* Mereworth), and their only son, who died before either of his parents; their alabaster effigies lie side by side, with the child's effigy kneeling to the w. of them and a shrouded skeleton to the E.

There are older things in the chancel: C. 13 arches on the N. side, and C. 13 sedilia on the s.; the vestry, leading out of the s. side of the chancel, has a C. 13 window against the chancel wall, blocked on the chancel side – it is at the back of the Brett monument. In fact the

Chartwell: the Library　　　　　　　　　　　　　　(A. F. Kersting)

WICKHAMBREAUX

vestry seems to be a sort of medieval lean-to, partly timber-framed: very odd.

To the s., the road passes between the handsome Douces Manor on the right and its lake on the left. The house is c. 18, with alterations of about 1840; it is now a training centre for an insurance company. Further along on the right is St Leonards Tower (D.O.E.), a late-c. 11 defensive tower, originally of three storeys, attributed to Bishop Gundulph, and standing on a knoll a little distance from the roadside. Two of the three storeys remain, though they are no more than an empty shell, with numerous pigeons in residence. Inside there is a stair turret in the NW. corner, and the stairs, which are covered with pigeon droppings, go as far as the top of the first storey. Not a place for a prolonged visit.

Wickhambreaux (*pron.* Wickmbroo)   Kent   H3

This place (which can be spelt with or without the second 'a') is a worthy claimant to the title of the perfect village, with an old water-mill and a mixture of houses and a pub ranged round a green. The flint church stands behind the NW. corner of the green, a late-c. 14 building in the Perpendicular style. Inside, the Victorians have been busy, painting murals round the nave arches, and the vault of heaven on the ceiling.

The *art nouveau* E. window of 1896 depicting the Annunciation, by an American glazier, Arild Rosen-krantz, commands attention if not unqualified admiration. There are ancient timbers everywhere. On the N. wall is an amusing c. 16 tapestry, after a picture by Titian. It shows Christ at Emmaeus: the figure of Christ himself is a portrait of Charles V of Spain; the man standing behind him is Charles's son, Philip II, who married Mary Tudor in 1554; on Christ's right is Francis I of France, while on his left is Cardinal Pole, the Papal legate in England during Mary's reign.

On the s. side of the green is the immensely tall weatherboarded mill, its large wheel, now stilled, housed in a slatted cage and poised over the Nail Bourne, which runs through the village. Opposite the mill is a Tudor brick and flint house that was formerly the post office. Beyond the SE. corner of the green is another pub, rejoicing in the name of the Hooden Horse. This curious name is connected with the grotesque horse's head worn by one of the members of a team of Morris dancers in commemoration of an ancient Christmas Eve custom, itself a christianized version of the much more basic pagan custom of eating horseflesh at midwinter.

Wilmington   E. Sussex   D6

Here is a pleasant village under the Downs just s. of the main Lewes–Eastbourne road, and famous for its 'Long Man', a figure cut out in the chalk of the hillside above the village, outlined in 1873 in yellow bricks for greater permanence. Its present outline, in white blocks, was laid in 1969.

The Long Man is now the property of the Sussex

St Leonard's Tower, West Malling
(Janet & Colin Bord)

Archaeological Trust. No one knows how old he is, but there is strong support for his having originated in the Bronze Age. He is a giant, nearly 230ft high, carrying two staves, which are slightly longer. The distance between the staves is just half their mean length, which owing to the slope of the hill and the consequent foreshortening is hard to believe: from a distance the figure appears broad and stocky. Nevertheless the foreshortening would be even greater if the figure had not been cut disproportionately long, which betokens a considerable degree of sophistication in the artist.

Wilmington has interesting remains of a Norman priory, which also now belongs to the Sussex Archaeological Trust. It was founded before 1100 for Benedictine monks from Grestain, which is on the left bank of the River Seine just E. of Honfleur. The abbey at Grestain was founded by Herluin de Conteville, whose son Robert de Mortain came over to England with his half-

The Long Man of Wilmington (A. F. Kersting)

brother William the Conqueror (*see* Pevensey). After the Battle of Hastings William gave Robert the Rape of Pevensey, and Robert gave the manor of Wilmington to his father's abbey.

The priory must be considered as all of a piece with the adjacent parish church, with which it was connected by the church's s. aisle. The c. 12 chancel of the church is unusually long, and no doubt served as the monks' quire, which explains the presence of the stone seats on the s. side. The nave would be used for lay, or parochial, worship.

In the Tudor house adjoining the priory remains is a fascinating collection of agricultural implements and the like, clearly displayed and labelled, which many visitors will find more interesting than the architectural fragments outside. Here are mole-traps, rat-traps, man-traps – one of these last is shown grabbing a wooden shin to demonstrate how it worked, its teeth embedded in the wood. Here, too, are ox-goads, 'horse-boots' worn by 'lawnmower ponies', and tubs used by smugglers for carrying contraband during the 'darks' or moonless nights.

The lower room of this upstairs museum is c. 15, but the upper part is older and was probably the prior's chapel. It has the remains of a c. 14 E. window, at the top of the steps connecting the two rooms.

There are other exhibits in the porch, which is immediately below the prior's chapel and has a ribbed vault with a large stone face where the ribs meet in the middle.

Over in the church, with its weatherboarded bell-tower and shingled cap, we see the long chancel already mentioned, with its low stone seats. The seated figure high up on the N. wall may be a Norman representation of the Virgin. There is a grandly self-confident Jacobean pulpit and sounding-board, with a curious 'obelisk' perched on top. The church was very thoroughly restored and the s. aisle rebuilt in 1883.

Outside, the enormous yew tree, held together by chains and supported by sturdy wooden props, may well be older than either church or priory. The Long Man probably knows.

Winchelsea E. Sussex F5

The original town of Winchelsea, of which nothing remains, was on the sea on a spit of land some distance to the SE. of the present town. In the c. 12 it was, like Rye, an important port. Like Rye, it early became a member of the confederation of the Cinque Ports. But during the following century the cruel sea subjected it to such a hammering as even Rye never suffered, and in the second half of the century, particularly in the storms of 1252 and 1287, it was finally destroyed.

Yet Winchelsea was too important for extinction; a new town must be built. Edward I, himself Warden of the Cinque Ports, put the work in hand, and a town laid out in squares, a planner's town, went up, on the hill where it stands today. Alas, what the sea did to old Winchelsea, the French did to the new; they ravaged it no less than three times, in 1360, 1380, and 1449, as well as carrying out several minor raids. Finally the sea completed its doom – not, this time, by storm, but by quietly withdrawing: suffocation by silt. By the middle of the c. 16 Winchelsea was no longer a port.

Immediate evidence that the town was once a proud place confronts the visitor coming from the direction of Rye, as he climbs the steep hill up to the Strand Gate – so called because it was once above the very banks of The River Brede. The Gate was built in the c. 14. Further round to the N. is Pipewell Gate, a rebuilding of about a hundred years later, while to the s. of the town, across fields well outside its present bounds, stand the forlorn ruins of the so-called New Gate, probably another rebuilding after one of the French raids.

Also witnessing to the town's former glory is the church. The building standing today is only the chancel and side chapels of the original church. The rest was a prey to the French raiders, who on one occasion surprised the inhabitants during mass, sacking the church and killing many of the worshippers. There are slight remains of the transepts, outside what is now the w. end the original nave and central tower have disappeared. Indeed it is not certain that the nave was ever built although there is strong evidence for it. The present porch was probably once the porch of the s. transept

WINCHELSEA

In the circumstances the wonder is not how little is left of the original church, but how much.

Even the fragment of the church that survives seems large for such a place. It contains much of interest, and has a mysterious, numinous atmosphere. The cost of its upkeep is high, and it may not be altogether a tragedy that so much of the original building is lost.

Perhaps the most immediately striking feature of the interior is the glass, designed by Dr Douglas Strachan in the early 1930s. The colours are admirable, but the sentimentality seems out of tune. Other objects that catch the eye are the piscina and sedilia, one group on the s. side of the High Altar, and the other, later and more elaborate, in the s. chapel; and the tombs in the N. and s. chapels, dating respectively from the late C. 13 and early C. 14.

The various parts of the church blend harmoniously. Only the rather clumsy late-Perpendicular porch and the E. window go far wrong. The story of the E. window is interesting. Originally in the Decorated style like the rest, it was probably smashed in one of the French raids. For whatever reason, it was replaced at about the end of the C. 15 by a Perpendicular window, and filled with the exquisite stained glass of the period. By 1850, however, the tracery had been allowed to crumble, and the restorers of that time decided to revert to 'Decorated'. Unfortunately, as well as being too anxiously 'correct', they were also too thorough, and the result is the present tracery, over-elaborate and as spiky as a holly tree. The lovely glass was broken up and dispersed, although bits were rescued and are now in the N. window of the sanctuary. The Victorian glass has, of course, itself been replaced by Dr Strachan's. Today the church stands, with the exceptions already mentioned, as a superb example of the Decorated style.

Winchelsea is a pleasant town to wander round, a town of well-maintained houses and carefully tended gardens. To the s. of the church, in the grounds of Greyfriars, a private house, are the early-C. 14 ruins of the chapel of a Franciscan convent; while across the road from the NW. corner of the churchyard is the C. 14 stone court house. On the upper floor of this is a museum, open in the summer; among the exhibits is a model showing what Winchelsea looked like in the old days of its prosperity.

Several of the houses have vaults, some with direct access from the road, which were used to store the wine imported from Gascony in the Middle Ages. Winchelsea was not built primarily as a military or naval town, but as a commercial one, and wine merchanting was its chief trade. One such vault is under the New Inn, just across the road from the w. side of the churchyard. Another is below an old ruined barn, opposite the red-brick Methodist church of 1785 in Rectory Lane. Beyond this, out in a field of mounds and depressions, sole remains of bustling streets and proud houses, stands a tarred C. 18 post-mill that has lost its sails.

Strand Gate, Winchelsea

From this point we look out over the valley of the River Brede, once busy with ships, now no more than a wide dyke traversing lush meadows nibbled by sheep; their peace may soon be disturbed by a bypass, whose route has been the subject of much argument.

Wingham Kent H3

In the reign of Edward III, one of the King's aides in the war against France was Sir Eustace d'Abrichecourt. On his return to England he sought out one Elizabeth Plantagenet, widow of John, Earl of Kent. The lady had become a nun, but, nothing daunted, the gallant knight abducted her from the convent and persuaded a priest to marry them in a room of a canonry opposite Wingham church. When this high-handed conduct was discovered, penances were imposed upon the erring couple: she had to recite 22 psalms and the litany every day, eat bread and water one day a week, and walk barefoot to Becket's shrine at Canterbury once a year; he had merely to say five Paternosters and five Aves morning and evening – which some might regard as a C. 14 example of sex discrimination.

The house where they were married still stands, a noble half-timbered house across the road on the s. side of Wingham church, where a college was founded in the late C. 13 consisting of a provost and six canons; the canons lived in a row of houses of which this was one. It is now known as The Old Canonry. It has close-set studs (uprights) and elaborately carved barge-boards, and bears the date 1286.

Wingham, a large village on the busy Canterbury–Sandwich road, has a High Street with a right-angled bend and several attractive houses. The Old Canonry is one; the Dog Inn, next to it, is another; this too was part of the canons' establishment (not, of course, an inn), as was the house on the other side of it. The group ends with the Red Lion on the corner, yet another timber-framed house with overhangs. After the corner the street runs gently downhill to the N.; there are more good houses, though perhaps none is outstanding. There are, however, two excellent c. 18 houses elsewhere: Delbridge House, standing well back from the road w. of the churchyard, and the Vicarage, in School Lane.

The church of St Mary's has a recessed green copper spire which does nothing to enhance its beauty but which acts as a useful landmark. The building is a noble one of flint, brick, rubble, and goodness knows what, with blocked-up doorways and windows all over the place to puzzle and confuse. Although parts go back earlier, the church was rebuilt in the late c. 13, when the college was founded.

At the Reformation, when the college was closed down, the church fell on evil days. Then in 1573 Queen Elizabeth I came to stay at Wingham and expressed her royal disapproval of the state of affairs, whereupon the nave and s. aisle were promptly rebuilt and the roof supported by six massive wooden pillars, five of them chestnut and the sixth, the easternmost, oak. There is a story that a certain Canterbury brewer, who had been collecting the money for the repairs, made off with it – hence, perhaps, the use of inexpensive wood for the pillars instead of stone.

There are two remarkable things in the church. One is the c. 15 stone reredos, with carvings in deep relief showing scenes from the Passion story. The other is the Oxenden monument in the s. chapel, erected in 1682, with elaborately carved cherubs and other conceits, and ponderous c. 18 eulogies of Sir George Oxenden.

Winkworth Arboretum Surrey *see* **Godalming**

Wisley Surrey B3
This place is famous for the garden owned by the Royal Horticultural Society. The garden first came into the Society's possession in 1903. At that time the area under cultivation was just over six acres; now it is about 200 acres. Apart from running a garden with a superb and most varied display of ornamental plants, the Society's objectives at Wisley are to provide an advisory service to Fellows of the Society, and to carry out horticultural experiments, training, and research. The garden is open to the public every day of the year except Christmas Day.

It is in fact not one but many gardens: formal garden, wild garden, rock garden, rose garden, summer garden, winter garden, herb garden, heather garden, fruit garden, vegetable garden, and – most imaginatively – a garden for the disabled, where disabled people can learn that their disabilities are not necessarily an absolute bar to their being able to do some gardening. (Incidentally almost all parts of the main garden can be reached by wheel-chair.)

Even this list is by no means exhaustive, and in addition to the garden itself there is a licensed restaurant, a general shop, an information centre, and a place where plants can be bought. Picnicking is not allowed, but there is an area just outside which is set apart for it.

It might be thought that the Society chose the site for the suitability of its soil and climate. Far from it; it was given in trust by its previous owner, and in fact the soil is very sandy, quick-draining, and acid, while the annual rainfall, 26in., is well below the national average.

The village of Wisley, with c. 12 church and c. 16 Church Farm, lies astride the River Wey to the N.

Withyham E. Sussex D4
'Idyllic' is the only word to describe the view from the little hill on which stands the church of St Mary and All Angels. Below is a pond, almost a lake, with ducks; over the hill beyond peeps the spire of Hartfield church.

Withyham too once had a spire, but in 1663 the church was struck by lightning and suffered severe damage. By 1672 restoration was complete, but the spire was never replaced.

The village is dominated by the memory of the Sackvilles, who owned the nearby manor house. The church's pride and glory is the Sackville Chapel, and the pub is the Dorset Arms, for the Sackvilles were Earls of Dorset. The chapel is chock-a-block with Sackville memorials, the most imposing being the one for which the chapel was erected, that of Thomas Sackville, son of the 5th Earl, who died in 1675 at the age of 13. He reclines on a tomb chest, while his disconsolate parents kneel beside him. He holds a skull, which symbolizes that he predeceased them. Carved on the sides of the chest are the figures of his six brothers and six sisters. The memorial is the work of C. G. Cibber, who later became official sculptor to William III. Among all the statuary in the chapel, however, the simple tablet commemorating Victoria Sackville-West, who died in 1962, scores highest marks for unpretentious dignity.

The E. window of the chapel consists of a genealogical table explaining the descent of the Sackville family from Herbrand de Sauqueville, who came over with William the Conqueror.

Another beautiful memorial is the tablet in the N. aisle commemorating Earl Kilmuir (David Maxwell-Fyfe), who died in 1967. But perhaps the best things in the church are over in the s. aisle, which was added by the Victorians and has odd-looking dormer windows: a c. 14 Italian altar-piece, and four c. 15 Italian paintings depicting scenes from the closing hours of the life of Christ.

Beside the church is the c. 18 rectory (parts, however, date from the c. 15 or earlier) and Rectory Cottage. Nothing is left of the old manor house of Buckhurst, the seat of the Sackvilles. The other half of Withyham is a short distance along the road towards Groombridge the Dorset Arms, the filling station, and the post office stores. Up a turn at the side of the pub is the village cricket ground, backed by trees, where all is peace.

Worth W. Sussex C4

A deep neglected cutting marks the line of the old Three Bridges–East Grinstead railway here. Once no doubt an occasional billow of smoke would envelop the watcher on the bridge above, as the engine huffed and puffed its way up the incline. Now, instead, a continuous sound somewhere between a hum and a roar assails his ears. It is the M23 motorway, which wraps itself round Worth to E. and s., as if trying to bind the place closer to its big-brother neighbour, Crawley.

A suburb with a noisy motorway and a disused railway line that nobody remembers: what should bring the traveller to such a place? Almost at the SE. corner of the village – for suburb though it be, Worth still retains something of a village atmosphere – is the answer: the Saxon church of St Nicholas.

One enters the churchyard through a restored C. 16 lychgate, roofed in Horsham slate, which even for this hospitable material has attracted an unusual quantity of vegetation. On the N. side of the church is a tower designed by Anthony Salvin and built in 1871. This is often criticized as out of keeping with the rest, but there are also those who hold it to be an improvement on the cumbersome timber bell-tower and spire that were formerly superimposed upon the N. transept.

All round this cruciform church are vertical stone strips, or pilasters, a form of decoration characteristic of the late-Saxon period and so suggesting an C. 11 date. Once inside, one experiences a thrill of excitement on first seeing the immensely strong and simple chancel arch, and the two smaller and lower but still impressive arches to the transepts. The simplicity of the arches has been carried through into the apsidal chancel itself, and indeed the whole church presents a wonderfully fresh and uncluttered appearance. Much of this is due to those oft-maligned Victorian restorers.

Salvin appears again at WORTH ABBEY, a mile and a half SE. on the B2110 road between Turners Hill and Handcross. This is now a Roman Catholic monastery and boys' boarding school, a jumble of buildings at whose core is Paddockhurst, Salvin's imitation-Tudor mansion built for Mr George Smith in 1869–72. In 1894 the house was bought by Sir Weetman Pearson, later Lord Cowdray, who made considerable additions and put up the Cowdray crest everywhere. The Benedictines bought the place in 1933, and the name Paddockhurst survives only in the park, over which the house commands a superb view southwards across the Sussex landscape, while the name of its former owner is preserved at the pub along the road, the Cowdray Arms.

Wye Kent G4

This delightful small town is in the valley of the Great Stour, under the escarpment of the North Downs. The Saxon church is mentioned in Domesday, but no trace of it remains. The church was rebuilt and enlarged in the C. 13, when it was given a cruciform shape and a central tower. Then in the C. 15 came John Kempe, Archbishop of York (and, later, of Canterbury), who had himself been born and bred in these parts. In 1447 he founded Wye College as a residence for secular priests, with the prime object of restoring the worship of God 'by the augmentation of God's ministers'. He also put in new windows in the church, exactly like the windows in his college next door.

Today Kempe's church and college still stand side by side at Wye, but both have undergone great changes. The original buildings of the college, ranged round a small quadrangle, remain more or less intact. But under Henry VIII the secular priests were swept away, only the grammar school, which formed part of the college, being allowed to continue, which it did until 1893. Then the school became an agricultural college, and finally the Agricultural Department of London University. So far as buildings are concerned, there are contributions from almost every period since the C. 15, with the C. 20 producing by far the most, for additions were made in Edwardian times and again after the Second World War. Today many of the houses in the town, too, belong to the college and are used as hostels.

As for the church, the changes have been even more drastic. In 1686 the central tower collapsed and the transepts and chancel were totally destroyed. In the following century a new tower was built at the SE. corner, this time on the ground, and a small chancel with apsidal sanctuary replaced the large medieval chancel, which extended 60ft beyond the present E. end. Now, therefore, the church consists of C. 13 nave and aisle with C. 15 windows, and C. 18 tower and chancel. The C. 18 tower fits in well with the old nave and aisles, but the Georgian chancel (well restored in recent times) is an anti-climax. The gargoyles all round the outside should not be missed, except by the squeamish.

The town, predominantly Georgian, is completely charming, with open spaces and vistas across the valley of the Great Stour to the gentle line of the Downs. On the hillside to the E. is a chalk crown cut out by the college students in 1902 to commemorate the coronation of Edward VII. Beyond that, about two miles SE. of the town, is the DEVIL'S KNEADING TROUGH, a glacial combe in the Wye and Crundale Down Nature Reserve and a popular viewpoint.

Further Reading

Aubrey, J. *A Perambulation of Surrey* included in *The Natural History and Antiquities of the County of Surrey* (1718–19, ed. Kohler and Coombes 1975).

Bede *A History of the English Church and People* (731, trans. Sherley-Price, L. 1955; rev. by Latham, R. E. 1968).

Brandon, P. *The Sussex Landscape* (1974; in 'The Making of the English Landscape' series ed. Hoskins, W. G.)

'Buildings of England' ed. Pevsner, N.

> Nairn, I. & Pevsner, N. *Surrey* (2nd edn. rev. by Cherry, B. 1971).

> Nairn, I. (West) & Pevsner, N. (East) *Sussex* (1965).

> Newman, J. *North East and East Kent* (2nd edn. 1976).

> Newman, J. *West Kent and the Weald* (2nd edn. 1976).

Church, R. *Kent* (1948).

Clifton-Taylor, A. *The Pattern of English Building* (1962).

Cobbett, W. *Rural Rides* (1821–30; edn. 1912).

Cottrell, L. *The Great Invasion* (1958). An account of the Roman invasion.

Cracknell, B. E. *Portrait of Surrey* (1970).

Crofts, J. *Packhorse, Waggon and Post* (1967).

Defoe, D. *A Tour through the Whole Island of Britain* (1724–7; edn. 1975).

Fisher, E. A. *The Saxon Churches of Sussex* (1970).

Gallois, R. W. *British Regional Geology: The Wealden District* (4th edn. 1965).

Glover, J. *The Place Names of Kent* (1976).

Glover, J. *The Place Names of Sussex* (1975).

Hall, P. *The Containment of Urban England* (1975).

'Highways and Byways' series:

> Jerrold, W. *Highways and Byways in Kent* (1907).

> Lucas, E. V. *Highways and Byways in Sussex* (1912).

> Parker, E. *Highways and Byways in Surrey* (1935).

HMSO *Strategic Plan for the South-East* (1970).

Hughes, P. *Shell Guide to Kent* (1969).

Kaye-Smith, S. *The Weald of Kent and Sussex* (1973).

Kenyon, G. H. *The Glass Industry of the Weald* (1967).

Lawrence, R. *Surrey* (1951).

'Little Guides' series:

> Cox, J. C. *Surrey* (rev. edn. Peeler, E. F. 1952).

> Jessup, R. F. *Kent* (7th edn. 1950).

> Jessup, R. F. *Sussex* (10th edn. 1949).

Lousley, J. E. *Wild Flowers in Chalk and Limestone* (2nd edn. 1969).

Margary, I. D. *Roman Ways in the Weald* (1949).

Mawer, A., *et al. The Place Names of Surrey* (1934).

Meynell, E. *Sussex* (1947).

Mitchell, W. S. *Shell Guide to East Sussex* (1978).

Renn, D. F. *Norman Castles in Britain* (1968).

Salmon, J. E. (ed.) *The Surrey Countryside* (1975).

Sankey, J. H. *Chalkland Ecology* (1966).

Spence, K. *The Companion Guide to Kent and Sussex* (1973).

Stamp, L. D. *Britain's Structure and Scenery* (1946).

Straker, E. *Wealden Iron* (1931).

Thomas, D. *London's Green Belt* (1970).

Trueman A. E. *Geology and Scenery in England and Wales* (rev. by Whittow, J. B. and Hardy, J. R. 1971).

Victoria County History Series:
      Victoria County History of Kent
      Victoria County History of Surrey
      Victoria County History of Sussex

Vine, P. A. L. *London's Lost Route to the Sea* (3rd edn. 1973).

Watkin, B. *Shell Guide to Surrey* (1977).

White, J. T. *The South-East. Down and Weald: Kent, Surrey and Sussex* (1977).

Wilkinson, F. *The Castles of England* (1973).

Winbolt, S. E. *With a Spade on Stane Street* (1936).

Wood, D. M. *On the Rocks – A Geology of Britain* (1978).

Wooldridge, S. W. & Goldring, F. *The Weald* (1953).

Wyndham, R. *South-East England* (1951).

Index

INDEX